LAW IN CONTEXT

Editors: Robert Stevens (University of California, Santa Cruz),
William Twining (University College, London) and
Christopher McCrudden (Lincoln College, Oxford)

REGULATION AND PUBLIC LAW

Regulation and Public Law

ROBERT BALDWIN
Lecturer in Law, London School of Economics

CHRISTOPHER McCRUDDEN
Fellow and Tutor in Law, Lincoln College, Oxford

With Contributions by

Paul Craig
Linda Dickens
David Miers
Alan Page
Iain Ramsay
Cento Veljanovski

WEIDENFELD AND NICOLSON
London

To our mothers

George Weidenfeld and Nicolson Ltd
91 Clapham High Street, London SW4 7TA

ISBN 0 297 78780 2 cased
ISBN 0 297 78781 0 paperback

Photoset by Deltatype Ltd., Ellesmere Port
Printed in Great Britain by
Butler & Tanner Ltd
Frome and London

CONTENTS

PREFACE

This book owes a great deal to a series of seminars on 'Law and the Administrative Process' which we have convened in Oxford for the past few years, initially at the suggestion of Richard Markovits. We take this opportunity to thank him for his support and all our students and our past seminar participants, academics and practitioners alike, for their stimulating contributions. A number are represented in the pages which follow. We are grateful to the Board of the Faculty of Law of Oxford University and the Oxford Centre for Socio-Legal Studies for providing assistance with that series and to Lincoln College, Oxford for granting sabbatical leave and a research grant to one of the authors during part of the writing of the book.

In putting this book together we owe a special debt to our contributors, Paul Craig, Linda Dickens, David Miers, Alan Page, Iain Ramsay and Cento Veljanovski, who delivered promptly and listened to our comments with good grace.

We are grateful, too, to our colleagues in Oxford, Brunel and Yale, and to all those who read and commented on drafts of all or part of the book, especially Rodney Austin, Harry Arthurs, Anthony Barker, Jack Beatson, Bill Bishop, Paul Burrows, Donald Elliot, Lucinda Finley, Tim Frazer, Mark Freedland, Hazel Genn, Carol Harlow, Geoffrey Hazard, Valentine Korah, L. T. McCrudden, Burke Marshall, Derek Morgan, Maimon Schwartzchild, Roger Shiner, Robert Stevens, William Twining and Toni Williams. We also join with our contributors in thanking those government departments and agencies which gave of their time and expertise in answering our questions and reading drafts of chapters.

We thank Julia Black, Sue Hardie, Cloe Stephenson and David Freedman for research assistance and the following for producing a final text from manuscripts of various descriptions: Donna Baston, Noel Blatchford, Jennifer Dix, Angela Duncan, Alison Marsland and Linda Peterson.

Robert Baldwin
Christopher McCrudden
Oxford
Easter, April 1987

CASES

STATUTES

GLOSSARY OF MAIN ABBREVIATIONS

ACAS	Advisory Conciliation and Arbitration Service
ACOP	Approved Code of Practice
AFBD	Association of Futures Brokers and Dealers
APA	Administrative Procedure Act (United States)
ATAC	Air Transport Advisory Council
ATLB	Air Transport Licensing Board
BA	British Airways
BBC	British Broadcasting Corporation
BCA	British Casino Association
BCal	British Caledonian Airways
BEA	British European Airways
BOAC	British Overseas Airways Corporation
BSAC	British South American Airways Corporation
BT	British Telecom
CA	Cable Authority
CAA	Civil Aviation Authority
CAC	Central Arbitration Committee
CAG	Comptroller and Auditor General
C&BA	Cable and Broadcasting Act 1984
CBI	Confederation of British Industry
CEB	Central Electricity Board
CIAC	Commonwealth Immigrants Advisory Council
CIR	Commission on Industrial Relations
CPAC	Consumer Protection Advisory Committee
CPRS	Central Policy Review Staff
CRE	Commission for Racial Equality
CRC	Community Relations Commission
crcs	community relations councils
CSI	Council for the Securities Industries
DBS	Direct Broadcast by Satellite
DE	Department of Employment
DEA	Department of Economic Affairs
DGFT	Director General of Fair Trading
DTI	Department of Trade and Industry
EA	Employment Act 1980

EDU	Enterprise and Deregulation Unit
EEC	European Economic Community
EEOC	Equal Employment Opportunities Commission (United States)
EOC	Equal Opportunities Commission
EOD	Equal Opportunities Division (CRE)
EP(C)A	Employment Protection (Consolidation) Act 1978
EMA	Engineers' and Managers' Association
EPA	Employment Protection Act 1975
ESRC	Economic and Social Research Council
FTA	Fair Trading Act 1973
FTC	Federal Trade Commission
FI	Factory Inspectorate
GB	Gaming Board
HSWA	Health and Safety at Work etc Act 1974
HIDB	Highlands and Islands Development Board
HSC/E	Health and Safety Commission/Executive
IAB	Industry Advisory Board
IBA	Independent Broadcasting Authority
IBOC	Investment Board Organising Committee
IBRO	Investment Brokers' Regulatory Organisation
ICAP	Independent Cable Advisory Panel
ICC	Interstate Commerce Commission (United States)
IMRO	Investment Management Regulatory Organisation
IRA	Industrial Relations Act 1971
IRC	Industrial Reorganisation Corporation
ISRO	International Securities Regulatory Organisation
ITA	Independent Television Authority
ITAP	Information Technology Advisory Panel
ITV	Independent Television
JRB	Joint Review Body
LAUTRO	Life Assurance and Unit Trust Regulatory Organisation
LRCC	Law Reform Commission of Canada
MIB	Marketing of Investments Board
MMC	Monopolies and Mergers Commission
MSC	Manpower Services Commission
NBPI	National Board for Prices and Incomes
NCC	National Consumer Council

NCCI	National Committee for Commonwealth Immigrants
NEB	National Enterprise Board
NEDC/O	National Economic Development Council/Office
NIC	National Incomes Commission
OFT	Office of Fair Trading
OFTEL	Office of Telecommunications
PCA	Parliamentary Commissioner for Administration
PEP	Political and Economic Planning
QBD	Queen's Bench Division
RPC	Restrictive Practices Court
RRB	Race Relations Board
SBC	Supplementary Benefits Commission
SIB	Securities and Investments Board
SRO	Self-Regulating Organisation
TSB	Trustee Savings Bank
TUC	Trades Union Congress
UKAPE	United Kingdom Association of Professional Engineers
vlcs	voluntary liaison committees

Part I

I
Regulatory Agencies: An Introduction

The influence of government over economic and social life is increasingly contentious. The methods by which government seeks to exercise that influence deserve intensive scrutiny. The particular concerns of this book are the increasing use of 'regulatory agencies' by government and the acute problems they pose for public law. These bodies undertake important government functions but are constitutionally awkward because they combine powers that have traditionally been kept separate. They act on behalf of central government, yet are not central Departments of State. They expend considerable resources in deciding disputes between parties and in interpreting a particular body of law, yet differ from courts and tribunals. They enforce the law as well as interpret it. They employ a substantial number of specialist staff. They exercise continuing influence over a specific industry, trade or social practice. They constitute an identifiable species, yet are of the broader genus variously referred to as quangos,[1] fringe bodies,[2] non-departmental public bodies[3] or public corporations.[4]

This species is here to stay. Any future government is likely to continue to employ agencies and to increase their use, whether through increased privatization (with agencies as a safeguard), or increased government control of the economy (with agencies as a buffer). A reluctance to accommodate agencies is, perhaps, understandable. Nevertheless, they are bodies that currently do, and will continue to, fulfil important functions. Their perceived effectiveness, moreover, derives from the same property which makes them constitutionally awkward: their ability to engage in disparate and apparently conflicting activities.

We shall consider subsequently the specifically public law issues raised by resort to agency regulation. Before doing so, however, it will help to consider why governments and administrators might find resort to regulatory agencies attractive; second, to examine some of the major choices governments or regulators confront when establishing or operating a regulatory agency; third, to anticipate some of the more common criticisms to which regulatory agencies have become liable.

1 Why Agencies?

Under which conditions may regulation by agency be seen to be preferable to government action through a Whitehall Department, to nationalisation, self-regulation, or to control by the ordinary courts, tribunals or local government? On a pragmatic level there are managerial reasons for resort to agencies. Thus, Frans Slatter[5] has noted how the rise of administrative agencies has paralleled a substantial increase in the overall size of government. He argues that one of the most obvious reasons for the creation of these bodies has been to take some of the workload off the more traditional branches of government, either by hiving-off old functions or giving new functions to administrative agencies.

A number of factors may influence the placing of new governmental burdens on agencies, rather than allocating them to the existing departments of the public service or giving more work to the courts. In some cases, the new activities would have been seen as awkward or burdensome bedfellows if added to already existing duties of departments or courts. In other cases, functions are thought likely to be better administered if they are the sole or central interest of the organization, and not just a peripheral matter dealt with by someone whose attentions are primarily directed elsewhere. A division of labour in this way may also help to develop specialization and expertise.

Greater government involvement with the economy combined with new and increasingly complex forms of technology, has led to the establishment of administrative agencies which are seen as experts in these substantive matters. The required expertise might have been developed inside existing departments or courts by appointing or retaining the appropriate personnel. However, the need for expertise is sometimes found in combination with a rule-making, decision-making or adjudicative function that is thought to be inappropriate for a government department or a court. Sometimes a department is seen as not able to provide the independence from government needed in some of these applications of expertise. Sometimes it is thought to be difficult to develop all the different kinds of expertise needed in courts without increasing their number and size. In any event, if new courts are needed, or if the existing courts have to function in divisions based on expertise, a new administrative agency might as well be used. In other cases the expenditure of the time and prestige of highly paid senior judges may be thought to be unjustified.

The advantages agencies are said to have over traditional courts are numerous. The sheer volume of decisions may call for a separate structure. Economy, speed in decision making, ability to adapt quickly to changing conditions, and freedom from technicality in procedures are other commonly cited advantages. Agencies are also thought to be able to relax the formal rules of evidence when appropriate, to avoid an over-reliance on adversarial techniques, and to avoid strict adherence to their own precedents. Administrative agencies are thought not to be as restricted to formulating policy on a case-by-case basis as are the courts.

As government expands into unfamiliar territory it is often hard to set fixed criteria that will adequately anticipate marginal cases. Sometimes it is simply not possible to foresee what circumstances will arise. In these cases a greater or lesser degree of discretionary power may need to be left to the administrator. A rule-making power is often found where regulation of a highly complex or technical nature is required. Delegation of rule-making powers may also be needed where constant fine-tuning of the rules and quick changes to meet new circumstances are required. Often the Cabinet cannot justify devoting the time needed to these matters, or else it is felt that it simply cannot act quickly enough. It would, of course, be wholly impractical to take the numerous amendments needed through Parliament. This is not to say that the impossibility of fixing criteria in advance and insufficient Cabinet and Parliamentary time lead inexorably to the establishment of an independent agency. Placing a wide discretion on the Minister or department has, in Britain, been a more common reaction.

Many of these factors have also been considered to represent advantages of agencies over the traditional central government department. The opportunity for consultations by way of a public hearing is often denied to departments because of the conventions under which they operate. An agency structure, however, may enable interested members of the public to participate in the making of the decision, rather than merely to react to the decision once it is made. Being able to use a modified adversarial system to decide between competing parties may be another advantage agencies have over departments.

Agencies' separateness from government may also make them a preferred mechanism for giving various interest groups a place in government policy-making through the appointments process. Agencies are also argued to be more suited than courts and probably than Whitehall departments to collegial decision-making. This facilitates the bringing together of many and diverse ideas, and can be used to encourage openness in decision-making. Groups that are co-opted into the system in this way may be more likely to support government activity in the field. An agency may be able to provide for greater continuity and stability in policy-making and implement-ation, being one step removed from the vagaries of Cabinet reshuffles and changes in government.

The exercise of a policy-making function by an administrative agency is said to provide flexibility not merely in policy formulation but also in the application of policy to particular circumstances. Agencies are said to be able to react to new circumstances more quickly than the departments of state, and are able to be more flexible in the application of standards than the judiciary. Somewhat paradoxically, as we have seen, they are also said to provide greater continuity than courts and greater stability than cabinets because the administrative agency is one step removed from the election returns.

In the discussion up to this point, one characteristic of administ-rative agencies has recurred: their independence from, or arm's-length relationship with, central government. In many cases this is the only reason why an agency is used rather than a more conventional department. Departments could generate advice, build expertise, develop new procedures, or manage programmes and projects. It is only an administrative agency, however, that can provide this added remoteness. In other cases the very function itself calls for independence. Adjudications, arbitrations, and the exercise of some statutory discretions are examples of this need. It is here that agencies are said to play an important role as insulators between government and the public.

There are several facets to the agencies' role as insulators. They may be used for dealing with 'hot potatoes', i.e. politically controversial decisions. Agencies have sometimes been used to give the appearance that the government was 'doing something' about some sensitive matter. The agency can then serve to deflect criticism and give the government time to examine the alternative solutions available. An agency may also be used where the administration of a particular policy is viewed as being politically dangerous. The use of an agency means that the Minister is not directly responsible for decisions taken, and so the government is protected.

Where valuable benefits such as licences or rate increases are at stake, an agency may be used to deflect lobbying and attempts at invoking political favours. It is easier for a government to say 'no' when it can say that the responsibility does not lie with it. The hope here is not that pressure groups will have no influence on government, but rather that their arguments will be evaluated more technically. An impartial decision-maker is useful whenever it is hoped to free government administration from partisan politics and party political influence. Adjudication and arbitration are examples where this is necessary, as are the granting of funds for research or cultural purposes. Where economic regulation interferes with vested private rights, the business community will usually be less antagonistic to government intervention if it is not a matter of party politics.

Finally, agencies have been justified as being able to 'raise and clarify arguments upon which political decisions depend'.[6] Regulatory agencies may help 'focus public attention on alleged harms and bring out issues in a way that enrich[es] political debate'.[7] In short, irrespective of their ability to command expertise they may be useful simply to enlarge the scope of political discussions.

These, then, are the main functional justifications for and the major roles performed by administrative agencies. While few of these functions could not be performed within more conventional government structures, agencies usually bring something to the particular role which departments and courts cannot. No agency is likely to perform only one of these roles. There are therefore technical reasons and justifications for using regulatory agencies, but there is also a variety of political motives for resort to such bodies. Thus Hood[8] has noted that in addition to a government's desire to distance itself from certain decisions or to co-opt certain groups into the decision-making process, it may often resort to agency control so as to create 'space' for a new policy within the machinery of government or to conceal the real size of state bureaucracy or to give the impression of taking firm action on an issue of concern.

2 Operational Choices

In establishing an agency, the government faces a number of choices. Where these are not made before legislation is passed, then they devolve, at least initially, on the agency itself. Three choices are particularly important. First, should the agency proceed by way of education, negotiation and bargaining, or by enforcement of established standards through the legal process? This may involve deciding whether the agency is to act as a pressure group and thus adopt a primarily representational role, or whether it is to remain 'neutral'. The government or agency may also have to consider whether a self-regulatory or more interventionist approach is more desirable.

A second choice is whether the agency is to adopt a reactive or a proactive enforcement strategy.[9] A proactive strategy would mean that the controlling body does not allow its priorities to be decided by outside forces (e.g. by those cases that happen to come into the agency of their own accord) but rather develops its own priorities (by way of, e.g., a strategic enforcement plan). Involved in this choice is the question whether the agency is to favour an 'incrementalist' or a 'comprehensive' approach to bringing about change. The characteristics of the former approach are a piecemeal development of policy, with a limited consideration of options and consequences. Regulation under this regime is a series of small-scale experiments and continual adjustments of differing interests and values. A comprehensive approach, often called 'comprehensive rationality',[10] emphasizes a clear specification of goals, choices and the consequences of alternative regulatory decisions. Systematic analysis (as represented by, for example, cost-benefit studies) is central. While some writers have doubted the feasibility in practice of this approach, and have drawn attention to the 'bounded rationality' of administrators,[11] it has had an important influence on attempts to improve the quality of policy-making.[12]

A third choice is necessary where some element of 'strategic' enforcement is adopted. This may involve concentrating on what might loosely be called 'rule-making', i.e. securing the promulgation of rules by the legislature or by the body itself through, e.g., codes of practice. Alternatively it may involve adjudicatory methods of enforcement: encouraging, planning and funding individual cases, or initiating investigations. Courts and tribunals tend to rely on adjudicatory and adversarial procedures rather than engage in consultative rule-making processes. Central government departments make many rules, but seldom adopt procedures that resemble trials. It is, as a consequence, rare to have to ask whether, in the development of policy or in deciding between parties, the appropriate procedure for courts or tribunals is rule-making or trial-based (or indeed some other form of adjudication). With regard to agencies, however, the advantages of rule-making procedures (wide consultation, prospectivity, research, etc.) have to be balanced against those of trial-type adjudication (the protection of individual rights, the 'day in court', etc.). Where rule-making is preferred, other choices are relevant: Is the purpose of the rule to be an aid to prosecution, or a means of promotion or consciousness raising? Which parties are sought to be addressed by the rule or code, and who is to participate in its making?

The different regulatory mechanisms implicit in these three choices may not formally conflict at the level of theory, and indeed may be complementary. However, scarce resources (in staff time, energy, and expertise) mean that these mechanisms may well conflict in practice. An agency cannot in the real world be all things to all people.

3 Pitfalls

A number of (sometimes inconsistent) criticisms have been made of the exercise of power by agencies. They have been accused, inter alia, of being slow, inefficient, unfair, unpredictable, corrupt, ill-managed, badly staffed, undemocratic, and unresponsive to changes in political opinion. It has been argued that it is inappropriate for those who make rules to be permitted also to sit in judgement on their application to individual cases;[13] that agency processes are run by people who do not have a sufficient appreciation of the problems of those who are subject to its rulings; that regulators make their decisions before the issues are sufficiently formalized for requirements of consultation to apply; and that agencies (like all bureaucracies) desire growth, seek new business to justify this growth, and thus produce ever increasing regulation.

Perhaps the most common form of attack is that agencies are too easily subject to influence by various outside interests; 'clientalism' and 'agency capture' are familiar terms. Several capture theories have been advanced. One common version is that capture is the process whereby agencies created in the public interest are subverted to the ends of those supposed to be regulated. The best known example of this theory argues that agencies go through a life-cycle of gestation, youth, maturity and old-age, ultimately becoming 'captured', so that the agency becomes 'the recognized protector' of the industry supposedly being regulated, rather than the champion of the public interest. This theory has been criticized as having surprisingly little empirical backing, and is inconsistent with specific industry studies in the United States and the growth of social regulation in the 1970s. It has also been criticized as apolitical in its concentration on the influence of the regulated industry to the exclusion of other political pressures.

A second variety of capture theory states that agencies are created in the first place in a manner that benefits existing industrial interests. The older 'public interest' theory conceived government intervention as a beneficial corrective for inefficiencies and inequities in the market-place. The 'public interest' was equated with remedying a list of 'market failures' which both explained and justified government intervention. Experience of regulatory programmes has suggested to some that they more often serve private rather than public interests.

A more promising variation on the theme of regulation serving private interests is the interest-group theory. This involves the familiar argument that the political process is a market-place in which rational, self-interested individuals attempt to maximize their utility. Regulation is a valuable commodity sold by politicians to the highest bidders. Thus, for example, consumers might 'buy' protection in return for votes. Given these assumptions, it is unlikely that the outcome of the regulatory process will have any necessary connection with efficiency, since the role of the state is essentially that of mediating distributive claims. Within this market there will be a variety of 'players': bureaucrats, politicians, voters, pressure groups and the media. The resources (legal, inform-ational) available to each group and the strength of incentives to obtain favourable regulation will have a decisive impact on the creation and implementation of regulatory schemes. The problems involved in organizing diffuse and fragmented groups such as consumers, and the limited incentives which individual consumers have to develop informed preferences on policy issues affecting them, suggest that they will be weak players in the regulation game. This economic theory has the merit of simplicity but it is as yet largely untested.

It is often unclear whether such accounts are intended to assess the *origins* or the *means of implementing* a regulatory programme. A theory of regulatory origin may not explain regulatory output. Moreover, the contrast of the 'public interest' and 'interest group' theories suggests different conceptions of rationality in the regulatory process. Within the former, technocratic rationality will be both necessary and possible. The interest-group theory seems, however, to deny the possibility of long-term planning; expert knowledge will be relevant primarily as support for particular political interests. Other theories argue that capture results from the bureaucratic and organizational make-up of agencies. Yet others argue that decision-making in these agencies 'is largely the result of coalitions of diverse participants – career bureaucrats, political appointees, agency professionals, public activists, and corporate managers – all with different motives and all interacting within complex institutional settings which provide changing patterns of incentives'.[14]

We will be concerned, therefore, to examine the extent to which the enabling statutes sufficiently control administrative discretion. Do regulators act as 'professionals' whose discretion is held in check by the tenets of their discipline? Is there effective control of the exercise of discretion through an internal administrative law of the agency? Questions with which public lawyers have been concerned for some years are thus posed in peculiarly acute form. The following are some of the issues on which the book will focus. What are the appropriate criteria for determining the use of rules and adjudicatory mechanisms, the exercise of discretion, the degree and role of participation and accountability, the external scrutiny of specialists and experts? Is there a relationship between the competence and the legitimacy of a decision-maker? How does procedure interrelate with substance? What makes (or should make) an issue justiciable? What is the appropriate relationship between the various agencies and the courts? A central issue is thus the basis upon which the courts should interfere with the decisions, actions and policies of regulatory agencies. Judicial review is only one form of control over agencies, but such influence must itself be based on justifiable criteria if it is to be legitimate. Is there, indeed, a legitimate basis for judicial review of agency action?

This book is in three parts. The first consists of four chapters and is concerned with general issues. Chapter 2 considers the rise of regulatory agencies in Britain and in particular the position of agencies in the politics of the 1980s. Chapter 3 discusses the standards for evaluating agency performance, and examines to what extent these criteria are taken into account in the internal and external oversight of existing agencies. It also considers what internal and other reforms might be introduced to satisfy these criteria of assessment. Chapter 4 considers judicial supervision of the existing agencies, in particular the incidence of judicial review, its effect, its functions, the competence of the judicial process, and possible changes in the approaches and procedures of judicial review which might prove more suitable for the scrutiny of regulatory agencies.

The second part of the book contains detailed case studies of selected agencies: the Advisory Conciliation and Arbitration Service (ACAS), the Civil Aviation Authority (CAA), the Commission for Racial Equality (CRE), the Gaming Board (GB), the Health and Safety Commission (HSC) and Executive (HSE), the Office of Fair Trading (OFT), the Monopolies and Mergers Commission (MMC), the Cable Authority (CA), and the new bodies established to regulate the financial markets of the City of London. From bodies with the characteristics of regulatory agencies we have selected a range of different types, e.g. social and economic agencies, existing and emerging agencies, rule-preferring and adjudicatory agencies, and those agencies affected and apparently unaffected by judicial review.

The third part of the book contains a brief discussion of a number of common themes which emerge from the case studies (chapter 14), and a detailed guide to further reading on many of the issues discussed (chapter 15). We turn first, however, to the rise of regulatory agencies in Britain.

2

The Rise of
Regulatory Agencies

The technical arguments for the establishment of agencies in Britain have often given way to political considerations. As in a number of other countries, the emergence of a complex administrative and governmental structure has not been the product of a well-defined approach or design. The comments of the Law Reform Commission of Canada apply to Britain: 'The growth of this structure is best described as an aspect of the evolution of government rather than as a planned constitutional development. It takes its shape from pragmatic responses to emerging problems over the years.'[1]

A commentator on government in the late nineteenth century might well have predicted the imminent demise of regulatory agencies. The growth of central government from 1830 to the end of the nineteenth century heralded the decline of the previously popular system of government by boards and commissions outside the central government departments.[2] Functions were also shifted from local authorities to central departments. The board system, with its control by appointees and independence from direct parliamentary supervision, was criticised as inconsistent with Parliament's growing desire to control administration.[3] Although of long and accepted tradition in both local and central government, the boards came under attack for their lack of accountability. Matters came to a head soon after the creation of the Poor Law Commissioners in 1834. The independence of the Commissioners from direct parliamentary control did not make for strong and fearless administration, as had been intended. Instead the commissioners were conscious of their lack of a political base. They were subject to intense political pressures and 'lived in dread of unpopularity and inquisitions'.[4]

A central cause of dissatisfaction was the lack of any board representative to answer to Parliament. Even in cases where board members happened also to be Members of Parliament, it could by no means be taken for granted that whoever was held accountable was in actual control of board policy.[5] These pressures contributed to the evolution of the modern Whitehall department, headed by a person both formally in control of policy and answerable for his or her department's actions to Parliament.

By 1847, for example, the three-man Poor Law Commission had been abolished in favour of ministerial control, and both the Railway Commission and the General Board of Health were similarly replaced in 1851 and 1854. By 1889 the same procedure had been followed in the fields of emigration, patents and lands.[6] The later Victorian era was what Willson has called the 'Golden Age of Ministerial Administration'[7] and at the turn of the century there remained only half a dozen or so boards with more than nominal independence of Ministers. During this period any regulatory function that was not given to a ministerial department tended to be allocated not to an independent agency but to a judicial authority or to Parliament itself.

Railway regulation exemplified the British approach.[8] The Railways Regulation Act of 1840 entrusted the task of reviewing the proposals of the private railway companies to the new Railway Department of the Board of Trade (a Whitehall department) rather than to an agency. In fact this system of regulation by inspectorate left effective control in the hands of the parliamentary committees that scrutinized Private Bills. Brief experiments with the Railway Board (a departmental body) and the under-powered Commissioners of Railways proved unsuccessful, and the next device to be employed was the tribunal-like Railway Commission of 1873. This tribunal took over from the Court of Common Pleas the task of making rulings on rates and preferences. Though the Commission was a weak body, little concerned with the wider issues of railway management, fifteen years later it was made permanent as the Railway and Canal Commission. Little had changed, however. Real control over railways policy remained with the parliamentary committees. A further tribunal-like body, the Railway Rates Tribunal, was set up in 1921 to control the charges set by private owners. In 1947 the railways were brought into public ownership and nationalized.

Such a pattern of control was typical of British utility regulation in the late nineteenth and early twentieth centuries. Other areas such as gas, water supplies and tramways relied heavily on parliamentary controls combined with systems of departmental inspection. Only in the electricity industry was there any indication of a willingness by central government to establish a body with a broader based regulatory power: the Electricity Commissioners were given both planning and adjudicatory functions in the Electricity Supply Act 1919. Even so, they lacked the resources with which to impose a structure on the industry and their regulatory functions were superceded when the Central Electricity Board (CEB) was set up in 1926.

The tendency, in short, was to treat regulatory issues as either administrative or executive (and so tasks for ministers), or as judicial (and so matters for determination by courts or court-like tribunals). The rise of social insurance and assistance brought with it a rise in the use of tribunals in the wake of the Liberal victory of 1906, but these bodies were modelled on the courts. Indeed tribunals, such as the Railways Commission, proved so common that by 1933 the regulation of British public utilities was viewed by some as considerably impaired by this reliance on the quasi-judicial method and by 'the resulting failure to develop the administrative commission'.[9] What was absent was a powerful agency that applied a special expertise, employed its own secretariat and regulated (in the sense of imposing a planned structure on an industry or social issue). Regulators, instead of instituting action, responded to the competing proposals of private interests.[10]

For a number of reasons that we discuss below, however, governments subsequently came to look on independent regulatory bodies as unavoidable (if in some respects undesirable) adjuncts of modern administration. Developments in relation to three related but distinct kinds of body can be traced; these are operational boards, tribunals and regulatory agencies.

Operational boards are public bodies that execute and manage certain functions themselves, rather than regulate the activities of private actors. Regulatory agencies should be distinguished from these operational bodies. Thus the Independent Broadcasting Authority (IBA) and the British Broadcasting Corporation (BBC) are quite different from one another in their functions. The IBA is principally regulatory:[11] rather than making programmes it leaves this to private television companies; it seeks instead to act in the public interest by imposing restrictions on the companies' activities. The BBC, on the other hand, is in charge of the production process itself and so is involved directly in operation. In this respect the BBC resembles public corporations and boards such as the British Railways Board and the Atomic Energy Authority.

Operating and regulatory bodies have some similarities, for example there is a common problem of subjection to ministerial control; and some bodies exercise both regulatory and operational functions (e.g. the Bank of England and the British National Oil Corporation as originally set up). In general, however, it is the regulatory body that gives rise to those issues of greatest interest to public lawyers. This is because the regulatory agency is perpetually sandwiched: it is invariably subject to overall governmental control but its *raison d'être* is the control of others. As a result it tends to come under attack from more than one set of interests. The role of law in resolving such tensions is a central concern of this book.

Especially after the Liberals came to power in 1906 the operating agency flourished. It provided a compromise between full government control and private ownership and operation. The Port of London Authority was set up in 1908, to be followed by the Road Board in 1909 and the Insurance Commission in 1911. In spite of the disfavour with which the Haldane Committee on the Machinery of Government[12] viewed the public corporation's lack of ministerial accountability, it continued to flourish, as exemplified by the Forestry Commission (1919), the British Broadcasting Corporation (1926) and the Central Electricity Board (1926). The feeling grew that there were good reasons for using such bodies as alternatives to central departments. With the support of champions like Herbert Morrison,[13] the London Passenger Transport Board developed in the 1930s to the accompaniment of the quasi-regulatory marketing boards for hops, pigs, milk, bacon, potatoes, etc. It was considered that these bodies allowed continuity of managerial expertise to develop; and that it was often more efficient to operate by small independent bodies than by large and amorphous government departments; and that they insulated industries from the vacillations of party politics (though the *Padfield* case[13a] showed a clear failure to achieve this in the case of milk).

Founded on such thinking, the operating agencies grew in number. From the 1940s onwards, with nationalization, they assumed more important functions. Further support for 'hiving-off' came when the Fulton Committee on the Civil Service accepted in 1967 that separation from the department would not only bring efficiency gains but would introduce more accountable management for many executive activities, especially in the provision of services to the community.[14] This aspect of the Fulton report was partly put into effect with the creation of the Post Office as a public corporation in 1969.[15]

Tribunals, too, have grown considerably in numbers with the development of the welfare state. Tribunals may be divided into (in Abel-Smith and Stevens'[16] terms) the court-substitute and policy-oriented types. Policy on which type of tribunal should be established has at times been highly contentious. More usually it has been the court-substitute variety which has eventually been favoured. Thus, one of the Franks Committee's more famous pronouncements was that tribunals should 'properly be regarded as machinery provided by Parliament for adjudication rather than as part of the machinery of administration'.[17] This view still influences current thinking. Thus conceived, tribunals present little threat to central government in respect of either their expertise or their policy-making power.

The policy-oriented tribunal, on the other hand, has been neglected by government, with the consequent indifference towards a group of agencies that serve an important function in government.[18] Moreover, the idea of the tribunal as properly only a court-substitute has added to other delays in the development of the regulatory agency in this country. Arguably it has also led to the allocation of decision-making functions to bodies ill-equipped to regulate in anything other than a reactive and haphazard fashion. Governments have in the past been more likely to set up tribunals or courts (such as the Restrictive Practices Court) and give them decision-making functions of an arguably non-justiciable nature.[19] Administrators have been slow to acknowledge the need for, the legitimacy of, and perhaps even the existence of, a more versatile kind of 'tribunal' – that, or they have shied away from the complex problems presented by such bodies.

Following the brief flurry of the Electricity Commissioners in the early 1920s, other bodies appeared that might have been given or have adopted a more adventurous regulatory role but failed to do so. The Traffic Commissioners were set up by 1930 to license public-service vehicles subject to ministerial appeals and policy controls. Even here, however, there was no body with a wide range of powers; the commissioners did not develop policies across the industry but adopted the stance of a specialist (court-substitute) tribunal. Real control of broad policy remained with the Minister and the industry itself. The road-haulage controls of the 1930s onwards were even more legalistic. A Traffic Commissioner licensed goods vehicle operations subject to appeals to the Road and Rail Traffic Appeal Tribunal (the Transport Tribunal after 1947). The system relied on judicial methods; policy-making evolved through a case-law that was later admitted to have been much more 'legal in flavour' than had been intended by its originators.[20]

In another respect, however, the marketing boards, with their mixed operational and regulatory functions, represented a step on the way to the regulatory agency. The Herring Industry Board (1935) and the White Fish Commission (1938) were empowered to make reorganization schemes, prescribe standards, give grants and act on behalf of the consumer. The White Fish Authority (1951) was given extensive powers to regulate by licensing, to impose conditions on licensees and to hold inquiries. In the post-war period, further marketing boards were set up to control such fields as Raw Cotton (1948), Crofting (1955), Sugar (1956), and Iron and Steel (1946–51).

In the late 1940s, another device designed to reconcile public and private interests was introduced. This was the ministerial public inquiry.[21] The origins of this process lie in the nineteenth-century Private Bill procedure, according to which undertakings wishing to acquire land by Private Bill had to allow objections to be lodged and parties to be heard by parliamentary committee. By the mid-nineteenth century the inquiry offered a means by which ministers could launch proposals and, through the appointment of inspectors and the holding of hearings, could receive information, consider public responses and give objectors a right to be heard. Inquiries might be statutory or non-statutory but, as the Franks Committee noted:[22] 'All involve the weighing of proposals or decisions or provisional proposals or decisions made by a public authority on the one hand against the views and interests of individuals affected by them on the other. All culminate in a ministerial decision in the making of which there is a wide discretion and which is final.'

Although the history of inquiries is long, particularly in the fields of public health and local government, it was the Town and Country Planning Act 1947 that dramatically multiplied the governmental role of inquiries.[23] By the end of the sixties the Ministry of Housing and Local Government was holding over 6,000 planning and 1,000 housing inquiries per annum and smaller numbers in public health and transportation.

The public inquiry process has been subject to a number of

criticisms[24] concerning, inter alia, their expense and delay; their inaccessibility to certain interests; their use of legalistic procedures; the opacity of their decisions; and failure to ensure the disclosure and debate of departmental facts, their figures and policies. Inquiries have, however, provided for some time an alternative to court or agency decision-making. The utility of the inquiry lies in its combining participatory rights with ministerial decisions. The advantages of the inquiry over the court or tribunal accordingly have lain in the breadth of representation that is possible; in the depth of policy discussion and prospectivity that is feasible, and in an ability to process and make openly political and large-scale decisions. The ministerial inquiry has tended to be preferred to the agency where large 'one-off' decisions have been called for and where ministers have been unwilling to delegate final decision-making powers.

The growth of inquiries in the fifties and sixties did not impede the rise of regulatory agencies unduly. Inquiries focused on planning, but agencies were to prove more suited to monitoring functions that required some independence and to the processing of smaller-scale decisions in numbers. Thus, following the development of the marketing boards a further step was taken in the broadcasting area with the 1954 Television Act and the advent of the Independent Television Authority. This body was given an independent status and powers to license programme-making companies in the public interest. Few wanted a directly government-controlled medium. The Authority was provided with a new and, for Britain, unique combination of powers. It adjudicated on issues between parties, it developed general policies and it enjoyed relative independence in a politically contentious area.[25]

A host of regulatory agencies followed in the 1960s. In this period some attention began to be paid to American experience. In the United States the pioneering body was the Interstate Commerce Commission (ICC) which was set up in 1887 to limit discriminatory pricing by railroads. The United States federal government quickly developed a penchant for independent regulatory agencies as the form of law enforcement best suited to offset the limitations of the civil legal process. Between the establishment of the ICC and the beginning of the Second World War at least eight major federal agencies had been established.

Certain powers were identified by R. E. Cushman as common to such agencies: a quasi-judicial power, often in the form of a power to issue injunctive-type 'cease and desist' orders; a quasi-legislative power to issue rules and regulations; a broad administrative or managerial power to conduct or closely direct the conduct of business operations; an enforcement power; and an investigation and planning power, e.g. to research problems and recommend new legislation.[26] Some of these bodies were essentially concerned with the economic functioning of a particular industry (e.g. the ICC) and others were given 'an extended policing function of a particular nature' (e.g. the National Labour Relations Board).[27] Resort to the administrative process for the latter purpose was said to spring 'from a distrust of the judicial process as a way of developing both law and regulatory methods that were sufficiently responsive to particular industrial problems'.[28]

During the 1930s, in the era of increasingly active intervention by the US federal government in social and economic policy known as the New Deal, United States independent commissions multiplied and their most rigorous academic defence was mounted. In 1938 James M. Landis published *The Administrative Process* – 'the most eloquent celebration of commission regulation ever written'[29] – affirming the validity of broad administrative discretions in pursuit of the public interest. Since the high point created by Landis, the United States agencies have felt the weight of almost fifty years of criticism.[30] We have considered some of the pros and cons in the first chapter and will consider them again in chapter 3. For present purposes what is important is that in the 1960s British civil servants and legislators became increasingly well-disposed towards agencies and began to take notice of the regulatory strategies that were being employed across the Atlantic while apparently downplaying the mounting criticism encountered in the United States. Thus, for example, the United States Equal Employment Opportunity Commission provided the precedent for the British anti-discrimination agencies.

The early sixties in Britain marked what has been called a movement from the 'mixed economy' towards the 'managed economy'[31] and this shift of political strategy was reflected in new institutional fashions. Instead of general arm's-length regulation of industry and society, more specific forms of state intervention came into favour. New attempts at national economic planning were made by a Conservative government that had been re-elected for a third term. The shape of government was redrawn on more 'corporatist' lines, in which major groupings and interests were encouraged to share in the processes of government. The Conservatives' belief at that time in planning led to the creation of the National Economic Development Council (NEDC), the National Economic Development Office (NEDO), and the National Incomes Commission (NIC). For our purposes, the NEDC was notable then as a non-departmental body set up on a tripartite basis, i.e. with representatives from the TUC, industrialists' organizations and from government. It marked the start of a period of sustained corporatist planning and heralded a new rise in agency fortunes.

The incoming Labour Government of 1964 created a new Department of Economic Affairs (DEA). A host of ancillary planning and regulatory agencies were set up to work alongside it. Foremost of these were the National Board for Prices and Incomes (NBPI) of 1965 and the Industrial Reorganisation Corporation (IRC) of 1966. At a greater distance from the planning hub were bodies such as the Highlands and Islands Development Board (HIDB, 1965); the Race Relations Board (RRB, 1965); the Monopolies Commission (1965); the Supplementary Benefits Commission (SBC, 1966); the Land Commission (1967); the Gaming Board (1968); the Community Relations Commission (1968); and the Commission on Industrial Relations (1969). As noted already, the Fulton Committee's endorsement of the public corporation in 1967 was mainly concerned with operational issues, but it also encouraged the use of agencies in their broader role.

Agencies also survived the next change in governmental philosophy. Although the notion of the managed economy had waned by the start of the seventies and the cult of economic liberalism had become stronger, the momentum of corporatism was sustained. The new aim was to make tripartism work – if not for the purposes of general planning, then in specific areas. New bodies were created taking this goal into account. The creation of the Manpower Services Commission (MSC, 1973), the Health and Safety Commission (HSC, 1974), the Advisory Conciliation and Arbitration Service (ACAS, 1974), the Equal Opportunities Commission (EOC, 1976), and the Commission for Racial Equality (CRE, 1977) reflected this concern. Consumer and social interests were represented by a large number of new groups and agencies (principally by the National Consumer Council (NCC, 1975)). More narrowly-defined planning functions were revived with the National Enterprise Board (NEB, 1975). Regulatory bodies such as the Civil Aviation Authority (CAA, 1972) and Independent Broadcasting Authority (IBA, 1972) appeared on the scene.

The reasons for the lateness of the agency's arrival on the political stage are, then, fairly clear. For many decades before the Second World War, governments and administrators had felt more comfortable with courts, tribunals and Whitehall departments. The explanations for agency growth go beyond political fashions. Four perceptions were of particular importance. First, certain areas of industrial activity and of social life were thought to require a special and continuing form of control. Thus in discrimination or broadcasting it was insufficient to rely on sporadic forays by individuals in the ordinary courts. Second, such fields demanded the development of regulatory strategies, and overall policies to guide individual decisions; a thinly-staffed court or tribunal was incapable of researching and applying such policies. Third, there was perceived to be the need to mix functions – bodies were required not only to decide issues between parties but to promote policies in the field, to fight political battles, to investigate and to enforce. Again, the traditional tribunal was ill-suited to the task. Fourth, the growth of particular social problems and the arrival of advanced technologies justified the creation of *expert* decision-makers capable of attracting staff of high calibre and of understanding the problems of regulating such complex matters as gaming, broadcasting, or civil aviation. By the mid-seventies the regulatory agency had proved to be a necessary and a resilient feature of government. It was considered to be an essential part of the planned economy; it was also central to a corporatist approach to the governmental function in a more liberal, capitalistic model of the economy.

The sixties, and to a lesser extent the seventies, were decades of economic growth. The idea of increased regulation was not so difficult to sell to politicians, the public and industry as it was to become in a recession. In a burgeoning economy relatively few people protested about compliance costs and those concerned to take action against social wrongs found more supporters than in harder times. Regulatory agencies are in a rather different situation in the very different political climate of the 1980s.

Developments on a number of fronts have had a direct effect on the use and operation of agencies since 1979 when the Conservative Government of Margaret Thatcher came to power. Policies on privatization, on deregulation and on the costs of complying with regulation affect the work which already established agencies undertake. They also influence the design of future institutions. Attitudes towards particular strategies also affect the nature of régimes: thus self-regulatory and incentive-based methods of control are less dependent on agency supervision than, say, licensing schemes. Developments in these policies and strategies will be considered first before commenting on some of the institutional and legal implications of recent events for agencies.

Civil servants concerned with regulation in Britain distinguish between three current strands of policy, all of which bear on the institutions and strategies of government control. *Privatization* principally aims to effect a movement from public to private ownership. It seeks to increase competition in the market-place, to improve management, to separate industrial from social policy, to increase efficiency, to broaden share ownership, and to 'roll back' the state.[32] It can also be seen as a useful way of financing such items as tax cuts. *Deregulation* is the process of reducing state control over an industry or activity so as to make it structurally more responsive to market forces. (The term 'liberalization' may be used to refer to less ambitious reductions in control.) *Disburdening* overlaps with deregulation but is less radical; it is aimed at reducing the compliance costs imposed on industry by regulation. A principal justification for disburdening has been the notion that a reduction in regulatory burdens will contribute significantly to employment.

The Conservative government adopted a three-pronged strategy of privatization. It sold off public assets to the private sector, opened state activities to competition and contracted out public-sector services.[33] Asset sales started with shares in British Petroleum and reached a peak with the floating of British Telecom, TSB and British Gas between 1984 and 1986. Other notable privatizations have concerned Cable and Wireless, Associated British Ports, Amersham International, British Aerospace, Britoil, the National Freight Corporation, Jaguar Cars, Enterprise Oil, Sealink Ferries, British Airways and the British Airports Authority. In 1987 proposals were at varying stages to privatize the National Bus Company and the Regional Water Authorities.

Restrictions on market entry have been lifted in a number of areas so as to allow the private sector to compete with the public. A principal example is the Government allowing Mercury to enter into competition with British Telecom (BT). This was achieved by removing BT's statutory monopoly over the supply and installation of subscriber equipment (e.g. phone sets). In 1983 private electricity producers were allowed to supply power directly to customers – and to do so they were permitted to use the public distribution network at pre-specified charges.

Contracting-out[34] is the third element of privatization. It involves putting out to competitive tender many of the services provided by local government and public bodies. Examples are refuse-collection services, school cleaning, hospital cleaning and hospital catering. Central departments such as the Ministry of Defence have contracted out services ranging from catering and cleaning to the refitting of warships.

Deregulation seeks to increase competition within and between sectors.[35] Thus express coaching services were deregulated in 1980. This removed route monopolies enjoyed by public and private operators. The Government instituted the deregulation of financial services, removed control on foreign exchange and dividends, opened the market for spectacles to competition, relaxed advertising restrictions on solicitors, accountants, stockbrokers, opticians and veterinary surgeons and limited the solicitors' monopoly on conveyancing. Competition on domestic air routes was allowed, the Civil Aviation Authority deregulated domestic air tariffs and the Government negotiated the liberalization of air services with Holland, Germany and Luxembourg.[36]

Disburdening stemmed from rather different roots. It was pressure from the small business lobby in the wake of the Conservatives' 1979 election victory that started the movement to reduce compliance costs. A first manifestation of this pressure came in the form of action by the Department of Trade and Industry (DTI) which was concerned mainly with employment (rather than, say, the inflationary effects of regulation). An attempt was made in the early eighties to identify those regulations that discouraged small businesses from expanding employment.

Such disburdening endeavours met with little enthusiasm within the civil service but in 1983 an internal report reached the Prime Minister who decided that insufficient attention had been given to the issue. By March 1985 the report *Burdens on Business*[37] had been produced and a task force, called the Enterprise Unit, had been set up under Lord Young in the Cabinet Office and served as a forum for proposals on disburdening and (to a lesser extent) deregulation.

The Department of Trade and Industry proposed to introduce a number of burden-reducing measures and a new regulatory review procedure. The details were spelled out in the ensuing White Paper, *Lifting the Burden*[38] and the mischief clearly spotlighted: 'The tide of legislation has risen inexorably over the years in all countries of the western world . . . overall there is no doubt that we suffer from the sheer weight of legislation and controls.'[39] The White Paper proposed such measures as: introducing simpler building regulations; reducing VAT form-filling requirements; training health and safety inspectors on small firms' interests; designating a Health and Safety Commissioner to represent small firms; abolishing road service licensing for local buses; abolishing restrictions on shop hours and improving the quality of Departmental guidance to businesses.

More adventurous was the proposal to set up a central task force in the Cabinet Office to scrutinize departmental regulations. In 1986, this unit was called the Enterprise and Deregulation Unit (EDU). It was set up initially for a three-year trial period and consisted of an Under-Secretary, two Assistant Secretaries, three Principals, and other staff up to a total of twenty. The EDU was assisted by an advisory panel on deregulation which was made up of practising businessmen. The procedures used were similar to (and were modelled on) those employed by President Reagan's Office of Management and Budget from 1981 onwards.[40] They were set out in the White Paper, *Building Business . . . Not Barriers* of May 1986[41] and required Departments to submit to the EDU their legislative and rule-making plans. Each new regulation was to be accompanied by a 'preliminary' compliance cost assessment in brief form and these assessments were to be carried out by departments' own 'deregulation units'. The 1986 White Paper set out a checklist on costs and benefits for use in carrying out such assessments.[42] The EDU would 'call in' problematic analyses by asking for a more detailed balancing of costs and benefits in a 'full compliance cost assessment'. The aim was to intervene in the policy-making process at an early stage in order to reduce the imposition of 'unnecessary' burdens on industry. The EDU was to react to proposals as they emerged from departments rather than to consider root and branch reforms. They were thus to focus on the department's ability to justify a particular proposed regulation rather than an analysis of whether another regulatory strategy would achieve the desired end more effectively.

In contrast, some academics and reformers in the United States have become concerned not only to trim existing regulatory mechanisms, but also to examine whether there is a match between a particular regulatory strategy and the activity under control. The objective of such inquiries has been to identify the 'least restrictive' form of regulation, i.e. the mode of control that would realize legislatively-defined objectives, but at the same time would most effectively give industrial managers freedom in their decision-making, and would reduce compliance costs. The less restrictive forms of regulation considered by Stephen Breyer[43] include such policies as: deregulation, coupled with increased use of antitrust laws; disclosure rules; taxation; the creation of marketable property rights; adjusted liability rules; bargaining; and public ownership.

There is little evidence that the British Government has taken steps to replace systems of control such as agency licensing and standard setting with these less restrictive regimes. Thus antitrust laws have not replaced command and control methods, nor has much use been made of rules on disclosure, taxes, marketable property rights, liability or bargaining processes. This is understandable given governments' reluctance (and lack of appropriate machinery) to effect a root and branch reappraisal of regulatory regimes.

There are, also, very few civil servants who are concerned with regulatory strategies. Those strategies that emerge do so not out of any consistent plan or programme but from a process of political and bureaucratic muddling-through. In 1986 the Department of Trade and Industry (DTI) contained a small branch dealing with competition aspects of regulation and, averaged out, the time of only one Principal (supervised by an Assistant-Secretary with broader responsibilities) was devoted to regulatory techniques. The EDU, as already noted, had in 1986 a staff of around twenty but was more specifically devoted to the question of regulatory strategy. Staff of the Treasury and of the Management and Personnel Office overviewed regulation on a less specialized basis.

No one branch of the civil service has a coordinating function. Experience of regulation in one area is not consistently passed on to those dealing with related systems of control. Considerable faith is still placed in the notion that each regulatory problem may be dealt with ad hoc by generalists. Individuals such as those engaged in parliamentary drafting have a limited role in drawing parallels between different areas but such bridges are built on a random basis only. Both regulation and, later, privatization are largely dealt with on a departmentally-sponsored basis and this strictly limits the flow of·ideas. As for knowledge of regulatory experience in other countries such as the USA, one senior official described this as 'negligible'.[44] The overriding factor in such matters is the pressure of time. Political timescales are short, workloads are heavy and civil servants are hard-pressed to meet immediate deadlines.

This is not to say that certain strategies do not become fashionable (or unpopular) through a process of osmosis or by derivation from the Government's broader position. A number deserve comment. The first is self-regulation. As will be seen in the chapters on health and safety at work, on conciliation and arbitration in industrial relations, and on financial services, the idea that regulation can be delegated to those participating in an activity (with or without a compulsory element incorporated in the scheme) has grown more popular with recent governments than it has been for some time. Self-regulation in this sense has succeeded tripartism, consensualism and arms-length regulation as the strategy in vogue. Thus, for example, from the 'regulation with a light touch' of civil aviation licensing in the 1970s, government has moved in the 1980s to self-regulation in the shadow of government in the area of financial services. Resource limitations also encourage this drift – hence the Health and Safety Commission's movement towards 'health and safety assurance'.

A related development is the increasing practice of regulating by administrative rather than statutory rules.[45] Thus, instead of relying on primary legislation enforced by officials, an increasing number of regulatory regimes now rely heavily on codes of practice, guidance and circulars, often of indeterminate legal status. Reliance on codes of practice has been officially sanctioned in the fields of arbitration, race and sex discrimination and health and safety at work. The code is also a central plank of self-regulatory systems of control.

One device now less fashionable in central government is the use by government of power to distribute government largess (for example in the form of contracts, grants and access to resources) to impose particular policies on the recipients in the private sector.[46] One of the most publicized uses of such a power was the attempt in the mid 1970s to impose wage restraint by such methods.[47] The collapse of this policy has increased the unpopularity of such measures. Successive governments have been hesitant, for example, to use their contracting powers to influence the employment practices of private companies in relation to race and sex discrimination, although a number of local authorities use contracts as a tool of anti-discrimination enforcement. The reluctance of the Conservative government to limit commercial interests in the public interest has also contributed to a lack of enthusiasm for contractual regulation. The power of the purse has, however, been used continuously and increasingly by central government to impose policies on local government.

Despite the relatively limited changes, however, these governmental policies have important implications for agencies, as do the attitudes of the party in power towards the actual institutions of government. Agencies come within the genus of 'quangos'[48] and therefore might be expected to suffer, with other fringe bodies, from the attacks that have been made on that genus. The latest assault began in 1978 when Phillip Holland and Michael Fallon published *The Quango Explosion* and criticized fringe bodies on three grounds: there were too many of them, they were too free from parliamentary control and they were founded upon an unhealthy system of ministerial patronage. Holland was supported by other Conservative commentators (such as Alfred Sherman[49]) in issuing what amounted to anti-quango propaganda.[50] From other political directions came numerous defences of these bodies.[51]

It was clear after the 1979 election that Conservative sentiments against quangos had been stirred. Less clear was the nature of the bodies involved and the value of the term 'quango' as an explanatory device. In 1979 Holland had listed 3,068 bodies, divided into 947 'types'. In his 1982 book on the subject, Anthony Barker, who had invented the word 'quango', complained that it was 'overused and uselessly vague'.[52] Undeterred, Mrs Thatcher examined the possibilities of reducing the number of such bodies by commissioning a report that would go beyond the Civil Service's 1978 survey of fringe bodies.[53] This report was undertaken by Sir Leo Pliatsky, who reviewed 'non-departmental public bodies' in 1980.[54] By this time there were already signs that no radical cull was to occur. Michael Heseltine, the then Environment Secretary, announced that he would abolish half the quangos under his department's control. But in the event few bodies of size or importance were affected and the exercise has been described as 'a massacre of gnats'.[55] Even after the Pliatsky report only 30 out of 489 executive bodies and six tribunals out of 67 tribunal *systems* were abolished. Commentators such as Hood[56] and Barker[57] have argued that non-departmental bodies have considerable tenacity, that they help to keep the centre of government small, that it is often difficult to find other bodies to fulfil the task at issue and that, as a result, culls tend to be either cosmetic (the squashing of gnats), or political (where one administration abolishes agencies that are peculiarly associated with an opposing party's politics), or take the form of an increase in constraints such as budget controls and the tightening of ministerial powers.

Regulatory agencies do not come into the class of gnats since they are on the whole sizeable and engaged in tasks that are seen as important. They have, as a result, managed to withstand the attack on quangos. The functions of regulatory agencies would be peculiarly difficult for a department to handle and agencies thus have a porcupine-like quality within government. Where they are most prone to abolition is, firstly, in cases where deregulation makes their skills redundant. Secondly, they may prove unnecessary where an alternative, less restrictive form of regulation is instituted – but, as we have seen, government is neither well equipped nor apparently inclined to effect such reforms.

Paradoxically, there are instances where the Government has given regulatory agencies greater freedom. Thus we shall see that the Civil Aviation Authority (CAA) was released from the system of ministerial policy guidance in 1980 so as to create (at least on the surface) a body of greater rather than less freedom from governmental control.[58] It is also the case that even an administration hostile to agencies may create new agencies where a new regulatory issue arises, for example because of technological developments, as with the Cable Authority. Central government may, moreover, prefer agency to local government control in certain circumstances. Thus the abolition of the Greater London Council[59] has resulted in control by commissions rather than by a directly elected body.

Where a nationalized industry is privatized even a Conservative administration may also decide to set up a new regulatory agency. Thus in the case of the British Telecom (BT) privatization, the options of creating competition for BT and breaking it up into smaller units were explored but rejected as being too difficult given the political timescale involved and, with regard to the latter, the size of such a task. The strategy pursued – the creation of a dominant private corporation – was not seen as inevitably requiring a specialist agency. However, the Government considered that to rely solely on competition legislation as applied by an adapted Office of Fair Trading would have been inappropriate given the market strength of BT. The political need as perceived by the Government was to propose privatization subject to discipline by an overseeing body. Serious consideration was given to adding a new regulatory role to the Office of Fair Trading's (OFT's) functions but this was rejected on the grounds that it would overshadow the OFT's other more general functions of promoting competition. As a result, the Office of Telecommunications (OFTEL) was chosen. A similar pattern is likely to occur in future privatizations.

Regulatory agencies thus occupy a peculiar position in the politics of the 1980s. They are relatively immune from root-and-branch attack because of the size, importance and specialization of their functions; on the other hand, they are involved in the practice of regulation and so might be expected to find life difficult under a Conservative administration committed to liberating the forces of free enterprise. The CAA may have been unshackled in one sense but other agencies, such as the Commission for Racial Equality (CRE), the Equal Opportunities Commission (EOC) and the Advisory Conciliation and Arbitration Service (ACAS) have found little support from a government elected on a mandate that was not in full harmony with their endeavours.

From the point of view of an agency, its life can be made uncomfortable in a number of ways in the face of an unsympathetic government. Ministerial controls tend to be exercised more severely and to make policy development more problematic. Agencies may be pushed into more conservative and more reactive regulatory stances. Since agency rules and policies often require ministerial approval the policy-making process may be slowed as well as narrowed by tight governmental control. Where disburdening involves a scheme of governmental review (e.g. as by the EDU), a certain amount of second-guessing is inevitable. The changing political context has resulted, therefore, in considerably increased interest in the processes of agency decision-making and the external controls to which agencies are subject.

The American regulatory agencies have long been criticized for their lack of accountability. They have been dubbed the 'headless fourth branch'[60] of government and their legitimacy has been much debated.[61] In Britain also the agencies have been attacked as uncontrolled and as illegitimate planks of the corporate state.[62] One response to such attacks, and to some of the agencies' operational failings, may lie in systems of control and accountability involving (singly or in combination) the judiciary, the legislature, central government and internal oversight within the agency itself. Agencies that are perceived as being appropriately restrained may more readily be seen as constitutionally and politically acceptable than those that are not. There are, however, problems in most systems of agency accountability and control. These issues are the subject of the next chapters. We turn first, in chapter 3, to systems of internal and political oversight. In chapter 4 we consider judicial review.

3

The Evaluation and Oversight of Regulatory Agencies

To criticize an agency, to advocate its reform, may be either to criticize the appropriateness of an overall regulatory programme, or to point to failings of agency performance in pursuit of that programme. In the case of the Commission for Racial Equality, for example, the attempt to achieve a reduction in discrimination may itself be the source of criticism. Alternatively, the Commission's programme and methods of attempting to achieve that objective may be the subject of complaint. This chapter focuses largely on the second alternative, on agency performance.

If the commentator is to engage in more than the expression of personal preference, and if he or she hopes to engage in debate with others on agency performance, on the operation of the agency or on oversight of the agency, then a common set of values that serves as a basis for such comments should be identified if possible. One attempt to identify such values was made by the Law Reform Commission of Canada (LRCC) in its final report on Independent Administrative Agencies. The LRCC argued that the processes through which independent administrative agencies make decisions should reflect an appropriate blend of the following values: accountability; authoritativeness; comprehensibility; effectiveness, economy and efficiency; fairness; integrity; openness; and principled decision-making.

The issue of 'legitimacy' lies at the heart of the matter and underpins many of these issues. But 'legitimacy' is a difficult and complex concept. Which elements within the constitutional system suffice to provide legitimacy as distinct from moral, constitutional, or indeed legal worth to an action? Are there alternative sources of legitimacy? Does legitimacy arise from a combination of sources? What criteria are used to establish the legitimacy of administrative action by regulatory agencies? These questions have to be disentangled before evaluations or reforms are contemplated. This process of disentanglement is relevant not only for discussing regulatory agencies but for issues of public law more generally. This is where the study of regulatory agencies touches the core of constitutional theory.

When there is talk of this or that agency action being legitimate or illegitimate, in the sense that certain values are satisfied or left unsatisfied by agency action, reference appears to be being made to one or more of five key criteria: Is it supported by legislative authority? Is it otherwise accountable? Does it carry out its tasks with due process? Is the body expert? Is it efficient? These five criteria constitute the limited vocabulary of the language of legitimacy.

1 Legislative Mandate

Agency action deserves support, according to this first criterion, when there exists an authorizing mandate from Parliament, the fountain of democratic authority within the British state. Citizens control the legislature and through it the actions of administrators.[1] The agency is 'a mere transmission belt for implementing legislative directives in particular cases'.[2]

The legislative mandate provides an essential core in assessing agency action. To move clearly outside legislative terms of reference results in illegitimacy. Evaluating agency action is thus different from making a moral judgement. One may morally applaud the action of the head of the regulatory agency who donates all of the organization's funds to Oxfam but this is unlikely to be endorsed as legitimate agency action.

There are, however, various problems with this criterion. The first lies in its lack of application where the legislature has provided administrators with broad discretions. In such cases it cannot simply be asserted that a mandate is being fulfilled. Implementing that mandate demands a process of interpretation. Where, as is often the case with regulatory bodies, the relevant statute sets out objectives that are not only stated in general terms but exist at mutual tension, it may not be possible to identify a single mandate at all. In his chapter on the Cable Authority (CA), Cento Veljanovski makes the point that where a government has confused its control strategies a regulatory mandate will be especially unclear. It is, furthermore, difficult to set down clear statutory standards insofar as a regulator's *judgement* is precisely what is sought. Second, if the statutory objectives are to be pursued with regard to fairness and due process, some source beyond the statute is often needed to bring these principles into operation. In short the nature of the modern administrative state demands that bureaucrats act on broad legislative directives and that they engage in a political function in interpreting and applying those directives. This leaves the legislative model as a powerful but incomplete basis for assessment.

Most of the agencies discussed in this volume operate broad mandates which are difficult to cite as convincing defences when they are under attack. The CRE is a prime example of an agency that lacks a mandate sufficient to withstand the predations of an apparently hostile judiciary.[3] Likewise, when CAA route licensing policies have been subject to criticism by the airlines or have been appealed to the Trade and Industry Secretary, the CAA has not been able to counter those criticisms by referring to precise authorizing provisions in the parent statute. Complaints that the inspectors of the HSE have made excessively burdensome demands on industry have not been easily dismissed by reference to the Health and Safety at Work Act 1974. Contributors to this volume will also draw attention to the vagueness of the mandates of the Gaming Board, ACAS, the OFT, the MMC and the Cable Authority. A number of further consequences appear to flow from such vague mandates. It has proved as difficult to assess whether an agency is *under*-performing as it has to assess whether it is going beyond its mandate. Those in whose interest the agency was established find it hard to challenge the non-exercise of broad powers.

Were agencies to be given precise mandates then clearer assertions of legitimacy could be made. In an ideal world, agencies might derive legitimacy through a legislative mandate in which Parliament would set down the tasks it wants agencies to achieve, attribute powers and designate both precise objectives and appropriate standards to govern agency behaviour. Such a mechanistic or 'transmission-belt' model may, however, be inappropriate in the case of regulatory agencies. These are bodies that are created to engage in complex tasks that are specialized and require the exercise of judgement. The notion that precise standards can be used to control agency activity has long been questioned in the USA where most agencies in fact enjoy highly discretionary powers and regulate in pursuit of objectives that are stated in the broadest terms.[4] It is not feasible for Parliament to create specialist regulatory bodies and at the same time specify policies and strategies in advance and in detail.[5] Such an approach would unduly fetter the agency. As importantly, Parliament has neither the time, inclination or knowledge to undertake such a task.

One device that may serve a useful purpose in rendering an agency's interpretation of its statutory mandate more continuously subject to parliamentary scrutiny is the requirement that administrative rules be subject to parliamentary approval. The process of rule-making may be left informal in the statute establishing the agency or it may be institutionalized by Parliament conferring on regulatory agencies an explicit power to issue guidelines in relation to the exercise of their statutory powers (the Civil Aviation Authority was given a duty to do this in the Civil Aviation Act 1980).[6] The power is sometimes made subject to duties of reasonable notice, comment and consultation. On occasion it has also been made subject to parliamentary approval or veto, as is the case with the power of the CRE to issue Codes of Practice. This endorsement by Parliament of agency rules may increase the legitimacy of agency action. Thus in health and safety regulation the HSE inspectors may assure factory managers that they are acting consistently by citing a guidance note or approved code of practice. This has a legitimizing effect. It is a practice common to many enforcement officials. Although some commentators have seen such rule-making as the most hopeful way of controlling regulatory discretion,[7] there are limits here also. Where agencies possess rule-making powers they may not necessarily use these to confine, structure or check discretion; they may in fact create further discretions.[8] The agency may not see it as in its own interest to develop rules and there may exist considerable tensions between rule-making and the other activities in which the agency is engaged – such as adjudication by trial-type procedures and enforcement. As importantly, scrutiny by the legislature of such rules is intermittent and arguably ineffective.

2 Accountability or Control

While legitimacy may ultimately derive from the assent of the people as expressed in Parliament, oversight of agencies has often been placed in the hands of others separate from the agency itself. Thus, an agency might be made accountable for its interpretation of its mandate to a representative body and this oversight renders exercise of its powers more acceptable.[9]

This criterion suffers from some of the same deficiencies as the legislative mandate criterion but there are often additional difficulties. The selection of the individuals or bodies to whom the bureaucrat is to be made accountable is controversial. Insofar as accountability and control are not exercised by Parliament or elected persons, it may in turn be criticized as unrepresentative. Thus, where a body such as the judiciary provides the basis for accountability and control through judicial review, it may be objected that the judges are not competent in the relevant area; that the process of going to law is inefficient; and that the legislature did not, in any event, intend that the courts rather than, say, the agency should decide this issue.

Can it be said that the systems of accountability and control to which most agencies are subject are sufficiently rigorous? It seems that there do exist real difficulties on this front. Many agencies discussed in this book are subject to powers of direction by a Secretary of State, they issue Annual Reports and are subject to varying forms of political influence. In spite of such factors, however, many agencies still control their own destinies and policies to an extent that exposes them to criticism as unaccountable and uncontrolled.

A review, moreover, of the agencies discussed in this volume reveals a wide variety of problems with and responses to accountability and control. For the self-regulatory agency, as encountered in the financial services area, legitimacy has a most insecure footing in accountability and control and must largely look to other criteria such as efficiency. Tripartite bodies such as the HSC and ACAS offer a ready-made response to the accountability and control issue insofar as major involved interests are represented at the highest levels of the agency. As the chapters on ACAS and HSC/E make clear, however, tripartism offers no easy or complete answer. There is the problem of representing the spectrum of interests adequately through limited board membership. The consensual approach does not make radical forms of regulation easy and it may produce regulatory regimes that are highly dependent on governmental support. When that support disappears then, as we shall see with ACAS, this may place the agency in a very difficult position. In contrast to areas of regulatory activity where political contentious ness highlights issues of legitimacy, the Gaming Board (GB) is a body engaged in relatively uncontroversial matters. In such a sphere the need for political controls and accountability may not be *perceived* as so pressing. The language of legitimacy does, nevertheless, imply that bodies such as the GB should not simply be left to their own devices.

In general, accountability to and control by ministers has operated in a piecemeal fashion and this is to some extent understandable. Ministerial powers of formal direction are frequently found but Ministers are reluctant to use these. They tend to prefer more discreet forms of influence which are less readily attributed legitimizing value by observers and those involved. Two factors, moreover, diminish ministerial incentives to make agencies controlled and accountable. First, the shadowing departments of state tend not to be able to match the specialist knowledge of the agencies. Second, Ministers are very often glad to preserve the autonomy of the agency so as to avoid potential political flak in a difficult area.

Agencies are accountable, to a limited extent, to the Parliamentary Commissioner for Administration (PCA) and the Comptroller and Auditor-General, both of whom scrutinize on behalf of Parliament. The Parliamentary Commissioner Act 1967 established the PCA to investigate maladministration by central government departments and certain other bodies acting on behalf of the Crown. Over the years a number of regulatory bodies have also become subject to the PCA, for example the Health and Safety Commission and Executive (in 1974); the Office of the Director General of Fair Trading (in 1975), the Advisory Conciliation and Arbitration Service (in 1977) and the Office of the Director General of Telecommunications (in 1984). The Select Committee on the PCA recommended in 1984[10] that the PCA's jurisdiction should be extended to cover a larger number of non-departmental bodies. The committee had been convinced by arguments from Sir Leo Pliatsky and the Civil Service Department that a means of obtaining independent investigation of complaints should be available against non-departmental bodies where the functions carried out by those bodies affect individual citizens or groups and where those functions might just as appropriately be those of central government. Non-departmental status was, accordingly, not to be a shelter from PCA investigation.

The Government responded to the Select Committee report in 1985 with a White Paper,[11] which agreed in principle to extend the PCA's jurisdiction to cover certain non-departmental bodies provided that the function involved affected individual citizens or groups of citizens and that the bodies were subject to some degree of ultimate ministerial accountability to Parliament. Financial dependency was to suffice for these purposes. The Government accepted the Select Committee's view that PCA scrutiny and sanctioning of non-departmental bodies did not require a new ministerial power to order compliance with PCA recommendations. It was thought that the authority of the PCA and the interest in these matters of Parliament and the Select Committee on the PCA would suffice. The White Paper accordingly proposed to amend the 1967 Act so as to put a series of non-departmental bodies under the PCA's scrutiny. Notably for our purposes, this included the Commission for Racial Equality and the Equal Opportunities Commission as well as a number of development boards, e.g. the Highlands and Islands Development Board. The Civil Aviation Authority was, however, not to be added: it was to be treated as a nationalized industry subject like others to the constraints of trading and in its regulatory functions it was said to be liable to the oversight of the Council on Tribunals. Action on these proposals is awaited.

The powers of the Comptroller and Auditor General (CAG) in relation to agencies were extended by the National Audit Act 1983. The CAG, assisted by a National Audit Office, was empowered[12] to carry out examination into the 'economy, efficiency and effectiveness' with which any department, authority or other body has used its resources in discharging its functions. This power covers any body believed to receive more than half its income from public funds. It does not, however, entitle the CAG to question the merits of the policy objectives of any such body.

Limits on accountability through the PCA and CAG flow from a number of features of these bodies. The PCA has pointed out[13] that the need for the PCA to take a personal interest in complaints restricts the number and scope of cases that his office can cover. The PCA is not a means of routinely controlling agency operations. The PCA may offer an avenue of redress in exceptional cases but does not provide continuous supervision of agencies. Similarly the CAG will investigate some agencies in depth but CAG actions will be sporadic and, crucially, will not address the merits of agency objectives or strategies.

Parliament also attempts to make agencies accountable and subject to control through its select committee system. But while this system has had its successes, there is no committee that takes a broad view of regulatory bodies. The investigations by the departmental select committees, though useful, do not provide consistent monitoring. The executive, for reasons already given, has neither a strong set of incentives nor great ability to control regulatory agencies. Overall it would be difficult to claim that *post*-legislative agency accountability to Parliament, to the executive or to the public provides a secure foundation for legitimacy.

These points suggest both that limited legitimacy flows to agencies through the machinery of accountability and control and that the system of government has largely failed to respond to these issues. What steps are available to increase potential legitimacy claims based on this criterion?

Parliament might, of course, take further steps to control agencies, for example by exercising direct *post*-legislative powers of scrutiny. One suggestion is the idea of a House of Commons Select Committee on Regulated Industries along the lines of the Select Committee on Nationalized Industries.[14] This might investigate both regulatory strategies and the effects of regulation and would add a dimension to Parliament's control. Suitably staffed such a committee might also be in a position to advise departments and agencies on the design of regulatory institutions and the match between regulatory strategy and task. Against this proposal, however, it has been argued that the effect of increasing parliamentary scrutiny is to encourage ministerial interference and the undermining of agency independence.[15] On this view Ministers are bound to assert control over bodies for which they are held responsible. For such reasons, controls other than direct parliamentary ones may be more appropriate in the case of independent bodies.

Executive direction has been the route favoured most recently in the United States, where the last decade has seen increasingly firm presidential control over agency action. Recent reforms have owed much to the Cutler-Johnson scheme which, as published in 1975,[16] would have allowed the President to modify or reverse agency decisions or to demand agency action within a prescribed time. The American Bar Association endorsed this approach in 1979 and urged that agencies be directed to prepare regulatory analyses when contemplating regulation.[17] President Reagan built on these suggestions by issuing Executive Order 12291 in February 1981. This order demanded that all new major regulatory rules promulgated by agencies should be submitted to cost-benefit testing.[18] Such tests are subject to review by the Office of Management and Budget, and it is argued that they have been effective in increasing presidential input into agency rule-making, in reducing the flow of new regulations and in increasing agency awareness of compliance costs.

Such a system of control might be introduced in this country, and applied to agencies. A move was made in this direction with the creation of the Enterprise and Deregulation Unit. The White Paper *Lifting the Burden*[19] was followed by a further White Paper calling for regulatory bodies such as the Health and Safety Commission to conduct compliance cost assessments before developing regulations.

As a general system of ministerial supervision over agencies, cost-benefit testing is nevertheless deficient. This is not simply because of those difficulties inherent in applying such tests in the field of regulation. There are other more general difficulties: the almost inevitable paucity of reliable data on effects; the assumptions to be made concerning enforcement; the problem of anticipating the behavioural responses of regulatees and the problems of pricing certain values such as life. It is because such a system is too reactive that it fails to satisfy Ministers. Even if it encourages agency attention to costings ex post facto, cost-benefit testing is of limited use in allowing Ministers to institute policies.

The issue here is how best formally to structure ministerial control of agencies rather than how to create ministerial influence. Ministers almost invariably do exert considerable influence even over the most independent of agencies: they control the purse strings, and the system of appointments, they can abolish the agency or institute radical reforms, they often decide appeals from agency decisions and the cooperation of central government departments is more often than not a precondition of effective agency action. This is why few people believe that it is merely a matter of coincidence when a body such as the IBA or BBC makes a programming decision consistent with the latest ministerial pronouncement.

The need to structure ministerial powers of control arises rather because unfiltered use of influence (often put into effect by the 'lunch-table directive') leads to a number of difficulties:[20] intermittent interventions disrupt agency policy-making; agency expertise and independence is undermined; two tiers of decision-making (agency and departmental) are in conflict; agency adjudications are reduced to the status of window-dressing; and policy-making becomes hidden from the view of both regulatees and public. In short, the agency's legitimacy is removed when Ministers fail to respect its sphere of independent operation. It is arguable[21] that unless their powers of intervention are structured, Ministers find it very difficult to exercise an appropriate degree of restraint.

One such method of structuring is for a Minister to give a written statement of policy guidance.[22] This, it is said, encourages more open discussion of policies and differences and discourages use of hidden threats. It also allows the agency to know more clearly where it stands in relation to government policy when the agency is both adjudicating and making its own policies. The system has been used in civil aviation regulation in Britain but was abandoned after legal challenge in the Court of Appeal.[23] It may, however, have been a mistake to reject this tool of control because of one instance of ill-advised use. A number of United States commentators have advocated systems of guidance[24] and the Law Reform Commission of Canada (LRCC) has argued that the directive power is particularly suitable for guiding the policies of independent regulatory agencies.[25] The LRCC has, however, cautioned[26] that policy directives should be used sparingly, that they should address general policy issues rather than specific cases, and that they should be issued as regulations and take the form of statutory instruments. This, it was argued, would make the legislative status of such directions clear. The LRCC has been concerned that the power to direct should not be used to undermine the agency but employed 'in a way that minimises interference with the role Parliament has given to the agency to perform'.[27]

Formal powers of direction, it could be argued, are often preferable to informal agreements between agencies and Ministers because the procedures accompanying that formality both create protections for affected parties and discourage excessive interference. Written guidance may also have advantages over control by statutory objectives. Guidance can be phrased in terms more consistent with a statement of economic and regulatory policies. As a result, guidance may prove a more effective as well as a more flexible system of control than statutory standards that, in any case, have to be phrased in such general terms as to be almost useless as effective guides.

A further alternative to written policy guidance as a means of influencing agency policy is through controlling the membership of the boards of agencies. Of the agencies which are discussed subsequently, all but one (the OFT) have a system of collegial decision-making. There are, however, a number of (overlapping) options available by which agency members may be chosen:

(i) providing for a quota of civil servants to sit on the board of an agency.

(ii) selection from a group of experienced and disinterested men and women recognised by Whitehall as respected in their field and likely to be influential more generally. This group is commonly called the 'great and good' (e.g. the Cable Authority, Gaming Board).

(iii) tripartism (e.g. the HSC, MSC, ACAS) where the two sides of industry are represented, supplemented by 'independent' members.

(iv) members nominated by relevant interest groups (e.g. the CRE).[28]

(v) members appointed short-term on an overtly political basis by the Minister.

(vi) membership by election.

(vii) membership by virtue of a position within the agency bureaucracy (e.g. the CAA).

The 'great and the good' option appears at first glance to be the most difficult of the above methods to justify. It does, however, possess two potential strengths. The group purports to contain persons of sufficient expertise to be able to wrestle with the central regulatory issues, and it holds out the possibility of a cohesive group of persons acting in pursuit of the public interest (as defined by the relevant statute) as opposed to the interest of a faction or group. Tripartism falls between a number of stools. It fails to represent all relevant interests. It provides preferential access to certain factions. It sets up barriers to radical regulation and innovation. The system of members delegated by interest groups does allow for the appointment of experts but, like tripartism, falls down on the basis of represent-ation. It would be difficult for any agency to claim legitimacy on a democratic or representative rationale when the agency could not justify the preferential access to membership that is allocated to certain groups.

Membership of the boards of agencies has been criticized as under-representing women, people under forty and those from outside the London and South East region.[29] Others have pointed to levels of political patronage and business interest representation.[30] Membership of boards is seldom publicly controversial, however, though on occasion there have been accusations that a government has stopped a critic being appointed. An example in 1986 was the reported blocking by the Treasury of an appointment to the Securities and Investments Board.[31]

More frequently there appears to be real difficulty in filling positions[32] because of the low recompense and the lack of a career structure. The vast majority of members of the boards of agencies are part-time and members are often provided with expenses and a per diem allowance only. In light of this, the membership of two of the agencies to be discussed subsequently is of interest. The Chairman of the ACAS Council, who is full-time, and the nine part-time members of the Council are appointed by the Secretary of State for Employment. In 1987 the Chairman was Mr Douglas Smith, formerly Deputy Secretary in the Department of Employment. Three of the members are appointed after consultation with such organizations representing workers as the Secretary of State thinks appropriate. One was the general secretary of a trade union; another was the head of the Organization and Industrial Relations Department of the TUC. Three are appointed after consultation with such organizations representing employers as the Secretary of State thinks appropriate. They included an executive deputy chairman of a large company and a member of the council of the CBI. Three are independent members. They were two professors, one of applied economics in the University of Glasgow (and chairman of the Post Office Arbitration Tribunal) and one a professor of industrial relations at London University.

The members of the Health and Safety Commission are also appointed by the Secretary of State for Employment. Three were appointed after consultation with the TUC. Of these, one was a general secretary of a trade union and past chairman of the TUC General Council; one was chairman of another large union and member of the General Council of the TUC; and the third was head of the TUC's Social Insurance and Industrial Welfare Department. Three were appointed after consultation with the CBI. Of these, one was Deputy Director of the Health and Safety and International Labour Division of the CBI; one was director of a large company and a member of the Council of the Chemical Industries Association; and the third was Chief Executive of the Engineering Employers West Midlands Association, and Deputy Chairman of the Engineering

Employers Federation's Health and Safety Committee. One member was appointed after consultation with local authority organizations and was Chairman of the Environmental Health Committee for the Convention of Scottish Local Authorities and a member of the Environmental Protection Committee for Glasgow District Council.

The Law Reform Commission of Canada's Report on Independent Administrative Agencies made a number of criticisms of the manner in which members are appointed in Canada and much the same may be said of appointments in Britain. The LRCC commented on the closed nature of the process, the absence of accountability for appointments and the vulnerability of the government to charges of patronage, with the attendant loss of prestige and public confidence in the agency.[33] Anne Davies has argued[34] that reforms should be introduced: 'to encourage more participation; to increase real public representation; to introduce greater democratic control over appoint-ments; and to extend open competition'. With regard to the last goal, she pointed in particular to the successful experiment in advertising carried out in 1976 for the post of Director General of Fair Trading, resulting in the appointment of Professor Gordon Borrie.[35]

The great strength of providing for agency members to be elected lies in the claim to legitimacy that can be made. The problems are that different voting systems would produce different spreads of interest representation, that there is no guarantee that experts would be elected, that certain active interests would gain disproportionate representation resulting in agency capture and that factionalism would lead to the pursuit of interests other than the public interest as defined by statute. The points relating to capture and interest representation are the most weighty but, while bearing in mind warnings concerning historical experience with elected boards,[36] there does appear to be some scope for new experiments with the system. That said, however, it is unlikely that Ministers will ever be inclined to create bodies in possession of a mandate directly from the electorate. Such bodies would be more powerful than present boards and more difficult for Ministers to control. This, of course, throws up a key point in looking at legitimacy. Ministers are disinclined to create fully legitimate bodies that would challenge their own authority. There should accordingly be limits to one's expectations of the degree of legitimacy accorded regulatory bodies within the present system of ministerial government.

A final note should be added here on the potential of monitoring bodies as enhancers of agency accountability. We have already suggested that a Select Committee on Regulated Industries might serve a useful control function over agencies. In relation to the activities of each particular agency there may be a place for a standing consumer body with monitoring functions that go beyond the consideration of complaints. The Air Transport Users Committee serves as an example here. This body does not simply consider airline-user complaints but considers air transport licensing policy issues and argues the consumer case at CAA public hearings and policy consultations. The idea might profitably be taken further with such bodies being given an express remit (and funding) to comment on regulatory practices. As a legitimizing factor such a body would have limited value if made up of consumer pressure group representatives rather than elected members but it would serve a useful role in exposing issues to a wider, more representative audience.

3 Due Process

The due process criterion assesses an agency's actions on the basis of the body's use of certain fair procedures, e.g. participation, consultation and openness. Actions are assessed by looking to the procedure by which decisions are arrived at, particularly in respect of their equality, fairness and consistency of treatment. It is inherent in this criterion that all the processes of decision-making should be carried out in a non-discriminatory and even-handed manner.

As a complete basis on which to build legitimacy, however, the criterion is again limited. Further guiding principles are required to explain *who* should be able to participate and in *what manner*. There is no guarantee that maximizing due process will produce an efficient decision (it may lead to stagnation and indecision); the dictates of the participatory procedure may not correspond with the legislative mandate. To expand participatory rights beyond a certain point may not be consistent with the development and exercise of necessary expertise and judgement.

Agencies come under greatest attack, certainly from lawyers, for failure to satisfy the requirements of due process. The due process rationale for legitimacy, it has been said, is based on the notion that democratic ideals are 'embodied at least partially, in administrative procedures that ensure the participation of affected interests in the process of administrative policy formulation'[37] and (one might add) implementation. Apart from its intrinsic value the recognition of due process rights allows broader values to be taken into account within the bureaucratic process. In 1975 the Independent Broadcasting Authority (IBA) was said to have 'gone nothing like far enough to satisfy the canons of open government' in allocating television programme contracts without public hearings or published reasons.[38]

There are a variety of ways in which agencies allow participation, argument and comment by affected parties and the wider public. They can encourage open decision and policy-making; develop and publish rules, policies and proposals; act on the basis of intelligible reasons; arrive at decisions after extensive consultations and public hearings and allow public participation in the process of rule-making and the making of routine decisions as well as adjudication. A review of the agencies discussed in this book shows, however, that tensions are almost inevitably inherent in such avenues of legitimation. Bodies that use trial-type procedures to decide regulatory or economic issues appear to be engaged in a more open and participatory procedure but they have to come to terms with the justiciability of the relevant questions. The chapters on the MMC and the CAA ask whether monopolies and civil aviation licensing issues are appropriately dealt with through trial-type processes. They describe the circumstances in which rule-making processes are necessary adjuncts to such forms of decision-making and the problems posed in setting up criteria for deciding economic issues at public trial-type hearings. The CAA has used public hearings extensively in both deciding individual route licensing cases and in developing policies and rules. Although the CAA has made considerable efforts to publish its criteria for decision-making and its policies, the very nature of the decisions that have to be made in aviation licensing (polycentric, technically complex and subject to a rapidly fluctuating economic background) has meant on occasions that trial-type procedures have left airline representatives confused.

The further problem that has faced bodies such as the IBA and CAA is that of eligibility to appear at public hearings. The CAA has exercised its discretion to hear different parties quite liberally but the objection can still be made that only well-organized and well-financed interests can actually participate and that logistical considerations impose a de facto limit on participation. It could thus be argued that only a set of 'preferred' parties are able to impose real influence on decisions and policies. The IBA's two-tier system of allocating franchises for independent local radio can similarly be questioned. The IBA holds public hearings at which franchise holders, competitors and IBA staff meet the public, answer questions and express views. The true decisions, however, it could be said, are not taken at these 'public relations' meetings but in closed sessions between the IBA and radio companies.[39] On the credit side it can however be argued that the experience of the CAA demonstrates how an agency, as distinct from a tribunal, can have some success in rendering difficult areas justiciable by linking trial-type procedures into a broader process of policy-making that operates at a number of levels through a number of different procedural devices.

Turning from trial-type procedures to rule-making and policy-making, it is clear that most of the agencies discussed subsequently engage in extensive processes of consultation. Thus the Health and Safety Executive allows 162 weeks to conduct the consultations required before the publication of an approved code of practice. The code of practice is used by nearly all the agencies to be discussed, either as an aid to enforcement activity (e.g. the OFT, HSE), for promotional reasons (e.g. ACAS, CRE) or as an element in policy-making (e.g. CAA). Combined with extensive consultation, sometimes with public hearing procedures, the administrative rule does allow extensive participation to affected or interested parties. It is not unproblematic, however. Legitimacy may be lacking from rule-making procedures when an unrepresentative group participates in rule-making, a *fait accompli* is presented to participants, or considerations of expertise and resources exclude groups or individuals from participation.

Little help is given to agencies in dealing with such procedural issues by the legislative or executive branches of government. There is, for instance, no Administrative Procedure Act (APA) as in the United States to provide standard requirements for the publication of rules and openness in rule-making, and there is no standard requirement established by statute that proposed rules be justified by reasons. Parliament, for reasons already given, is unable, through its committees, directly to scrutinize the workings of agencies in this regard.[40]

Could Parliament take legislative action to increase agency legitimacy on the due process rationale? A statute providing for open government and free access to information, one covering agencies as well as central departments, would broadly have this effect if it were accompanied or followed by increased participation. This proposal will merely be noted here, however, since the arguments for and against such a statute go beyond our present scope. An APA would subject rules to publication and comment but the issue would be 'which rules?'. In the United States the problems of distinguishing mere policy discussions from rules subject to the publishing requirements of the APA have been immense. There does seem to be a case, nevertheless, for developing, either by statute or through the common law, duties on agencies and other officials: (a) to disclose to parties, and to publish generally, rules that are being operated and which affect interests, and (b) to consult when making rules. For reasons argued at length elsewhere,[41] it seems preferable not to follow the APA route with its emphasis on classifications of rules that do and do not have to follow set procedures and instead to incorporate a requirement of reasonable consultation for both types of proposed rules. Thus the duties of disclosure and consultation would be less onerous in relation to a new policy development on a broad subject than they would in the case of a firm statement of policy of direct influence on agency decisions that affect interests. At present there is no general duty to consult when involved in rule-making activity.[42] Given the difficulty of distinguishing between rule-making and adjudication (in which there are clearer rights of participation), the absence of such a duty is a matter that should be remedied and would generally increase agency legitimacy.

Executive action might also be taken so as further to legitimize agency procedures. Principally this would take the form of ministerial monitoring of those procedures. Thus in cases where the Secretary of State's approval is required in the process of rule-making or in devising hearings procedures, those powers of approbation can be used to encourage reasonableness in agency disclosure, consultation and reason-giving, though at the risk that more substantive political concerns would intrude.

4 Expertise

Certain bureaucratic or regulatory functions seem to require an expert judgement. In these cases the decision-maker has to consider a number of competing options and values and come to a balanced judgement on incomplete and shifting information. Where this is so, it is inappropriate to demand reasons and justifications beyond a certain point. The expert, it is said, will come to the most appropriate decision when left alone and his or her performance will improve over time.[43] The greater the expertise, the more acceptable is the agency decision.

In such fields as gaming, civil aviation, monopolies and mergers, discrimination, health and safety and financial services, the need for an expert body was a particularly important factor in creating a certain regulatory regime.

The problems with this criterion of assessment are ones of measurement and process. It may be difficult to understand the basis for the expert's judgement and it may be impossible to assess whether the decisions arrived at have been effective. Observers may not know what would have happened if alternative choices had been adopted. The claim to acceptability on the basis of expertise may also be questionable where the expert fails to explain why *this* issue demands expert judgement. Attacks on the competence and independence of experts serve further to undermine legitimacy claims. These attacks are encouraged by a natural distrust of those who claim to 'know best', those who fail to give full reasons and those who pursue a narrow or arcane mode of analysis. The conflicting opinions of experts within a field and between fields further serves to render the expertise rationale dubious. Nor is it the case that the expert is a neutral actor. The main justification for 'decision by expert' is the existence of a wide range of goals, values and choices. Inevitably, therefore, the expert's decision has a political aspect. There is no single goal to be achieved but a set of competing interests. The expert's resolution of those interests may be as contentious as the non-expert's. Of the agencies we discuss, the CAA has made one of the most sustained attempts to combine judgmental decisions with recognition of due process rights but this has not placated those who advocate that markets rather than experts should be given the upper hand in regulation.[44] The Gaming Board relies heavily on its expert judgement rather than on precisely formulated tests in assessing applicants for gaming certificates. As a result it can hardly rely on detailed reason-giving as a means of demonstrating its expertise.

The expertise rationale can most effectively be strengthened within the system of government by the legislature maximizing the clarity with which it makes an issue a matter of judgement for a particular agency rather than anyone else (e.g. the courts); and for the executive to respect the sphere of expertise of the agency. The ACAS, CRE and CAA studies all document the effect of governmental interference on the agency's ability to make and put into effect judgements based on special expertise.

5 Efficiency

Two main types of assessment may be made on the basis of efficiency. First, the agency may be scrutinized by seeing whether given objectives are pursued in an effective manner (the 'weak efficiency' rationale). Second, the agency may be assessed to see whether it is making economically efficient decisions (the 'strong efficiency' rationale).

On the first criterion, of 'weak efficiency', difficulties arise from its failure to define what are the 'given objectives'. The problems of the legislative mandate remain unsolved. Nor does weak efficiency in itself provide a means of designating procedures as appropriate, or otherwise. Reference again has to be made back to the 'proper' objectives of the agency and to the claims of those asserting due process rights.

A number of significant difficulties in the application of this criterion are raised in the studies of the specific agencies. First, in the case of a number of agencies, for example ACAS, OFT, the Gaming Board and the Cable Authority, our contributors emphasize the practical implications of the absence of a ready yardstick by which to measure regulatory performance. In the case of ACAS, Linda Dickens argues subsequently that this has been a contributory factor in the agency's weak political position. This may yet become a problem for the OFT, but might be expected to be a less serious problem in the case of the GB which relies to a less pronounced extent on government support. Second, it is particularly difficult to measure effectiveness or efficiency when the agency lacks coherent objectives. Veljanovski's chapter on Cable Television stresses the contradictions inherent in the government's regulatory strategy. Placed in such a context it will be very difficult for the regulatory body to claim legitimacy by effectiveness or efficiency of action. A similar predicament is faced by an agency whose functions intermesh with those of other agencies and departments. Craig's chapter describes how this is a particular problem for the MMC, and the same difficulty is faced acutely by ACAS and the CAA.

Third, even if objectives are clear, the agency has to pursue these by the most effective *means* available if it is to base its legitimacy on this rationale. Thus bodies such as the GB and HSE face the problems of regulation by standard setting and the MMC has to choose between control based on legal form versus that based on economic effect. A particular difficulty for certain bodies (e.g. the GB, IBA, CA and CAA) is that of finding a substitute operator where a present incumbent proves unsatisfactory. Where substitution is difficult, the 'least worst' rather than the optimal scenario becomes the regulatory aim and the claims to efficiency are correspondingly weakened. Enforcement activity almost inevitably involves agencies in the choice between negotiating compliance and a strategy of compulsion based on action through the courts. The chapters on the CRE, MMC, HSE and OFT detail how these agencies seek a balance on this front. Since a different pattern of successes and failures flows from each blend of regulatory strategies, it becomes in these conditions almost impossible to demonstrate that the most effective approach is being taken at any one time or even over a period of time.

Fourth, certain types of agency – those based on the tripartite model (ACAS and HSC/E) and those incorporating a high degree of self-regulation (the City, ACAS, HSE, OFT) – involve a particular slant on the efficiency argument. Both forms generally lead to less radical regulation. Tripartism, as we have noted, tends to give powerful interests a veto. Self-regulatory systems operate to entrench existing interests. In short, a trade-off has been made from the start: political stability has been bought at the price of radical, and possibly optimally efficient, regulation. Again, therefore, the case for legitimacy under an efficiency criterion will tend to be weak.

Fifth, agencies with a process of decision-making based on a board of appointed members have been seen to produce 'compromises that are antithetical to the setting of coherent policy',[45] to 'foster irresponsibility by cloaking individual decision makers in anonymity',[46] to have 'difficulty managing the bureaucracy',[47] and to encourage long delays resulting 'in severe backlogs'.[48] Katzman has argued, however, that collegial decision-making 'is not inherently unworkable and that the single-headed form of administration is not necessarily more effective'.[49] The case studies in Part II provide examples of agencies controlled by boards, as well as one headed by a single person (the OFT).

Sixth, a common problem faced by enforcement agencies is how to apply resources where they will be most productive. Thus in the chapters on the HSC and OFT the arguments for 'targeting' enforcement are considered and the dangers of focusing regulation on 'easy' targets is pointed out. Where an agency has failed to conduct such research as will demonstrate that it is targeting optimally, it will be difficult to show that it is acting efficiently – even in cases where it can demonstrate that existing policies are being carried out in a cost-effective manner.

Finally, a fundamental and recurring cause of inefficient regulation is the existence of a mismatch between regulatory institution or strategy and the task in hand. Thus the discussions of the MMC and Cable Authority question the appropriateness of both procedures and regulatory policies. Again, such difficulties undermine an agency's case for legitimacy. It can hardly be argued that an agency is acting efficiently when it is either the wrong kind of body for the job, its strategies are misguided or its policies uncertain. Although the effectiveness of an agency is not guaranteed by a parliamentary grant of powers, it will clearly be crucially affected by it: adequate legislative empowerment of the agency in the initial statute is a necessary but not a sufficient condition of an effective agency. The Law Reform Commission of Canada has recommended that Parliament should enable an agency to give fuller effect to the legislated standards by including a number of specific powers in the statute establishing the agency: a power to secure information that is relevant to the matter in question, including the power to summon witnesses and documents; the power to maintain control over its proceedings and to remove disruptive persons; the power to initiate contempt proceedings; the power to compel preliminary sessions; the power to adjourn proceedings; the power to make interim orders and to provide interim relief; the power to move from an adjudicative to a rule-making format; the power to add participants; and the power to consolidate proceedings.[50]

The second efficiency criterion, that of 'strong efficiency', is both more ambitious and more contentious. If it were the only criterion of assessment, this would assume the maximization of allocational efficiency to be a value in itself. It has been argued convincingly, however, that efficiency is not a value independent of distributional considerations, since it provides no answer to distributional issues. Economic analysis may be relevant in assessing the consequences of various policies but it provides no secure basis for distributional decisions.[51] It may conflict with legislative statements on distributional matters.[52] The appropriateness of 'strong efficiency' as a dominant criterion of assessment is thus especially questionable in those spheres of regulation where distributive concerns are central.

What can be done to improve legitimacy claims on the basis of efficiency? If legislators were to set out clearer statutory objectives then it would be easier to demonstrate at least efficient pursuit of these. For reasons given above, however, it is unrealistic to expect that Parliament will ever be able to devise clear and simple guidelines for regulatory agencies. Parliament sets up these bodies in order to resolve contradictions, not because matters are clear and simple.

It is the executive branch, however, that might be expected to take more rigorous action to test the efficiency of regulation. In the United States, as we have already noted, such tests were applied with new vigour when in 1982 President Reagan passed Executive Order 12291. This Order subjects all major regulatory rules to a cost-benefit test. The regulatory agency submits a cost-benefit analysis of a new regulation to the President's Office of Management and Budget and, if the test is not passed, approval for the regulation will not be given. Influenced by the Reagan system the British Conservative Government established an Enterprise and Deregulation Unit, and during 1986 proposals were introduced to increase the cost-benefit testing of regulations along American lines.

The agency whose regulations have 'passed' such an efficiency test will have a strengthened case for stating that its activities are efficient and on that basis are legitimate. There are, however, considerable difficulties in this approach. First, as we have noted, 'strong' efficiency is not uncontentiously a value in itself and it does not have an undisputed claim for inclusion as one of our five headings of legitimacy. Second, 'strong' efficiency may not be the test that the relevant statute has created for the agency. Where there is a conflict between statutory ends and the dictates of strong efficiency this may undermine the efficiency rationale. Third, strong efficiency cannot be carried out in an unproblematic fashion. Assumptions have to be made and values placed on matters such as life and health. It can thus be argued that the strong efficiency test buries real policy issues in economic analysis and accordingly that, even if efficiency were to offer a yardstick, satisfaction or otherwise of an efficiency test is too contentious a matter to be a workable basis for legitimacy.

6 Conclusions

A number of points may, then, be made on the problem of evaluating agency performance. First, most of the agencies discussed below would encounter problems if they sought to establish legitimacy under only one of the rationales we describe. Second, this does not mean that the institution of the regulatory agency or any particular agency that we discuss lacks all legitimacy. Third, there are trade-offs of performance under the different heads and each agency or agency action must be judged as a particular package. Fourth, the British Constitution has not fully embraced the regulatory agency insofar as it has failed to take action to maximize the potential legitimacy claims of agencies under the various headings. Fifth, administrative rule-making provides a means of clarifying mandates and increasing openness, participation, control and accountability. Rule-making does, however, need to be used on the appropriate occasions and has itself to be regulated by rules on disclosure, consultation and reason-giving. Sixth, written ministerial policy guidance may provide a way to increase legitimizing controls. Seventh, there is a case for a Select Committee on Regulated Industries. Eighth, complaints bodies may usefully legitimize if given broader remits. Ninth, legislation on open government may produce a broad legitimizing effect. Tenth, Ministers are disinclined to create agencies of real legitimacy, and weak legitimacy may therefore be a fact of life for regulatory bodies.

For advocates of social change through regulatory agencies, the fact that their legitimacy is never beyond question is important in two respects. This uncertainty encourages agencies to act defensively. For a reforming government the implications of this are profound. Compromises in policies at the legislative and pre-legislative stage will not readily be made good by the agency itself. The agency may succeed for a limited period but, as has been seen in the United States, a backlash is almost inevitable when agency activity comes to public attention. The moral is clear. Radical agencies need as clear a mandate as possible.

4
The Courts and Regulatory Agencies

Some of the concerns expressed in the last chapter would be reduced if regulatory agencies were subject to expert, efficient and convincing control by the courts. Commentators have seen such accountability before the ordinary courts as significant for future policy towards regulatory agencies. *The Economist* argued in 1977, for example, that: '. . . the more independent of ministers [agencies] become, the less accountable they are to anybody, as the thin strand of accountability to parliament withers. Their use of discretionary power becomes nearly absolute. Most important, the possibilities of appeal – because Britain lacks a proper structure of administrative law – are limited.'[1] Nevil Johnson has argued more recently that, '[g]iven the inevitable weakness of traditional forms of political and administrative control or accountability through Ministers to Parliament, it seems only reasonable to look for some strengthening of the more formal legal checks on the activities of governmental bodies'.[2]

On the other hand, many share the concern of the Law Reform Commission of Canada's Final Report on Independent Administrative Agencies about the effect judicial intervention can have on the authoritativeness and integrity of an agency's decision making process.[3] 'Courts', it observed, 'typically intervene in the administrative process on an *ex post facto* basis, and only where it is alleged that something has gone wrong. Those who perceive administration principally through the lens of judicial review can acquire a distorted view of the performance of agencies, one focussed more on their "pathology" than on their normal operations'.[4] Clearly, then, the courts may play an important role in affecting the mix of values which were considered in the last chapter to amount to the core of an agency's legitimacy.

This chapter considers whether an appropriate system of judicial oversight has developed. We assess whether certain deficiencies of current judicial approaches become particularly apparent when the courts review agencies, and the scope for potentially useful reforms. We consider, first, what the impact of judicial review on agency operations has actually been; second, the competence of the courts in this field; and third, the functions of judicial intervention that are implicit in existing court decisions. We suggest a number of changes designed to reconcile legitimate judicial oversight with effective regulatory action.

Before turning to these issues, it is important to note that this chapter concentrates largely on judicial review of administrative action under Order 53 of the Rules of the Supreme Court, not with other methods by which the courts may review agencies. The most important additional method is by way of claims for damages, for example for negligent advice or actions.[5] We touch on these other controls only sporadically. Nevertheless, despite their differences, we believe that what is argued subsequently regarding judicial review is, in general, applicable also to these other methods of oversight.

1 The Impact of Judicial Review

When judges review the activities of regulatory agencies this has an effect both across the general system of government and on the internal operation of the agency itself. Before considering those effects, however, it is important to look at the *incidence* of such review and some of the factors that govern that incidence.

Unfortunately, however, there is a dearth of empirical information about the interrelationship between the courts and regulatory agencies in Britain.[6] Some at least of the theoretical debate in Britain has, therefore, taken place on rather shaky factual foundations. This is particularly true with regard to the incidence and the effects of judicial review. The studies of particular agencies in this book lead us to draw some tentative conclusions. As a number of other writers have found, the incidence of judicial review is tiny in comparison with the number of decisions these bodies take. The studies of the OFT and the MMC later in this book, for example, show that there have been few instances of judicial review or judicial appeals from these bodies. Even where judicial review has been sought comparatively often, it is still infrequent and discontinuous. Judicial review has played an important role in regulating some bodies such as the CRE, for example. The sporadic nature of appeals and reviews means, however, that they are not substitutes for a system of continuing supervision. Though the CRE has been subject to considerable restraints through judicial review this does not mean that CRE policies are regularly scrutinized by the judiciary. The judiciary does exercise influence, but this is intermittent, and depends on the instigation of some aggrieved party.

Why is there an apparent reluctance to involve the courts? The study of the CAA suggests some reasons: a reluctance by parties to impose the considerable expense and delay upon themselves; the closeness of the community of airlines, Department and the CAA; the likelihood that a victory at law might achieve little since an error by the CAA or Secretary of State might well be corrected in a re-made decision; the availability of a 'political' appeal which reduces the incentive to challenge CAA decisions or procedures. The extent to which these elements also dampen the resort to litigation in other areas is unclear.

While the number of cases of appeal or review is therefore small, and while there are persuasive reasons why an aggrieved person may well decide not to go to court, the incidence of judicial review is increasing. There has been a steady growth since the mid 1960s, especially after the introduction of Order 53. Sir Michael Kerry, former Treasury Solicitor, observed in 1982 that such cases 'increased from a handful a year in the 60s to 50–100 in the early 70s, to a rate of about 400 a year in the first six months of [1982]'. He reported that most of these cases 'come under two main heads, applications to quash planning decisions . . . and immigration cases.'[7] By 1985 the number of cases was running at over 1,200 a year, double that of five years previously.[8] 'Judicial review', according to the *Financial Times* in 1986, had 'become the growth area in the law.'[9] Recourse to judicial review is also likely to increase, it has been observed, with a more active regulatory system of the City of London's financial services.[10] The number of cases taken concerning regulatory agencies also appears to have increased.[11] And the number of reported cases is fewer than the number of threats to resort to judicial review, as will be seen in the study of the CRE.

Why has there been this apparent growth in judicial review? A number of possible reasons may be put forward. Some have argued that there is an increased need to intervene. Sir Harry Woolf, a Lord Justice and former judge of the Divisional Court responsible for adjudicating many of the applications for judicial review in the 1970s, has argued that '[i]t used to be the case that, if the legality of a course of action was in doubt, it was not adopted. Now it appears to be becoming a case of anything is permissible unless and until it is stopped by the courts.'[12] Hugo Young, the noted political journalist, has offered a similar explanation. 'A remarkable change has come over the political atmosphere in the last decade,' he has written, '. . . Judges are now accepted as a perfectly normal element of the process by which power is exercised in at least some areas of government. Ministers fight their corner and retain the best lawyers to help them. But submission to a judicial verdict is no longer a badge of ministerial incompetence or dishonour, so much as an emblem of the judges' expanding role as the citizen's policeman of the executive.' A first reason, therefore, may be that Ministers are less concerned than before at losing in court. Some have also argued that the introduction into government of 'brusque public sector management techniques' has encouraged a greater number of mistakes in the making of decisions and that this too has increased the number of aggrieved persons prepared to go to court.[13]

A second reason may be a lack of awareness by government generally and agencies specifically of developments in administrative law. In turn this may be due in part to the relatively peripheral role lawyers play in British administration. We shall see in chapter 6, for example, how resistant ACAS was to employing lawyers in-house. We shall see also how this may have adversely affected ACAS's ability to anticipate judicial hostility to certain policies which the agency adopted. Though this may have had much to do with the idea of voluntarism that pervaded ACAS particularly, it is a noteable feature of British administration generally. Louis Blom-Cooper, QC, for example, has described the situation in the Whitehall departments as one where '[p]ublic administrators . . . , wielding extensive statutory powers and duties which have increasingly come under judicial scrutiny, have remained largely an elitist group, separate and distinct from those professionally versed in the legal framework of those very same statutory powers and duties. Lawyers in government service have failed to attain anything more than formal equality of status within the hierarchy of the Civil Service'.[14] Sir Michael Kerry echoes these views:

Administrators and politicians have been very suspicious of legal interference in the decision-making processes. . . . Of course, there are many administrators who have a sound knowledge of and interest in, the law as it affects their work. But this is, I think, far from universal. New cases are continuously coming to the attention of myself and my colleagues in which senior administrators show a surprising ignorance of elementary legal principle. . . . At present, in spite of the degree of training available, administrators can reach positions of responsibility without any clear understanding of the extent or nature of the legal limitations imposed by the law on their activities.[15]

A third reason for the apparent growth of judicial review has been put forward. This is the advent of a period in which political divisions have become increasingly accentuated in Britain. Years of broad consensus as to policy have gone. Thus the decisions of a central or local government of a particular political complexion are more likely to give rise to strong disagreement by those of differing political complexions. This provides a strong impetus towards seeing whether there is any legal remedy available. As Hugo Young has observed: '. . . the plethora of developing case law is in part a product of the conflict between local and central government. Many of the cases against [the Department of the] Environment and the DHSS originate with eagle-eyed local authority lawyers using the fine print of statutes as defensive weapons against a government that has declared war on them. To that extent the picture is not one of valiant citizens fighting off an overmighty government, more one of Leviathan locked in a struggle for power within itself.'[16] This has enabled, according to *The Economist*, 'swarms of able young lawyers' to transform 'the Cinderella practice of local government into one of the bar's trendiest specialities'.[17] Nor is this development restricted to local government. An increasing number of cases involving regulatory agencies arise out of disputes with other branches of government.[18]

Lastly, of course, success breeds success. Challenging some decisions successfully has led to an increase in the number of such challenges. Not surprisingly, enthusiasm for mounting challenges grows throughout the legal profession in proportion to their success.

Turning now to the *impact* of judicial review and appeals on the internal operation of the body reviewed, this may be said to depend on three interlinking conditions. The first is the extent to which openings are taken advantage of by other litigants. It is arguable that the availability of judicial review has to some extent transferred power of a kind to interest groups able to become involved in litigation, particularly insofar as they are now able, at a minimum, to delay decisions with which they disagree. (Tony Prosser has further suggested that welfare rights groups have benefitted from the use of law not in terms of substantive results but in terms of the development of skills and opportunities for the use of a range of forums apart from the courts.[19]) The second reason is the perceived capacity of the agency to respond to and accommodate judicial direction should they so desire – 'the uneven capacity of agencies to implement judicial direction may make the ultimate effects of judicial review quite unpredictable at the time of decision'.[20] The third reason is the extent of agency recalcitrance, either open and direct, or based on avoidance and subterfuge. An agency can attempt to circumvent unpopular decisions 'through the time honoured method of distinguishing them from a case currently under consideration before it'.[21] From the studies in this volume, there is little evidence of sustained attempts at evasion of the consequences of judicial decisions. Indeed, in the case of the CRE, the opposite appears to be the case. The case studies also point to a number of potentially adverse effects of judicial review.

First, long-range planning may be discouraged. Despite the importance of non-decision-making by agencies, it is action rather than inaction which tends to be challenged. Court scrutiny of agency *inaction* seldom happens.[22] The effect may be to pull agencies away from longer-term planning in order to deal with specific *ad hoc* challenges. Ackerman and Hassler discuss some of the reasons for this in their study of the effect of litigation on environmental protection in the United States:

Environmental litigation is typically generated by actions in the here and now that catalyze environmental anxieties – the building of a new plant, the refusal to clean up an old one. No less important, a successful lawsuit against a particular plant will (ultimately) yield a palpable sense of victory for both the environmental lawyer and his clients. In contrast, a lawsuit to compel the agency to engage in sophisticated long-range planning is a daunting prospect. Not only is it harder to sustain public interest in a complex and esoteric debate, but there is a danger that the lawsuit will never end – with the lawyers sinking without trace in an endless series of remands and reconsiderations.[23]

Second, judicial review may discourage the pursuit of radical initiatives. 'The stricter the review and the more clearly and convincingly the agency must explain the need for any change, the more reluctant the agency will be to change the status quo.'[24]

Third, judicial review may bring about a fundamental redistribution of powers within the group of bodies affected. One effect of judicial review of the Secretary of State in the *Laker*[25] case in the civil aviation area was that departmental lawyers were by no means confident that a guidance of useful precision could be drafted so as to avoid judicial review. The effect of this was to contribute to a substantial revision of the relationship between the Secretary of State and the CAA.

Fourth, judicial review may increase resort to non-reviewable regulatory techniques by the body reviewed. Using other forms of regulation may be thought to avoid the problem of intrusive judicial review. Thus, for example, regulation by bargaining, and rule-making became more popular with the CRE after the consistently hostile reception given by the judges to the exercise of their power to conduct formal investigations.

Fifth, it may increase the use and influence of lawyers. Blom-Cooper has observed how 'in those departments which have in recent years experienced the impact of administrative law . . . the trend to direct lawyer involvement in administration is plainly noticeable. In these departments there has been evident a degree of "cordial co-operation" . . . and an awareness of the impact of administrative law . . .'[26]

These effects may well cause administrators some concern. Whitehall Departments have become much more aware of the potentialities of judicial review but have reacted in different ways. In addition to the changing role of government lawyers, there appears to be an increasing attempt to take more radical evasive action. The exclusion and control of judicial review in new statutes lies to a large extent with the executive and Parliament, and thus they are able to redirect judicial review by manipulation of the statute book.[27] The use of this power has varied. There have been a number of recent attempts to prevent or restrict judicial review when establishing new bodies, and allocating powers by statute, either directly[28] or indirectly.[29] In addition, the Financial Services Act 1986 granted legal immunity from suit in negligence for bona fide regulatory action[30] by the Securities and Investments Board and the self-regulatory organizations.

The establishment and structure of agencies has also been affected by the perceived likelihood of judicial review and the extent to which it could be excluded (at least without causing a rumpus). On other occasions the government has sought to restrict the opportunities for judicial review as a whole. A controversial attempt was the proposal in the Administration of Justice Bill in 1985 to do away with the right of appeal to the Court of Appeal against a judge's refusal to grant leave to apply for judicial review. This proposal was subsequently withdrawn after a backbench revolt in the House of Lords.[31] On the other hand, the availability of judicial review has, on occasion, been made use of when setting up some bodies outside central government which are viewed with suspicion.[32] The establishment of both ACAS and the CRE, for example, involved consideration of the extent to which the judiciary should or should not be excluded.

How important, then, is judicial review? To some extent different perceptions of importance reflect differences in the interpretation of what little empirical information we have. It would miss an important element in the debate, however, to assume that this is the only reason for disagreement. There is in addition an ideological assumption behind some at least of the claims that administrative law is relatively unimportant: a position which involves viewing the role of law as inevitably merely peripheral rather than as potentially more funda-mental.[33] We do not seek to enter that debate. Instead, we offer a few tentative empirical observations. Though the incidence of judicial review does not necessarily reflect its actual importance in terms of affecting agency decision-making, arguably judicial review litigation has more effect on the subsequent conduct of the regulatory agencies than some have thought.[34] It may also be that the law has more effect on the conduct of the regulatory agencies even in the absence of litigation than some commentators have hitherto believed.

Are the effects of judicial review on the whole beneficial? The following issues need to be addressed in order to answer this question: Does it provide greater protection from the extremes of incompetence or clear illegality? Does it make agency procedures more accessible and thus play a democratising role? Does it, by 'providing the assurance that the courts remain open to check administrative lawlessness . . . [accommodate] the administrative apparatus of the modern welfare state to an historically liberal individualist political ideology'?[35] Or does it incline the agencies to defensive (and disfunctional) administrative actions? These are even more difficult questions to answer, and responses will depend in part on a view as to what the functions of judicial review are and should be. These issues are discussed further below and in the chapters on ACAS and the CRE.

It is clear that the courts could take steps to make the substance of agency actions more controlled and accountable.

These procedures do little, in themselves, to alleviate the problems which courts have in reviewing agencies. Our concern, as will become clear subsequently, is not so much that the courts have exercised the wrong amount of judicial review over agencies but whether they have dealt with the issues in an appropriate fashion. Whether the courts have developed principles on *when* to exercise review, and made the *objectives* of review clear is at least important. Before examining these issues, however, we turn to a related issue: the ability of the judicial process as an institution to handle the issues thrown up in the course of public law and regulatory litigation.

2 The Competence of the Judicial Process

The current procedure for the application for judicial review is, briefly, a two-stage process. The applicant first applies to the Divisional Court of the QBD for leave to apply for review. His or her application is accompanied by affidavits (sworn written statements) setting out the facts. The application can be heard by a single judge in chambers. In practice, however, most are dealt with, without an oral hearing, 'on the papers', which include the applicant's affidavit evidence. If the applicant is given leave, he or she then applies for review by notice of motion, and this, plus the affidavits, are served on the body whose action or decision is to be reviewed. That body then replies by way of affidavits and the Divisional Court, as a general rule, decides the matter on the basis of the affidavits alone. Despite there being provision for discovery, interrogatories, oral testimony and cross-examination, these are not available as of right, as they are in many other actions, and the court rarely allows their use.

These procedures do little, in themselves, to alleviate the problems which courts have in reviewing agencies. Courts may, for a number of reasons, be less able than the traditional political process to provide solutions to problems requiring consideration of issues other than those raised in individual cases.[36] The classic law case often involves only isolated aspects of a larger issue. Certain issues, however, have been said to be 'polycentric':[37] they have 'many centres of stress and direction of force, only some of which are likely to be the focus of attention when a decision in the area is made'.[38] The consequences of making a decision in an area of polycentricity are complex. 'Because it has these many different critical areas and because they are all inter-related, a decision's immediate effects are likely to be communicated in many unforeseeable ways and affect many other areas of human concern.'[39] The metaphor of a spider's web illustrates the issue – pulling one thread affects each of the other parts of the web. The reactions of Maurice Stonefrost, the then Comptroller of the GLC, to the trial of the *Bromley*[40] case well illustrates the point from an administrator's perspective:

I was continually troubled during the judicial process with the limitations which the judiciary applied to itself both for practical reasons and for judicial process reasons. In brief, in order for the judiciary to have a practical framework within which to review a major policy decision, it is forced to assume that the 'administrative' decisions should be taken and are taken in a manner closer to that appropriate to a judicial decision than to that appropriate for a democratically elected body taking a major policy decision.[41]

This is not to say, however, that a judge deciding issues in an ordinary case is divorced from policy problems. In all decisions on what the judge perceives to be points of law or judgement, he or she is likely to take into account the consequences (again, as perceived) of one decision rather than another. Even if the matter is being decided between individuals the question of the general public good is likely to arise in formulating the legal principle which is applied to the specific case. Decision-making in areas with polycentric characteristics is probably not different in kind: the difference lies in the extent to which the judge is unaware of the policy arguments which ought to be brought to bear.

To solve the problem effectively, the decision-maker is likely to need information of two broad types: facts concerning the events which have transpired between the parties to the law suit (what Horowitz[42] calls 'historical' facts), and facts which help in the ascertainment of the current patterns of behaviour on which policy should be based (Horowitz's 'social' facts[43]). Yet a party-initiated and party-controlled process, with the primary focus on the parties rather than the larger issues, is unlikely to provide a suitable structure in which to solve polycentric problems. As Griffith has argued, the courts of law are not designed as research centres: 'the traditional practices and procedures [of the court] frequently preclude them from acquiring the relevant information without which such decisions are inevitably less good than they should be.'[44]

Furthermore, injuries to a group of people may well occur in circumstances in which those involved are in a poor position to seek legal redress individually, either because they do not know enough or because such redress is disproportionately expensive. There are problems relating to the representativeness of the plaintiff. The reactive nature of the courts makes it difficult for them to know the extent to which the situation of litigants illustrates the dimensions of the problem they bring to court. Restricting the judicial role to that of an umpire also presumes that litigants are equally *able* to put forward facts in support of their claims. In the absence of equal power, the umpire theory of administering law is almost certain to fail. Stonefrost's question on the conduct of the *Bromley* case is again apposite: 'is it appropriate', he asked, 'that such cases, which affect the public far beyond individual participants, should be argued solely by the individual parties without the aid of some form of *amicus curiae*?'[45]

Yet the aim of the judicial process, as traditionally viewed, is not the fair disposition of the controversy, it is the fair disposition of the controversy *upon the record as made by the parties*. Breyer puts it thus: '. . . the courts work within institutional constraints that limit their inquiry. An appellate judge, for example, cannot ask an expert to answer his technical questions or go outside the record to determine the present state of scientific or technical knowledge. But the record itself tells only part of the story – the part the advocates have chosen to let the court see.'[46] To Stonefrost,

the [judicial] process [in the *Bromley* case] was more in the nature of an intellectual marauding over a wide area of hunting territory rather than an ordered, structured, predictable and prepared process. Some issues were dealt with comprehensively and with full intellectual rigour. But others were not and it was not possible to predict on which of many issues a member of the court might concentrate upon at any one time. The basic judicial process of adversarial advocacy, punctuated courteously but irregularly, unpredictably and frequently by important court questions and interjections working from a mound of papers within a necessarily highly concentrated but limited time scale contrasts sharply with an administrative policy decision which may be an important final expression of widespread political struggle and practical pressures over a very long period of time.[47]

Further problems of using the traditional judicial process to solve polycentric problems have been identified. There are problems of timing; it is often uncertain when or whether intervention by a plaintiff will take place. There are problems involving the sequencing of change, where the court considers change to be necessary. There is the difficulty that once intervention takes place, it is usually all or nothing; one side wins, the other loses. There are problems of co-ordination of cases seeking change in a particular area. There are problems concerning review of any policy decided on by the court; the reactive nature of the judicial process makes no provision for automatic examination of the success or even the implementation of the policy decided upon by the court. There are, finally, problems arising from the generalist nature of the personnel in the judicial process, both counsel and judges. As Breyer asks: '. . . how well can courts understand an agency's problems when it [the agency] seeks to set technical standards in complex areas?'[48]

Some changes in the process of judicial review are taking place: in the *Brent*[50] case, for example, counsel advocated, and the trial judge accepted, that because of the complexity of the issues, the court should experiment with the use of reading days, and an opportunity was given to submit written briefs containing submissions on law and fact. Such changes are not confined to judicial review. The use of skeletal arguments in the Court of Appeal and the constant process of streamlining in the Commercial Court are further examples outside the administrative law context. It is arguable, however, that considerably more radical changes may be necessary in order to suit the courts to their expanded task. Sir Harry Woolf, for example, has questioned the appropriateness of the adversarial procedures and asked whether it provides sufficient public safeguards. He has suggested that a new 'director of civil proceedings' might be appropriate. Such an officer would have a similar status in civil proceedings as the Director of Public Prosecutions has in criminal proceedings – to bring proceedings on his or her own initiative, to monitor applications and ensure that relevant arguments are put before the court, and perhaps to play a role in the discovery process.[51] Similarly, Griffith[52] has argued 'for a movement from the adversarial towards the inquisitorial'. More specifically, he has called 'for the appointment of a public officer whose responsibility it would be to act as an advocate-general, to present such evidence as he considered necessary in the public interest, and more generally draw the attention of the court to those matters affecting the public interest which he considered the court should take into account. He would also be empowered to cross examine witnesses called by the parties where their evidence was relevant to the public interest.'

The Committee of Inquiry into the Conduct of Local Authority Business recommended in 1986[53] that to offset the cost of judicial proceedings there should be a new statutory power of assistance for individuals wishing to challenge a decision by their local authority in the courts in the public interest. This power should be exercised in cases where: (i) there are implications for an Authority's services at large or, on procedural issues, for its conduct of business generally; or (ii) there are important issues of principle where clarification of the law is desirable; or (iii) there is evidence of persistent breaches of the law.[54] The Committee considered whether to recommend that a High Court judge should have power to guarantee that costs would be met from the public purse in advance of the case being brought, say at the leave stage. However, the Committee recommended instead that the new power should be vested in the three local ombudsmen (the Commissions for Local Administration).[55]

United States federal courts have gone even further in adapting their procedures, though in a different direction.[56] They have been expected to adapt and have adapted to tasks very different from those of traditional adjudication, arguably without the loss of their already existing expertise, legitimacy or impartiality. These courts have adapted their procedures in a number of ways: reliance on expert witnesses; permitting wide discovery of evidence; widespread use and encouragement of suits which enable large numbers of complainants to seek redress of similar issues together in one action ('class action suits'); relaxation of standing requirements; permitting arguments by those interested in the outcome of a case but with no legal standing ('amicus curiae arguments'); encouragement of arguments which explain the social facts (so-called 'Brandeis briefs'); acceptance of the expertise of specialist government agencies; and lastly, willingness to examine the background to the Act they are interpreting with considerable particularity.

To sum up this section: there are a number of procedural characteristics associated with the current exercise of judicial review which give rise to difficulties; a number of proposals for reform have been proposed. How are these proposals likely to be viewed? The extent to which it is believed that legal processes and institutions are malleable and adaptable to new demands placed on them will influence the decision whether or not to place greater responsibility for carrying out these new tasks with reformed courts. If, on the one hand, it is believed that the undoubted benefits of expertise in historical fact-finding, legitimacy and impartiality can be retained even after adapting the courts the better to equip them for their new tasks, then their modification is likely to be seen as preferable to their replacement. If, on the other hand, it is believed that different types of institutions have an 'inner integrity of their own', are not 'all-purpose tools of unlimited pliability' and have 'distinctive uses and limits',[49] the opposite conclusion is more likely.

3 Functions of Judicial Review

What, then, is the function of judicial review, given its limited incidence and effect, and given also the existing limitations of the judicial process? Lord Diplock, in *Council of Civil Service Unions* v. *Minister for the Civil Service*,[57] has recently set out what is likely to become a classic statement of the *grounds* on which intervention by the courts may take place:

. . . one can conveniently classify under three heads the grounds on which administrative action is subject to control by judicial review. The first ground I would call 'illegality', the second 'irrationality' and the third 'procedural impropriety'. . . . By 'illegality' as a ground for judicial review I mean that the decision-maker must understand correctly the law that regulates his decision-making power and must give effect to it. . . . By 'irrationality' I mean . . . a decision which is so outrageous in its defiance of logic or of accepted moral standards that no sensible person who had applied his mind to the question to be decided could have arrived at it.

'Procedural impropriety' involves 'failure to observe basic rules of natural justice or failure to act with procedural fairness towards the person who will be affected by the decision . . .' and 'failure by an administrative tribunal to observe procedural rules that are expressly laid down in the legislative instrument by which its jurisdiction is conferred, even where such failure does not involve any denial of natural justice.' For the purposes of this chapter, these *grounds* of judicial review may conveniently be reduced to two. Judicial review is concerned with *legality* and with *process*. However, the *function* which judicial review plays in our current constitutional structure still needs to be considered.

Traditionally the legitimacy of judicial review was said to derive solely from the doctrine of parliamentary sovereignty. The institution of judicial review is justified, it was said, because Parliament has made it clear on the face of particular statutes that it intends a particular result or interpretation. When a public body does not achieve that result, or adopt that interpretation, the court is justified in keeping that body within the confines dictated by Parliament. This seems undoubtedly still the approach which dominates the run-of-the-mill cases. Kerr LJ's *obiter* in *R*. v. *London Transport Executive, ex p. Greater London Council*[58] is a good recent example: 'The interpretation of the intention of Parliament as expressed in our statutes is a matter for the courts. . . . This does not involve any substitution of the views of the judges on questions of policy or discretion . . . but merely the interpretation of the will of Parliament as expressed in its enactments.'[59] Indeed such cases may well still be paradigmatic examples of judicial review.

Parliamentary sovereignty seems a weak basis, however, on which to build the legitimacy of much that is now happening in the area of judicial review. It is now by no means clear that judges are solely involved in doing Parliament's will. (In any case, as we noted in chapter 3, the legislative mandate is problematic.) In reviewing the appropriateness of the decision-making process used by administrators, the courts appear to impose values of their own. In *R*. v. *Attorney General, ex p. ICI*,[60] for example, the court held that,

. . . proceedings for judicial review are not concerned with the correctness of the decision reached by the body whose decision is sought to be reviewed, but with the means by which the decision was reached. It is no part of the court's function in such proceedings to make a new decision for the body concerned, but to consider the legitimacy of the process by which the decision was reached, the relevance or validity of the considerations of which account was taken, and the admissibility or probative value of the evidence upon which the decision was based.[61]

These process values espoused may or may not reflect parliamentary preferences. The number of fictions necessary to sustain the argument that they do strains credibility: the fiction of legislative intent; the fiction of non-displacement of common law; the fiction of a common law fixed and unchanging. The judiciary are also concerned, jealously and with few exceptions, to keep issues of legality as the primary preserve of the courts.[62] In *Re Energy Conversion Devices Incorporated*, Lord Diplock, with whom the other members of the House of Lords agreed, reaffirmed (*obiter*) his view that there is an 'important constitutional principle that questions of construction of all legislation primary or secondary are questions of law to be determined authoritatively by courts of law, that errors in construing primary or secondary legislation made by inferior tribunals that are not courts of law, however specialised and prestigious they may be, are subject to correction by judicial review . . .'[63]

Increasingly, therefore, a supplementary justification is claimed by the judges and attributed by commentators to the judges to explain their exercise of judicial review in hard cases. This emphasizes that the judges are also concerned with setting standards of good or fair administration. Their practice increasingly seems to demand a standard-setting justification.[64] Acting on the basis of a standard-setting justification involves at a minimum acting according to some set of normative values which are espoused by the judge irrespective of whether they have been adopted by Parliament. In a number of hard cases a set of sometimes unarticulated values must be supplied by a reader of administrative law judgments in order to justify, or indeed to make sense of, what the judge is doing. The courts' role, under this rationale, is to set standards in cases where the proper standards are unclear or contested. Some commentators approve of this,[65] some do not,[66] but most acknowledge it to be important.[67]

Criticism of standard setting has focused on three problems: the problem of uncertainty, the problem of inconsistency, and the problem of inappropriate values. The judiciary are seen by some as supporting individuals who challenge the use of governmental powers in certain types of area but not in others, without any coherent expression of the differences between the cases. They are also seen as in some cases espousing standards that are inappropriate. We consider first the problems of uncertainty and inconsistency.

Let us imagine that a person living near an airport wishes to appear at a CAA public hearing to argue against the licensing of a second (and night-time) operation to serve that airport. The CAA states that it will consider written representations from that person but will not hear oral representations from them. The resident seeks judicial review of this CAA decision. As things stand at present, it is difficult to predict the basis on which the courts would decide such a case. They would examine the standing of the applicant, they would analyse the relevant statute and regulations and would no doubt construe the extent of the CAA's discretion to hear or refuse to hear private individuals at public hearings. They would be likely then to weigh whether the private interest is sufficiently weighty to render the CAA's exercise of its discretion unreasonable. The court *might* consider the extent to which the CAA has to account for its decisions to other bodies or groups. It *might* look at the applicant's access to other groups able to influence the CAA. It *might* consider the appeal function and regulatory role of the Secretary of State. It *might* consider whether access to the public hearing is a matter so close to the effective working of the licensing system as to be a matter best left to the CAA's expert judgement. It *might* consider the implications of allowing access for the CAA's effective attainment of its statutory objectives. The point is that, in relation to all the matters prefaced by 'might', it is difficult to predict what part they will play in the judicial decision. The judges appear to decide such cases without an agenda. They tend either to locate one dominant rule and apply it, or to react to the factual circumstances of the particular case.

A better way to decide such cases may be to deal with the array of relevant arguments and to choose on the basis of articulated principles. In order to set standards, judges should instead identify more clearly their value premises and articulate which values they adopt in particular situations, for three main reasons. First, all relevant matters are more likely to be considered; second, it should encourage a broader view of appropriate regulatory activity; and third, it should discourage the arbitrary selection of certain principles as relevant and the omission from analysis of others. It will then be possible for those involved and affected to engage in a 'constitutional conversation'. Without knowing what is going on in a conversation it is rather difficult to contribute, and this seems the case for many participants at the moment. The justification for engaging in this conversation is clear, where the values that are in issue are as highly contested as these are. Indeed it may be said that in determining these questions the courts are increasingly being asked to shape out public political philosophy.

The idea of constitutional law as best involving a conversation between those who govern and those who are governed, and among those who govern, does, however, give rise to a number of problems. Given that the values which are likely to be articulated are almost inevitably in conflict, we cannot say that one all-encompassing, all-embracing synthesis can emerge. We are not urging, nor do we believe it is possible or desirable, that one should. Rather we envisage a better informed, more coherent choice among these values. This does not necessarily give greater power to the judges, it merely recognizes the power they already have.

It may also be argued that to urge judges to articulate the principles governing judicial intervention may be naive and unwise. First, because although '[t]he case law may tempt one to believe that the courts possess no coherent approach towards reviewing agency decisions of questions of law, [p]erhaps one should not expect judicial coherence. After all, these questions range from very minor to very major in importance.'[68] A second objection is that to do so might prevent the judges from continuing to do a necessary job. That job is the limiting of the 'excesses' of Parliament by the application of common law principles in spite of indirect, and sometimes in the face of direct, parliamentary intention. It could be argued, for example, that where Parliament passes a highly illiberal measure that sets out to exclude judicial review, it is desirable that the courts should temper Parliament's will by undermining exclusion clauses so as to offer some remedies to affected parties. This judicial function is now made possible by jurisdictional testing of the *Anismic*[69] kind and facilitated by the non-articulation of underlying principles. If greater openness were encouraged, the argument runs, the courts would be less willing to act as a backdoor Supreme Court on the American model and would have to sit back and watch Parliament legislate away long-established common law protections. A strategy of openness, it might be said, is feasible where there is a Supreme Court which has an explicitly counter-majoritarian function, but where this is not so, to advocate a strategy which would indirectly result in the reduction of judicial intervention would be undesirable. However imperfect, we do have hidden checks and balances now and we would be in danger of losing them. There is some danger that courts will be less inclined to overrule Parliament's wishes if they have to do so openly.

In reply, a number of arguments may be put forward. For every occasion in which the courts overrule Parliament to protect liberties, there are a score of other occasions when courts move in the other direction – for example under the banner of 'national security'[70] or 'ministerial prerogative'.[71] Judges have, on occasion, failed to protect liberties and one reason for this has been their slowness in developing common law and other principles and in applying them to the actions of modern government. Although there are prominent examples to the contrary,[72] it sometimes seems that the more important the powers given by statute, the less judicial review is likely to take place. (Does judicial review, indeed, take place in inverse proportion to the importance of the powers exercised?) The basis of the argument for unarticulated review is a greater confidence in the liberality of the institution than the evidence bears out. Indeed it may be that unless a coherent, convincing basis for intervention is developed and articulated, judges may feel more and more *constrained* from intervening. Some have argued that this is beginning to happen already.[73] Unarticulated review is thus founded on peculiar assumptions about the judiciary. In addition, it demonstrates a preference for vagueness in law that is difficult to justify. Courts are good at exposing the reasoning behind a particular administrative decision, in bringing decisions into the light of day. Similar principles should apply to the decisions of judges.[74]

Let us turn now to the third criticism of judicial standard-setting: that inappropriate standards are adopted. We shall concentrate, in particular, on the values adopted in the determination of what is an appropriate and legitimate administrative process. The courts are criticized as preferring a procedural model closer to that which judges themselves would use in the context of ordinary civil litigation; the so-called 'trial type' or 'adjudicatory' process. There is broad agreement among commentators that a trial type or adjudicatory process includes several features: '(1) timely and specific notice of the issues to be resolved at a hearing; (2) the right of affected parties to appear personally or through representatives for purposes of presenting evidence and arguing their positions; (3) confrontation and cross-examination of opposing witnesses; (4) public proceedings; (5) an impartial decision maker; (6) a decision based exclusively on the evidence and argument submitted at the hearing; and (7) written findings of fact and conclusions of law.'[75] Judicial review of administrative action and in particular the application of the principle of natural justice (or fairness) has been centrally concerned with 'the appropriate extent of departures from that model in the non-judicial context'.[76]

According to Mashaw and Merrill, two features of administrative bodies, and in particular of the way in which such bodies take decisions, give rise to tensions if the process model were to be imposed as the only legitimate procedure for administrative agencies. 'The first is the bureaucratic character of modern government. One of the great strengths of administrative organization is its capacity – through the combination of specialization and coordination – to utilize the talent, knowledge, and energy of many persons to achieve a common goal. The customary routines of bureaucratic decision making thus emphasize particularized expertise and dispersed responsibility, unified ultimately through hierarchical control.'[77] The result is what Mashaw and Merrill have termed an 'institutional decision', a decision 'that is the product of many hands and minds but that is the final responsibility of those at the top of the agency hierarchy.'[78] Second, most bureaucracies exist 'primarily to pursue positive programs, not to resolve individualized disputes ... Adjudication in such a context is a means of implementation, a device for achieving general goals in particular cases. Moreover, implementation of a continuing national program extends across space and through time. Each adjudicatory decision, therefore, is but a part of an overall scheme whose ultimate, aggregate success provides the agency's *raison d'être*.'[79] Mashaw and Merrill continue:

The superimposition of trial-type procedures on the process of bureaucratic implementation produces some discordant notes, for the techniques of trial are borrowed from a different institutional context. Courts have no institutional responsibility to seek out crimes, torts, or breaches of contract or to 'implement' bodies of law governing these categories of activity; nor do they possess armies of specialists who can pursue the technical facts germane to legal disputes. Courts decide disputes within a particularistic microcosm of fact and law, developed and presented by outsiders, shaped to suit those parties' particular purposes, and related primarily to their past conduct.[80]

Lastly, we may note that the expectations of participants may become more and more inflated if such procedures are used routinely.[81] These points are illustrated by looking in more detail at the treatment by the courts of the Commission for Racial Equality's exercise of its formal investigation powers.[82] This example illustrates also a reluctance in the courts to surrender issues of legality which makes the task of the agency potentially (and sometimes actually) of considerable difficulty.

While the courts may *over*emphasize the process values of adjudicatory mechanisms and case-by-case decision-making,[83] they may *under*estimate other process values. In considering whether to apply a strict or a lax standard of scrutiny, judicial review tends to give too much weight, for example, to whether there is ministerial responsibility or House of Commons involvement in decisions, and too little to other methods of accountability and control. Actions involving traditional ministerial responsibility to Parliament are accorded inappropriately loose scrutiny.[84] On the other hand, bodies without such traditional relationships with Parliament are accorded unduly strict scrutiny, despite the multifarious other methods of control normally governing these bodies.

In order to assess the potential of a revised approach to issues of legality and process, it will be helpful to consider the case-studies of the regulatory agencies. From these, two changes may be thought necessary if judicial review is to play a more constructive role. First, the courts should recognize that forms of scrutiny other than judicial review are valuable and should appreciate more both the differences between the different procedures, and their relative value. Secondly, the courts should approach questions of legality recognizing a principle of pluralism in interpretation. Other bodies, in other words, should be accorded a legitimate role in interpreting the law. Variations in interpretation between what the judiciary might decide and what a regulatory agency did decide should not necessarily lead to the agency being overruled. The Law Reform Commission of Canada's Final Report recommended, indeed, that legislation should provide that courts show 'reasonable deference' to agency expertise. Such a provision 'should direct courts to show deference to agency expertise and, therefore, not to exercise their discretion to intervene [where error of law is alleged] unless the interpretation placed by an agency on a legislative provision it is required to administer is patently unreasonable'.[85]

This is not to say that adequate recognition of the value in alternative *processes* has been absent in all cases. There are a number of examples of better practice. So, too, though *legality* is considered almost entirely the preserve of the courts, examples of a more pluralistic approach are available.[86] In *R. v. Monopolies and Mergers Commission, ex p. Argyll Group plc*,[87] both 'legality' and 'process' issues were centrally concerned. Taking into account 'the practicalities' involved, Sir John Donaldson MR held that the issue involving the question of legality was 'always . . . a question of fact and degree. . . . This is supremely a matter for the commission.'[88] On the process issue, in the absence of express or implied power in the Act, the chairman of the MMC had acted incorrectly. However, this was not a case in which judicial review should be granted. 'We are sitting as a public law court concerned to review an administrative decision, albeit one which has to be reached by the application of judicial or quasi-judicial principles. We have to approach our duties with a proper awareness of the needs of public administration.'[89] Sir John Donaldson stated that these included: concern with substance, not form; speed, decisiveness and finality of decisions so as to avoid uncertainty in the market; the availability of alternative sources of redress through ministerial scrutiny; and the legitimate interests of individual persons or companies in the light of the purpose of the administrative process concerned.[90]

The apparent inconsistencies in judicial approach discussed in this section indicate a deep uncertainty as to how best to interpret the constitutional function of judicial review. What is the way forward? A number of approaches have been suggested in the United States. One of the better-known discussions of how courts might, for example, take other process values into account in the context of judicial review of administrative action is that found in the discussion of the so-called 'interest representation model'. Associated with the work of Richard Stewart in relation to administrative law in the United States, the judicial function is seen as that of providing an alternative to the political process for the assertion of group interests in certain circumstances.[91] John Hart Ely has developed a sophisticated constitutional theory based on the argument that the proper function of the judiciary under the United States Constitution is that of intervening only when the political process malfunctions.[92] A third, very different, analysis is to be found in the work of Jerry Mashaw, who advocates an approach to securing administrative justice which emphasizes bureaucratic rationality, coupled with internal systems of management and control to ensure consistency, rather than judicial activism.[93]

The need for such theory has been recognized for some time in the United States. The willingness of a growing number of British judges to reconsider the functions of judicial review is also apparent. A broader willingness to undertake this reconsideration is now necessary. British courts will continue to muddle through until they develop a clearer conception of their role in reviewing administrative action, a conception which is more sensitive to the changing shape of government. Indeed, failure to do so may lead to the courts themselves being brought into disrepute.

At the inaugural meeting of the Administrative Law Bar Association in 1986, Sir Harry Woolf warned that undue interference 'could result in the government of the day, out of a sense of frustration, seeking to exclude the supervision of the courts. . . .'[94] This chapter has argued for a clarification in the relationship between the judiciary and regulators, partly to reduce that sense of frustration. So far as the problems in the relationship lie with the judges (and we have seen in chapter 3 that a significant number do not), we have argued that a more articulate, a more structured, and a more consistent approach to judicial review is necessary. In addition, we have argued for an approach which treats the different institutional characteristics and relationships of regulatory agencies more sympathetically. In short, we urge that the judges should take institutions more seriously. To do so, however, requires more systematic information about how the specific institutions in question actually work. It is to this that we now turn in the following chapters.

Part II

5
The Gaming Board for Great Britain: Enforcement and Judicial Restraint

David Miers

The Gaming Board for Great Britain was established by the Gaming Act 1968 as the agency whose primary responsibility would be the implementation of a complex and sophisticated regime designed to regulate the commercial gaming market.[1] As a regulatory agency the Gaming Board is of a special interest for a number of reasons. Firstly, it is engaged in a highly discretionary screening and policing function. It has wide powers to vet and to monitor entrepreneurs and to expel those who are deviant or potentially deviant from the market, all on the basis of deliberately indeterminate criteria. These criteria have been given some specific content during the life of the agency, which is in many respects responsive to the commercial practices of those established in the market, but it retains and continues to exercise a broad measure of independent non-reviewable judgement.

Secondly, the Gaming Board regulates not to reproduce or substitute for competition, but to avoid it. It is the Board's task to recommend the local adjustment of facilities so that the quantity and variety of gaming opportunities in any area should neither stimulate demand nor fail to satisfy such unstimulated demand as may exist. Competition is evidence of the efforts of particular entrepreneurs to influence their market share, and as such is a cue for the agency to seek the correction of any tendency to disequilibrium between the supply of and the demand for gaming facilities.

Beyond these primary tasks, the Gaming Board differs from other economic regulatory agencies in having no broad policy-making role.

While the Board has encouraged some development in market segmentation and would not wish to see large operators achieve a monopoly position in a particular location, the Act gives the Board no power to employ the structure of the market as a criterion when exercising its screening functions over aspirant licence holders. Beyond satisfying the controversial notion of unstimulated demand, the Board has no remit to direct how the market should operate.

The Gaming Board is thus called upon to exercise its discretion in a specialist area characterized by a structural tension between the commercial acquisitiveness of the entrepreneur and the anti-market sentiments of the legislation. Unlike many enforcement agencies, this discretion substantially entails judgements about the potential rather than the proven risks of non-compliance among applicants to the Board. Given the commercial significance of these judgements and the possibility of their being based on unattributable and uncorroborated sources, it is perhaps surprising that they have given rise to so little public controversy. Where judicial review has been sought, the courts have acquiesced in the procedures devised and practised by the Board.

My main concerns are to explain how the Board goes about its tasks and to consider the role of the courts in reviewing the manner in which it has undertaken them. The discussion will consider whether the system of relatively unconstrained regulation is an unavoidable response to particular problems which were perceived as requiring the rigorous, specific and powerful controls exercised by the Board, and whether the Board can be regarded as being sufficiently accountable for its actions.

1 Establishing the Regulatory Regime

Earlier legislation, the Betting and Gaming Act 1960, had failed to prevent the commercial exploitation of gaming. That Act had legalized behaviour which had been unlawful in varying manner and under a number of enactments since 1541. By limiting the financial interest of the promoter in the conduct and outcome of the gaming and by maintaining the legal unenforceability of gaming debts, it was hoped that the 1960 Act would reduce the attractiveness of commercial gaming to such a level that entrepreneurs would not consider its exploitation commercially worthwhile. Given that public and parliamentary attention to the 1960 Act was principally focused on its provisions legalizing off-track cash betting, it is perhaps not surprising that the few sections designed to permit sociable and small-scale gaming for charitable purposes were largely overlooked in debate.

The social costs that were incurred by the Betting and Gaming Act 1960 were of two main kinds. Firstly, the absence of controls restricting the availability of gaming facilities encouraged excessive consumption leading to consumer indebtedness, insolvency, addiction and criminality. Concern was expressed about the debilitating effects of excessive consumption more generally upon the values of thrift and industry and upon the personal worth of the gambler. The number of gaming outlets (around 1,200 throughout Great Britain when the Gaming Act became law), the substantial scale of the 'drop' (money exchanged for chips) in casinos and frequent publicity that moral entrepreneurs gave to 'jackpot fever', contributed to the public perception of a growing social problem.

Secondly, the absence of controls vetting the quality and monitoring the performance of casino management permitted the acquisitive to exploit systematically and to the detriment of consumers those opportunities in the 1960 Act for accumulating profit. Given the abundant and untraceable supplies of ready money, it also encouraged involvement in sundry unlawful enterprises. Casino management was further associated in a number of instances with blackmail, extortion and protection rackets and with a generally robust attitude towards debt enforcement and compliance with house rules.

The perceived seriousness of these pathological aspects of commercial gaming under the 1960 Act dictated both the remedy and the instrument of its realization. Prohibition, which had at one stage been considered by the Home Office, was soon acknowledged to be self-defeating; the costs of policing an illicit market would be far greater than those of policing one recognized by law: 'The one hope of controlling or even containing [commercial gaming] is to make it lawful – but on our terms.'[2] Equally there was absolutely no question of the Government in 1968 permitting market forces alone or even primarily (and monitored by government-encouraged self-regulation) to be responsible for bringing about a reduction in the quantity, or an improvement in the quality, of gaming facilities. The Government's terms included controls over 'the nature, siting and standards of the premises and the antecedents of the proprietors and management'[3] to be imposed by a 'really expert body maintaining a constant watch over gaming of every description, and capable of meeting or anticipating the moves of those seeking to bend the law to their advantage'.[4] Significant aspects of these controls, notably the creation of a statutory body with powers to vet aspirant licence holders, were suggested and developed by the Casino Association, representing the more respectable entrepreneurs. No doubt inspired by commercial self-interest, these proposals nevertheless formed the basis from which the Gaming Board for Great Britain and the consent procedure (described in the next section) emerged.

The Government's objectives (to manipulate the supply of gaming facilities so as to produce tolerable levels of consumption, to eliminate those who might exploit and to expel those who had exploited the market) could probably have been as well achieved by nationalization. Though unusual, the nationalization of gambling opportunities in this country is not without precedent: the Horserace Totalisator Board is a nationalised industry enjoying a statutory monopoly over on- and off-track pool betting. However, while nationalization might once have been a candidate in Home Office thinking, commercial gaming was, by the mid 1960s, held in such odium that it was then impossible to bring it into public ownership. There was also a significant symbolic dimension. It is typically 'national assets' that are brought into public ownership; however else commercial gaming may have been described, it certainly was not valued as an asset, on any scale. Commercial gaming was, to the contrary, seen in 1968 as an essentially undesirable (though inevitable) social activity with few, if any, redeeming economic features. This attitude is well reflected in the Government's view that no one could claim a right to make a living from it; 'it is a privilege albeit a doubtful one', to be enjoyed only by those who are absolutely trustworthy.[5]

Given the moral panic associated with a number of gaming scandals of the 1960s, the creation of an extremely powerful body having a pronounced law-enforcement function and possessing arbitrary powers of an extreme and unprecedented kind quickly became the preferred instrument of policy. When established, the Gaming Board for Great Britain was indeed given powers unusual in their imagination and scope. While opinions continue to differ as to their appropriateness and implementation, the Gaming Board remains a paradigm of industry-specific regulation.

2 Implementing the Regulatory Regime

Quality Control over Market Entry

One of the Government's two primary objectives was to improve the quality of gaming facilities. There was a widespread agreement that the main task was to eliminate from the market those entrepreneurs who might be likely to adopt exploitative practices either because of their undesirable associations or unstable financial arrangements, or because of their predicted inability or unwillingness to comply with standards to be imposed on the conduct of the gaming. This task was to be achieved in a number of ways including the standard status requirements concerning age, nationality/residence or place of incorporation. Unquestionably the most important, however, was and remains the system of individualized screening through which entrepreneurs must pass before they may even apply for a gaming licence. Under the Gaming Act, no gaming may take place on commercial premises unless a gaming licence is in force in respect of them. But before a person may apply to the justices for a gaming licence the Gaming Board must first 'have issued to the applicant a certificate consenting to his applying for such a licence in respect of those premises'.[6] Of the various prior clearance schemes contained in the Act, this process of certification represents the most substantial hurdle to any prospective supplier of gaming facilities.

'Individualized screening' is that regulatory style which in Breyer's analysis[7] is employed when the regulator desires to eliminate from a market those who are 'unfit', but in respect of which 'fitness' is not a readily determinable quality. He contrasts with this a 'standard setting' approach, the success of which depends upon the ease with which fairly precise standards of competence, skill, capitation, prior experience, etc. can be formulated and applied. In many situations, however, the variety of applicants and their backgrounds, the levels of competence and honesty, and the sources of temptations for non-compliance may be but uncertainly known. In these situations, a system of individualized screening involving the application of general standards to screen out, on a case-by-case basis, unacceptable persons (processes or products), may be preferred. It may also be that even where some precision in standards is possible, it will be thought undesirable to do more than establish this kind of regulatory style, even though such indeterminate standards may cause problems both for the regulator and the would-be regulatee.

These points are well illustrated by the scope and implementation of the Gaming Board's discretion to grant a certificate of consent. Paragraph 4(5) to Schedule 2 instructs the Board to have regard only to the applicant's likely capability and diligence in securing that the Act will be complied with, the gaming will be fairly and properly conducted and that premises will be conducted without disorder or disturbance. It was considered 'unnecessary and perhaps hampering to the Board to attempt a comprehensive description' of those circumstances relating to an applicant's 'record, experience and backing'[8] that might be considered relevant to the determination of such questions. The Act, therefore, while requiring it to take some specific (though imprecise) considerations into account, leaves the Board to be the sole judge of other relevant circumstances. Paragraph 4 thus requires the Board to take into consideration the character, reputation and financial standing of the applicant and of any other person who stands to benefit from the operation of the casino, but proceeds to give it a discretion to 'take into consideration any other circumstances appearing to them to be relevant in determining whether the applicant is likely to be capable of, and diligent in' securing compliance with the legislation.

Capacity refers primarily to the ability of the applicant to comply. Relevant considerations are prior experience (if any) of commercial gaming, clarity of lines of authority and communication within the managerial infrastructure, and financial stability and autonomy. The Board is particularly concerned to identify clearly where financial control over the aspirant licence-holder lies. Where others do have a call upon the applicants' assets, the Board will seek to establish whether this is likely to generate pressures weakening ability to control the conduct of the gaming or the destination of the gaming revenue. Diligence contemplates the applicant's disposition to comply. Financial considerations are relevant here also: the object is to identify those who might be tempted (whether because of their own uncertain financial position or because of pressure from others) to exploit the market beyond the limits set by the legislation and the Board. In this connection, investigation of the character and reputation of applicants and their backers is routine. Reliance is placed upon the results of informal inquiries made of a variety of sources, as well as upon formal records of proved deviance.

The open-ended terms of paragraph 4 were needed 'because of the paramount importance of excluding criminals from the field of commercial gaming, which may often have to be done on the grounds of reasonable suspicion rather than absolute proof, or on the basis of information which could not be presented in open court'.[9] The indeterminacy was deliberate, but was made more problematic given the nature of the regulatory objective. While it may be relatively easy to screen out those who are *obviously* unfit, it is very much more difficult (as is required by the consent procedure) to screen out *all* those who are, or might prove to be, unfit. Where the regulatory agency itself cannot formulate accurately and comprehensively the circumstances under which a licence-holder may prove not to be capable of and diligent in complying with the law, it will be difficult for it to identify in advance those characteristics of applicants that pose *risks* of unfitness. In short, the agency will be screening applicants but without knowing clearly what to look for. As the agency's experience grows, so greater definition can be given to such open-ended criteria, but there may be some holders of certificates of consent from the early 1970s who would not now satisfy the Board.

For the regulated, too, such indeterminacy poses problems. Since they are unaware of the precise criteria by which they are to be judged, they will be unable either to address these criteria as they might wish or to determine in what manner they are deficient (so as to take remedial action) should their application be rejected. In practice the Board does give the applicant detailed reasons for its refusal to issue a consent, and these will frequently have been canvassed at length in private interviews with the Board, but attempts to obtain, by means of judicial review, greater precision in the *public* formulation of the criteria contained in paragraph 4, have signally failed. In *R. v. Gaming Board for Great Britain, ex parte Benaim and Khaida*,[10] the ground of the complaint was indeed that the Board had refused to give the specific reason(s) why it had rejected the application, beyond reiterating a number of matters that had troubled it at the interview, and had also refused to disclose the evidence upon which it relied when identifying those matters and formulating its judgement upon them. Dismissing applications for *certiorari* and *mandamus*, the Court of Appeal held that while the Board had a duty to give the applicants an opportunity to satisfy it as to the requirements of paragraph 4(5) and to let them know what its impressions were so that they could disabuse the Board of them, it was not under a duty to give reasons for rejecting their application. The Court also held that the Board had no duty to disclose its sources of information or to reveal details if that would indicate the source. In this connection, however, the decision in *Rogers* v. *Secretary of State for the Home Department*[11] is of greater significance. There the House of Lords was unanimously of the opinion that the public interest required that communications to the Board concerning the character, reputation and financial standing of the applicant should be immune from disclosure, no matter that they might be based on hearsay, involve unsubstantiated allegations or be actuated by malice.

Ex parte Benaim is of course an important illustration of the limits that public interest demands may impose upon an applicant's right to adequate disclosure in an administrative hearing. The duty to act fairly does not impose an identical content in all cases. De Smith, for example, argues that there is a sliding scale of procedural rights: the further removed from the judicial paradigm a particular function is, the weaker the analogy between the conduct appropriate for its exercise and that followed in a court of law.[12] This clearly holds for the present context, in which it was specifically contemplated that the Board would be relying on evidence inadmissible in court. While *Ridge* v. *Baldwin*[13] suggests that the duty to act fairly extends, *inter alia*, to decisions in which applicants have reasonable expectations of preserving or even of acquiring such benefits as licences, the tenor of Lord Denning MR's judgment in *ex parte Benaim* nevertheless appears to indicate that the acquisition of a licence involves a mere privilege; and that, in the case of commercial gaming, this privilege is itself weak. Certainly *dicta* in *ex parte Benaim* and *Rogers* v. *Secretary of State etc.* reflect the high degree of consensus that accompanied the passage of the Bill as to the diagnosis of the mischiefs to be remedied and the appropriateness of the remedies finally contained in the Act.[14]

These two decisions were, and continue to be, of considerable significance to the Board. They delimit its statutory obligations with regard to the public formulation of criteria upon which applications will be determined. They also protect the acquisition, use and legal reliability of 'soft' information. In these respects the implementation of these market entry controls is as we have seen strikingly different from that which obtains in other commercial activities. The Board's ability to continue in this way is largely due to its success in withstanding judicial review in these two cases.

The need for its procedures and decisions to survive judicial review is a significant theoretical constraint upon the exercise by a regulatory agency of its discretion. In the case of the Gaming Board this has not, however, been so in practice. Has greater openness or fairness been achieved by the establishment of other institutional arrangements designed to monitor compliance with these associated values? When the consent procedure was first proposed to Parliament, the Bill made provision for an appeal against refusal to be made to the Secretary of State. But because of the overriding importance of cleansing commercial gaming of the 'criminal element', the proposal was dropped as being an undesirable constraint on the Board's ability to achieve this objective. That the Board would be required to comply with the rules of natural justice was thought to be a sufficient safeguard.

However, because of the essential subjectivity of the statutory test, and because of what were perceived to be the 'significant limitations' of the prerogative orders as a means of reviewing the Board's decisions, the Rothschild (Royal) Commission later proposed 'that any person who has been notified of a decision to refuse or revoke a certificate of consent should be given the right to have the decision reviewed by a specially constituted Gaming Review Board'.[15] This Board would have available to it all the information upon which the original decision was taken and would, like the Gaming Board, give applicants the opportunity to make representations to it, and be legally represented if they wished. The object was that justice be seen to be done. But at the same time, the Rothschild Commission repeatedly emphasized that this recommendation should not be seen as a reflection on the way in which the Board had exercised its powers under the Act.

Two observations may be made about this recommendation and the accompanying clean bill of health given to the Board by the Royal Commission. Firstly, it was made abundantly clear that the secrecy and the reliance upon 'soft' information which characterizes the Gaming Board's enquiries would also be a guaranteed feature of the Review Board's procedures. It was agreed 'that the need to preserve the confidentiality of the Board's information *makes it impossible to have an open review procedure*'.[16] A clearer statement of the impact of the ethos that informed the enactment of the legislation, and that continues to govern its implementation, could not be found: commercial gaming is to be tolerated by law so as, and only, to prevent the creation of an illicit market. To be licensed to run a casino is a privilege to be jealously guarded, and every effort must be made to ensure that the market is not adulterated by the kind of entrepreneur who exploited the 1960 Act. To this end, the Gaming Board must be allowed procedurally unrestricted reliance upon any evidence of actual or potential deviance. The scandals of the late 1970s involving such substantial public companies as Playboy, Ladbrokes and Coral are, in the Board's judgement, amply demonstrative of the continuing need for firm and vigilant control.[17] This judgement is evidently shared by its parent department, since the Home Office shows no sign of wishing to implement this or any similar proposal to institutionalize review of Board decisions.

Given the relatively unconstrained system of regulation permitted by *ex parte Benaim* there is, on the face of it, ample scope for the Board to adopt unconventional forms of enquiry into the background of applicants or to lean on licence-holders to obtain compliance with its requests for cooperation. Since that case there have been several unsuccessful applications for judical review but virtually no other complaints about the exercise of powers of certification. Such evidence does not of course support the view that all who come into contact with the Board are happy with the manner in which it deals with them, but *Rothschild* was nevertheless 'impressed by the general respect in which the Board is held and its reputation for fairness in virtually all responsible sectors of the gaming industry'.[18] Of the non-judicial factors that might explain this attitude, the most persuasive lies in the success with which the Board has projected a self-image: 'tough but fair' might be its motto. Gaming is universally associated with corrupt practices, bent rules and collusive agreements. Contact with the Gaming Board gives one the impression of an agency doing its level best to follow the standards of fairness which it has set for itself while dealing with some devious but mostly acquisitive entrepreneurs. As confirmed by *ex parte Benaim* these standards may well fall below those applicable in other regulatory contexts, but de Smith's sanguine conclusion on that case was that it was 'better to recognise that notwithstanding the impact of the Board's decisions on private interests, the public interest exempts the Board from an ostensible duty to observe certain basic standards of procedural fairness'.[19]

Quantity Control over Market Entry

Possession of a certificate of consent is only the first step for the entrepreneur who is now authorized to apply for a gaming licence and who must satisfy a further set of market entry controls. Of these, the most important are the controls over demand for gaming facilities. In this respect the Gaming Board can quite consistently regard an applicant for a consent as 'likely to be capable of, and diligent in' complying with the legislation, while objecting to the application for a licence on the ground that there is no demand in that locality. The second of the two primary objectives of the Gaming Act was to bring about a reduction in levels of consumption. There are particular features of gaming that encourage high levels of consumption and, to control these features, the Board has powers to define, and to set the odds payable in, those games lawfully provided by casinos. However, the Government's wish to control patterns of consumption went considerably further than this.

Demand for gaming facilities was thought to be of two kinds. There was a comparatively small population whose demand subsisted irrespective of the presence of any incentives (for example, advertising, the easy availability of casinos or of credit for play) or disincentives (for example, the illegality of the behaviour, or having to wait 48 hours after joining a club before one could play). In addition, there was a much larger population whose demand levels were elastic. This hypothesis finds expression in the conceptually and empirically problematic notion of unstimulated demand: it is the Board's function to bring about that number, variety and distribution of gaming facilities which is sufficient 'to satisfy an unstimulated demand for gaming that might otherwise seek an illegal outlet',[20] but no more. Such demand was considered to require at most 20–25 per cent of the casinos operating in 1968. To bring about the desired reduction in the level of 'stimulated demand', the Board implemented the policy (foreshadowed in the parliamentary debates)[21] of restricting casinos to certain parts of the country. As availability depends not just upon the quantity of outlets, further restrictions were placed upon access to those casinos that are licensed. The 1,200 casinos in operation prior to the full commencement of the Gaming Act in 1970 were reduced to 120 by the application of these geographical restrictions, and of the statutory test of demand.

This test provides that the justices may refuse to grant a licence if they are not satisfied that a substantial demand already exists on the part of the prospective players for gaming facilities of the kind proposed to be provided by the entrepreneur. Even if there is such a demand, the justices may still refuse to grant a licence if they are not satisfied that that demand cannot be met by a casino which is reasonably accessible to those players. To assist licensing justices to apply this test, the Board has power to advise them 'as to the extent of the demand on the part of prospective players for gaming facilities of any particular kind, either generally in Great Britain or in any particular part of Great Britain'.[22] The justices must take this advice into account. It was envisaged that this blend of national and local responsibilities would enable consistent and considered policy on the supply of gaming facilities to be successfully implemented. Opinions differ as to the desirability of the results that have been achieved.

The initial declared policy of reduction followed by the adoption of measures designed 'to discourage further propagation',[23] leaves little scope for alternatives. Unlike other commercial enterprises, there is also restricted opportunity for product or process development and diversification. The only area in which improvement was actively encouraged by the Board during the mid 1970s was in the standards of accommodation and amenities offered by casinos, but such improvements were nevertheless constrained by the governing policy, as the Board's advice for each year's Licensing Sessions makes clear.[24]

A persistent difficulty lies in the qualification that the demand which is to be satisfied must itself be 'unstimulated'.[25] Apart from the questionable assumption that there exist natural and artificial levels of demand, this notion is not easily translated into standards susceptible to empirical measurement; indeed no national research into levels of demand for gaming outlets has been undertaken by the Board. It is therefore not surprising that it has had 'no general advice to offer over the whole field',[26] beyond reiteration of the governing policy.

The Home Office predicted in 1968 that if licensing were conducted by the Board and not the local justices (as was proposed by some), rigid patterns would be imposed based on partial local knowledge. Ironically, this has substantially transpired in practice. In December 1986 there were 114 casinos in Great Britain[27] distributed in largely the same manner as in 1970; no new 'permitted areas' have been established and, in the 100 or so provincial casinos, income and expenditure have remained (inflation aside) largely constant. This homogeneity is accentuated in the provincial clubs by the impact of the rules governing the conduct of the gaming. Beyond some permitted variations in the ambience of a club, and in the mix and number (and table limits) of the games offered, clubs cannot provide games other than those specified in the Regulations, cannot uni-laterally change their variety or the location of the premises, cannot offer preferential credit terms or other inducements to play. Because it admits of minimal variation, their regulatory policy has resulted in the creation of a market whose parameters are substantially the same as they were in 1970.

These results are not altogether welcome to some entrepreneurs; nor are the implications for their future profits of a regulatory policy that is essentially inimical to market development. It is hardly surprising that there are differences of opinion between the Board and the industry as to what constitutes 'a substantial demand' for gaming facilities of the kind which an applicant proposes to supply, and concerning the methods by which patterns of consumption are to be assessed. Casino entrepreneurs, however, find themselves, like others who enjoy the benefits of a regulatory fold, in two minds on agency policy. It is unquestionably true that the particular advice of the Gaming Board concerning demand can, as was the case in London in 1982, have the most substantial commercial impact upon entre-preneurs' profitability, share value and therefore upon their share-holders.[28] Nevertheless, the financial rewards for London casino entrepreneurs in the recent past have been immense, in one instance both covering a \$15 million loss incurred by its American parent and showing a \$25 million pre-tax profit. Here again what was perceived to be an objectionable state of affairs, that those who receive licences will be 'left in the enjoyment of a local monopoly',[29] has occured in practice. Unlike other situations where capture of the agency may protect the regulated from competition, it is the regulatory policy itself which achieves this: the policy *is* to discourage competition, both within and without, since competition presupposes (for the purpose of this regime) that supply exceeds, in quantity or quality, the 'unstimulated' demand that exists for gaming facilities.

Setting Performance Standards

The Gaming Act imposes on licence-holders a number of standards regulating the manner in which gaming is to be conducted on their premises and their financial interests in the level and outcome of the betting. Some of these are specified in the Act or in Regulations made under it; others are particularized in the licence.

A persistent issue in the regulation literature concerns the difficulties that attend the formulation and implementation of the standards with which the regulated are to comply. For the purposes of enforcement,

regulators must have standards that are practicably and readily enforceable. Tests to determine compliance must be capable of simple application by the industry and agency staff. This need will bias the standard towards enforceability rather than achieving the ends sought.[30]

From the regulator's point of view, simplified and standardized expectations of the regulated have their value, but this presupposes, as we noted earlier in connection with the consent procedure, that it is both possible and desirable to determine accurately what these expectations should be in given instances. There is therefore a tendency to formulate standards permitting leeway in their application, lest the agency's hands be tied in the future. The regulated, too, have an interest in clear standards, but may also desire flexibility and so welcome standards of indeterminate scope while, like the agency, regretting their over-inclusiveness.

A good example of these difficulties is provided by the power to cancel or to refuse to renew a gaming licence on the deliberately indeterminate ground that the holder is not a 'fit and proper' person. Problems arose over its application to certain cheque transactions in casinos. Under Section 16, no credit may be given for gaming. It is, however, lawful to obtain chips for gaming on the strength of a cheque which, for these purposes, is enforceable at law.[31] Such cheques are sometimes dishonoured and controversy arose between the Gaming Board and the industry as to what constituted 'fit and proper' behaviour in respect of them.[32] Two main issues were at stake: whether it was proper for a casino to accept a cheque for gaming while a dishonoured cheque drawn by the player remained unpaid (thus raising the possibility that subsequent cheques would also be dishonoured); and secondly, whether it was proper for a casino to compromise a dishonoured cheque, settling with the player for a less sum or allowing time to pay. The point behind both issues is that if such dealings were lawful, a casino could freely provide what is in effect credit for gaming, the only constraint being its commercial judgement. Many London casinos took advantage of the uncertain scope of section 16 which, besides bringing them into conflict with the Gaming Board, in extreme cases brought them into conflict with those casino proprietors who, while seeking some commercial legroom, preferred a more cooperative relationship with the Board.

The legal arguments are too intricate to be rehearsed here, but essentially the Board took the view that it was neither fit and proper for a proprietor to compromise a dishonoured cheque, nor to accept further cheques for gaming until the previous debt so incurred had been discharged. The advantage of this view was that it contained a clear, if commercially arbitrary line which, when the casino's books were examined, permitted a simple test of compliance. From the industry's point of view it was unnecessarily inflexible in that it did not, for example, account for genuine instances in which the *particular* facts of a series of cheque transactions suggested no more than a temporary loss of liquidity in the bank upon which the dishonoured cheque was drawn, and were not indicative of any sustained or systematic attempts to provide credit for gaming. Moreover, in the view of the more compliant licence-holders, the problems were aggravated by the all-or-nothing character of the formal sanctions of cancellation or non-renewal of the gaming licence, which caught both the marginal and the extreme deviant. But, apart from enforcement practicalities, the Board was also concerned that the less compliant proprietors would exploit any commercial flexibility which was permitted, a concern amply justified by some of the events of the late 1970s.

In 1982 the Court of Appeal held that 'the only lawful cheque contemplated by section 16 is one in which there is a common expectation of payment'[33] and that the compromise of a dishonoured cheque is, prima facie, unlawful. Since then the Board and industry have reached agreement over cheque-cashing facilities,[34] but these past disagreements illustrate well the difficulties that regulatory agencies face when they have to give specific content to open-ended performance standards.

Securing Compliance

Compliance with the Act is monitored by a specially appointed Inspectorate within the Board, although there are occasions on which the police (in their general capacity or in the pursuit of more specialized enquiries) and other agencies have a role to play. We shall be concerned here only with the Board's own staff.

The Gaming Board for Great Britain consists of a Chairman, a Secretary, four part-time members and, in 1986, 73 full-time employees of whom 35–40 were members of the Inspectorate.[35] The Inspectorate is differentiated both geographically and hierarchically.

The country is divided into six roughly comparable regions, within which each divisional team is responsible for monitoring compliance with the Act of gaming machine operators and their suppliers, casino licence-holders, and bingo licence-holders. A Senior Inspector is in charge of each region and below him are usually five inspectors who deal on a daily basis with the various responsibilities imposed by the legislation. The Senior Inspector reports routinely to a Deputy Chief Inspector in London who, with the other DCIs, is responsible to the Board's Chief Inspector.

The Inspectors themselves tend to be drawn largely from the police, or from the armed services. In the former organization they may have had some acquaintance with the Gaming Act but all undergo training once within the Inspectorate. They are expected to have a general knowledge of the relevant law and to be familiar with the details of particular licence-holders in their region; complex or unusual problems are referred initially to the Senior Inspector and thereafter to one of the London inspectors who specializes in the area of concern. As with other regulatory agencies, the inspectors have two broad functions to perform: one is giving advice to licence-holders; the other has a more pronounced law enforcement function. Regarding the former, typical matters include the mix of games, the disposition of the tables and the licence-holder's wish to vary these features, variations in licensing procedures and in the certification of employees and the more general concerns of running a business generating a large turnover of ready money.

Apart from maintaining regular contact with the local police, standing instructions to inspectors require them to visit the casinos in their region at least once a month. In practice they will make 3–4 visits a month, without pre-arrangement with the licence-holder. There are routine matters which the inspectors will examine: the signing-in book and the membership list (to check for evasion of section 12); the cheque list and bank receipt book (to check for evasions of section 16); accounting and auditing procedures; table use (to assess demand) and more generally the conduct of the staff at all levels. The Board has a work programme which indicates what inspectors should look for to detect non-compliance, and encourages them to follow through the internal management of each casino so that the inspector will know who is responsible for each aspect of the conduct of the gaming. Sometimes the inspector will have particular aspects of the gaming to scrutinize. This may be the result of a policy direction by the Board, for example, that inspectors should pay close attention to the competence of dealers or supervisors because it is concerned about the quality of applicants for certificates of approval. On other occasions, the inspector may be looking for evidence of non-compliance in response to a particular complaint made against the club. This may come from a disgruntled punter, from employees or former employees, and sometimes from other casinos.

Faced with what he perceives to be non-compliance with the legislation, the inspector's decision to report the matter to his regional superior (and to the police) or to request the licence-holder to comply by the next visit is largely dependent on the gravity of the deviance. If it relates to what the Board regards as a critical feature of the legislation, for example granting unlawful credit, the inspector is bound to report the matter, unless there is a wholly convincing explanation. His discretion is less fettered with less serious in-fractions, where the response resembles the 'serial and incremental nature'[36] of compliance enforcement in other regulatory contexts. If, for example, an inspector considers that the club has inadequate table supervision, he will usually request the licence-holder to remedy matters. Only if the licence-holder dissents from his diagnosis, or compliance is not forthcoming by a subsequent visit, will the matter be reported.

When reported, the Senior Inspector may decide to forward the report to the Gaming Board for further action (which may include recommending to the police that they bring criminal proceedings or building a case for objecting to the renewal of the licence). He may send a warning letter on his own authority to the licence-holder or, if less serious or if the fact or degree of non-compliance is uncertain, may require the inspector to investigate further. Generally speaking, the big stick is seldom waved by the inspectors; casinos are for the most part well-managed and honest operations, although there continue to be instances of mismanagement of varying seriousness.

The relationship that develops between inspectors and licence-holders appears much as that described in other regulatory contexts. Either may appear to the other as by turns helpful, conciliatory, co-operative or obstructionist, though in London casinos where the stakes and the rewards are *much* higher, points of conflict are of greater sensitivity. To the Board, the licence-holders may also be overly exploitative of the market or downright dishonest; in either event it will seek to close the casino. The commercial impact of closure means, as Wade and Schwartz observed of the sanctioning powers of American regulatory commissions, that those engaged in the commercial gaming market 'simply cannot afford to risk having to live with a [Commission] that is hostile to them'.[37] Not that this implies any significant problems of substitution. If an entrepreneur is expelled from the market, there is no obligation on the Board to invite competition for the vacant place. There is, firstly, no such conception under the legislation of a 'place' in the market to which applicants may aspire. Secondly, unlike, for example, television broadcasting, the Board does not have to consider the competing claims of substitute operators.[38] In broadcasting, as in the allocation of such other scarce resources as airline routes or communications more generally, the agency typically has to consider who is the best supplier of the services contemplated by the legislation or the agency's interpretation of it and its policy. It is true that the Board will have to consider, should anyone seek a licence, the nature and variety of gaming facilities that the aspirant operator proposes to supply, and compare them, in terms of the Act's conception of supply and demand, with the facilities being supplied by existing operators. What it does not have to do is to consider whether what is proposed is a complete substitution for what has disappeared; indeed, if the previous operator was expelled for seeking to influence demand in favour of the facilities he was supplying, the Board may object to any substitution at all being made.

Sanctioning the Deviant Entrepreneur: Legislative Sanctions

Part Two of the Gaming Act creates a number of offences which may be committed on premises licensed for gaming, and which attract fines and imprisonment. 'The chief deterrent',[39] however, was intended to be the withdrawal of official approval instituted by the Board objecting to the renewal of the gaming licence, applying at any time for the cancellation of the licence, or by the licensing justices disqualifying the premises from being used for gaming on proof of specified deviations from the legislation. As these are the only serious legal sanctions for non-compliance, the Gaming Board and the police must, in almost any case that involves more than a technical breach of the law, seek to persuade the justices to apply them. Their 'all or nothing' quality thus offers an inflexible response to a range of deviant behaviour that arguably requires differential treatment. The Board acknowledged this problem in its evidence to Rothschild. The matter is made more contentious where, as in the example of transactions with dishonoured cheques discussed above, both the immorality and the unlawfulness of the actions complained of were by no means certain.

The lack of discrimination in these sanctions is not, however, their only problematic aspect. From the Gaming Board's point of view, they have lacked the legal bite that they were intended to have. Between 1979 and 1982 the licences of 12 of the 25 London casinos were either cancelled or not renewed on the evidence of substantial and chronic deviance. Pending the outcome of appeals, many of the premises under threat of closure were sold to 'fit and proper' purchasers who were subsequently successful in the appeals they took over and were thus able to continue trading. In this way the deviant licence-holder avoided the *legal* consequences of closure, though not the commercial impact of the threat measured in terms of the reduced market value of the premises.

A noteworthy but unsuccessful attempt by the Gaming Board to prevent what it perceived to be the commercial subversion of legislative sanction arose in *Playboy Club* v. *Gaming Board for Great Britain*.[40] In December 1978 the police raided the premises of the Victoria Sporting Club. A number of prosecutions were brought against persons involved in the management of the club, where it was alleged that some £1.8 million had been skimmed from the casino's take. In April 1979 the police and the Gaming Board applied for the cancellation of the gaming licence. The application, which was not heard until March 1980, was successful: the licence was cancelled and the premises disqualified for three years. In the meantime, in October 1979, aware of these pending proceedings, Playboy Ltd bought the entire share capital of the club's holding company. Because Playboy wished to have the licence transferred to its own name, it was required by the Act to apply to the Gaming Board for a certificate of consent to apply to the justices for the transfer of the licence. The Board (which had no objection to Playboy at that time) declined to consider the application until the outcome of the various licensing and criminal proceedings was final. The Board had no statutory authority for this refusal to exercise its discretion, and Playboy successfully applied for *mandamus*. Of interest were the reasons that the Board gave for its refusal to hear Playboy's application for a consent. They reflected a particular view on the way in which the gaming industry should be conducted, a recognition that the Act did not explicitly confer on the Board a power to put this opinion directly into practice and a decision to give effect to it indirectly, by holding up the consent application. In essence, it was the view of the Board that a casino operator who had so misconducted himself as no longer to be worthy of a licence 'should not be able to salvage his position by transferring at full value the operation of the casino to a buyer who is not personally open to objection'.[41] Although not required to pass any comment on the validity of this view, Mustill J did observe that so far as the present case was concerned, the goal was beyond realization, as the sale had been completed nearly a year earlier. 'The only effect of blocking the application will be to ensure that the buyer loses money on the transaction: and hence no doubt to discourage similar transactions in the future.'[42]

In terms of the impact of sanctions upon those gaming entrepreneurs perceived as 'amoral calculators',[43] this case is of some importance. This is so not because of the particular result, nor even because of the Board's conception of the proper way in which the gaming industry should be conducted; it is because it reveals the powerlessness of the Board under the Act to insist upon realization of sanctions which have *legal* authority rather than those which are imposed by the market-place. The degree to which deviant entrepreneurs suffer financially following legal proceedings depends substantially not on legal values, but on the commercial values of potential purchasers, including some who are themselves involved in the gaming industry. The commercial sanction is out of the hands of the authorities and thus they cannot control its impact or its severity. As Mustill J said, 'The reality is that the Board wishes to use delay as an instrument for achieving what is in practice the same result as a refusal. . . .'[44]

Sanctioning the Deviant Entrepreneur: Market Sanctions

The benefits which accompany an entrepreneur's uninterrupted membership of the regulatory fold are sufficient to outweigh either the disadvantage of his activities being monitored by agency personnel or the possibility of expulsion from it. Entrepreneurs may thus be expected to take steps to protect their position within the market, both as individuals and collectively, at least where their commercial interest and the agency's requirements coincide. In this connection a significant stimulant to compliance with the Gaming Board's requirements is the collective view of the majority of licence-holders as expressed through the British Casino Association (BCA).

This Association, which represents 90 per cent of licence-holders, imposes a code of conduct upon its members to 'conduct gaming and related business affairs with due regard to the spirit and intention of the Gaming Act 1968 as well as to the letter of the law'.[45] The Gaming Board relies to a great extent upon the goodwill and co-operation of the BCA in the implementation of the Act and is prepared to accede to self-regulation within the market on various matters. Nevertheless, the Association is also concerned to promote the commercial interests of its members, and this may bring it into conflict with the Board. The BCA's commercial interests are tempered by the recognition that its members enjoy the evident advantages of a protected market, and that it has as much interest as the Gaming Board in presenting and maintaining a clean image. This is reflected in the public statements of some of its past members, and in its endeavours to impose its own performance standards on licence-holders and to monitor their compliance with them. The BCA's regulatory stance was well illustrated by its criticism of Ladbroke's Unit Six operation,[46] in which that company, by seeking to poach players from other clubs, broke the tacit conventions governing competition within the industry.

3 Evaluating the Regulatory Regime

Although, as Fels has noted, the definition of regulation 'varies with the purpose of the discussion'[47] and is often used in different senses, the regime regulating commercial gaming presents structural characteristics that are persistent and shared features of other regimes regulating for example, communications[48] and pollution.[49] The collective aspects of a given enterprise are subject to a regime under which either entry is validated or practice is monitored (or both) by an agency which is formally independent of the enterprise, and which has powers to set or to modify standards of entry and/or practice and in the event of non-compliance may invoke sanctions which particularly involve temporary or permanent suspension from the enterprise. It is this structural coherence that distinguishes a regulatory regime from a mere congeries of rules enforced by private individuals or by agencies of general social or fiscal control. In this connection, Breyer[50] has argued that all regulatory regimes present, to a greater or lesser degree, the same issues which include, as we have seen, the familiar problems associated with standard setting, compliance seeking, tendencies to monopoly, bargaining, moral ambivalence and so on.[51]

The regime regulating the commercial gaming market is, however, unusual in at least one respect, and this difference accounts for some of the tension that has existed between the Gaming Board and the industry. In his discussion of the differences between specialized regulatory enforcement and general policing, Kagan says of the nature of the offenders subject to general policing:

> The burglars, drunks, heroin peddlers, and other criminal offenders encountered by police officers are rarely engaged in what are thought to be socially useful occupations. In the case of regulated businesses, however, their offences, even if irresponsible or socially harmful in and of themselves, are more likely to be viewed as negligent, non-malicious *side effects of socially useful activities*.[52]

The implications of this distinction lie in the perception of the former as 'thoroughgoing "bad apples"' and of the latter as 'essentially decent human beings who have "gone wrong"'[53] under market pressures and so affect the selection of appropriate enforcement and penalty strategies. However, the distinction is based on an assumption which is controversial in the case of commercial gaming, namely that the activity being regulated *is* socially useful.

As we have seen, the regulatory regime was structured in 1968 so as to exclude those who, motivated entirely by profit seeking, carefully and competently assess opportunities and risks and are prepared to disobey the law when the anticipated legal penalties and the probability of being caught are small in relation to the profits to be gained by non-compliance. Unlike other regulated businesses, however, commercial gaming was also regarded in 1968 as performing neither any desirable nor any productive economic function. The irony is that gaming is now regulated in a manner akin to those activities which *are* considered socially useful. Such treatment legitimizes the activity and attracts entrepreneurs (sometimes from other regulated industries) who subsequently become frustrated by the anti-market sentiments of the policies endorsed by the legislation and implemented by the agency. Not surprisingly, this frustration leads to difficulties, for in practice contemporary gaming entrepreneurs fall more squarely within Kagan and Scholz's description of entrepreneurs who are 'ordinarily inclined to comply with the law' (partly as a matter of long-term self-interest), but will 'adopt a strategy of selective non-compliance when regulations and government officials treat them arbitrarily or impose unreasonable burdens'.[54] A clear instance of such non-compliance concerned dealings with dishonoured cheques, discussed earlier.

These two images of corporate criminality underlie the perception and evaluation that the Gaming Board makes of the industry, and that the industry makes of itself. The Board has wide powers to control entry to the market, to regulate levels of supply, to set and monitor business practices and to expel the deviant. All these, and more, are required in its judgment to ensure the continued public health of commercial gaming. While the Board does generally acknowledge the legitimacy of most entrepreneurs (in particular as represented by the British Casino Association), it is acutely sensitive to the opportunities for abuse of the market that are open to the amoral calculator. In much the same way as the pathology of gaming informed the content of the regulatory regime, so the awareness of these opportunities continues to inform much of the Board's efforts to convince the Home Office to increase its powers. The London scandals of the late 1970s are, for the Board, ample evidence that its suspicions are well founded.

For the regulated, the Gaming Board is a source both of frustration and of protection. The commercial gaming market is characterized by a relatively high degree of consensus as to the desirability of the regulatory regime, if for no other reason than the commercial self-interest of those within the fold, who are thereby protected from competition from without. The Board has no remit to consider who might be a 'better' (more competitive, more efficient) supplier of gaming facilities than an existing licence-holder.[55] Generally, entrepreneurs cannot afford to lose the Board's confidence in them, but there are tensions. Thus, established entrepreneurs, who 'grew up' with the Board and were instrumental in giving content to the Act, have, in the past, regarded the Board's response to their deviance as heavy-handed, where official tolerance of legitimate commercial judgment would have resolved their difficulty. Originally inclined to comply with the law, these entrepreneurs were also affronted by what they perceived to be a lack of differentiation in the Board's response between their 'legitimate' deviance and the systematic and exploitative deviance of those who more squarely fitted the image of amoral calculator.

Newer entrants to the market, on the other hand, may have been surprised both by the closeness of the relationship between established entrepreneurs and the Board and, following the scandals of the late 1970s, by a tougher attitude on the part of the Board to compliance with the rules. These entrants may also have brought more assertive marketing practices to the industry which in turn were resented by the Board, licensing justices and older licence-holders. A matter which continues to excite controversy, therefore, is the Board's willingness to intervene on the issue of demand. Here entrepreneurs are resentful of what they perceive to be the inappropriateness of the Board for determining what are essentially matters of commercial judgment. The point is, of course, that the issue of demand was never intended to be so flexible as to allow variations in the commercial judgment of what the market will bear to affect the quantity of gaming outlets beyond the most marginal increases or decreases in supply. Such resentment may particularly be expressed by licence-holders with experience of other regulated industries where issues of demand are more significantly affected by market values.

However, beyond the continuing efforts of the British Casino Association and the Gaming Board to negotiate mutually acceptable rules for the management of commercial gaming, there are few suggestions for radical change; certainly deregulation of this market is not on the political agenda.[56] From the Home Office's standpoint, the criteria of efficacy set for this regime in 1968 – to control and contain a social mischief – have substantially been realized. From the entrepreneur's standpoint, the regime is efficacious if for no other reason than that their oligopoly continues to generate substantial profits. In 1986 the 'drop' in casinos in Great Britain was £1,604 million, producing a 'win' (income before any expenditure, taxation or duty payable) of £312 million.[57] While it is the case that this figure is disproportionately distributed among casinos (some 73 per cent of the total is shared by the 20 London clubs), neither the wealthy nor the less profitable entrepreneur has any great incentive to advocate radical change to a regulatory regime which offers significant opportunities to the licence-holder who can match the extent of his commercial acquisitiveness to the limits of what the Board regards as compliant behaviour.

A notable feature of the regulation of the commercial gaming market was the paucity, until recent years, of outside scrutiny of the way in which the Gaming Board and the entrepreneurs have managed the regime. Between 1970 and 1978 when the Rothschild Commission published its final report, the implementation of the legislation received little public attention, notwithstanding its significant commercial implications for a number of major public companies. Nor do the activities of the Board or the entrepreneurs generate much political interest. Commercial gaming presents no party political issues, nor any significant conflicts of economic theory or practice. Decisions of the Board, while of legal and commercial importance to the entrepreneur, do not involve the balancing of competing personal and collective values that characterize the decisions for example of the Parole Board or the Commission for Racial Equality. Nevertheless, the structure and implementation of the regime continue to present the same (problematic) features that characterize attempts to regulate other economic and social activities attracting greater publicity.

It remains striking that over its 15 years, there have only been a handful of applications for judicial review of the Board's decisions. Whether the Board's decisions have indeed been procedurally beyond reproach, or its staff are unusually adept at deflecting complainants from seeking public review of its decisions, or agreements are reached with those affected by them, remains a matter of speculation. There is some evidence, for example in the *Playboy* case, that earlier distinctions between rights and privileges, and refusal and revocation of licences, have been 'in large part abandoned in favour of . . . a more realistic assessment of the economic effect [of such decisions] upon the individual'.[58] Nevertheless, given the complaisant response of the Court of Appeal in *ex parte Benaim*, the Board remains possessed of a wide measure of protection from judicial review. The *Playboy* case is a rare example of a successful application for judicial review of a decision of the Gaming Board. Beyond such instances where the Board was plainly acting without authority, it is difficult to see what further protection judicial review can afford. Gaming club proprietors are a class of person (along with aliens and scientologists) whose interests the courts have been less than enthusiastic to secure. Certainly their interests were conclusively displaced in *ex parte Benaim* and *Rogers* v. *Secretary of State* by the interest of the public in ensuring the realization of the legislation's objectives.

To the extent that public lawyers are concerned with the accountability of regulatory agencies, a common response to the relatively unconstrained discretion exercised by the Gaming Board would be to measure the existing arrangements for review against some constitutional ideal combining efficiency with justice and then to conclude that the arrangements are, in this particular case, deficient. Implicit in this ideal is an approach to the constitution that emphasizes the efficacy of law to secure such values as 'the protection of individual rights, observance of due process, the avoidance of arbitrariness and the promotion of certainty, predictability and uniformity in decision making'.[59] Where these values are apparently not secured by existing legal arrangements, the constitutionalist response is to press for 'an increase in the role of law in government'. Such a conception of constitutional values and of the role of law to secure them has been frequently and critically challenged,[60] though this is not the place to detail these criticisms. Nevertheless, the practices generated and sustained by the Gaming Board in the pursuit of its statutory duties are further evidence of an approach to regulatory legislation that attaches little importance to judicial review, but emphasizes the place of negotiation and the formulation of procedures between the participants directly affected by the legislation. The crucial point is that most entrepreneurs both embrace the regime's objectives and share the Gaming Board's projection of what standards of fair dealing can be expected. Measured against an idealized version of accountability, or against the standards publicly approved and required to be met in other regulatory contexts, these standards fall short. But by the consensus generated within this regime, they meet, for the most part, the participants' expectations.

6

The Advisory Conciliation and Arbitration Service: Regulation and Voluntarism in Industrial Relations

Linda Dickens

ACAS has existed for well over a decade. During that time the political and legislative context within which it operates has changed considerably; the philosophy on which it was based has lost favour and it has found its values and approach in conflict with those of the courts. Yet it survives. This chapter describes and evaluates how ACAS has performed its different and changing functions and the problems encountered through judicial review. It explores whether there is a role for such an agency in the current relationship between the state and the processes of industrial relations.

1 Continuity and Change

ACAS was set up on a non-statutory basis as the Conciliation and Arbitration Service in September 1974. It adopted its present title by adding 'advisory' in January 1975 and was established as a statutory Crown body on 1 January 1976 under the Employment Protection Act (EPA) 1975. It took over from the Department of Employment (DE) long-established collective dispute settlement functions, and a more recent conciliation role in individual rights claims. Thus, it continued the tradition of providing a 'breakdown' or peace-keeping service for the British voluntary system of industrial relations, a system which gave preference to self-regulation over legal regulation.

But ACAS was founded in a period of what may be called

'enhanced voluntarism'. The voluntary system of autonomous regulation through collective bargaining was not merely supported by the state, it was actively promoted, and the so-called Social Contract with the Labour Government accorded the trade unions the status of partners in the economic and industrial management of Britain. ACAS's tripartite governing Council reflects this. So does the range of functions it was given, including a role in operating such provisions as the EPA recognition procedure which embodied a view that law should be used directly to promote and support trade unionism and collective bargaining. ACAS was also heir to functions previously performed by the Commission on Industrial Relations (CIR) which had an industrial relations reform role of the kind envisaged by the Royal Commission on Trade Unions and Employers' Associations (the Donovan Commission) in the late 1960s. The EPA (section 1) charged ACAS with the general duty of 'promoting the improvement of industrial relations, and in particular of encouraging the extension of collective bargaining and the development and, where necessary, reform of collective bargaining machinery'. This general duty remains unchanged but the context within which ACAS operates has changed dramatically.

The reform strategy, exemplified by the Donovan Report, while conceding some role for law, saw 'virtue in the autonomous collective system and wished to expand both its scope and coverage'.[1] Since ACAS was established, however, there has been a marked shift away from a reform strategy towards one of 'restriction'[2] or even 'ultra-restriction'.[3] Such a strategy aims to 'restrict the social power of trade unions through the use (or threatened use) of legal sanctions'[4] and embodies individualist rather than collectivist values. One consequence of the withdrawal of public policy support for collective bargaining and trade unionism was the repeal of the legislative 'props' to the voluntary system,[5] such as the union recognition procedure in which ACAS played the major role, and the enactment of legal provisions designed to promote non-unionism.[6]

Proposed at one time as 'an alternative to law',[7] ACAS now operates in a political context where the law, rather than the parties to collective bargaining aided by an external agency, is 'an important, or even ... a main instrument of achieving the reconstruction of industrial relations'.[8] Furthermore, in the 1980s the tripartism, or corporatism, fostered by previous governments is out of political favour. Just as collective bargaining is no longer promoted by the state as the best method of conducting industrial relations at workplace or company level, trade unions no longer have the status of equal partners at national level. The move away from corporatist arrangements partly reflects a different ideology but also results from the adoption of a different economic policy after 1979. National-level tripartism can be seen as a pragmatic way in which past governments have come to terms with, or attempted to contain, the ability of trade unions and their members to disrupt their economic policies. This disruptive potential is being dealt with by means other than corporatism, in particular restrictive labour legislation and high unemployment. Nor does the free-market economic policy, as exemplified by the Conservative Government since 1979, require an incomes policy deal of the kind which underpinned the Social Contract.

An agency governed by a Council containing representatives of the Trade Union Congress (TUC) and the Confederation of British Industry (CBI) thus appears anachronistic after 1979. This corporatist arrangement nonetheless has a continuing utility in providing ACAS with its badge of independence from government.

2 Voluntarism and the Need for an Independent Service

In Britain, legal enforcement in industrial relations has traditionally taken second place to regulation through collective bargaining. This is largely a consequence of historical circumstance, in particular the fact that the industrial strength of the male working class and the development of collective bargaining predated political enfranchisement and parliamentary links, and the adverse experience which unions and their members had of the courts and thereby of 'law'.[9] The preference for collective bargaining between unions and employers, rather than legislation, as a means of regulating jobs meant that the settlement of disputes over job regulation was left also to voluntary procedures and arrangements.

The state's interest in maintaining industrial peace was pursued by the provision of bargaining assistance. This included conciliation (aiding the parties to reach their own settlement) and arbitration (handing down an award where the parties sought external determination of the issue). In peacetime such assistance has been voluntary and non-coercive. ACAS's functions of conciliation and arbitration can be traced back to the Conciliation Act 1896 and the Industrial Courts Act 1919. The 1896 Act was an outcome of the Report of the Royal Commission on Labour 1894 and provided the legal basis for the conciliation services operated by the DE and its predecessors. It, and the 1919 Act, as Kahn-Freund noted, 'took industrial relations as they were and enlisted the law in their support'.[10]

ACAS's advisory role, giving industrial relations advice to employers, workers and their organizations, derives from the Manpower Advisers in the DE, descendants of the Personnel Management Advisory Service which had grown up after the Second World War in the Ministry of Labour. The transfer of these third-party dispute-settlement and advisory services from the DE was to meet the demand for a service which was independent of government.

The same economic pressures which in the 1960s had led to a questioning of the 'voluntary tradition' (see below) also led to interventionist incomes policies and the Government became concerned that the third-party services provided by the DE should aim not merely at securing peace at any price but peace at the right price. Thus, for example, in 1971 the DE withdrew its conciliation services where an agreement above the incomes policy norm appeared likely. Such interference led the parties to collective bargaining to perceive the need for a dispute-resolution service independent of government.[11] In 1972 the TUC and CBI had made moves to establish their own independent service, a factor which no doubt influenced the new Labour Government in 1974 to set up what was to become ACAS.

ACAS is governed by a Council which may consist of as many as fifteen members but has always numbered nine, in addition to the chairperson who is the only full-time member. The nine members, who have appropriate specialist knowledge and experience, are appointed for not more than five-year periods (usually two years) by the Secretary of State and may be re-appointed. Three members are appointed after consultation with the TUC (often union general secretaries or, more recently, TUC officials) and three after consultation with the CBI (senior business people and CBI officials). The other three members are not representatives but 'independents', to date all academics. The first ACAS Chairman was Mr Jim Mortimer, who had considerable experience in both union and management posts. He was succeeded by Sir Pat Lowry, a leading management figure in the motor industry. The latest appointment is something of a departure in that the Chairman comes from within the civil service – Mr Douglas Smith, formerly Deputy Secretary (Industrial Relations) at the DE. Although the Secretary of State appoints the Council, ACAS's constitution provides that 'the Service shall not be subject to directions of any kind from any Minister of the Crown as to the manner in which it is to exercise any of its functions under any enactment'.[12]

The Council, which meets ten times a year, exercises minimal control over the day-to-day operations of ACAS's six hundred or so staff who work in the London head office, in Scotland, Wales or one of the seven English regional offices. Further, the potential strategic policy-making functions of Council appear limited now that the recognition procedure has been repealed, the code-making function has fallen into virtual disuse (see below, p. 121), and ACAS's mode of operation has become well-established. Indeed, the mode of operation was largely inherited along with the staff. The regional organization of ACAS was formed by taking over the regional conciliation and advisory staff of the DE, while staff of the defunct CIR were employed to undertake inquiry work at head office.

Inheriting an organizational pattern and functions, together with the staff already performing them, provided ACAS with expertise and experience. But it reduced the likelihood of any radical rethinking or restructuring. Further, the existing staff were averse to losing their civil service status which they considered guaranteed their careers, job security, and terms and conditions of employment. Some members of ACAS Council thought civil service staffing might appear to identify ACAS too closely with the Department, would prevent the recruitment of high-calibre people from industry and the unions, and would impose a staffing/grading ratio which would be constraining on the organization. Ultimately, however, and not least because of pressure from the civil service unions, the status of ACAS staff as civil servants was confirmed. People from outside the civil service are recruited in small numbers as 'period appointments', but after a maximum of five years they have to gain appointment as established civil servants or leave the Service.

For administration purposes, the staff of ACAS are part of the 'DE group'. Consequently their career progression is not simply within ACAS. There has been a considerable amount of cross transference between the ACAS head office and other parts of the DE group, for example the Manpower Services Commission and the DE itself. The

ACAS staff perform all of ACAS's functions except mediation and arbitration. These services, which require the third party to express a view or impose an outcome, rather than simply assist the disputing parties to reach their own solution, are performed by independent outsiders on a list maintained by ACAS. They are mainly academics, some retired civil servants and certain retired employer and union officials.[13] A separate list of experts for appointment to investigate claims for equal pay for work of equal value under the amended Equal Pay Act is also maintained.[14]

The civil service status of its staff, the way in which its Council is appointed, and the fact that the Government holds the purse strings may all make ACAS vulnerable to indirect, subtle forms of government influence or interference. The change in the identity of independent members of ACAS Council appears to reflect change in the government appointing them, with a move to the right in terms of the academic political continuum. It is likely also that ACAS, which cost some £13 million to run in the year 1984–5 (a fall in real terms over the previous year), feels as vulnerable as other government-funded agencies in a time of reduced public expenditure. It has experienced a reduction in staff in common with government departments, losing some 200 staff since 1979. Some of this reduction, however, reflects a loss of certain statutory functions.

There is no evidence to suggest that the Government has sought to use the various channels of influence open to it to influence ACAS's performance of its various functions, although a politically insensitive incident in 1984 highlighted the potentially fragile nature of the Service's independence. A senior member of ACAS staff was transferred back to the DE, under government instruction, to help establish an in-house staff association at the Government's Communications Headquarters at Cheltenham following the banning of trade unions there. ACAS protested to the Government and indicated that it would not be prepared to take back the officer. It could not afford to be so associated with an act which had outraged the trade union movement.[15] Generally, however, governments appear to have respected the need for ACAS to be, and to be seen to be, free from government interference and ACAS has passed the various tests with which it has been faced.

Importantly, in view of its genesis, ACAS passed the incomes policy test in the 1970s. It was undoubtedly helped in this by the fact that, initially at least, the policy had the support of the union movement as part of the Social Contract. Nor did ACAS act as an interpreter of the policy. Rather than give its view on whether proposed conciliation settlements conformed with the policy, ACAS referred the parties elsewhere – to the DE or TUC and CBI – and thus could stand apart from rulings the parties might find unsatisfactory. Similarly, arbitrators on the ACAS list, who were sent a copy of the Government's White Paper *The Attack on Inflation* (1975), were recommended by ACAS to include in their awards a statement that they were not empowered to give an authoritative ruling as to whether the award conformed with the pay policy.

Another test of its perceived independence from government is its willingness to intervene, and its acceptability as an external party in public-sector disputes. It has been accepted as conciliator not only in disputes concerning nationalized industries such as the railways and coal mining, and utilities such as water, but also more recently by civil servants, although not over matters of direct concern to other civil servants, including ACAS's own staff.[16] Government pressure in such public-sector disputes is more likely to be exerted via the 'employer' in the dispute than through ACAS. This is nonetheless a difficult area for ACAS, and outcomes unfavourable from the government point of view might put the Service in some disfavour, as appears to have been the case following ACAS intervention in the Water dispute in 1983. In such circumstances, ACAS Council can play an important 'buffer' role between the Government and the Service.

The limited role of ACAS Council, detailed above, does not detract from its importance as a guarantee or symbol of the Service's independence from government. Its composition, involving in effect nominees from the TUC and CBI, is also an important aspect of its acceptability, symbolizing ACAS's impartiality as between the parties in industrial relations and providing another buffer, this time between ACAS and any major union or large employer who may be upset by outcomes resulting from the involvement of the Service.

Some non-TUC organizations and companies outside the CBI, especially small employers, have questioned the composition of the Council, which arguably embodies a collectivist view of industrial relations. But only during the period when ACAS was centrally involved in operating the avowedly pro-union legislation of the Social Contract period was its impartiality really questioned. Even then, research evidence, such as a survey of manufacturing industry,[17] revealed a high regard among unions and employers generally for ACAS's independence and neutrality.

Evaluation of the Voluntarist Functions

The peace-keeping or breakdown service which ACAS provides for British industrial relations rests on its inherited role as provider and facilitator of voluntary third-party dispute-settlement processes. ACAS is empowered, under EPA, section 2, to provide assistance by way of conciliation 'or by other means', including mediation, where a trade dispute exists or is apprehended and can, under EPA, section 3, arrange arbitration. In *conciliation* the outsider, or 'third party', aims to assist the disputing parties to reach their own resolution of the dispute. *Mediation* is a more positive form of conciliation, with the third party advocating solutions, although in practice the line between these two processes can blur. In *arbitration* the parties hand over determination of the dispute to a third party. Whereas they may accept, reject or modify the mediator's suggestions or recommendations, they agree beforehand to accept the arbitrator's award. Together with its advisory work, which ranges from responding to queries (often concerning employment legislation) to in-depth work, possibly involving diagnostic analysis, surveys or training exercises or the setting up of a joint working party, these dispute-settlement services are expected to contribute to 'promoting the improvement of industrial relations' as required by statute.

The lack of a yardstick as to what constitutes 'good industrial relations', the problem of identifying improvements in industrial relations and of attributing cause to any which may be perceived, make evaluation of ACAS's work particularly difficult. Although this may be a problem for ACAS in seeking to justify itself, would-be critics of the Service are similarly handicapped. On the face of it, evaluation of its peace-keeping role should be easier where ACAS provides its conciliation or other services in the context of an immediate dispute. As most ACAS conciliation occurs in disputes where no industrial action is being taken,[18] however, any assessment of its contribution to industrial peace can rest only on guesses as to the likelihood of industrial action being taken in the absence of such intervention. ACAS itself claims a very high rate of success in its collective conciliation: 86 per cent in 1984 and 84 per cent in 1985.[19] ACAS's definition of success, however, includes progress towards a settlement as well as settlement, and research by Jones and his colleagues found that settlement actually occurred in about half the collective conciliation cases which they surveyed.[20]

In 1985 the Service handled 1,337 collective conciliation cases and referred 162 disputes to arbitration and mediation.[21] This means ACAS gets involved in only a tiny minority of disputes, most being settled through the parties' own voluntary procedures.[22] But the use made of ACAS services is higher than when the DE was providing them. Given the non-coercive, voluntary nature of the third-party services, the current usage may be seen – and is presented by ACAS – as evidence of the Service's continued acceptability and perceived effectiveness. Similarly, lacking any other agreed criteria, both ACAS and independent observers tend to use the evaluations of users of the Service as a gauge of its effectiveness. On this measure, ACAS scores well. Surveys of parties who have used ACAS for collective conciliation[23] and in its advisory capacity[24] report favourable responses.

The research also highlights the essentially passive rather than active nature of ACAS involvement which has been the subject of some criticism. Criticism has been made also of the essentially marginal, reactive and non-strategic role of the Service.[25] In 1984, as in previous years, about 4 per cent of ACAS's collective conciliation caseload arose from direct ACAS-initiated intervention. This declined to 2.4 per cent in 1985, as opposed to a request from one of the parties to the dispute (most often the union) or, increasingly commonly, both parties jointly. It is, however, perhaps this very passivity and marginality (in terms of proportion of disputes involving the Service) together with the acceptability and appreciation of its involvement where it *is* used, which has helped ACAS to survive.

As the demand for ACAS's dispute-settlement services has declined during the recession, it has placed increased emphasis on its advisory work, trying to increase the amount of work undertaken on what it sees as 'fundamental industrial relations and manpower issues'.[26] A total of 842 in-depth work exercises were completed in 1984 and 946 in 1985.[27] The transfer of the Work Research Unit to ACAS from the DE has widened the range of advisory services which can be provided. It is principally through its advisory work that ACAS sees itself as promoting the improvement of industrial relations.[28]

The role of a third-party agency in improving industrial relations may be seen (as by McCarthy and Ellis, following Kerr) as strategic or tactical.[29] A strategic role demands that the agency act as a powerful catalyst for change, taking the initiative in promoting long-run reform; whereas a tactical role centres on the avoidance or resolution of immediate disputes. The conciliation work of ACAS and the mediation and arbitration which it arranges, clearly fall within the tactical mode. Its advisory work has elements of a strategic role, as no immediate dispute needs resolution, but here too there is a strong 'fire fighting by prevention' aspect. A strategic body would play a positive and innovative role in stimulating demand, not waiting to be asked, and not necessarily only providing services in response to the immediate needs of the parties involved. Although ACAS's advisory work may result from uninvited visits from ACAS officers, this function, like other aspects of the Service, is mainly demand-led, arising where management (or occasionally unions) have identified an immediate problem.

As noted, ACAS's advisory function is properly seen as a descendant of the DE breakdown service rather than of the 'enhanced voluntarism', reforming function of the CIR which operated from 1969 to 1974. Some of its other powers – to inquire into any industrial relations matter and to issue Codes of Practice containing practical guidance for promoting good industrial relations – are, however, part of the reform role which ACAS inherited from that body.

3 Enhanced Voluntarism – Towards Regulation

ACAS had a mixed parentage, as we have seen. The DE provided the traditional peace-keeping and advisory functions discussed above but the abolition of the CIR, tainted by its association with the Industrial Relations Act (IRA) 1971, created a space for an investigatory, reform agency of the kind advocated by the Donovan Commission.[30] The tradition of legal abstention from industrial relations, with primacy accorded to autonomous, unregulated collective bargaining, came under attack in the 1960s. The postwar acceptability of 'voluntarism', as Wedderburn notes, rested on a 'middle class acquiescence in the current balance of industrial power'.[31] Changing economic and social circumstances shook that acquiescence and demands grew that 'something should be done' to overcome the perceived failings of self-regulation.

It is not necessary to go into detail here, but it should be noted that strategies based on direct legal regulation and suppression of industrial action were not favoured by the Donovan Commission. The Commission doubted the efficacy of direct legal regulation of collective bargaining (at least until it had been reformed) and was anxious to find solutions which kept the courts out of industrial relations disputes. The preferred approach of the majority of the Commissioners was to aid the development and spread of collective bargaining, while also introducing measures designed to stimulate its reform, in order to overcome the disorder and loss of managerial control which it had identified as problems. Among these measures was the creation of a public agency with special responsibility for promoting reform in industrial relations.

As a result of the Donovan Commission, the CIR was set up under Royal Warrant in 1969 to be concerned with the examination and improvement of the institutions and procedures for the conduct of industrial relations, acting on references made to it by the Secretary of State for Employment. These would include the reference of trade union recognition disputes. The need for third-party intervention in this area – partly to avoid costly recognition strikes and partly to aid workers in no position to strike to obtain recognition – had been accepted by the Royal Commission. Under the IRA 1971, the CIR's recognition inquiry function was subsumed under the Act's recognition procedure.[32]

The procedure disappeared when the IRA was repealed in 1974, but the EPA 1975 had its own recognition procedure designed to assist unions faced with employers who refused to bargain with them and ACAS was given the central role in it.[33] Thus, between 1976 and 1980 a duty to inquire into and make recommendations where appropriate on recognition issues was grafted on to ACAS's other functions. During the same period other statutory rights for trade unions, including information disclosure and 'fair wages' provisions, enforceable by the Central Arbitration Committee (CAC), involved ACAS in a conciliation role.

The recognition procedure, whereby unions could claim bargaining rights from unwilling employers, gave ACAS a role which differed significantly from its voluntarist peace-keeping functions. It was no longer only an agency to be called in by collective bargaining parties voluntarily; it could be involved unilaterally by a union in a dispute with an employer over recognition and, rather than distancing itself from the nature of the outcome of the dispute, ACAS was required ultimately to express its own views as to the desirability and appropriateness of collective bargaining in particular circumstances and its level and extent. This was a more controversial and higher-profile role than any of its DE-inherited functions and one which ACAS came to feel sat uneasily with its voluntary dispute-settlement role. The confrontation between ACAS and the courts over its operation of the recognition procedure is discussed below (p. 124).

Other reform functions inherited from the CIR – inquiry and code-making – proved less problematic. Partly this is because they have been used less but also because, unlike the recognition procedure, they ultimately operate at the level of advice and guidance and so appear to clash less with ACAS's voluntary functions.

Inquiry and Code-Making

Under EPA, section 5, ACAS is empowered to inquire into industrial relations generally or in any particular firm. This function supplements the power of the Secretary of State to set up an inquiry under the Industrial Courts Act 1919, section 4, which is now used only exceptionally. The Secretary of State may also request ACAS to inquire into a wages council or statutory joint industrial council industry.[34]

These powers have been used but ACAS has not sought to use its section 5 inquiry power to develop the kind of strategic, catalytic and innovative role discussed earlier. Such a reforming role demands a direction for reform, a strong concept of what constitutes good industrial relations. The CIR had its direction provided by the Donovan Report,[35] but ACAS lacks any such brief.[36] The consensus concerning the problems and solutions around the time of Donovan may have been more apparent than real,[37] but today there is not even an apparent consensus. A more 'positive' role in promoting industrial relations reform rather than its present essentially reactive role would demand, as a minimum, that the members of ACAS Council reach a common view on fundamental issues. This prerequisite appears unlikely to be achieved, as ACAS's record in code-making indicates.

The Service has general powers to issue Codes of Practice containing practical guidance to promote the improvement of industrial relations. In two areas – disclosure of information for the purpose of collective bargaining, and time off for union officials and trade union members – the issuing of guidance through Codes was made mandatory.[38] Of its own volition ACAS has issued only one Code, on disciplinary practice and procedures, which was revised in 1986 but has not yet been approved by the Secretary of State. The code-making reform function is in keeping with the voluntary, self-regulatory system of industrial relations, since the Codes operate at the level of education and persuasion rather than compulsion. They dispense 'benevolent advice or admonition'[39] rather than give rise to legal rights and duties. A failure to observe the provisions of a Code does not 'of itself' render a person liable to any legal proceedings but the Code is admissible in evidence in proceedings before an industrial tribunal or the CAC, and any provision of a Code which appears relevant shall be taken into account.[40]

The industrial relations standards which ACAS embodies in its Codes therefore can be, and have been, influential in judicial decision-making. This was certainly the case in the early industrial tribunal and higher court decisions concerning unfair dismissal where the Code on *Disciplinary Practice and Procedure in Employment* was looked to for guidance as to procedural fairness.[41] But, as Elias documents,[42] procedural fairness was weakened by subsequent appeal decisions which also diminished the importance and relevance of the Code. In practice, tribunals today rarely refer to the ACAS Codes of Practice but look rather to decisions of the appellate courts for guidance on reasonableness, for example in dismissing for ill-health or redundancy.

The Code on *Disclosure of Information to Trade Unions for Collective Bargaining Purposes* gives examples of information which 'could be relevant in certain bargaining situations' but fails to address itself specifically to what good industrial relations practice in this area might be. The CAC itself on occasion has found the Code of little assistance to it and has noted the lack of consensus on good practice in this area.[43] Gospel has suggested that the weakness of the disclosure Code stems from its attempting to steer a middle course between the views of the CBI and TUC as represented via ACAS Council.[44]

The impact of the Codes is to be sought not only in their influence on judicial decision-making. The guidance they provide is also directed at the parties to industrial relations. Along with other ACAS publications, such as its advisory booklets on matters including payment systems, absence, recruitment and selection, and workplace communications, they thus contribute to the fulfilment of the general duty of promoting an improvement in industrial relations, but it is difficult to assess their impact.

Inasmuch as the Codes seek to distil and generalize existing good practice, large, well-organized companies in the private and public sector may be expected to adopt already the approach they advocate. In such employment the Codes may provide an additional reference point in any negotiations. Where union recognition is being accorded for the first time, the Codes do provide useful benchmarks, for example on facilities for shop stewards. The generality of the Codes, however, may reduce their utility. As the Code on *Time Off for Trade Union Duties and Activities* stresses, in view of 'the wide variety of circumstances and problems, employers and unions should reach agreement on arrangements for handling time off in ways appropriate to their own situations'. Similarly, the Code on information disclosure recommends 'employers and trade unions should endeavour to arrive at a joint understanding on how the provisions on the disclosure of information can be implemented most effectively'. Few 'information agreements', however, have been negotiated.[45] Evidence suggests that small companies, particularly if not unionized, are unlikely to be aware in detail, if at all, of the Codes' provisions.[46] Where unions are not recognized, only the Code on discipline is relevant.

Generally speaking it is the Code on discipline which appears to have had the greatest impact, largely because of the statutory provisions with which it is associated. Employers are required under the Employment Protection (Consolidation) Act (EP(C)A) 1978, s.1(4), for example, to specify disciplinary rules applicable to workers and the procedure to be followed if a worker is dissatisfied with a disciplinary decision. This provision, together with the unfair dismissal provisions,[47] has stimulated procedural development and reform in this area along the lines advocated by the Code.[48] As some changes will be no more than formalization of existing practices, however, and because one cannot 'read off' practice from procedure, it is uncertain to what extent the procedural reform reflects a real move as advocated by ACAS towards a 'corrective', rather than 'punitive', approach to discipline in companies where this disciplinary technique was not already predominant.

ACAS has adopted an approach to code-making which may be described as consensual. Its ability to produce a Code depends on a degree of consensus at the level of its Council which is obtained in part by being non-directive. This is done by stressing the desirability of the collective bargaining parties arriving at their own consensus over the matters addressed by the Code. This approach, and the limited use made of the code-making power, minimizes its reform potential.

In sharp contrast to ACAS's approach stand the Codes on the closed shop and picketing issued by the Secretary of State under a provision in the Employment Act 1980. The Secretary of State's *Code of Practice on Closed Shop Agreements and Arrangements*, for instance, contains very specific guidance rather than 'benevolent advice' for tribunals and courts on various aspects of the legislation. This attempt to 'legislate by the back door' by including such directive provisions in a Code rather than in the main body of the law has been criticized.[49]

The Codes issued by the Secretary of State reflect the legislative policy of restriction, discussed earlier. They cover areas where ACAS would have found it impossible to produce detailed guidance because of strongly divergent views concerning the legislation among those represented on ACAS Council. The TUC rejected the legislation and began campaigning against it, while the CBI welcomed it as providing necessary reforms. This split prevented ACAS from even participating in the consultative process on the Employment Bill and from making representations concerning the Codes issued by the Secretary of State. Only where common ground can be found between the CBI and TUC representatives on its Council is ACAS able to make representations to government, as was the case recently concerning proposed changes to legislation regulating the payment of wages.[50]

The ACAS code-making function thus appears to have been overtaken by the Secretary of State's new role in this area. The downgrading of ACAS's function here is seen also in the fact that a Code issued by the Secretary of State may expressly supersede all or part of an ACAS Code.[51]

The mid-1970s saw not only the enactment of collective rights for trade unions, referred to earlier, but also an extension of individual legal rights enforceable in the industrial tribunals. Viewed as building blocks for collective rights,[52] these individual rights appeared in keeping with enhanced voluntarism. These rights, later consolidated in the EP(C)A 1978, and supplemented by separate statutes on race and sex discrimination, considerably extended the individual conciliation function ACAS had taken over from the DE.

Individual Conciliation
ACAS has a duty to provide conciliation in cases which are, or would be, the subject of complaints by individuals alleging infringement of specified rights arising under the employment legislation (notably EP(C)A 1978) and sex and race discrimination legislation. In 1985,

39,797 individual conciliation cases were dealt with by ACAS, accounting for a large part of its operational resources. The majority of these cases were disposed of by ACAS without the need for a tribunal hearing.[53]

Despite the expanding jurisdiction of the tribunals, most of ACAS's work in this area still concerns applications alleging unfair dismissal. Under EP(C)A 1978, section 134, ACAS individual conciliation officers have a duty 'to endeavour to promote a settlement of the complaint without its being determined by the tribunal' and are instructed in particular to seek the re-employment of the applicant. If this is not wanted by the applicant or is 'not practicable' then some other form of settlement is to be attempted. Where an agreement is reached or applications withdrawn after the conciliation officer has 'taken action' under this section then, under section 140, the tribunal is barred from hearing the case. ACAS disposed of 26,422 applications without a tribunal hearing in 1985, 68 per cent of which were withdrawn on the basis of a settlement, generally money.[54] Re-employment of the applicant was agreed in only 2 per cent of the cases settled in 1984. The median average money settlement was £709, about half the level of the median tribunal award.[55]

The special status accorded to agreements made with ACAS involvement has led some observers[56] to argue that ACAS should take a view of the fairness of any settlement reached and that some positive initiative to promote re-employment of the applicant is needed to satisfy the statutory duty. This is not, however, the construction which ACAS has placed on its statutory duty[57] and its interpretation has been upheld by the courts when asked to decide whether an industrial tribunal is barred under section 140 from hearing a case.

The courts have been willing to read a phrase into ACAS's statutory duty so that it need pursue re-employment only 'so far as applicable in the circumstances of the particular case'. The courts have also confirmed ACAS's view that in promoting monetary settlements it is not required to be concerned with equity. They have held that a conciliation officer need do no more than record settlement terms, having ensured that the parties understand them, in order to have 'taken action'.[58] There is no obligation on the conciliation officer to go through the whole framework of the legislation and inform claimants of their rights.[59] Nor does the settlement need to be in writing for it to be binding on the parties.[60]

Only about one third of unfair dismissal applications handled by

ACAS go through to a tribunal hearing. Its value as a filter, and as an aid to efficiency in the tribunal system, is thus evident. Its effectiveness in fulfilling the intentions and expectations which lay behind the inclusion of a conciliation stage is more open to question. These expectations concerned the method by which settlements would be reached (voluntary agreement rather than imposed outcome) and the, unrealized, assumption that re-employment was more likely to result from conciliation than tribunal imposition. Although ACAS is offering conciliation here as in collective disputes, the context in which it occurs is quite different. Rather than bargaining over outcomes, the context is one where applicants are likely to accept whatever offer of settlement the employer cares to make.[61]

A smaller proportion of cases are disposed of by ACAS under the discrimination jurisdictions, possibly because such issues are seen by those concerned to be less 'compromisable' than is dismissal. Where alleged discrimination cases are disposed of without need of a tribunal hearing, they are more likely to be abandoned by the applicant than to result in a conciliated settlement.[62] It is in these jurisdictions in particular that the neutral stance of ACAS, which assumes an equality between the parties and requires no commitment to the spirit of the anti-discrimination legislation, has been most criticized.[63] This neutrality can be seen, however, as allowing the individual conciliation function to operate in a way which is compatible with the continued acceptance of its voluntary dispute-settlement functions. This appears to be ACAS's view.

In no sense does ACAS perform a rights-enforcement or applicant-assistance role, and it has been held that no such role is required by the statute. It is not ACAS's duty to attempt to reduce the inequality in the relationship between the employer and the worker; an inequality which is part of the explanation for the frequency and nature of settlements and uncompensated withdrawals of claims. The adoption of a rights-enforcement stance – or even a more active approach towards obtaining re-employment of dismissed workers – might upset employers and thus jeopardize ACAS's acceptability in voluntary dispute settlement, which is seen to rest on its not antagonising either side.

ACAS's conciliation in the context of the EPA recognition procedure, discussed below, demonstrates how a form of conciliation designed to bring about agreed settlements promoting certain desired ends may be devised,[64] but illustrates also the problems such a role may cause for a body which strives to maintain an impartial stance. The operation of the recognition procedure ran into a variety of problems which, in combination, finally led the Council of the Service to inform the Secretary of State that it could not 'satisfactorily operate the statutory recognition procedures as they stand'.[65] The problems concerned judicial review, which did not leave ACAS a viable task and undermined its expert tripartite status; the difficulty of obtaining consensus on ACAS Council; and ACAS's assessment that its role in the recognition procedure led to perceptions among some organizations that it was biased in favour of trade unions, which undermined its acceptability to employers as a provider of third-party services.[66]

4 The Recognition Procedure and Judicial Review

The Social Contract legislation (notably the Trade Union and Labour Relations Act 1974–6 and the EPA 1975) not only repealed the IRA 1971 and restored the trade unions to the *status quo ante*, but, as noted earlier, enacted provisions which, as part of a quid pro quo for wage restraint, were designed to help unions in their bargaining with employers and in establishing new bargaining arrangements. The unions, wary as ever of the judiciary (who, history taught, displayed little understanding of, or sympathy for, the realities and values of collective labour relations), wanted legislation which would not involve the courts. As Flanders noted,[67] the 'voluntary principle' of British industrial relations did not rule out legal enactment but it did embrace a desire to keep the courts out of industrial relations matters. The new collective legal rights, therefore, such as information disclosure (EPA, sections 17–21), depended for their enforcement on the CAC, an arbitral body, and not on legal sanctions imposed by the courts. Similarly, the recognition procedure (EPA, sections 11–16), in contrast to that of the IRA 1971 which had given the courts a formal role,[68] was designed to exclude the judges. The task of inquiry and recommendation was entrusted to ACAS as an expert body and there was no right of appeal. The sanction for failure to comply with an ACAS recognition recommendation was not a fine or injunction obtainable from the courts, but an arbitration award on the terms and conditions of employees concerned in the recommendation.[69]

The statutory provisions (EPA, sections 11–14) provided little specific guidance to ACAS on how it was to determine the recognition issues which unions referred to it. It was to 'examine the issue, consult all the parties who it considers will be affected by the outcome of the reference and make such inquiries as it thinks fit'. In the course of its inquiries ACAS had to 'ascertain the opinions of workers to whom the issue relates by any means it thinks fit' and could hold a formal ballot, in accordance with certain requirements, if it wished. The Service was required at all times to have regard to the desirability of the issue being settled voluntarily and to promote such agreement by conciliation. If no settlement occurred, ACAS was required to report on the reference, 'setting out its findings, any advice in connection with those findings and any recommendation for recognition' with reasons, or reasons for not making a recommendation.

The statute's 'as it thinks fit' approach to ACAS operation, and particularly the lack of criteria for recognition, were intended to give the Service flexibility and scope for the exercise of discretion. The absence of prescriptive principles also reflected British practice: union jurisdiction follows no neat nor necessarily agreed pattern, bargaining occurs at various levels, and recognition may be granted to a union with anything from 100 per cent membership to none. There is, therefore, no one 'correct' answer to such questions as when recognition is appropriate and in respect of which union or which workers. In entrusting determination of recognition issues to the wide discretion of a body with non-justiciable objectives, and expertise in industrial relations rather than law, Parliament apparently did not regard recognition as a problem of a legal character at all. The more discretion allowed by statute, the less scope there was thought to be for judicial intervention.

Although the courts were given no explicit role in the procedure, they were not explicitly excluded and ACAS was subject to the supervisory jurisdiction of the High Court on the traditional grounds of error on the face of the record, abuse of discretion, lack of natural justice, or excess of jurisdiction. ACAS was challenged in the courts on the method and scope of its recognition inquiries, its discretion as to proceeding with a reference, and the criteria by which it decided whether or not to recommend recognition. The courts, particularly the Court of Appeal, seemed keen, for reasons considered below, to subject the Service to judicial scrutiny and control.

Judicial decisions led to ACAS changing the format of the questionnaire used to ascertain employee opinion and modifying the format of the reports it published. But some of the implications of the judgments could not be accommodated so easily and by 1979 the Chairman of ACAS was advising the Secretary of State that the Service could no longer operate the statutory recognition procedure as it stood: the courts had not left a viable task for the agency.[70]

In *Grunwick*[71] the House of Lords had held that ACAS's statutory duty required it to ascertain and take into consideration the opinions held by every group of workers of any significant size in the workforce that would be affected by any recognition recommendation but, at the same time, employers had no legal duty to give ACAS access to employees or provide their names and addresses. Employer obstruction therefore could, and did in this case and several subsequent ones, successfully thwart ACAS's attempt to carry out its statutory duty. ACAS considered that Parliament had intended ACAS to have a wide discretion where to recommend recognition by not specifying recognition criteria in the statute. The Court of Appeal also, in *UKAPE*,[72] had severely reduced this discretion. In this case, UKAPE, a non-TUC union which for some years had been attempting to gain recognition in the engineering industry,[73] had been refused recognition in respect of certain employees among whom it had very strong support. ACAS's decision not to recommend recognition was influenced by various factors, among them the existing bargaining arrangements in engineering and the support for them by the union confederation and employers' association in the industry; the desire to avoid fragmentation of bargaining by introducing a new union; and the opposition which recognition of the new union would provoke. Although a recommendation that UKAPE be recognized would extend collective bargaining, it would not promote an improvement in industrial relations and ACAS gave precedence to this part of its general duty.

It is clear that Parliament intended ACAS to be more than just a balloting agency; the wishes of employees were only one consideration. Thus recognition might be, and was in 36 cases, recommended by ACAS where the union had only minority support but where, in ACAS's view, effective collective bargaining could be sustained. Similarly, recognition could be denied, and was in 19 cases, despite majority support where the designated negotiating group was considered inappropriate or where, for other reasons, it was deemed not to be in the interests of good industrial relations.[74]

The notion of 'good industrial relations' was necessarily vague and rested on a pragmatic, common-sense approach to each case as it arose. ACAS Council rejected the view that any single set of criteria or general principles could be evolved to cover the diversity of cases with which ACAS was faced. Its Annual Report for 1978 stressed how experience had shown that there were difficulties in attempting to define strict criteria which could be applied automatically in all cases. It commented that any general guidelines 'must take account both of the diversity of circumstances surrounding recognition issues and of the different view of employers and unions'. The difficulties came not only from the diversity of cases but also from the divergent views of the TUC and CBI representatives on Council which eventually made agreement even on a case-by-case basis hard to achieve and consensual decision-making was replaced by vote-taking.[75]

This pragmatic, case-by-case approach – like the industrial relations language of the ACAS reports – was alien to the courts, who demanded reference to general principles. Their rulings required ACAS to adopt an increasingly legalistic approach to its recognition work. Thus the Court of Appeal expressed a view as to the range of matters on which the Service was obliged to make findings even though the Service might consider them irrelevant or unnecessary or harmful to industrial relations.[76] The Court also considered that ACAS was to be regarded as a tribunal when considering recognition issues.[77] The implication of this was that Council members should not take part in recognition decisions in which they might be seen to have an interest, a decision particularly affecting the trade union members. The Chairman of ACAS pointed out that given the nature of the constitution of the Council, which the statute intended should draw experience from both sides of industry, it was 'clearly unrealistic to expect some of those same members not to take part in the deliberations on an important industrial relations matter'.[78] The Court of Appeal's decision clashed with the rationale behind the tripartite composition of ACAS's Council.

Ultimately the House of Lords, in two important decisions (*UKAPE* and *EMA*),[79] appeared to restore to ACAS the discretion in procedural and substantive matters which ACAS had thought it possessed – though the *Grunwick* problem of employer non-cooperation remained. Whether in practice the Lords' judgments in these cases would have allowed ACAS to operate unhampered by further judicial interference is unknown, as the procedure was repealed by the time the decisions were handed down. Elliott has argued that the 'courts did not establish for all time a set of discretions that ACAS could operate sensibly. They simply granted some discretion to ACAS in language that enables this discretion to be legitimately removed if fashions change.'[80]

Certainly neither the 'legalistic' nor the 'individualistic' approach of the judges documented by Simpson[81] revealed any real understanding of, or sympathy for, the third-party role which ACAS has been given. Indeed, as in other cases, it is possible to detect some judicial hostility towards third-party agencies which have powers to interfere in the individual employment relation.[82] A failure to recognize the subordination inherent in the contract of employment[83] leads to collective bargaining being viewed as an interference with individual liberty. The enforcement powers of the recognition procedure (an arbitration award by the CAC which could not be adversely varied) was weak in intention[84] and weaker still in operation because of the approach adopted by the CAC.[85] Yet they were considered by one judge to be 'every bit as large as powers of compulsory acquisition of property' because they represented the 'compulsory acquisition of an individual's right to regulate his working life'.[86] Similar sentiments were expressed by Lord Salmon and Lord Denning in *UKAPE*. The latter saw the recognition procedure as 'an interference with individual liberty' which 'could hardly be tolerated in a free society unless there were safeguards against abuse'.[87] This individualistic perspective, rather than viewing collective organization and collective bargaining as a means whereby workers gain protection from their employer, sees collective bargaining as an interference with individual freedom of contract – as something *from which* workers need judicial protection. Such attitudes inevitably clash with the underlying rationale of a third-party agency charged with promoting collective bargaining.

But the clash between ACAS and the courts was not just between collective and individual values. It also derived from ACAS's pragmatic concern with making industrial relations 'work' rather than the pursuit of abstract rights and general principles. The courts, on the other hand, were concerned with the vindication of rights and with ensuring that administrative decisions display regularity and due process. The differences between the Court of Appeal and the House of Lords did not arise from different views as to the desired outcomes of the recognition issues (that is whether, in Lord Denning's analogy, the 'David' of new unions should triumph over the 'Goliath' of established unions and employers' associations, or not), but from different views as to the proper role for the courts. ACAS was caught up in a wider battle taking place between the Appeal Court and the House of Lords at that time which flowed from differing views about the creative function of the judiciary.[88] In the recognition area the Court of Appeal was using judicial review to champion what it saw as the reasonable rights and expectations of affected parties, while the Lords were concerned to delineate a field of operation for administrative law which did not involve itself in the value conflicts of the particular area of dispute.

The recognition procedure was repealed by the EA 1980. By that time a total of 1,610 references had been received and some form of recognition established in 573 or 36 per cent of the cases, covering 65,000 employees.[89] Although this direct impact of the procedure on union recognition may be thought marginal, the indirect impact of the existence of a procedure on the industrial relations climate must also be taken into account.[90] Many recognition issues were either settled without ACAS involvement or under the voluntary collective conciliation machinery discussed above. This was used for 2,292 recognition disputes during the lifetime of the statutory procedure and some form of recognition was established in 981 or 43 per cent of them, covering approximately 77,500 employees.[91]

Nonetheless the unions were disappointed with the operation of the procedure and ACAS became overwhelmed by the problems outlined above. The repeal was in keeping with the shift in public policy away from support for union growth and collective bargaining, but the fact that few were prepared to argue in defence of the procedure marks the extent of the disillusionment with it. There were various problems with the procedure itself, including its weak enforcement sanction, but the disillusionment owed much to judicial intervention. This exposed and exacerbated weaknesses in the procedure and prevented ACAS applying the very industrial relations expertise which was part of the rationale for giving the Service, and not the courts, responsibility for recognition issues.

5 Conclusions

ACAS's conflict with the courts – the clash of collectivist and individualist values and ideology, of pragmatism and legalism – was 'resolved' by the repeal of the recognition procedure. The repeal of this and other 'enhanced voluntarism' provisions in 1980 marked the switch to a policy of restriction, using the law and the courts more directly in an attempt to restructure industrial relations. The policy of restriction requires no reform-oriented third-party agency and where reform functions remain, for example code-making, they have been marginalized. In the new context ACAS has, and seeks, a fairly narrow remit involving it mainly in relatively low-profile activity based on the invitation or acquiescence of the parties concerned. Indeed, such a narrow remit appears to be a prerequisite for the continued support of both sides of industry, symbolized by their representation on ACAS's Council.

The composition of the ACAS Council provides ACAS with its strength and, to some extent, its weakness. It gives ACAS its status as an expert, independent body and enhances its acceptability, but in practice prevents the agency adopting a positive role in the reform of industrial relations. A reforming role demands a direction for reform, and consensus as to what constitutes 'good industrial relations' and how they might be achieved. Such consensus is lacking. Consequently ACAS is confined to a restricted sphere of activity where agreement on objectives can be reached.

A potential alternative role for the Service, other than as a reform body, is a regulatory role on behalf of the Government which is, among other things, attempting to increase external supervision of the affairs and conduct of trade unions. But it is a role which it would find difficult to embrace, given its tripartite composition (particularly the presence of trade union representatives). Recent legislation has conferred functions relating to inquiries into the conduct of union elections on the Certification Officer. Although ACAS is responsible for providing the Certification Officer with finances and support services, he functions independently from it and so the Service has been able to distance itself from the operation of controversial labour legislation.

ACAS's present activity extends little further than the voluntary dispute-settlement processes performed by the DE and its pre-decessors. This raises the question of whether there is still a need for ACAS as a third-party agency or whether these functions could be returned to the DE. The changed context of industrial relations, however, although associated with the removal or marginalization of aspects of ACAS's activity, paradoxically may also give the Service a continuing utility.

The performance of third-party functions by a government department really was possible only in the days of the old Ministry of Labour and voluntarism. Interventionism of governments through incomes policies (whether named as such or not) and in industrial relations generally is unlikely to diminish. Further, the growth in public-sector employment since 1945 and the increase in public-sector industrial action in recent years[92] underlines the need for a dispute settlement service independent of government. The restrictionist strategy, with its increased emphasis on legal remedies in industrial disputes, may reduce the scope for, or success of, third-party dispute settlement. But as long as a need for services of conciliation, arbitration and the like continues, there will be a need for an independent agency to provide them. What ACAS can do to some extent, therefore, which the DE cannot, is distance itself from government policy and the political aspects of industrial conflict. As long as this is perceived as useful by governments, ACAS is likely to continue, albeit as an institution of far less significance in British industrial relations than appeared likely at its birth.

7
Health and Safety at Work: Consensus and Self-Regulation

Robert Baldwin

The Health and Safety Commission (HSC) was set up in 1974 and was followed by its Executive (HSE) in 1975. These agencies followed intensive reappraisal of controls over health and safety at work, a period of scrutiny that produced not only novel regulatory institutions but a new view of legal rules in regulation and a new approach to enforcement. This chapter looks at how such changes came about and examines the significance of the HSC/E in institutional, legal and enforcement terms. These linked bodies represented an attempt to regulate by new, consensual means. Particular attention will, therefore, be paid to the strengths and weaknesses of such a strategy.

1 Disenchantment and the Robens Reforms

The Robens Committee of 1970–72[1] was asked by Barbara Castle, the then Secretary of State for Employment and Productivity, to review the existing provisions governing the safety and health of persons at work. What *Robens* found was a hugely complicated system of control in which nine separate groups of statutes were separately administered by five central government departments through seven separate central inspectorates.[2] The Committee concluded that there was too much law;[3] apart from the statutes, there were 500 subordinate statutory instruments. Not only that, but the law was failing to operate as a useful regulatory tool. The sheer mass of law had become counter-productive, it had an 'all-pervading psychological effect'[4] in which people were conditioned to think of safety and health at work as a matter of detailed rules imposed by external agencies. *Robens* believed that *apathy* was the greatest single contributing factor to accidents at work and that this attitude would prevail so long as people thought that safety could be ensured by ever more inspectors and legal regulations. The way forward was to take a new tack in which 'the primary responsibility for doing something about the present levels of occupational accidents and disease lies with those who create the risks and those who work with them.'[5]

Here was the new philosophy: more emphasis was to be placed on voluntary action, less on state regulation. The role of legislation had to move from detailed prescription to the creation of a framework of rules that would influence attitudes and encourage effective self-regulation.

On institutional arrangements, *Robens* was clear that if health and safety regulation was to be organized coherently there were four major requirements: control had to be given to a self-contained organization clearly responsible for the area; it should have day-to-day autonomy; it should be organized in a fashion consistent with responsible and accountable management; and finally, those involved in the field – employers, workers, local authorities and so on – should be fully involved in managing the new institution. Self-regulation and shared responsibility was said to call for real participation in decisions at all levels.

The new agency was to be a national body with comprehensive responsibility for promoting safety and health at work. It would have the maximum budgetary and operational autonomy and be directed by an executive Managing Board. There would be a full-time Chairman of the Board (the 'authoritative voice'[6]) and the board members would be drawn from industrial management, trade unions, the professions and local authorities.

The idea that such a body could form part of a central department was rejected. This would have detracted from its identity and caused diffusion of responsibility. On the other hand, there were problems with a completely independent body: there would have to be government control over budgets and overall policies; the public interest in health and safety called for a more direct link with government and Parliament than a completely non-departmental body could offer; and, finally, the preparation, revision and enforcement of legislative provisions called for some degree of ministerial control.

For these reasons, *Robens* advocated that the Authority be a separate body with its own budget and staff but functioning under the broad policy directives of a Minister who would be responsible for the Authority's relations with government and Parliament. Enforcement would be carried out by a unified inspectorate – one thoroughly integrated at all levels and controlled by the Authority.

Other organizational changes reflected *Robens'* philosophy of increased self-regulation and an emphasis on consensual systems of control. Within firms, safety and health objectives were to be clearly defined at all levels and employers were to be required to set out written statements of their safety and health policies. Workers would also be offered an increased role in monitoring safety. Thus encouragement was to be given to a system of workers' safety representation and, to this end, employers were to be given a statutory duty to consult employees or their representatives on health and safety matters.

The machinery of enforcement was similarly to give effect to the cooperative strategy. Thus *Robens* looked for ways to 'reduce the negative influence of an excessively regulatory approach'[7] and suggested that the basic function of state inspection should be the provision of advice and assistance towards better safety standards. Their position was quite clear:

. . . any idea that standards generally should be rigorously enforced through the extensive use of legal sanctions is one that runs counter to our general philosophy.[8]

This was not, however, said to be opting for a milder, more tolerant system of control. After all, prosecutions for health and safety had long been small in number and had resulted in low fines (in 1970 the average fine imposed under the Factories Act 1961 was £40). *Robens* saw more effective sanctions in the form of administrative directions to those who failed in their obligations. Two important measures were thus to be introduced. Inspectors would be empowered to issue formal *Improvement Notices* requiring employers to remedy specific faults within a specific time or, in more urgent cases, inspectors would be able to issue *Prohibition Notices*. The latter notices might contain a direction that, in the event of non-compliance within the time stated, the use of specific plant or machinery must be discontinued.

To summarize, then, *Robens* rejected mandated as opposed to negotiated or self-imposed solutions to regulatory problems. The new approach was to be coordinated by a central institution that emphasized advice and assistance rather than prosecution. This body was to operate according to rules marked by accessibility and clarity rather than detailed instruction. Finally, since enforcement was not to be based on commands, it was to rely to a great extent on the worker's motivation in monitoring health and safety, on the employer's willingness to negotiate and on the agency's ability to advise, assist and educate. Whether or not the 'negotiated-self-regulatory' approach would operate in an effective or radical fashion remained to be seen.[9]

2 Institutions and Regulatory Strategies

When the Health and Safety at Work Act 1974 came to give effect to *Robens* it was decided, as has been noted, to set up two linked bodies rather than one agency. The Health and Safety Commission (HSC) consists of a Chair, appointed by the Secretary of State, plus three employers' representatives, nominated by the CBI; three employees' representatives, nominated by the TUC, and two local authority representatives. It is thus a tripartite body. The local authority representatives are there to represent the general interests of society. It is notable that in the case of the CBI and TUC, those organizations rather than the Secretary of State select the individuals to be appointed.[10]

The Commission is required to gain the Secretary of State's approval for the work that it intends to do, and it submits a Plan of Work to him or her, usually every other year in the Autumn. The HSC meets fortnightly and decides the strategic plans of the HSC/E. Thus it sets objectives, allocates resources and reviews priorities, normally on the basis of HSE proposals. It is a policy-making body rather than one concerned to develop detailed expertise.[11] The HSC has the Executive as its expert adviser.

The Executive is a three-person statutory body, headed by the Director General and responsible for enforcing health and safety legislation and for carrying out the directions of the Commission. It meets at least fortnightly and is responsible for allocating resources within the HSE, subject to Commission decisions. It is aided by two important institutions within the HSE, the Management Board, made up largely of the heads of all HSE divisions, and the Field Operations Group, a subcommittee of the Management Board and containing representatives of all the Divisions carrying out field operations. This group provides a forum for discussing enforcement and field activities.

The identities of six inspectorates have (in contrast to *Robens'* advocacy of a unified inspectorate[12]) been retained. They are the Factories, Mines and Quarries, Nuclear Installations, Industrial Air Pollution, Agriculture and Explosives inspectorates. A workforce of 1,242 permanent inspectors was employed at April 1984 and this represented a third of HSE staff.

Why were two bodies set up? In the case of the Manpower Services Commission (MSC) and its agencies, such an arrangement was justified by the need to manage two different services and to co-ordinate those functions separately.[13] In the case of the HSC/E the primary concern was with the regulatory functions involved. The Executive was to be given considerable powers to instruct individuals on actions to be taken and to use sanctions if necessary. Since the Commission was to be a largely industry-based body, it was seen as necessary to insert a degree of insulation between these industry interests and the work of enforcement. This was designed to enhance the Commission's reputation for impartiality and to protect HSE staff from undue pressure.

Both the Commission and the Executive were to be Crown bodies, staffed by civil servants and, on the latter point, constitutional arguments were used once more. The MSC and its agencies had been set up as non-Crown bodies with non-civil service staff.[14] The position for the new health and safety agencies was seen as quite different. Whereas the MSC was established to offer services, to advise and to play a strategic role in the labour market, the HSC/E were also engaged in regulation and enforcement. The Government considered that it would be more acceptable to Parliament and the public if powers to mandate individuals, to investigate and to prosecute were exercised by Crown servants, who were thought to be more directly controllable than public authority employees.

For the purpose of this book, however, it is the tripartism and consensual basis of health and safety regulation that is its most notable feature. Shared responsibility provided the foundation upon which *Robens'* co-operative and self-regulatory system of control was built. Thus the Committee stated that there was a greater 'natural identity of interest' between 'the two sides' in relation to safety and health problems than in most other matters. Indeed, no such distinction was to be drawn between the 'two sides' of industry. There was no legitimate scope for 'bargaining' on safety and health issues, but much scope for constructive decision-making, joint inspection and participation in working out solutions. Self-regulation and self-inspection were said to be 'basic themes' of the Report. If progress was to be made there had to be adequate arrangements for both management and work people to play their full part.[15]

This approach was common to the Manpower Services Commission (MSC), the Advisory Conciliation and Arbitration Service (ACAS) and the HSC/E, but in the early seventies the effectiveness of tripartism as a regulatory strategy was untried. In health and safety this tripartism is reflected not merely in the HSC/E's framework but in the roles given to both sides of industry in the continuing process of regulation. The 1974 Act imposes on employers the duties to provide written safety policies[16] and to provide information, instruction, training and supervision.[17] On top of this there is the general duty of every employer to ensure so far as is reasonably practicable the health, safety and welfare at work of his or her employees.[18]

The union part is played through the innovatory system of safety representatives and safety committees. The Act provided for recognized trade unions to be given the right to appoint safety representatives from amongst the employees and the employer must consult these individuals.[19] Representatives also have the right to call for the creation of a safety committee.[20] The functions of the representatives are principally to investigate complaints, potential hazards, dangerous occurrences and accidents; to make representations to employers on these or on general health and safety matters; and to inspect the workplace either routinely or after an incident. The employer must assist the safety representative to carry out these tasks, documents may be copied and paid time-off shall be given for the performance of these duties and for training. As for the safety committees, they have a general function of reviewing health and safety matters and of reporting to management on such matters as trends in accidents and diseases at the workplace.

A number of questions arise concerning the role of tripartite structures in the policy-making and enforcement processes. Have they really led to agreed policies, effective enforcement and account-able regulation? What happens to agency tripartism when the underlying philosophy is alien to the government of the day? An examination of policy-making procedures (for enforcement, see p. 148 below) reveals the extent to which tripartism infuses the HSC/E system. A new regulation or approved code of practice will typically be produced in the following manner.

Action may be set in motion by an HSE policy branch or by one of the Executives' tripartite advisory committees or working parties. In the case of an HSE policy branch initiative, this can result from a variety of circumstances.[21] These are, principally, where a new hazard comes to light; where existing standards appear unacceptably low; to respond to a growing or sudden public concern; to put into effect proposals from an HSC advisory committee or to respond to problems identified by field forces, policy staff, industry, trade unions or other bodies; to effect an EEC initiative; to adapt to technology changes; or to meet a need for information and advice.

At the preliminary stage, the policy branch works towards a submission that will be put to the Commission through the Executive for authority to conduct detailed work. It will consult with the inspectorate's National Industry Groups (NIGs) and solicitor's branch on the need for new rules and consider the adequacy of existing legislation. The costs and benefits of any proposed change will be analysed. The regulation, approved code of practice (ACOP) or other guidance is then drafted, bearing in mind the need to make the information or rule accessible to those involved. Policy branches and working parties are especially concerned during this period to iron out problems through informal consultations with industry. Commission approval is then obtained through the Management Board of the Executive. At this stage, a case will be made for the package of proposals (regulations, approved codes, guidance notes, etc.), the costs and benefits will be set out and a timetable offered.

Once the HSC approves action, government departments are notified of the work in hand and a period of internal discussion and revision begins. Instructions will go to the HSE solicitor to draft regulations or to seek approval for a draft code. These drafts will be sent to interested branches and inspectorates, advisory committees and, where appropriate, working parties.

Tripartism feeds into the policy-making process at all stages, not least through informal consultations. The Commission represents industry, unions and local authorities but so do the advisory committees and working parties that are set up on a standing or ad hoc basis. Foremost in importance are the subject advisory committees (i.e. those organized according to a type of hazard) and the Industry Advisory Committees (IACs). Both types of committee involve the representatives of unions and management, and (serviced by HSE staff) they develop and coordinate proposals on health and safety strategies on particular topics and specific industries. The advisory committees, where they do not develop their own proposals, will comment on the effect of draft proposals on their subject area or industry.

Once developmental discussions are complete, a formal consultative document is produced and circulated. At this time the HSE goes public with press notices. Comments are then received, the drafts are revised and circulated to the same parties, including the Confederation of British Industry (CBI), the Trades Union Congress (TUC), all interested branches, secretaries and working groups. The regulations then go back to the Commission for approval and then they are submitted to the Secretary of State. In the case of codes, these are formally issued by the HSC and the Minister consents to Commission approval. With regulations, the Department takes over responsibility for processing drafts and the Minister both signs them and lays them before Parliament.

Such an account indicates the *procedures* for taking into account the views of all sides of industry. The *substantive* issue is whether this extensive process is conducive to agreed policies, easy enforcement or accountable regulation.

It could be argued that nothing in this procedure goes beyond the potential achievements of rigorous consultation. Any agreement reached is clearly of a restricted nature. However hard the HSE tries, there are limits to the representativeness of, say, an industry advisory committee. The accusation is liable to be made that large organized firms and groups are well represented in policy-making in contrast with smaller firms. Any one new regulation may affect a huge variety of industries and workforces. The views of all those concerned, therefore, cannot be assumed to have been taken on board in HSE policy-making.

What this means is not that the consultative process is worthless – it has considerable value in appraising the HSE staff of the problems raised by regulatory proposals. It does, however, indicate the rashness of assuming universal consent. It further suggests that the consultative process has a limited role in providing relevant information to those who are affected by a new rule.

Having said that, regulation is facilitated by such procedures to the extent that unworkable regulations can sometimes be weeded out. The inspectorates have an opportunity to comment on enforceability at an early stage and either side of industry can object to the costs of compliance or the poor protections inherent in a new provision. The system is, however, more responsive to industry objections than to inspectorate assessments on enforceability. Thus when, in 1977, the HSE proposed new and detailed regulations on lifting gear they were (as will be described below) very quickly dropped when industry and the CBI condemned them as impracticable. This reaction contrasts with the policy-makers' more sceptical view of inspectorate complaints that new rules will be difficult to apply in the field.

Tripartism in HSE policy-making leads to accountability only insofar as it gives a voice to those involved. Where tripartism may be weakest in health and safety regulation is in representing the interests of a particular sector of the general public. Thus, in the case of a group of residents living around a hazardous installation, there is often no pressure group to put forward their views and they must rely to a great extent on local authority representatives to argue their case in HSC/E policy-making.[22] In terms of the broader public interest, the HSC/E's accountability is limited in a way common to other agencies. It is the Secretary of State who issues new regulations and it is, therefore, he or she who accounts to Parliament for these. The Secretary of State has a number of other powers with which to control the Commission. He or she may modify proposed regulations after consulting the Commission[23] or may refuse consent to a code of practice.[24] The HSC must submit particulars of its proposals to the Secretary of State, and must annually submit a report and accounts. Finally, the Secretary of State may give the HSC general directions regarding its functions (including those depriving it of functions). These are provisions familiar in the field of operating and regulatory agencies, and the HSC/E is no more or less accountable by virtue of its tripartism.

As for the operation of tripartism in a shifting political climate, three factors can be noted. First, there is evidence that even a tripartite body like the HSC will not waste its time in putting up regulations to the Secretary of State when these are likely to be rejected. Thus during the administration of Margaret Thatcher, the HSC/E were concerned to have in hand a good case for regulations in cost-benefit terms before submitting these to the Secretary of State. This approach was reflected in the comment of one HSE official: 'There are some things one simply would not bother trying with certain Secretaries of State, that is merely understanding the politics.'

Commenting on disagreements with Ministers in 1981, the then Director General of the HSE, John Locke, said that Ministers might disagree with HSC/E decisions, regulations or codes but that this had until then been a 'theoretical not a real problem'. He admitted, however, that in the end Ministers would always prevail and that in certain narrow areas there had been disagreements and regulations had been delayed by such disagreements (e.g. those relating to Safety Representatives).[25]

Second, it is also clear that the tripartite agency is no more immune to general mistrust of regulation than any other body. Thus the Department of Trade and Industry's Report *Burdens on Business*[26] advocated the simplification and rationalization of statutory health and safety provisions as part of a broader attempt to lift the burdens on small firms. The tripartite structure may, however, prove effective in reducing the danger that one side of industry will mount a concerted attack on the agency. Thus, the HSC/E has for some time seen itself as involved in negotiation, not 'a crusade'[27] and, since representatives of management and unions have been given considerable opportunity to feed their views into the policy-making process, this to some extent militates against this kind of assault.

A third factor to bear in mind in considering how political opinions and changes affect a tripartite body is the area of potential disagreement. In this respect, health and safety might be expected to be relatively uncontentious. Ministers are never in office for periods long enough to institute major substantive reforms in health and safety controls and this is an area less susceptible or amenable than, say, civil aviation licensing, to sweeping policy changes. Ministers may therefore be less interested in radical revisions of policy than in responding to disasters and other issues of more immediate concern. Thus Ministers may be seen to call for action after a catastrophe and they may claim to be instituting action on a matter of topical concern (e.g. asbestos), but such types of action leave the HSC/E relatively free to make policy on other long-term issues. This is not, therefore, an agency system that is liable to devastating ministerial interference on matters of substance.

3 Regulation and Rule-Types

A major contention of *Robens* was, as we have seen, that health and safety regulation was hindered by the nature of the rules being enforced. They were inappropriately detailed, they presumed a system of regulation based on external commands and they created an undesirable climate for the control of work hazards. Such comments invite public lawyers to consider the kinds of rule structure that might be workable in different kinds of regulatory context. The *Robens* argument at least assumed that the type of rule structure adopted by an agency actually made a difference to the enforcement process.

Robens wanted a general movement away from fragmented and complex statutory rules towards a mixture of statutory regulations and voluntary codes that clearly stated principles, was intelligible and was 'constructive rather than prohibitory'.[28] Moreover it was said:

> We recommend that in future no statutory regulation should be made before detailed consideration has been given to whether the objectives might adequately be met by a non-statutory code of practice or standard.'[29]

It was acknowledged that increased reliance would be placed on rules that were subject to little parliamentary control, but *Robens* thought that this was necessary. Full scrutiny of all health and safety rules was, in any case, not practicable and Ministers would be responsible for the rules that they made.

So as to effect this approach, section 1(2) of the HSWA 1974 provided for the HSC/E's progressive replacement of existing statutory provisions by a new system of regulations and approved codes. The Act provided HSC/E policy-makers with a hierarchy of rule-types. This was headed by the general statutory duties set down in sections 2–9 of the 1974 Act. Regulations provide the next layer of rules. Section 15 of the Act gave the Secretary of State powers to make regulations for any of the general purposes of the Act and these regulations might not only repeal or modify existing statutory provisions but could also exclude or modify the general duties of sections 2–9. They were meant to provide the main means of replacing outdated statutory provisions.

The 'Approved Code of Practice' (ACOP) was the next device introduced by the Act and attempted to reap the benefits of responsiveness whilst at the same time operating with some legal force. The ACOP provides 'practical guidance' in relation to the requirements of either regulations or the Act. Failure to observe a code provision does not render a person automatically liable to civil or criminal proceedings. If, however, it is shown that there was a failure to observe a code on a matter relevant to the contravention of a requirement or prohibition, that matter is taken as proved unless it can be shown that compliance was achieved in a manner other than by observing the code.

Codes are approved by the HSC, not by the Secretary of State, but the HSC does have to obtain the Secretary of State's consent beforehand and must consult appropriate government departments and other interested parties. They were seen by the Government as useful in a number of respects: they could be written in lay language more easily than statutory instruments; they could spell out technical matters in detail; they could specify *alternative* ways of doing a thing and incorporate flexibility in that manner; they could be updated readily in the light of technological developments or operational experience; they provided a way to involve both sides of industry; and they supplemented regulations without determining an exclusive mode of compliance.

A constitutional issue arose concerning the codes. They did have some legislative force but were not made by Parliament or by a person immediately responsible to Parliament. The government thinking here covered two main points. In view of the anticipated volume of approved codes and the need to have them approved quickly, it was not thought practicable for all of them to be laid before Parliament. On the other hand, some form of accountability that went beyond the HSC's overall answerability to Ministers was considered to be necessary. The requirement of the Secretary of State's consent was a compromise – one that was adhered to in spite of opposition arguments that an expert body should be fully responsible for the codes and should be able to issue them without the delay inherent in seeking consent.

The lowest tier of control in health and safety matters consists of guidance notes. These may be developed by the HSC or the HSE, by Industry Advisory Committees or by industry itself. Guidance notes have no formal legal significance but aim to assist employers and others to comply with the law.

Examination of the HSE's use of different rule-types shows how difficult it is to measure the performance of different kinds of rule. Within three years of the HSWA 1974, the HSE Management Board had agreed a general approach. *Regulations* were to set out specific aims, principles, objectives of control or numerical standards which were important enough to be mandatory. They would generally be wide in application and apply across-the-board to some risk or subject. *Approved Codes of Practice* (ACOPs) would set out the preferred methods for meeting the mandatory requirements of regulations. Only exceptionally would a code be linked directly to a statutory duty (which would be too general in most cases). *Guidance* would constitute authoritative advice of an explanatory or descriptive nature and could frequently be process or industry-specific in scope.

By 1982 HSE staff were considering the feasibility of a 'standard package' of control measures. At that time varying approaches to rule selection had been taken in different areas. Thus, simple regulations were coupled with detailed guidance in the areas of *lead, pressurised systems, electricity* and *first aid*, but in such fields as *diving*, very detailed regulations were still employed. Other matters such as *substances hazardous to health* and *asbestos* involved more complex packages that relied heavily on both statutory duties and general regulations. Proposals under discussion in that period suggested that the 'standard package' of control measures to be preferred in future should be the ACOP (plus guidance if necessary) linked to the general duties of the Act. Regulations were considered to be rigid and inflexible, their application to different industries was difficult and they had high resource implications, a built-in obsolescence that inhibited technological development, an inability to deal with technical, medical and scientific matters and an inaccessibility to lay persons. ACOPs were thought to perform much better on all the above fronts and non-statutory guidance was said to be even more adaptable. These suggested guidelines were thought to be a deliberate and positive movement away from detailed regulation.

These proposals were discussed by senior staff and a revised paper issued in March 1984. This acknowledged that in practice some parts of a package would require the legislative authority of regulations, but in most cases a simple framework of regulations was envisaged as most appropriate. Codes and guidance would give the necessary detailed requirement and practical advice and could do so in language that was transparent and accessible to the people who had to put the provisions into effect.

The general philosophy of the paper was agreed by the HSE Management Board in April 1984 and it was decided that policy sections should be issued with guidance on those lines. Regulations were normally to concern themselves with objectives, not means of achievement. Wherever possible, packages would consist of two tiers only and, as a general principle, material was to be included in the lowest possible tier, namely guidance.

The problems of rule-selection on a particular regulatory issue can be demonstrated by outlining HSE policy-making concerning lifting gear in the period 1977 to 1983. Here the HSE came up with an old-fashioned package of regulations and was forced to rethink its approach. 'Getting it wrong' on this matter made it clear that choice of rule-type would not merely affect enforcement strategy but would have considerable political consequences within the organization. The experience is noteworthy for three reasons. A regulatory regime based on detailed legal commands was abandoned, an alternative scheme was prepared and HSE staff began to look more closely at the effects of rule-type on regulation.

The trigger for reform was an EEC Directive, which resulted in the (draft) Lifting Gear (Testing and Use) Regulations (1977). These required all items of lifting gear to be supplied with a manufacturer's certificate designating safety limits. They covered not only the hooks, ropes, slings and chains mentioned in existing legislation but other items such as lifting eyes, beams and frames. The aim was to replace scattered legislation by a single code.

The draft regulations were approved by the HSC for consultation in May 1977 and copies went out to industry groups, unions, inspectors and other interested parties. The remarkable aspect of the regulations was their detail. There were lengthy definitions of such items as 'hook', 'lifting appliance' and 'multi-legged sling'. Even what constituted a 'thorough examination' was subject to minute definition. What the manufacturer had to certify in relation to a chain took more than a page to outline.

Why were detailed regulations used and not, say, approved codes of practice (ACOPs) or guidance notes? HSE staff gave three reasons for this:

1 Much material was carried over in modified form from past legislation or was determined by the EEC Directive and so was best dealt with by regulations.

2 The use of lifting gear was a hazardous area of work that warranted mandatory treatment.
3 The requirements consisted of precise, sharply-defined rules which were best expressed as regulations and would lose clarity if treated in the language appropriate to a guidance note.

In the consultation process, industry gave a decidely negative response. Two hundred and sixty-three organizations offered comments and the great majority opposed the new regulations. Established industries already covered by legislation considered that existing provisions were adequate, while those newly covered by the rules objected that across-the-board proposals could not be applied to them.

There were contrasting submissions from the TUC and CBI. The TUC generally welcomed the proposals but the CBI found them wholly unacceptable, arguing that accident statistics did not justify any change and that considerable costs would be imposed on industry (£25m on the construction industry alone). Several organizations urged that detailed legal requirements were inappropriate and respondents frequently used words such as 'complex', 'confusing', 'lengthy', 'unnecessary', 'too detailed', 'too wide in scope', 'badly drafted', 'impracticable', 'costly' and 'legalistic'. A number, including the CBI, suggested that if regulations were required, they should be short and general in content and supplemented by codes of practice. Many quoted from *Robens* on the use of simple regulations supplemented by codes. It was thus not only the content but the form of the legislation that drew fire.

The HSE drew two principal lessons from the consultation. First, the format of the draft rules had been inappropriate and, second, there was a need to have more effective and earlier consultations with industry on new proposals. Senior staff put the proposals on ice and started a less ambitious programme of guidance notes. At the same time a set of 'phantom' regulations was placed on file without plans for implementation. A period of discontinuity followed when a new team of staff took up responsibility, but by 1982 an overall definition of policy had been drawn up and was based on a number of propositions.

1 There was a need for flexible policies that could respond to society's changing views on acceptable risks. Lifting gear was an important area since in 1980 there were 3,500 injuries and 28 fatalities resulting from such gear.

2 The exhaustive or 'across the board' kind of regulations had a limited relevance and applicability – as had been shown by the 1977 regulations. The 1982 approach emphasized greater selectivity and more analysis of certain key questions. What were the most hazardous pieces of equipment? What were the hazards? How could these best be minimized?

3 The main cause of lifting-gear accidents was not so much plant failure but system defect and abuse of equipment.

4 The state of existing legislation was not a real problem – the trouble lay in low standards of compliance.

5 Guidance notes were respected in industry and inspectors were constantly asked for them. Respect for guidance notes was increased by the process of consultation preceeding their issue.

The way forward was thus seen as relying on existing legislation but identifying particular areas of activity or items of equipment where limited legislation or ACOPs or guidance were useful. In this strategy of 'selective action', guidance was to pay particular attention to training, supervision and the system of work. It was decided that the programme of guidance notes should be continued and encouragement given to users and manufacturers to draw up their own Codes of Practice. In 1983 the HSE Management Board and the HSC endorsed a programme of work in pursuance of the new more specific policy.

This glance at one small area of HSE rule-making indicates the range of issues involved in the problem of rule choice. Not only had the enforceability and political acceptability of rules to be considered but their scope, transparency, accessibility and justiciability also. In the end, the pragmatic approach prevailed. The 'blockbuster' attempt to regulate lifting gear across-the-board failed. From 1982 onwards it was clear that more was required of policy-makers than the updating of old regulations or the routine application of new regulations. A good deal of attention had to be given to the correspondence between rule-type and regulatory task.

Such endeavours, however, have tended to assume that there are significant differences between rule-types. Thus, contrasts are drawn between ACOPs and regulations, and the two sides of industry argue at length that certain provisions should take a particular form. What tends to happen in such circumstances is that procedures become more rigorous and consultations become more onerous as concessions are made to various parties.[30] Thus the HSE's procedures for producing an ACOP and a regulation (described above) have become very similar. The average time that the HSE assumes is necessary to produce a regulation is 144 weeks, but an ACOP takes even longer at 151 weeks.[31] It would accordingly be easy to exaggerate the speed with which ACOPs and guidance notes can be adapted to cope with, for example, technological changes.

The danger is, as one trade union official put it, that: 'All the rules rise up a tier.' Thus, if the ACOP is to operate as a regulation and the guidance note is itself subjected to lengthy consultation, many of the advantages of the lower tiers of rules may disappear. The ACOP may still differ in style or content from the regulation but the procedures for making it are not marked by their responsiveness.

A fundamental issue raised by the whole discussion of rule-types is whether such choices make any difference at all. This turns on the role that legal and other rules play in health and safety regulation. To answer this we have to consider the nature of enforcement under the consensual system of regulation.

4 Enforcement and Consensus

The six inspectorates of the HSE are faced with a daunting set of tasks. They inspect work activities; provide advice to employers, workers and public; investigate accidents and ill-health; consider complaints; and enforce relevant health and safety legislation.

In looking at enforcement it would be rash to assume that all the inspectorates, with their different traditions, have a common philosophy. They do not.[32] Thus the prosecution policies and enforcement strategies of the Factory Inspectorate (FI) contrast with those of the Nuclear Installations Inspectorate which has powers under the Nuclear Installations Act 1965 that make prosecution look a very blunt and unresponsive tool.

Here I will focus on enforcement by the FI, the largest of the HSE's field divisions. This division in 1985/6 operated with around 530 general inspectors and around 700 support staff. They carried out a total number of 185,000 visits to premises in 1983. As well as routine visits, the FI staff run a number of campaigns to respond to particularly acute or contentious risks. Thus their current 'preemptive inspection programmes' target hazards from noise, asbestos and the conveyance of dangerous substances by road.[33] Another range of actions comes under the heading of 'Planned Special Visits' and are more sharply focused on specific hazards. The FI has also developed initiatives on installations handling hazardous substances, major accident hazards and gas safety.

Inspections of premises are relatively rare. According to the HSE: 'Only a handful of workplaces will be visited by an inspector as often as three or four times a year – once a year is relatively frequent and many workplaces will not see an inspector for several years.'[34] In the case of, say, a medium-sized garment factory it would not be exceptional to have four- or five-year gaps between visits. The FI, after all, has to deal with over 460,000 establishments, many of which have multiple or transient sites. The frequency of visits is governed by a number of factors: the present standards of health and safety in the workplace; the nature of the worst problem that might arise; management's ability and attitudes; and the possibility of changes in standards or hazards between visits.[35]

Inspectors are given authority by a battery of powers. Section 20 of the HSWA 1974 enables them to take a number of steps to put relevant statutory provisions into effect. Thus there are powers to enter (with police and equipment if necessary) to examine and investigate; to direct premises to be left undisturbed until examined; to measure and record; to take samples; to order dismantling or testing; to take possession of articles; to require answers and information; and to inspect, copy and order production of documents.

The new administrative sanctions that *Robens* thought would be far more flexible than prosecutions are provided for in sections 21 and 22. An inspector can issue an *Improvement Notice* when he or she thinks a contravention of a statutory provision has occurred. The notice requires remedial action to be taken within a limited period. It may specify the remedial steps to be taken and must give reasons for deeming a contravention to have occurred. A *Prohibition Notice* under section 22 can be issued to order the discontinuance of a hazardous activity and may either have immediate effect or give a fixed period of notice. There must, however, be a danger of 'serious personal injury' involved.

Robens' consensual mode of regulation is thus marked by low reliance on prosecution and increased use of adminstrative powers.

But what changes were effected by the *Robens* package? On the one hand it can be argued that enforcement has changed very little under the new regulatory philosophy. HSE inspectors are inclined to argue that *Robens* overstated the extent to which the 'mandatory' model of enforcement applied before 1972. As one HSE staff member put it:

The reality of pre-*Robens* was exaggerated. We were not going around prosecuting everyone. That was never the way. And nowadays there is the perception that we go around 'knocking hell out of people'. That perception is incredible given our prosecution record.[36]

According to this view, there only ever has been one principal way to enforce and that is to advise, negotiate and persuade. The threat of prosecution has always been held in reserve and prosecutions themselves have been rare. (To prosecute, one is reminded, takes up a great deal of time and results in comparatively low fines.) The figures support this contention. In 1970 some 300,000 visits by factory inspectors resulted in the prosecution of under 3,000 offences. By the mid-eighties the number of visits had been almost halved but the ratio of visits to prosecutions remained similar. Thus there were only 1,431 prosecutions by the factory inspectorate in the 15 months to April 1985.

The role of prosecution in preventing accidents is even less than these figures seem to indicate, since of those 1,431 prosecutions, 775 followed accidents. Although the prosecution that follows an accident will have some preventative role, more than half of the prosecutions brought to April 1985 may be seen as *responses* to events rather than purely anticipatory actions.

Any changes effected by Robens were thus unlikely to relate to the use of prosecutions since these have long played a relatively marginal role in health and safety regulation. The real possibilities for a new consensual scheme of control lay in stimulating cooperative responsibility and self-regulation and in improving the inspector's non-prosecutorial powers.

On the latter point, the evidence is that the system of notices introduced by the 1974 Act has provided inspectors with a new and highly effective scheme of administratively issued and legally endorsed sanctions that plays a key role between the stages of advice or persuasion and criminal prosecution. The statistics on fatal injuries to employees at work, moreover, have been taken by the HSC as an indication that the general regulatory package has been reasonably successful. Thus, it is said that there has been a consistent drop from 4.0 fatal injuries per 100,000 employees in 1971 to 2.4 such injuries in 1982, and that this drop is more than can be explained by reference to the decline in manufacturing as opposed to other forms of employment over this period.[37] Although such figures are not unproblematic (the total of weekly hours worked by all operatives in manufacturing in 1984 was only 53 per cent of that worked in 1964), they do offer the HSC a favourable comparison between performance pre and post the 1974 Act.

The success of consensual regulation in stimulating more safety consciousness and better self-regulation is more difficult to assess.[38] Comments may, however, be made on the HSE's 'advice and assistance'[39] role, what might be termed the 'consensual paradox' and the problems of controlling health as opposed to safety hazards.

The HSE advises and assists not merely through inspections but by means of the consultative and tripartite processes, by use of the media and by the dissemination of published information in the form of codes and guidance. A central question here is whether the supply of information to industry is to be seen as a supplement to or substitute for inspection. Some inspectors and trade unionists argue that leaflets and guidance are only of value when there is an inspector to advise on them. *Robens*, it is said, took this point in stating that the provision of advice and the enforcement of sanctions where necessary were 'two inseparable elements' of inspection work.[40] The real need, it is argued, is for more inspectors and more frequent inspection. To issue guidance on its own, these commentators argue, is to paper over the HSC/E's insufficient and shrinking inspectoral resources.[41] Inspectors do see advice as a central aspect of their role but they do not issue multiple copies of guidance free of charge. The position of the HSC[42] is that the Act[43] imposes on employers, not the Commission, the primary duty to provide information on health and safety matters to employees. Nevertheless, in recognition of its own duties to communicate information,[44] the HSC sees inspectors as having 'an important complementary role in providing information and advice from their own knowledge'.[45]

Insofar as the consultative and tripartite processes advise and inform, much depends on the communications networks created by trade unions or the employers' associations. Where such organizations are well-developed in an industry, the policy-making processes of the HSE work highly successfully. When agreements are made as to controls, the unions' and employers' representatives will report back to their members by means of, for example, trade newspapers or newsletters and information is rapidly and widely disseminated. Such information, moreover, is passed on in a form that those close to the ground consider is most useful to their members.

Where employers and workers are ill-organized or, because of the nature of the industry, fragmented, such information lines do not exist to the same extent or even at all. Nor can it be assumed that the widest range of interests are represented in consultations. The value of policy-making procedures in terms of advice and assistance is, therefore, highly variable in the HSE system. Insofar as the shape of industrial activity changes with the decline of large-scale manufacturing enterprises in favour of smaller service industries,[46] the quality of information channels so crucial to the HSE cannot be guaranteed to remain constant. The Chief Inspector of Factories has himself noted that industry, because of structural changes, is less able to take on a self-regulatory role than it was.[47]

In using the media, a main objective of the HSE is to foster awareness of legislative requirements and to encourage good practice on all sides of industry.[48] To this end, the HSE press office is in daily contact with the national press, radio and TV in an attempt to raise consciousness, explain HSE activities and stimulate debate. A problem, however, for press officers is that technical changes in standards do not make headlines. Nor do the modest fines that result from HSE prosecutions. (In 1985 a magistrate's court gave the first prison sentence on a health and safety (asbestos) charge – but that sentence was suspended. Thus prompted, major unions began in autumn 1985 a new campaign for more severe punishment of health and safety offenders.)

The HSE can of itself do relatively little to increase the newsworthiness of its activities but it is affected by media attention in another respect. It is clear that where a sudden burst of public concern is voiced in the newspapers, TV or radio (over, for example, asbestos hazards) the HSE will respond to that concern. Staff acknowledge that such attention will allow an issue to 'leapfrog' others in the policy pipeline and accept this as part of living in a political world. As we have seen, one of the HSC's published factors for consideration in preparing its plans of work is 'to respond to public concern'.[49]

The great mass of HSC/E information comes through its own publications and the output is huge. In 1983/4 the HSE issued 173 press notices, 292,000 leaflets, 10,476 pages of translations and publications, 6 newsletters and it published 114 new titles. Again there are problems. Apart from the questionable value of information without inspection, the HSE's strategy in sending out leaflets by mail may be somewhat speculative. It is difficult to assess the percentage of documents that fail to reach their intended destinations (due to changes of address, etc.) and the treatment received by a leaflet on arrival at the appropriate premises is uncertain. The cost of HSE documentation is also an issue. The HSE publisher is Her Majesty's Stationery Office (HMSO) and prices are charged on a commercial basis. Of the list of publication-types (regulations, codes of practice, discussion documents, research papers, guidance notes, notes of best practical means and advisory leaflets) only leaflets are routinely issued free of charge. Self-regulation here means that the small enterprise that operates on a shoestring has to make time to organize the purchase of relevant documents and has to pay for the information that is there to encourage it to improve health and safety measures. Such a strategy is seen by critics as excessively optimistic.

Here the 'consensual paradox' is evidenced. It can be stated thus. Consensual regulation, as well as assuming that optimal safety conditions coincide with optimal profit-maximizing conditions, is aimed at the well-informed, well-intentioned and well-organized employer who would present few problems if left wholly to self-regulate. But many hazards relate to the ill-informed, ill-intentioned and ill-organized employer who is left untouched by consensual regulation.

This is a key problem for the HSE. The methods of advising and assisting noted above all work acceptably well where employers and workers are organized and willing to negotiate. Indeed this was the industrial model implicit in *Robens* – both sides of industry were reasonable, well intentioned and communicative, they had common interests in health and safety and simply needed relevant advice. Where this model does not apply, however, it is especially difficult to advise and assist through inspection, consultation, use of the media or by published material. The HSC/E is aware of this problem in observing that 'not all men are reasonable . . . legislative packages need in the end to be enforceable'.[50] In the final analysis, however, neither prosecution nor advice and assistance offers a highly effective response to the activities of a certain group of employers.

The statement that legislative packages have to be enforceable brings us back to rule-making and to another key question: What are the various kinds of HSE rule attempting to achieve? Rules may be designed for a number of purposes. They may aim, for example, to set standards which, if not followed, will be enforced by prosecutions; to promote, educate and raise consciousness; to control officials; to facilitate negotiated compliance; or to encourage self-regulation. Rules may possess different qualities that correspond to these objectives, for example specificity, inclusiveness, accessibility, status and type of sanction. It may, for instance, not be the case that the type of rule that best raises consciousness is that one most amenable to prosecution. In health and safety, as in other areas of regulation, it tends to be assumed that 'good' rules will achieve all desirable objectives equally. This is not the case. What has so far been missing in HSE rule-making is any sustained attempt to correlate rule-types and regulatory objectives and to build into that analysis models of the different types of employer and workforce.

Another difficulty arises in relation to the use of resources. For an agency in the HSE's position it would be very tempting to focus staff time on amenable employers – or at least those who are easily identified, large in scale and who are in a position to act on HSE advice. Thus the FI's criteria governing the frequency of inspection look, inter alia, to the worst contingency forseeable at a workplace.[51] This, it could be argued, almost inevitably biases inspection towards large-scale industry rather than smaller enterprises where very serious (but numerically less newsworthy) injuries may occur.

In order to counter such tendencies, the HSE would have to undertake research to correlate hazards with sizes and types of enterprise as well as types of employer and employee organization. Only then could the agency be sure that it was employing its resources in the most efficient manner. At present the HSE's accident data are by no means so highly developed. The HSC has itself admitted that its information as to accidents and ill-health is 'seriously deficient'.[52] Accurate figures on fatal injuries are available but no reliable data on non-fatal injuries exist. Before 1981 a system based on employers' statutory returns operated but this was shown to suffer badly from under-reporting when, in that year, the DHSS forwarded to the HSE its computerized data on claims for industrial injuries benefit (which were based on accidents at work). For two years there were useful statistics, until industrial injury benefit was withdrawn in 1983. Since then the HSE has worked on a new employers' reporting system but has conceded its 'lamentable' lack of injuries data. In the case of illness and non-obvious injuries the HSE has had no basis for determining its enforcement priorities other than the 'feel' of its staff.[53]

An alternative strategy for deployment, and one under consideration, is more contentious. It is to devote fewer resources to inspecting 'good' premises by employing a system of 'health and safety assurance'.[54] The HSC is considering whether it can formalize arrangements under which firms can satisfy it in a general way as to their safety policies and conduct 'without the need for continuous intervention on our part beyond what the essential need to investigate accidents might require'. The Commission, in dealing with large industrial units, would thus prefer to devote attention to 'the main organizational factors' which determine their health and safety performance rather than use scarce inspectorate resources on a continuing basis in order to cope with the effects of organizational shortcomings.

On its face, such an approach appears sensible, but it encapsulates the dilemma of the HSC/E. Unless it takes such steps it ties up a certain amount of resources (as yet unspecified). On the other hand, if it does so, it is open to accusations of abdicating its responsibilities in the face of large industrial interests. This will be a long-running debate.

Finally, mention has to be made of the HSC/E's major substantive problem – that of regulating health as opposed to safety. As has been noted, the statistics indicate to the HSC a gradual decline in fatal injuries over the last decade and this is of some comfort to its staff. In contrast, however, the HSC perceives there to be growing public concern over long-term health hazards and puts this down to increasing industrial use of substances that are known to be carcinogenic or toxic.[55]

For the HSE, regulating health can be particularly problematic insofar as harms are hidden rather than manifest. Establishing the causal connection between disease and occupation is often a first concern and is complicated by non-occupational and multiple-employment factors. The considerable time-lag between exposure and effect often compounds such difficulties, as does the task of identifying the health effects of new materials and substances.

Problems of uncertainty and causation are not absent from safety regulation but they occur with special frequency and force in relation to health matters.[56]

Nor have critics been slow to point to the HSE's failings in developing research into occupational health. In 1983 the House of Lords Select Committee on Science and Technology looked at Occupational Health and Hygiene Services and concluded that British research efforts were insufficiently coordinated by the HSE.[57] The HSE, the committee was told,[58] spent £1.2 million on occupational health research, compared to the US National Institute of Occupational Safety and Health (NIOSH)'s $40 million – a sum four times higher in relation to GNP. The TUC argued that at national level there were virtually no statistics to illustrate the degree to which different classes of disease are related to occupational factors.[59] The Committee itself thought that the Medical Division of the HSE was understaffed, under-resourced and so was insufficiently active in providing advice.[60] It recommended that more resources be devoted to health matters and that the HSE should play a stronger role in coordinating occupational health research.

The direction in which the HSE may be called to travel on health issues is indicated by the strong demands being made by the TUC, and some unions.[61] The TUC has criticized the present 'reactive and laissez-faire' policies towards occupational health[62] and calls have been made, inter alia, for large-scale surveying of occupational disease in the UK; for a statutory system of reporting probable occupational diseases at the workplace; for a similar reporting system linking occupational histories of individuals to their health; for a statutory employers' duty to report ill-health that is related to occupational factors; for greater training for doctors in occupational health and certification on death of occupational causes; for more training for inspectors and more information to workers on health hazards; and for the statutory provision of workplace health services by employers.

The HSC has indicated that it will shift resources from safety to health regulation in response to public concern and to the increasing prevalence of the more insidious hazards.[63] For the Commission, however, there is considerable work to be done and, for the HSC/E, the significance of a shift from safety to health regulation lies in any accompanying change in regulatory strategy. The HSE increasingly will be compelled to rely on data of a highly specialized and often contentious nature. It will depend even more than at present on 'advice and assistance' but will find its advice to be of a kind that both demands high training for inspectors and that is most difficult to put in convincing fashion to employers. Such developments are not likely to lead to any drastic change in the consensual model of regulation now in force. They will, however, make the obtaining of consent a more difficult process.

In another important aspect, focusing on health will bring about a change in the HSC/E. It would be impossible for the agency to do this job properly were it to adopt a reactive standpoint only. Already, signficant steps have been taken towards adopting a preventative role in relation to occupational health in such fields as lead, asbestos, vinyl chloride exposure, generic manipulation, dangerous pathogens and the notification of new substances. Given HSC perceptions, this trend is likely to continue. This will lead the HSC/E to adopt an increasingly strong preventative role both in its data collecting and enforcement activities. This is liable both to result in an agency of far higher profile and to put the tripartite system under increased stress. The principal alternative is a 'do nothing' approach. The HSC/E could spend time and resources on data collection, modelling and researching whilst indefinitely postponing action on the basis that proof is as yet inconclusive. A prioritising of research over enforce-ment would avoid certain stresses but would place the agency's credibility at risk and, politically, might be sustainable only for a limited period.

5 Conclusions

As agencies the Commission and Executive have offered new institutions, new procedures and new enforcement strategies in an attempt to regulate in a complex and difficult area. Institutionally the tripartite arrangement has been useful in some respects but less so in others. It has encouraged wide consultation, it has produced agreement in certain notable areas. On the other hand, some of the consultative procedures are liable to criticism as over-extended, the tripartite structure can operate as a veto[64] and, as a result, may encourage the HSC/E to take a reactive role rather than to exercise a positive lead over industry. It is, furthermore, argued by some trade unionists that tripartism neutralizes the progressive wing of the employers' side which, throughout the history of health and safety regulation, has played a key role in applying new standards across industry.

HSE rule-making procedures have attempted to adapt to particular circumstances but the promotional value of certain forms of rule is uncertain, the time taken to produce many rules is prolonged, there is a tendency for different types of rule to merge functions and the regulatory strategy implicit in rules is often unexplored.

As for enforcement under consensual self-regulation, the *Robens* philosophy has been criticized principally on the grounds that interests in safety and in profits cannot be assumed always to coincide, that vigorous enforcement has never been tried in this area but has a useful regulatory role, and that greater resources, powers and penalties offer more for inspectors than calls to increase advice and assistance. It is debatable, furthermore, whether promotional and advisory work can operate as an effective substitute for inspection. The consensual paradox applies insofar as the HSE is far more comfortable with organised industries than others that may be at least as hazardous. One precondition for responding to this problem, and to that of regulating occupational health, lies in developing research into accidents and disease so that an effective information base can be built up. The weakness of the HSE in this respect reflects its past willingness to settle for a more reactive role than was perhaps appropriate. In so far as the HSC/E chooses to respond to both health and safety problems by a course that combines increased research with effective enforcement – that is, by a more pro-active role – then it might well prepare for an increased political profile. In the past the agencies have become involved in political contention only sporadically and have been able to make a claim to reasonable success on the safety front. In placing greater emphasis on health matters, the HSC/E will find it more difficult to measure and demonstrate its own success. Consensual self-regulation will continue in its developing forms but an increasing number of critics will demand positive justification for HSC/E regulation.

8

Civil Aviation Regulation: From Tribunal to Regulatory Agency

Robert Baldwin

This chapter explains how British civil aviation has come to be regulated in a particular fashion and explores the implications of regulating by agency as opposed to tribunal. The Civil Aviation Authority (CAA) is a powerful agency, combining executive, judicial and legislative functions. It is of interest to public lawyers in four main respects: in its links with central government; its relationship to the courts; its use of trial-type procedures in a peculiarly difficult area; and its incorporation of a specialist expertise into policy-making. In the second part of the chapter, I consider how the agency has responded to considerable difficulties on these four fronts. First though, an account of how agency regulation came about.

1 The Evolution of a Regulatory System

In looking at how a particular regulatory regime came into existence it is worth bearing in mind the question: Why was it deemed necessary to regulate the civil aviation industry at all? These two issues are closely related and light is thrown on them by tracing developments in attitudes not merely to regulatory strategies but also to the civil aviation industry itself.[1] In the twenty years following the first commercial flight (in 1910), the main objective of regulation was to ensure that there was some degree of continuity in the supply of air services. In the early 1920s the Air Ministry operated a subsidy scheme which allowed the individual promotion of continental services by small operators. This policy was revised so as to concentrate state support on one single 'chosen instrument', and Imperial Airways was created in 1924. Although a private company, Imperial enjoyed a monopoly of subsidies and developed a considerable network of international scheduled services.[2]

By the mid-thirties British Airways had been formed by the merger of a number of private unsubsidized airlines and was endorsed as a second 'chosen instrument'. Competition on both domestic and international routes was intense. Within Britain, twenty operators struggled to keep 76 routes open. There were ad hoc subsidies with airmail contracts but most operators were small, ill-equipped and made losses.[3]

The Maybury Committee reported to the Government on the state of the industry in 1937.[4] Six years earlier the Royal Commission on Transport had responded to fierce competition on the roads between bus and coach operators by instituting a system of licensing by Traffic Commissioners.[5] In similar vein, *Maybury* advocated rationalization and the elimination of cut-throat competition by 'provisional regulation' of selected air routes so as to make them self-supporting.[6] A licensing system was advocated to cover both traffic and safety issues.

Another investigatory committee[7] was again to urge action (and to criticize Imperial Airways for taking an 'over-commercial' view of its responsibilities[8]) before a licensing body for civil aviation was eventually set up. The Air Transport Licensing Authority (ATLA) was established in 1938[9] so as to administer a system of subsidies and licensing by formal hearing. What the effect of such controls might have been we do not know, since any opportunities to effect changes were cut short by the war and revocation of the licensing scheme.

When hostilities ceased, the Conservative members of the coalition Government advocated the reintroduction of a large element of private ownership into British aviation. The recently-formed British Overseas Airways Corporation (BOAC) was to be privatized and regulation used to encourage the controlled development of routes. For their part, the independent operators pushed for a new ATLA. They urged that a semi-judicial body, independent of government, would provide the regulated competition that they considered was conducive to efficiency.[10]

The new Labour Government of July 1945 had different plans. Herbert Morrison, champion of the public service board,[11] introduced the Civil Aviation Bill of 1946, saying that unregulated competition had been tried and had failed, that regulated private enterprise would founder in red tape and that there was no alternative to nationalization. To the modified BOAC were added two new public corporations, British European Airways (BEA) and the British South American Airways Corporation. All scheduled services from the UK were reserved for the public sector.

What was notable about the Conservative response was that, more than a decade after the American New Deal, the Conservatives did not want an expert American-style regulatory commission, they wanted a court-like body,[12] one that was 'judicial with full legal powers and sitting under a legal chairman'.[13]

Although the 1946 Act opted for nationalization, a small step was taken in the direction of formal regulation. The Air Transport Advisory Council (ATAC) was set up to consider representations and complaints concerning the facilities offered by the Corporation and to advise the Minister on these. The ATAC, however, soon assumed larger functions.

It was the Minister's function to grant private operators permission to run services as 'associates' of the corporations[14] but the ATAC became a *de facto* licensing authority and, by 1949, was putting into effect ministerial directives on licensing policy.

By 1950 judicialized licensing systems for road goods and passenger transport had been in operation for twenty years. In aviation, however, the regulators had muddled through to produce a makeshift regime. Instead of controlling routes and prices by an expert, judicial or executive licensing body, nationalization had been combined with informal control by the ATAC, which was a body badly equipped for the job. When the Conservatives were in power and willing to allow more scope to independent airlines, the process of licensing by consumer/advisory body became even more overloaded. By 1958 the ATAC was considering 600 applications per year. Structurally the ATAC fell between a number of stools. It was neither judicial nor departmental, neither expert nor independent.

The movement for regulatory reform began in 1958. The (Conservative) Minister, Mr Watkinson, considered that matters were becoming 'too complicated' for the ATAC and his department to handle and that an independent body was called for. It was thought that change was needed for a number of reasons: the ATAC was not equipped for the job; the fiction of the 'associate agreement' (that was

used to circumvent the monopoly provisions of the Airways Corporations Act 1949) seemed out of place; the ATAC system only covered
scheduled services and yet charter operations needed at least safety
controls; and the independent operators wanted to compete for
licences on an equal footing with the corporations. It was this last
consideration that pointed most strongly in the direction of a judicial
body – any prospect of an independent decision-maker operating
trial-type procedures was viewed by the private sector as opening the
way to exciting opportunities.

The Civil Aviation (Licensing) Act 1960 provided the response
with the new Air Transport Licensing Board (ATLB). This was a
traditional body quite unlike its successor, the Civil Aviation
Authority (CAA). To see this it helps to distinguish the judicialized
tribunal from the *regulatory agency* (Abel-Smith and Stevens use the
terms 'court-substitute' tribunal and 'policy-oriented' tribunal).[15]
The tribunal is an adjudicating body akin to a court, whereas the
regulatory agency is specially equipped (in terms of expertise, staffing
and other resources) to develop and apply policies in a particular
area. The history of the ATLB indicates that the regulatory
performance of a tribunal may be very different from that of an
agency.

The ATLB had a licensing staff of about 25 and controlled both
route entry (domestic and international) and prices (domestic only).
It relied heavily on public trial-type hearings both to allocate licences
and to develop policy. This was part and parcel of its approach as
tribunal. The Minister responsible for creating the new ATLB spoke
of the pattern of aviation policy emerging from ATLB decisions and 'a
kind of case law' building up.[16]

In three major respects, however, the 'tribunal' approach failed.
The Board had severe problems in its relationship to government, in
its ability to formulate policy and in its development and application
of expertise. Analysis of these failings allows comparison with the
regulatory agency that replaced it.

The ATLB and Government

On nearly all fronts the ATLB failed to develop a working relationship with the Minister. From the Board's earliest days, appeals from
the ATLB's air transport licensing decisions were allowed with
alarming regularity. Since a third of all appeals were successful, it was
exceedingly difficult for the ATLB to sustain a competition policy
and, because new evidence could be submitted to an appeal, the

ATLB soon became a 'stepping stone' en route to the real decision-maker. Even when precedents were supposedly set on appeal, the ATLB declined to follow these.[17] Further conflicts arose over traffic rights (the internationally agreed permissions to fly that governments negotiate in order to put into effect the licensing decisions of national regulatory bodies). The ATLB did not consider the traffic rights implication of licensing decisions.[18] Serious confusion often arose with operators being licensed but not obtaining the rights that would allow the licences to be used.[19] Again with international air fares, divergent policies between the ATLB and the Board of Trade resulted in what the ATLB itself eventually admitted was a complete lack of rational control.[20]

What might have led to a degree of coordination between ATLB and Ministers was some system of policy guidance. The ATLB, however, was strict in looking only at its statutory objectives, not ministerial policy statements, and when the Minister, Roy Jenkins, attempted to lay down his own guidelines on licensing policy, the ATLB continued to ignore these in favour of direct reference to the aims of the 1960 Act.[21]

Policy Development by the ATLB

The ATLB failed to develop either durable policies or standards of sufficient precision to guide its licensing decisions. Thus in the early sixties it espoused a formula to govern its licensing of competition on scheduled service routes based on the forecast growth of the route.[22] By 1967, however, the 'growth formula' had been abandoned in favour of an ad hoc 'practical' approach. When it attempted to publish policy in its periodic licensing notices (notably on inclusive tours policy), it was undermined on appeal and was discouraged from further rule-making. Having set out as a court-like body, the ATLB conspicuously failed to develop a convincing case-law or to supplement this with alternative guidance on policy. With increasing frequency its decisions were condemned as 'arbitrary' or 'capricious'.

The ATLB as Expert

The ATLB lacked the resources with which to develop positive regulatory policies and to consider the wider aspects of its licencing decisions. As a result, it did not have the muscle to resist the Board of Trade. Nor could it plan for the industry in a rational fashion – it tended to await airline applications and react to these rather than develop policies and programmes.

In short, the tribunal failed as an all-purpose agency. It offered an unadventurous blend of the judicial with the managerial, of expertise with independence. It failed to develop case-law or policies, it managed inefficiently, it lacked the staff to generate expertise and it grew pale and weak under the shadowing wing of government.

The Agency Option

Complete deregulation of the airline industry was not considered a serious proposition in the late sixties. Drastic revision of the machinery of regulation was, however, on the agenda. The Select Committee on Nationalised Industries looked at the ATLB in 1967[23] and recommended that an end be made to the 'facade of independence'.[24] The ATLB should be wound up, they said, the Board of Trade should regulate competition, there should be no appeals system and direct price regulation should be ended.

More significantly (and before any action was taken), the forward-looking Edwards Committee on 'Air Transport in the Seventies'[25] was again highly critical of the ATLB's structure and performance, in particular of its *ad hocery*, its failure to develop policy and its lack of case-law. The suggested way to reform matters, however, was neither to improve the ATLB nor to hand matters over to the Department. To continue with the ATLB would perpetuate an undesirable separation between economic and safety licensing.[26] To opt for departmental licensing was unacceptable because the independent airlines feared that they would not be given a fair deal.[27] Thus, by the elimination of the alternatives rather than driven by a strong preference, *Edwards* came to advocate the setting-up of a large independent agency – the Civil Aviation Authority (CAA) – to be responsible not only for economic regulation but also for safety controls, traffic rights negotiations and air traffic controls, matters that had previously been divided between the independent Air Registration Board and the Board of Trade.

Significantly for our purposes, *Edwards* was aware that to create a powerful agency involved problems of ministerial control which also presented 'parliamentary and constitutional difficulties'.[28] The solution lay, they thought, in a system of written policy guidance.[29] This was the key to the new framework. It would eliminate the disguised conflicts of policy that had dogged relationships between the ATLB and the Board of Trade and it would force both the Minister and CAA to be clear and open about their respective strategies. Inconsistency with such written policy would be a basis for appeals which, *Edwards* said, should lie not to the Minister but to the courts or a special tribunal.

The general strategy of the Edwards report was endorsed by both the major parties, in and out of power.[30] The notion of a multi-powered agency was accepted quite readily, as was the device of written policy guidance. Predictably, however, Ministers were reluctant to give up those powers with direct policy and international implications. The appeals and traffic rights negotiating functions were accordingly retained in government hands.

How the CAA system compares in performance with that of the ATLB is a matter which will be considered later. Before moving on, however, it is worth summarizing the evolution described above and the major features of the new agency. Justifications for regulation[31] in this area have consistently emphasized the dangers of excessive competition. Whatever the bases of such arguments,[32] their durability has served to focus debate (at least until very recently) on 'how to regulate' rather than 'whether to regulate'. As a result, this has been a field in which some attention has been given to the question of agency design. There were clear reasons why other types of institution were deemed inappropriate – the tribunal had been a failure and the department lacked independence.

The new CAA was established as a public corporation. This, it was thought, would both force the Government to make clear its policies on aviation and allow those heading the agency to 'speak on and for aviation with greater freedom than civil servants'.[33] In spite of resistance in Whitehall and in the Civil Service unions to this hiving-off of functions and personnel, the CAA was staffed not by civil servants but by people on independent contracts. This had been seen by *Edwards* as necessary to attract regulators of sufficient calibre. It was also intended to underline the need for skills and loyalties that were directed to civil aviation rather than to general public service.[34] The balance of expertise between agency and department was changed dramatically. Instead of the staff ratio of 25 at the ATLB to 150 at the Board of Trade, this was reversed. In the early 1970s there were around 160 CAA staff devoted to economic and licensing matters compared to a skeletal 30 in the Department.

The CAA was created with a small in-house legal section and a number of economists were set to work on regulatory issues. Over the years a notable aspect of the balance between these two professions has been the manner in which economic argumentation has gained in currency as the CAA has become more experienced. In the early days the agency made policy with close reference to relevant legal provisions and then consulted the economists. The assumption by 1980 was that the economic merits of different arguments would be assessed at each stage of the policy-making process and not just by economists. The generalist policy-makers had educated themselves in what was seen as the dominant discipline.

What made the CAA a 'constitutional innovation',[35] however, was its combination of functions and techniques. Not merely was it made responsible for economic and safety regulation, advice on airports and the provision of air traffic control services, it combined public trial-type hearings with policy-making and did so under ministerial control. It sought to gain the best of a number of worlds where direct ministerial regulation was not feasible, where deregulation was not on the cards and where the tribunal had failed. Let us consider how it fared.

2 The Agency in Operation

The CAA and Government

As noted above, the Edwards Committee saw the written policy guidance system as the key to the CAA regulatory system, the way to yoke the powerful agency to the government machine. By 1980, however, the policy guidance system had been abolished. What went wrong, and where did this leave the agency?[36]

Until 1977 the guidance served a useful purpose in a number of respects. It replaced appeals and traffic rights to become the new medium of governmental control, it provided a framework for the CAA's own case-law and policy-making, and it allowed longer-term policies to be developed on the basis of research and a developing expertise.

The decline of the guidance system began in the Spring of 1976 when Peter Shore, the Labour Secretary of State for Trade, issued a revised policy to the CAA. Paragraphs 7 and 8 of the new guidance bridled the CAA in one major respect: they ruled out competition on long-haul scheduled services in favour of 'spheres of interest' for British Airways (BA) and British Caledonian Airways (B.Cal.). In particular, the CAA was instructed to revoke the licence that it had granted to Laker Airways in 1975 and which allowed that airline to operate the first 'Skytrain'. This was a new type of 'no frills' cheap scheduled service that was to run from London to New York on a walk-on, no- reservation basis. Mr Shore, moreover, decided to withdraw Laker's designation under the UK/USA air services agreement so as to deprive Laker of the traffic rights necessary to operate Skytrain.

Mr Freddie Laker took the matter to the Court of Appeal[37] where Lord Justices Denning, Roskill and Lawton were essentially in agreement in declaring both that the contentious paragraphs went beyond Mr Shore's powers and that the Secretary of State was not entitled to withdraw designation until the existing CAA licence expired. Guidance, said Lord Denning, could supplement the CAA's statutory objectives; it could not replace them. Not only did this guidance contradict the CAA's statutory objectives by imposing excessive restrictions on competition, but, in issuing peremptory instructions to the CAA it constituted direction rather than guidance. It thus fell foul of the statutory limitations that were placed on the direction power by the 1971 Civil Aviation Act. As for the withdrawal of designation, their Lordships said that the prerogative power could not be used to circumvent the provisions of the 1971 Act. Parliament could not have set up an elaborate licensing code, subject to limited powers of direction, only to allow the Crown to render licences useless by use of the prerogative power.

After the Court of Appeal's decision, the feasibility of the guidance system was called into question both in Parliament[38] and in the agency. At the CAA, senior staff sat round the table and, literally, began to delete those other sections of the guidance that they feared would be open to legal attack.

Another development also brought the value of the guidance into question. CAA staff were becoming capable of producing their own guidance. Especially after 1977, the CAA produced a number of 'brown books', termed 'consultative documents', 'discussion documents' or 'reviews of policy', to deal with various aspects of policy. Those papers gave the industry far more precise indications of relevant policies than the written guidance was ever able to do. Different layers of material emerged. Some offered 'licensing criteria' of a specific kind, others set down general regulatory philosophies.

Given such developments – the precarious position of the written guidance system and the growing role of informal CAA rule-making – the Conservative Government of 1979 came to consider abolishing the guidance system. The view of senior CAA staff was that guidance was necessarily flawed. It took so long to produce that, in a fast-changing climate, it was always likely to be out of date by the time it was issued. Within the Department, the lawyers were by no means confident that guidance of useful precision could be drafted whilst avoiding judicial review. The two views combined so as to favour abolition of the guidance and its replacement with an instruction that the CAA should publish its own policy statements. In addition, there would be expanded statutory objectives for the CAA to observe.

Abolition, together with new instructions and revised statutory objectives, came with the Civil Aviation Act 1980. Such a change, however, raised issues that went beyond civil aviation. On the one hand it could be argued that the written guidance system had emerged as a peculiarly appropriate method of linking regulatory bodies into government[39] and that it was wrong to dismiss the device. On the other hand there were questions as to the utility of the guidance system in an area of rapid economic change.

Experience in civil aviation indicates that abolition may have been based on unrealistic assumptions. The CAA showed itself clearly to be capable of publishing its own statements of licensing policy, but the issue remained – did abolition leave an appropriate system of government control?

On this question, two points can be taken as given. First, Ministers will exercise final control over civil aviation licensing policy by some means or other and, second, contentious decisions will continue to occur in aviation licensing. Since 1980 the evidence is that the Government has been far less reluctant than formerly to interfere with CAA decisions and that it is resorting to tactics that were familiar to the ATLB. Whereas in the period 1972–80 no appeal was allowed by the Secretary of State against a CAA decision, 18 appeals succeeded either wholly or in part between 1980 and April 1987. The CAA has also expressed concern in at least one case[40] that the licensing procedure has been pre-empted by the traffic rights negotiating process.

The danger lies in repeating the history of the ATLB. Some staff of the CAA believed in 1980 that to abolish the guidance was to set the agency free. As further CAA decisions are overruled on political grounds, such optimism appears misplaced.[41]

The CAA and the Courts

For lawyers, the implications of the CAA system of regulation are various. As will be seen below, some comfort may be taken from evidence that trial-type procedures may have a more flexible regulatory function than traditional theory would have us believe. On the other hand, less clear conclusions may be drawn about the role of the judiciary in relation to an agency like the CAA.

The Court of Appeal's decision in the *Skytrain* case was critical in restructuring the machinery for ministerial control over the CAA. In such terms the courts have been important in CAA regulation. On the other hand, it should be noted that in the period 1972–87 a CAA licensing decision has been contested in a court of law only once – and then unsuccessfully. The *Skytrain* case itself involved a challenge to the Minister rather than to any act or decision of the CAA. It could thus be said that the judges have exercised little direct supervision of the CAA.

The CAA's freedom from legal attack is remarkable given the degree to which other British agencies have been subjected to judicial review. Why should this be so? It cannot be said that the legislators deliberately went out of their way to insulate the CAA from judicial review. The authority does have powers and duties of some breadth but so do other, more frequently reviewed bodies.

Those in the industry give a number of reasons for their reluctance to involve the courts. First, they suggest a general reluctance to impose expense and delay on the decision-making process when in the longer term this may not affect an operator's overall share of routes – a 'swings and roundabouts' philosophy. Second, this is a close community in which operators have a continuing relationship with other airlines, the Department and the CAA. There may then be times when it is inopportune to go to law. In any event, a victory at law might achieve little, since an error by the CAA or Secretary of State might well be corrected in a re-made decision. Third, and perhaps most importantly in recent years, airlines have come to view the 'political' appeal as all-important and so have lacked the motivation to challenge CAA decisions or procedures. If dissatisfied with a CAA decision on procedural or substantive grounds, an operator will appeal to the Trade Secretary rather than go to the courts. Since the Secretary of State can call on the CAA to expand its reasons for decision on appeal, a further incentive to pursue this route is offered.

Trial-type Procedures and CAA Policies
Although aviation regulation is largely carried out beyond the view of

the courts, solicitors and barristers are involved on a daily basis in CAA licensing decisions. The CAA regularly holds public hearings which employ those procedures that are commonly associated with trials. What is notable about this agency is how it has attempted to incorporate trial-type procedures into its broader decision and policy-making processes.

Again it is useful to bear in mind the distinction between the *tribunal* and the *regulatory agency*. At the root of the ATLB's failings was its self-image as a judicial tribunal. It made little attempt to probe regulatory issues in the depth that would have allowed consistent standards or longer-term strategies to be developed. It fell back on the public hearings system but was increasingly accused of acting in a 'capricious' manner.

Has the regulatory agency improved on the tribunal's performance? Arguably the CAA has put trial-type procedures to more intelligent use than the ATLB ever did. It has done so by adopting two strategies that were either not available to or were ignored by its predecessor. The first of these has been to use the trial-type procedure in harness with a variety of other methods of decision and policy-making. The second has been to develop different packages of procedures in response to different kinds of regulatory issue. These strategies recognize certain limitations of the trial-type process: its dependence on cases that recur yet its inability to process large numbers of cases; its shortcomings as a forum for planning future policies and its lack of a broad consultative base.

On the recurrence of similar cases, it has been argued by some commentators[42] that, although it is reasonable to expect trial-type procedures to produce durable standards where issues do recur, it is unrealistic to expect this where most cases are highly individual in character. Examination of CAA decisions and policies on certain issues does, indeed, show that varying techniques have been seen as appropriate to different issue-types. Thus, questions on long-haul scheduled-service competition policy have been dealt with very differently from those on short-haul competition or cargo charters.

Long-haul competition throughout the seventies involved a relatively small number of highly contentious cases. Relevant policy owed a great deal to the written policy guidance issued by the Government and each case was dealt with ad hoc. Case-law, as such, failed to develop because each issue possessed highly individual characteristics. Any attempt to have developed standards through the trial-type process would have been upset by changes in the policy guidance. In any event, an airline's chances of flying a particular route were largely governed by the Government's political position and the Department's success in negotiating traffic rights.[43] Expectations both of the CAA policy-making and of the trial-type process were low on all sides although the public hearings procedures of the CAA were seen as useful in giving the airlines their 'day in court'.

In contrast, issues relating to route entry on short-haul routes have been less politically contentious but far greater in number. This has been an area in which the same issues have recurred and where more has been possible to structure CAA discretion by developing standards through case-law. CAA strategy in this area has also indicated how the regulatory agency can supplement trial-type procedures.

Early in its life the CAA sought to apply to particular short-haul cases the sometimes contradictory statements to be found in the Civil Aviation Act 1971 and the guidance. Soon, however, more detailed considerations played a part in public hearings as principles emerged from cases. One such principle was developed early in the 1970s: that an operator's initial investment on a route would be protected for a 'honeymoon' period.[44] As more cases were decided, the CAA developed its position and made rulings on such matters as the weight to be attached to promises of service from the non-operating licence-holder who objected to a potential competitor's licensing application.[45] These were middle-range issues: there was some recurrence of common elements but intermittent factors intruded. Up to 1974, therefore, individual decisions supplemented the guidance but on relatively few topics did well-defined standards govern decisions. Thus, no specific period was set down for the 'honeymoon', nor was there a set period by the end of which viability had to be achieved on a route.

At that time the CAA had not developed its expertise sufficiently to move from ad hoc policies and imperfect case-law towards a planned strategy. The first step in such a direction came in the mid-1970s when the CAA conducted a series of studies in relation to short-haul services and fares. As a result, CAA staff became willing to supplement the case-law with rules of their own. Those rules emerged in March 1976 as the 'Criteria for Licensing Competing Airlines on Short-Haul Routes'.

These criteria gave a more precise outline of policies than was available previously. They were, for example, more clear on the honeymoon. New services would have to cover direct operating costs within a year of first operating and would have to become fully remunerative in the third year. As licensing guides, the criteria brought some stability and have been subject to relatively minor changes over the years. Exceptions to them have been allowed (usually to meet special needs) but as they have been applied more frequently in trial-type hearings they have served to focus arguments.

In 1979 another level of guidance to short-haul license applicants was provided when the CAA published 'Domestic Air Services: A Review of Regulatory Policy'.[46] This document did not offer more criteria but described itself as a consultative document setting down the CAA's findings following an internal review of policy. This discussion of the CAA's regulatory philosophy provided a background against which the criteria, the policy guidance and the statutory objectives could be read. At public hearings, barristers would refer to any of these classes of document. The short-haul area was thus marked by a reliance on the trial-type process but it involved detailed support in the form of rule-making and consultative publications.

A further contrast in issue-types is presented by the cargo charter field where, over the years, large numbers of similar applications have had to be processed and the CAA has taken steps to streamline the use of trial-type proceedings. The first move was to liberalize regulation and to issue licences at general, multi-party hearings held on an annual basis. These hearings took on a restricted role as policy-making was removed to the consultative and research process. By 1977, operators who applied for freight licences did so not with an eye to any case-law but to the CAA's own consultation documents. During that year the CAA took the further step of issuing all 'standard' freight licences for five-year periods and it signalled the end of the large annual freight hearing. Here was a field in which recurrence of similar issues led not to emphasis on the trial-type procedure but to its phasing-out.

These brief sketches of issue-types and procedural responses in different areas, demonstrate how the CAA has reacted to the limitations of the trial-type process. Depending to some extent on the degree of recurrence in an area, different expectations and procedural packages have resulted. Where there has been a need and ability to consider a wide range of views and plan future policies this task has been allocated to the rule-making and consultative processes. The use of trial-type procedures in harness with other devices, as encountered particularly in the short-haul and cargo charter fields, has brought with it another advantage. This might be called the 'layering' of discretion.

Layering here refers to a decision-making body's practice of structuring its discretion at a number of different levels and by reference to different types of pronouncement. Thus the applicant for a CAA licence may look not merely to the principles of past case-law but to the statute, the written policy guidance (now succeeded by the CAA's own Statement of Policies on Air Transport Licensing) and to the CAA's own discussion documents, published criteria, consultative documents and reviews of policy.

The advantages of layering in regulatory decision-making are principally twofold. First, the reasoning behind individual decisions is rendered more intelligible when statements of broader policies and regulatory philosophies are available to affected parties. Second, where issues and contexts are rapidly changing (for example for political, economic or technical reasons) layering can create a greater continuity and consistency in policy-making. A change at one level will often be bridged at another policy level.

This is the significance of the CAA as an institution. In going beyond the trial-type process and operating at a number of decision and policy-making levels, it has rendered issues justiciable in a way that the ATLB could not. There is an irony here. Commentators most readily demand the development of standards from bodies that are modelled on courts and tribunals (usually with the expectation that this will be done through case-law). In practical regulation, however, it is the body with extensive resources – the regulatory agency as opposed to the tribunal or court – that may be most able to develop and sustain standards and policies.

The CAA and Expertise
The CAA, with six times more staff, is clearly able to take a broader approach to licensing than the ATLB found possible. The CAA has thus created briefing procedures so that the panels that hear licensing cases do not do so in a vacuum but are able to take into account detailed analyses of such matters as safety, foreign relations, traffic rights and current policies. It has a vastly improved data-collection system and can question airline costings and traffic data in some

detail. The CAA can develop and sustain medium and longer-term policies in a way that the ATLB at no time attempted. Its multi-layered decision and policy-making can take on board arguments of a detailed and technical nature. Similarly, the agency can take a more positive role than the tribunal in relation to new developments. Thus the CAA took a major part in introducing Advanced Booking Charters (ABCs) and Advanced Purchase Excursion (APEX) fares on the North Atlantic in the early seventies. It changed scheduled-service licences to allow 50 per cent charter capacity and deregulated inclusive tours and cargo charters.

All such developments, as well as a sensitivity to the burdens imposed by regulation, are the kinds of fruit that might be expected (indeed demanded) of a powerful agency. There are, however, at least two general arguments why expenditure on such expertise can be money wasted. These arguments go beyond mere criticism of the agencies' accountability and constitutional status. The first is made by Stephen Breyer[47] in relation to US civil aviation regulation. Paraphrased, it says that civil aviation is a structurally competitive industry, that it is a mismatch to apply classical price and entry regulation to such an industry and that it would be better to deregulate and rely on antitrust laws.

It is not the concern of this chapter to review the arguments for and against regulating entry and prices in civil aviation. The general point is that there is a relationship to be borne in mind between the level of resources worth applying to regulation and the type of regulatory regime sought. Deregulation strongly implies the appropriateness of streamlined and less sophisticated institutions and systems of regulation. A related point is that, in the absence of good market-based data (an absence common in regulation almost by necessity), regulation is a fairly blunt instrument – Breyer calls it a 'blunderbuss not a rifle'.[48] This means that increased fine-tuning and increased expertise will often fail to yield improved results. There is accordingly a limit to the amount of money worth spending on CAA expertise and this varies according to both the type of regulation attempted and the degree of fine-tuning that is feasible.

The second general argument questions how an agency's expertise is put to use. There is little point in having even an optimally expert CAA if governments allow it no scope. If Ministers overrule expert agency decisions and interfere beyond a certain point then the rationale for the agency is lost – the government may as well do away with the dog if it is going to bark itself. The resolution of this point lies in governmental attitudes – the task of commentators is to identify cases where agency expertise is wasted and where those bodies are used as 'fronts' for government.

3 Conclusions

The record of the CAA since 1972 demonstrates the problematic position of the regulatory agency within the British Constitution. This agency was innovatory and ambitious in its combination of powers, it has succeeded on some fronts but on others is highly vulnerable.

The CAA's strengths are made clear by juxtaposing it with the ATLB. CAA licensing has indicated that one way out of the justiciability problem is to combine trial-type procedures and public hearings with a variety of other processes. It has shown that attention to issue-types and the tailoring of procedural packages does offer greater potential than more strict reliance on trials. Again, it has been demonstrated that regulatory bodies that have to choose between competing parties do not have to give up hope of developing policies, of planning for the future or of engaging in consultation. The layering of discretion offers further assurance to those who demand both coherence and consistency from regulatory decision-makers. Layering offers an answer also to those who see trials and case-law as the only sources of administrative justice.

It is on the political front, however, that the CAA is exposed. In three respects it has difficulties. It may have no job to do, it may be unable to carry out its appointed task and it may not be allowed to do the work that it has been given.

The CAA would have no job to do if the Government opted for full deregulation. Already the CAA has decided to modify its policies so as to suspend controls over entry and over the details of fares on domestic scheduled services. There is, of course, nothing inherently wrong in the self-imposed sunset. It would, however, be wasteful for the CAA merely to anticipate government policies rather than exercise its own judgement and develop its own strategies. Increased deregulation would also make it wasteful to fund and run the CAA at levels appropriate to a highly interventionist regulatory regime. Should the CAA be perceived by those with political power as being unable to regulate efficiently then it would soon come under attack. There are few signs, however, that such criticisms are yet widespread. What disagreements there have been have tended to focus on particular aspects of the CAA's policies rather than its competence.[49]

Finally, there is the issue of greatest concern. The CAA, like other agencies, is subject to government control. As has been said above, its expensive operation and its powers of judgement only have value within the governmental system in so far as the government in power respects the CAA's spheres of decision and policy-making. The contribution of the policy guidance system lay in insulating the CAA to some extent from the more disruptive forms of government interference – by appeals, traffic rights negotiations or other more clandestine methods of control. The abolition of guidance has, as a result, left the CAA exposed. The CAA's worth as a regulatory agency now depends upon little more than the restraint of Ministers. Past experience is not reassuring.

9

The Office of
Fair Trading:
Policing the Consumer
Market-Place

Iain Ramsay

The rationale for creating the Office of Director General of Fair Trading in 1973 was to remove the regulation of competition and consumer protection from political involvement, permitting continuity and expertise in the development of policy on a long-term basis. Administrative regulation was justified as a response to the limitations of the judicial and legislative process. This rationale mirrored the US 'New Deal' conception of the regulatory agency as a politically insulated body with broad powers, rationally developing policy on the basis of 'scientific' expertise.[1] Successive Directors General have described the Office as a regulatory agency inviting comparison with the US Federal Trade Commission (FTC).[2] A study of the Office of Fair Trading (OFT) provides, therefore, a valuable opportunity to reflect on the persuasive force of some conventional explanations of regulation which have emerged from the North American literature.

This chapter is divided into two parts. In the first part, I shall describe the role of the Office of Fair Trading in the area of consumer protection. In the second, I shall place this description against the background of theories which attempt to explain the creation, implementation and administration of programmes of government regulation of the market-place. Although I focus on the role of the OFT in the area of consumer protection, some of the discussion is also of more general relevance in assessing the OFT's work in the broader field of competition policy which is discussed in greater depth in chapter 10.

1 Regulatory Origins: the Fair Trading Act 1973

The introduction of the Fair Trading Bill was justified to Parliament as a rationalization of regulation of 'market failures' attributable to abuse of monopoly market power, restrictive practices, information failures and unfair and misleading marketing techniques in the consumer market-place.[3] The major innovation in the Bill was the creation of a central government agency to monitor and police these failures on a continuing basis. At the head of this agency was the new Office of Director General of Fair Trading. A variety of powers and functions was conferred upon this independent and non-political office. In relation to consumer protection he was to have a watching brief over business practices affecting the interests of consumers and power to make recommendations for reform to the Secretary of State.[4] He was also given an important new rule-making initiative to propose regulations for those practices which appeared adversely to affect consumers' economic interests.[5] These proposals would be scrutinized by the newly created Consumer Protection Advisory Committee[6] (CPAC) which might, if it deemed necessary, modify the Director General's proposals, submitting its recommendations to the Secretary of State, who in turn had a discretion to adopt by statutory instrument either the Director General's or Committee's proposals or take no action.[7] Additional functions included the duty to seek assurances from individual traders that they would refrain from persisting in a course of conduct which was detrimental and unfair to the interests of consumers,[8] power to provide consumers with information[9] and a duty to encourage trade association codes of practice.[10]

·The Bill also reorganized the institutional structure of competition policy.[11] The Director General assumed the duties of the Registrar of Restrictive Trading Agreements and came under a general duty to monitor commercial activities in order to be aware of monopolies or uncompetitive practices.[12] He might refer such situations to the Monopolies and Mergers Commission (MMC) and, although given no power to refer potential mergers to the Commission, was to provide expert advice to the Secretary of State on the desirability of making a reference. The Director General therefore became the focal point for monitoring UK competition regulation, a role underlined by the further powers conferred upon him by the Competition Act 1980.[13]

The institutional coupling of consumer protection and competition policy in one agency, following the model of the US Federal Trade Commission, was intended to underline their functional correspondence in contributing to consumer sovereignty in an efficient marketplace. The role of the OFT in maintaining and promoting an effective market mechanism rather than redistributing resources to particular groups is well illustrated by Sir Geoffrey Howe's analysis of the role of the OFT at the time of its creation. 'The sovereignty of the consumer which is the most important element in the operation of the free . . . market . . . requires that the consumer should be adequately informed . . . and protected against unfair or misleading marketing techniques . . . and adequately protected . . . against abuses of market power, monopoly . . . or aspects of imperfect competition'.[14]

The creation of the OFT reflected the Conservative Government's commitment both to more rational long-term planning in government and to enhancing the market mechanism.[15] This explanation suggests, first, that one important standard for evaluating the output of the agency is that of the extent to which it promotes efficiency in the market: the ability to correct or propose correctives for those market failures where consumers are unlikely to be able to protect themselves through the market or private law. Second, economic analysis ought to play a major role in decision-making.

Analysis of the background to the introduction of the Fair Trading Bill by Roberts[16] suggests, however, a more complex explanation for the creation of the agency and a potentially different understanding of its role than the technocratic one implicit in the above explanation. This alternative draws on an interest-group explanation.

There were no plans for consumer legislation in the Conservative manifesto of 1970. Indeed, one of the first actions of the new Government was the abolition of the Consumer Council. The public resentment over this surprised the Government and sensitized it to the electoral advantages of pro-consumer legislation. The Government was faced therefore with the necessity of developing a consumer policy. The consumer measures of the 1960s, following the recommendations of the Molony Report,[17] had drawn heavily on long-established patterns of regulation[18] and there were no obvious regulatory models which did not appear to be either an electoral gimmick or an admission that the axing of the Consumer Council had been a mistake. It was against this background that the newly created

Central Policy Review Staff (CPRS) were able to play a significant role. They provided ideas to the relevant interdepartmental committee, drawing its attention to the models of the US Federal Trade Commission and the Swedish Market Court. The CPRS also maintained pressure for the new consumer policy and, when it seemed the impetus for new legislation was being lost, helped to convince the Cabinet and the relevant sections of the Department of Trade that consumer issues ought to be integrated with the scheduled reforms of monopolies and mergers legislation. A key factor was, however, the creation in Autumn 1972 of the new Cabinet rank office of Minister for Consumer Affairs. This post was filled by Sir Geoffrey Howe, regarded by many as an energetic reformer. He had several ideas for consumer-law reform and pressed ahead with what were to become the main consumer sections (Parts II and III) of the Fair Trading Bill. The opportunity to integrate these reforms with those revisions of competition policy which were envisaged within the Department in 1972–3, created great pressure for immediate action and there was consequently no opportunity to publish a White Paper on the Fair Trading Bill. There was some hesitation concerning the title of this composite Bill, which, had it been restricted to competition matters, might probably have been rather mundane – for example, the Monopolies, Mergers and Restrictive Practices (Amendment) Bill. The idea of 'fair trading' and a Director General of Fair Trading gave it significantly greater consumer appeal.

Though the enactment of this legislation may thus be viewed as a general response to consumer demand, consumer interest groups played little role in influencing the form of the legislation. The genesis of the Bill had been in reforms of the institutional structure of competition policy. It was fortuitous that the consumer interest coincided with the interests of strong government 'players' in the creation of a more competitive economy. Producer interests lacked strong incentives to oppose the legislation, since the costs of regulation would be spread widely throughout industry and it was possible that many producers might imagine potential benefits from regulation of unfair competition.

The precise form of the regulatory instrument – the creation of a high-profile Director General of Fair Trading with a somewhat open-ended mandate to monitor the consumer market-place – was a shrewd policy choice. The high symbolic effect implicit in the creation of the Office of Director General might reassure the widely dispersed and diffuse consumer interest, providing compensation for the axing of the Consumer Council. Yet it was far from clear exactly how the mandate would be implemented. Within this framework of interest-group conflict an important consequence of the Fair Trading Act 1973 was not solely the alteration of substantive rules but also the creation of a new 'player' in the political game, who might provide a natural coalition partner for consumer groups and a focus for the consumer protection community. Such a role might require significantly different expertise from that envisaged under the market failure rationale.

Structure and Staffing

It is clear from the legislative history of the Fair Trading Act that the OFT was intended to be a departure from the traditional departmental structure and civil service staffing.[19] The Director General, appointed on a five-year term, would have experience 'much wider than that which the normal civil servant is able to obtain'.[20] It was also assumed that specialist 'outsiders' from industry and consumer affairs would be hired for senior positions and that the importance of economic expertise would be reflected in the organizational structure.[21] The first Director General, Sir John Methven, appointed several outsiders to key positions.[22] His rationale was primarily that regulators with detailed knowledge of industry could move more quickly and effectively than those coming fresh to a problem.[23] This mirrors the justification for the US style of government regulation with a small professional bureaucracy and significant interchange of personnel between government, industry and other institutions. In addition, the senior positions in consumer protection were representative of the main constituencies affected by the activities of the Office. This would, it was hoped, provide the Office with credibility in its dealings with these groups.

However, apart from the current Director General himself, Sir Gordon Borrie, the influx of outside expertise to the OFT was relatively small and of limited duration. Since 1976 only one position has been advertised outside the civil service (Director of Consumer Affairs), the present holder being an outsider (Richard Thomas, previously head of resources, National Consumer Council). The office is currently organized on the traditional civil service model with parallel hierarchies for specialists (lawyers and economists) and generalists, and the generalist administrator playing a key role in policy development. One reason for this situation has been the influence of the civil service unions, who have a 'strong understanding' with the Director General that posts will be filled from within the Civil Service.[24] Lawyers play a significant role in consumer protection since the Director General must ensure that any policy or regulatory initiative is within his statutory powers. In addition, they may anticipate potential problems of judicial review in the exercise of the Director's regulatory powers.

It is difficult to measure the effect of staffing patterns on regulatory output. The advantages of civil service staffing are impartiality and stability and the experience of administrators familiar with the special problems of English public administration, 'deciding what to do and getting things done in a political context'.[25] The disadvantages are the lack of information and expertise which necessitates extensive consultation with outside sources (for example trade associations). In addition, there is also in the OFT the problem of a relatively high turnover of staff at a senior level. This is caused by the small size and consequently limited career hierarchy within the agency. Individuals may often be seconded to the Office for a few years before returning to the Department of Trade. It has also been suggested that civil service staffing has weakened its credibility to external constituencies.[26] The much greater interchange of 'outsiders' and 'insiders' in US agencies has led, however, to the system being dubbed 'the revolving door'.[27] Critics have argued that regulators have often been more interested in optimizing their chances of future employment in industry rather than achieving regulatory goals.

Classified as a non-ministerial government department,[28] the agency is headed by an individual Director General rather than a Commission or Board. The concept of a Director General of Fair Trading emerged out of modifications to the powers of the Registrar of Restrictive Trading Practices. The general advantages of individual as opposed to collegial decision-making have been debated at length elsewhere.[29] It is often argued that agencies headed by a single official are more efficient and allow for clearer lines of authority and responsibility.

The Director General is, within his consumer protection mandate, politically autonomous. He is required to prepare an annual report to the Secretary of State for Trade and Industry.[30] In theory the Office might be investigated by a parliamentary Select Committee; in practice this has never occurred. The Office is financed by a separate vote through the Treasury and is therefore subject to the annual budgetary procedure and the financial and manpower constraints imposed by the Treasury. The small size of the Office and the absence of a Minister within the Cabinet may reduce its bargaining power in this annual process. Notwithstanding the lack of active parliamentary monitoring of the Office, it has been reasonably sensitive throughout its history to changes in public and political opinion.

Both Directors General (Sir John Methven and Sir Gordon Borrie) have deliberately fostered a relatively high public profile. They have often used the media to 'sound off' on consumer themes and to develop issues raised by consumer groups. This activity is consistent with the conception of the Director General as a 'political player', who might occasionally act as a coalition partner to pressure groups. The media are regarded as a valuable resource by the OFT, underlining its importance in the regulatory process. If a consumer issue is picked up by the media then the Director General has usually made some response.

It is instructive at this point to mention briefly the role of the National Consumer Council (NCC), established in 1975. This non-departmental consumer advisory body[31] was established to represent the consumer interest, particularly those consumers most vulnerable in the market-place, for example the elderly or low-income groups.[32] The Council has no statutory basis and no legislative powers. It was to be a counterweight to the TUC and CBI in the policy process. In economic terms it was an attempt to overcome the difficulties associated with the political representation of large, diffuse and fragmented constituencies such as consumers.[33] Since it is often difficult within a voluntary system to restrict the benefits of consumer protection (e.g. better information) to those who have paid for the benefits, there will be a tendency for individuals to hide their true willingness to pay for the benefits. They will 'free ride' on the efforts of others.[34] Government subsidy of the NCC coerced the free rider. The aim of the NCC is primarily distributive – to obtain benefits for consumers in the political market-place. Its structure and staffing more closely resemble the 'freewheeling' model originally envisaged for the OFT. The staff are not civil servants and are drawn from a variety of backgrounds. Aware of the difficulties of mobilizing public opinion, its style is media-oriented and campaigning. Given its limited resources this is probably the most cost-effective method of attempting to obtain change. It may often therefore complement the work of the OFT.

2 The Experience of Regulation

The output of the OFT might be divided loosely into two: general law-reform activity and the regulation of individual trading practices. Within the former category are the rule-making initiatives under Part II of the Fair Trading Act 1973; the negotiation of codes of practice; recommendations for specific legislative changes to the Secretary of State; the production of consultative papers and reports; and the provision of consumer information. The latter category includes the power to seek assurances from persistently unfair traders under Part III of the Act, and, since 1974, the monitoring, licensing, and enforcement functions under the Consumer Credit Act 1974.[35] The distinction between individual regulation and general law reform is not completely satisfactory; for example individual adjudication under the Consumer Credit Act may provide an opportunity for making a statement of general policy and Part II regulates individual trading practices. However, the distinction is useful in the context of this chapter for drawing attention to the differing impact of a variety of constraints io the achievement of regulatory objectives.

OFT consumer activity may also be divided into two chronological periods: the crusading and the transitional.[36] The former refers to the early period of the Office (approximately 1973–78) when there was both a strong public opinion and political support behind government intervention in the consumer market-place. The approach was often quasi-legislative, attempting to use the 'command and control' type regulation of the Part II rule-making powers, or the negotiation of codes of practice.

The later transition period (from 1979) describes a more reflective approach to the objectives and instruments of regulation. The OFT is currently searching for a consumer protection role (hence the description 'transition') in an era when consumer protectionism is no longer a major political issue. There is greater interest in harnessing market incentives, for example through the provision of information and in the use of cost-effectiveness studies.[37]

After its creation in 1973 the OFT faced several tasks in carrying out its mandate. First, it had to identify the market problems which it wished to solve. This involved reflection on legislative objectives, diagnosis of potential problem areas and the collection of evidence to substantiate any policy initiative. Second, it had to choose the appropriate regulatory instrument, for example a statutory regulation or code of practice. In the context of public policy-making, resolution of these issues also involved questions of process, for example the degree of public consultation and participation.

All agencies operate within certain internal and external constraints in making these decisions.[38] These include limitations on resources (legal mandate, information, manpower), the requirements of administrative law, organizational problems, and external political constraints. In addition, public bureaucracies, unlike private companies, will rarely have any obvious measure of success. The vaguer the mandate, the greater the likelihood of the development of surrogates, for example the number of licences refused, and also of external pressure-group activity on the agency.[39]

Problem Identification – Law Reform

The first Director General had several important policy choices in this area of consumer protection. For example, he had to identify areas for Part II rule-making and those sectors where codes of practice might be desirable. There was no existing agenda of issues provided by civil servants to incoming directors of the consumer protection branch.[40] The first Annual Report indicated that the Office was concerned to plan these priorities carefully on a long-term basis, and not react to every issue highlighted by the media or individual complaints.[41] Given the rationale for the establishment of the agency, careful planning seemed obligatory. This approach required the development of a sophisticated information system, a clear ranking of objectives and a coherent framework to identify areas of consumer detriment. In practice, however, the attempt at comprehensive rationality in the early years of the OFT was far from complete.

Obtaining reliable and expert information on market problems is extremely costly for an agency like the OFT whose mandate spans many industries. In developing an information base for identifying priorities, the OFT relied heavily on consumer complaints collected by local authorities and Citizens Advice Bureaux.[42] The media also provided a source for early policy initiatives, and the Office quickly established consultative links with trade associations and consumer organizations to supplement this information. Consumer complaints have continued to provide the basis for subsequent OFT initiatives in consumer affairs.

The problems with using this source of data as a guide to problem identification are legion. For example, recorded complaints under-estimate the problems of certain groups (e.g. the elderly or vulner-able), fail to measure 'hidden costs' where consumers may be unaware of problems (e.g. carcinogens, or quality problems of the appropriate level of quality of legal services) and may give an undue influence to private groups in policy development. A further criticism is that a high level of consumer complaints indicates that consumers are already making a market response – through voicing com-plaints.[43] Government intervention in these areas may appear to correct market failures which would in time have been solved in any event by the market, without the potential distortions caused by government intervention.

In using these complaint statistics there seemed to be little attempt to fit them within a coherent economic theory of consumer protection which might identify clearly the source of consumer problems. If a theory did exist it was probably a somewhat muted version of the then dominant 'exploitation theory' which viewed exclusion clauses, advertising and other seller practices as primarily devices to exploit the unequal bargaining power of the consumer.[44] The market-place was an arena in which consumers seemed rarely to have any comparative advantage.

Given the market failure measure of regulatory output outlined on p. 179, it might be argued that this method of problem identification did not always result in an optimal choice of regulatory priorities. For example, the major focus on misleading pricing and bargain offers might be criticized.[45] Many pricing claims relate to low-cost repeat-purchase goods where consumer experience may often provide self-protection. The evaluation of price claims does not involve high search costs and many consumers are sceptical of exaggerated price claims.[46] In addition, price claims are often an important means of market entry and vigorous enforcement of misleading (as opposed to fraudulent) claims might dampen competition. It is relevant to mention in this context that these reasons encouraged the US Federal Trade Commission in the 1970s to transfer resources from the enforcement of misleading pricing to regulation of product quality and performance claims.[47]

It is important, however, to place this complaints-based approach within the political context of the period. First, there was during the early history of the Office, significant political and media pressure on the agency to 'do something' about a number of perceived abuses in the consumer market-place.[48] The media often play a vital role in the emergence of political issues – media coverage often being regarded as a surrogate form of political demand – and there was a continuing series of 'atrocity stories' which stimulated public concern. Against this background, complaints statistics were a relatively low-cost source of initial information. In addition, a response to those areas where consumer dissatisfaction appeared highest served an important political function by symbolizing a response to consumer demand. Given these facts and the limited resources of the agency, a 'scientific' approach to consumer protection was perceived to be neither necessary nor practicable. The political role of consumer complaints suggests that, whatever their technical defects, they will continue to play a role in establishing priorities. It is unlikely that any consumer protection initiative would be regarded as politically practicable if the Office could not refer to a significant body of consumer complaints. Complaints therefore still play an important role. In recent years, however, there has been an interest in integrating 'market failure' analysis into the process of problem identification. This coincides with a decline in political and media interest in consumerism and greater pressures to provide coherent justifications (e.g. through the use of cost-effectiveness analysis) for any policy initiatives.

Second, there was at this time no coherent economic theory of consumer protection beyond bland references to information failures. This was in contrast to the availability of relatively well developed theories in the area of monopolies and mergers. It is only in recent years that the law and economics literature has begun to provide a systematic rationale for government intervention to protect consumers.[49] These factors may partly explain the relatively limited role which the economics branch of the Office has had in the development of consumer protection policy.

Law Reform: The Choice of Instrument

It was anticipated by many in 1973 that the Part II rule-making powers would play a central role in the rational development of consumer policy. For example, those within the agency viewed it as an important measure of output, success to be measured by the ability of the Office to obtain a string of Part II orders.[50] It was assumed that reforms could be achieved through this procedure without the high rule-making costs associated with legislative change. Thus one 'insider' commented that it would be 'speedier and more effective [than parliamentary legislation], when it was necessary to mobilize public opinion, convince politicians of the need for change, draft new legislation, find space in the Parliamentary timetable and have the Bill passed by Parliament'.[51]

In practice, rule-making was initiated by preliminary informal consultation with trade and consumer interests.[52] At this stage the OFT floated the possibility of controlling a practice and obtained information and views on whether there would be substantial opposition to any proposals. A 'dossier' was subsequently prepared to support the reference to the CPAC. This outlined the nature of the practices and provided evidence of their adverse effects upon consumers, arguments in support of the practice (usually referring to material obtained in consultation), references to experience in other countries, the 'balance of arguments' in favour of controls, and the content of the proposed order. These dossiers contained a modest amount of economic and empirical analysis and a limited evaluation of the consequences of alternative regulatory decisions.

The CPAC, a part-time body with few research facilities, was intended to be a 'broad representative group with a wide range of experience.'[53] It was required to include among its members individuals with experience in consumer organizations, trading standards and the supply of goods.[54] In the case of regulatory proposals, it was under a duty to take into consideration represent-ations by those appearing to have a substantial interest in the reference.[55] During legislative debates a variety of metaphors was used to describe the role of the CPAC; as a 'bridge' between the OFT and the Department of Prices and Consumer Protection, as a 'touchstone' of the value of proposals – and as a 'jury'.[56] Certainly its existence appeared to respond partly to an unease at the potential power of the Secretary of State and the Director General of Fair Trading to create new criminal offences by statutory instrument. In its role of 'lay assessor', the committee scrutinized the *vires* of the rule-making initiative, examined whether there was evidence that the practice was relatively widespread and responded to the arguments made by the various intervenors. It primarily provided a focus for interest representation and technical legal scrutiny. In the latter role it was not dissimilar to the traditional function of judicial review.

There was in practice considerable delay between the CPAC report and implementation by statutory order.[57] In one case no order was made. The Secretary of State in several cases engaged in further consultation and continued to take representations from interested groups. The average period between the OFT reference and an order was two years.

By 1976 it was clear that the rule-making powers were a broken reed. Four references had been made in relation to exemption clauses, prepayments in mail-order transactions and shops, disguised business sales and VAT exclusive prices; three had been adopted. No further references have been made, the CPAC has been disbanded and the Director General does not anticipate making any reference in the near future.[58]

Why has Part II rule-making not lived up to its expectations? First, it seems that the OFT had anticipated that the CPAC would give a relatively cursory examination to its proposals and that the Secretary of State would 'rubberstamp' the regulatory recommendations. It has been suggested, for example, that the CPAC was established intentionally with a 'fifth wheel' constitution.[59] This implies a body whose powers and procedures are such that it will neither be effective nor attract a high calibre of membership. Yet neither consequence seems to have occurred in this case since the Committee, notwithstanding its resource limitations, exercised close scrutiny over the references, modifying and in some cases rejecting the Director General's recommendations. For example, in the first reference it rejected drafting which appeared wider than was necessary to correct the mischief.[60] This required the Office to be extremely meticulous in drafting regulatory recommendations, significantly raising rule-making costs. In addition, after submission of the CPAC report to the Department the relevant civil servants reopened the consultation process. They felt that they could not adequately advise the Minister unless they were 'in touch' with the views of interested parties. The Minister after consultation with relevant groups ultimately made a decision on political grounds. This result was perhaps inevitable given the structure of Part II which, although taking the rule-making initiative out of the political arena, left ultimate control with the

Secretary of State. The hesitation to delegate full rule-making powers to the OFT perhaps reflected an unease within the civil service at policy initiatives going outside the traditional departmental structure. One advantage of the structure was that it permitted the Department to ensure that the agency's policy-making was not out of step with the current political temper or other government objectives. This might be contrasted with the greater delegation of rule-making powers to US agencies such as the FTC which resulted in the late 1970s in significant conflicts with the executive branch.

The second reason for failure lay in the requirement that in order to justify a regulatory proposal under Part II, the Office had to demonstrate that a practice had resulted in 'economic detriment' to consumers. It had great difficulty in identifying, measuring and assembling evidence on consumer welfare losses resulting from a practice. Indeed, these problems led to the establishment of an external academic project to investigate the concept of the 'economic interests' of consumers and their policy consequences.[61] It has also been suggested that a third reason was that there had been some hesitation in using the criminal powers which provided the only sanction for breach of a Part II order. The criminal sanction may also have stimulated the close scrutiny of drafting detail by the CPAC. Finally, my researches on Part II have suggested a genuine lack of consensus of view as to the role of the different actors involved. The Department, for example, had not expected the Office to provide a detailed draft order.[62]

The failure of Part II to be a 'reasonably swift and sensitive piece of machinery'[63] probably led the Office to channel greater energy into the development of trade association codes of practice drawn up voluntarily by an association but in consultation and negotiation with the Office. The duty to encourage the development of codes of practice was very much a legislative afterthought, but they have become the main output of the Office.[64] Since 1973 over 20 codes have been negotiated. Common features of these codes are the provision of consumer information, detailed performance standards, the prohibition of 'unfair' practices (e.g. exclusion clauses) and the establishment of redress procedures.

The primary economic justifications for such codes as an alternative to government regulation in this area are the reduction in rule-making and enforcement costs.[65] The main potential costs are those of increased cartelization (particularly in light of its history among trade associations in the UK), and possible restrictions on consumer choice. During the period 1973–79 there was a flourishing market for codes of practice. Trade associations had strong incentives to negotiate codes both to raise a trade's public image and to forestall administrative regulation. Moreover, OFT approval could exempt codes from the scrutiny of the Restrictive Practices Court. It is not surprising, therefore, that in a number of cases, trade associations themselves initiated the process of code adoption.

The development of a code might go through several successive drafts, with negotiations on particular features. After approving a code, the OFT periodically monitors its performance, giving publicity to cases of significant non-compliance, and threatening the possibility of primary legislation[66] or a Part II reference if standards are not improved. The primary characteristic of this style of regulation is therefore that of a continuing 'bargaining process'. Since about 1978 the bargaining power of the OFT has been relatively weak. The change in political climate towards the desirability of consumer regulation makes the threat of legislation or Part II rule-making something of a paper tiger.

There are some relevant procedural issues involved in the negoti-ation of codes. First, the Office of Fair Trading has never issued guidelines for trades on certain key issues in codes. While annual reports have outlined the desirable contents of codes, each code is treated as a separate package. This approach may increase its bargaining power but might be subject to criticism. Second, third parties are not generally involved in code negotiations. This may be justified by the argument that codes have no 'legal effect' and apply only to trade association members. Yet they are clearly not merely private bargains between government and a trade association. Recent proposals have been made to introduce a legislative 'duty to trade fairly'[67] which would be fleshed out through detailed codes of practice drawn up by the OFT in consultation with trade associ-ations. This extension of the scope of codes of practice clearly raises issues concerning the participation of affected groups in the rule-making process. Trade association codes of practices are often described as an example of self-regulation. However, the above description indicates that these codes exist in the shadow of government regulation, and that significant public resources may be channelled into monitoring their performance. The only economic study of their impact suggested that, in general, their benefits exceeded their costs.[68] However, the data on which this conclusion rested were relatively soft and the authors also drew attention to problems of particular sectors, for example used cars. Certainly the social desirability of codes must be assessed against the background of the structure of particular industries. The OFT itself is not optimistic about the efficacy of codes of practice. Yet the limitations on its Part II rule-making powers make codes an important measure of regulatory output, tangible evidence of the activity of the Office in protecting the consumer.

Discussion of codes also draws private groups into the development and implementation of policy. Trade Associations are a continuing source of information on industry practices and attitudes, and dissemination of policy through a trade association may significantly reduce enforcement costs. An association and the Office may be regarded as 'bargaining agents', each attempting to reflect the preferences of its constituency.

Several additional law-reform roles ought to be briefly mentioned. The Office has produced consultative papers and reports on a wide variety of topics, including, for example, used cars, household insurance, home improvements and consumer guarantees. Legislative implementation of reform recommendations in these reports has been a rare occurrence. The Office seems to have been more successful in its information activities – its booklet, *Fair Deal*, has figured on a list of the 15 best-selling paperback books.

A final important area of general reform activity is the role which the Office plays in complementing the market mechanism in areas of new technology. Hirschman[69] has argued that in new markets there may be significant ignorance on *both* sides of the market-place concerning the best way to market a service. The classic mechanism of leaving the market place ('exit') may be deficient in these situations in facilitating the flow of information from consumers to producers. He argues that it might therefore be complemented by consumer 'voice' – providing feedback to producers on consumer preferences. The OFT has attempted to play the role of providing a focus for consumer and producer voices on such issues, for example credit scoring, Electronic Funds transfer. The dangers of this approach are that the representative 'voicers' may not accurately anticipate the market responses, causing potential distortions in the market.

Regulation of Individual Trading Practices
The regulation of individual trading practices involves the Office in a

close relationship with the 'frontline' consumer enforcement agencies in the UK, the Local Authorities Trading Standards Officers. The Office shares joint responsibility with these authorities for the enforcement of the Consumer Credit Act 1974 and depends heavily on local authority cooperation in the exercise of its powers under Part III of the FTA 1973. A central issue in this area therefore, concerns the respective roles of central and local government.

The Consumer Credit Act, described recently by one judge as 'an Act of extraordinary length and complexity'[70] provides a comprehensive and detailed regulation of the consumer credit market-place. In addition to enforcement the OFT monitors and evaluates the impact of the Act, provides interpretation advice to local agencies, particularly on difficult issues or points of national importance, explanatory material for business and consumers, and administers the Act's licensing procedures. Since the licensing net is extremely broad, the establishment and administration of licensing has consumed resources of the Office. By 1983 over 100,000 licences had been granted. The rationale for licensing appears to have been to provide a degree of *ex ante* protection to consumers of credit and a uniform treatment of the variety of differing credit types.[71] It was argued that the high error costs for uninformed consumers in credit transactions and the inadequacy of private law rights to police malpractices justified the requirement of licensing. It seems also to have been intended to have a distributional effect by protecting those most vulnerable in the marketplace.[72]

The Director General has a broad discretion in exercising his quasi-judicial power to grant, refuse, renew and revoke licences.[73] In deciding whether an applicant is a fit person he may make reference to any circumstances appearing to him to be relevant, and the list of grounds which may justify a finding of unfitness includes the open-textured category of 'practices appearing to the Director to be deceitful or oppressive or otherwise unfair or improper (whether unlawful or not)'.[74] Decisions of the Director General may be appealed to the Secretary of State and a further appeal on questions of law may be made to the High Court. There is annually only a handful of appeals to the Secretary of State and during the period 1980–82 only one appeal to the High Court.[75]

I indicated that individual regulation provides an opportunity for policy development. A conception of 'unfair practices' might for example be expected to emerge from the licensing process. During the early years of licensing practice, unfairness was restricted primarily to breaches of existing legal rules. In recent years more complex cases are being investigated which do not involve any clear breach of an existing rule. Whatever the substantive policy emerging from this process it is clear that it is being used to develop rules on unfair consumer practices. Unfair practices revealed by licensing are published in annual reports and press releases.[76] They are regarded merely as guidelines, on the theory that the Office cannot fetter its discretion. However, it is intriguing to speculate whether this process may provide a partial substitute for the general rule-making power in Part II. If this were to occur it would raise questions concerning the opportunity for notice and comment by third parties, the retroactivity of the rules created through adjudication and the binding effect of the rules on the agency.

It is not proposed to discuss at length the effectiveness of licensing as an instrument for regulating unfair trading practices. The OFT seem to regard it as a valuable regulatory weapon.[77] The broad nature and scope of the licensing power make it a powerful bargaining lever in securing compliance with a wide variety of consumer legislation, in chilling potentially unfair behaviour, and deterring unscrupulous operators from entering the legal consumer credit market. It has also been used to secure compensation for consumers notwithstanding the absence of statutory authorization to use it for this purpose.[78] Critics have, however, drawn attention to its high administration and enforcement costs, arguing that it is a blunt and overinclusive approach to regulation of the relatively small minority of unscrupulous traders.[79] It is also argued that the 'chilling effect' of the broad discretionary powers may induce a shift at the margin of reputable financiers into the less regulated area of commercial finance. Finally, it may be difficult to use licensing to protect those most vulnerable in the credit market. Many lenders in low-income markets operate illegally anyway and the consensual nature of illegal moneylending and hesitation of borrowers in these markets to complain, significantly raise enforcement costs.[80] The costs of licensing the whole credit market may draw resources away from a more finely tuned attack against unfair practices in these low-income markets.

The Office has instituted a limited number of test cases under the

Act.[81] In general, however, enforcement through education and advice is regarded as more cost-effective. Resources have been channelled into explaining the complexities of the Act to business. There is a general expectation that most businesses will accept the Office's interpretation and only large organizations with significant resources are likely to be able or willing to challenge this interpretation.

The powers in Part III are intended to reinforce criminal enforcement of trading standards at the local level against traders who have persisted in a course of conduct which is detrimental and unfair to consumers (defined as contraventions of the civil or criminal law). If such a course of conduct is identified, the Director General is under a duty to 'use his best endeavours'[82] to obtain an assurance from the relevant trader that he will refrain from the conduct. If an assurance is refused or subsequently broken then a court order may be obtained. Breach of this order will be contempt of court. Publicity is also given to this procedure, and this may provide an additional deterrent.[83] By July 1984 the Office had obtained 449 assurances. A subsequent court order was necessary in under 5 per cent of cases and in only one case has there been proceedings for contempt of court.[84] In practice the successful operation of these powers depends heavily on information provided by local Trading Standards Departments. Without this input the Office would face an insurmountable information gap in detecting and obtaining evidence of unfair trading. The Office has in turn issued guidelines to local authorities on the application of the statutory criteria, for example concerning the number of contraventions which might constitute 'persistent conduct' and has its own internal guidelines on enforcement. These guidelines are merely one example of the pervasive need which all bureaucracies have to clarify broad discretionary mandates by creating concrete rules which can be understood and administered with relative ease. If the Office is effectively adopting a selective enforcement policy then ought the guidelines to be set out in a formal instrument and consequently give rise to justiciable issues in a court of law? It is impossible in this chapter to discuss this issue at length. The choice of informal versus formal guidelines must involve a complex balancing of rule-making costs and justice concerns.[85] These issues would, however, be relevant to any attempt by a private individual or group to review the exercise of the Director General's discretion in allocating enforcement priorities.[86]

There is no study of the effectiveness of Part III in reducing residual unfair trading not caught by criminal or private enforcement.[87] The Director General is of the opinion that although 'there is no precise way of measuring the extent to which the Part III powers have achieved their objective . . . the general consensus is that Part III is a useful sanction'.[88] The majority of assurances have been sought against small firms or individual traders primarily in the used-car, home improvements, mail order and electrical businesses.[89] The majority of these traders ceased to trade some time after giving an assurance, suggesting the hypothesis that unfair trading may be inefficient. It is also plausible to hypothesize that this pattern of enforcement is cost-effective since the sectors covered include those where consumers may expend large amounts on a single transaction and may have difficulties in measuring product performance, and where sellers may lack incentives (through the repeat purchase mechanism or reputation) to provide consumers with adequate information.[90] Market forces may provide a greater discipline on national firms. The existing pattern may also partly be attributable to the higher costs (evidence, legal resources) in attempting to bring undertakings against large firms which can command sophisticated legal resources. Yet there might be a high deterrence effect from an action (with the attendant publicity) brought against a national business which was trading unfairly.[91]

A major emerging issue in this area concerns the comparative advantage of central and local government in administering Part III. Local authorities argue strongly that they have more information and greater expertise than central government, allowing them to move more swiftly and expertly to eradicate instances of unfair trading. Concern has been expressed by these authorities at the lack of expertise within the OFT in this area of enforcing trading standards. Certainly if the problems addressed by Part III are primarily those of the small trader or 'fly-by-night' and require swift action, local authorities may be better placed to administer the section. In addition the network of information exchange between authorities on trading practices, fostered in part by the Local Authorities Co-ordinating Body on Trading Standards, may deal with the problem of the trader whose activities cover several local jurisdictions.

The Office, however, seems unwilling to relinquish its powers in this area and the Director General gave a prominent place in his 1982 Annual Report to setting out arguments in favour of national enforcement.[92] Citing the severity of potential sanctions under Part III, which necessitated 'due consideration of the evidence at national level' and the need for 'consistent application of principle' throughout the UK, he concluded that 'it would not be feasible or efficient for over 90 separate local authorities to fulfil these objectives.'[93] The argument from consistency loses some of its appeal if those potentially subject to the legislation do not know the internal guidelines on enforcement. Indeed a certain degree of unpredictability may have a 'chilling' effect on the Holmesian 'bad men' operating on the fringes of the market-place. Whatever the judgment on the appropriate enforcement authority, Part III is a potential source of continuing friction between central and local government in the area of consumer protection.

3 Conclusion: The OFT and Theories of Regulation

This brief outline of the OFT's regulatory powers, both in relation to general law reform and individual trade practice, underlines the fact that – like most agencies – regulation is often informal, characterized by negotiation, persuasion and cajoling. It has bargained with individual firms to remove exclusion clauses, used its licensing powers to persuade firms to compensate consumers, and periodically used the media to threaten dire consequences if particular sectors do not improve their practices.[94] Its powers provide a variety of resources and inputs into this process. For example, the Office has shown interest in regulating the continued use of terms excluding liability for death and personal injury which are void under the Unfair Contract Terms Act 1977. Its information sources on the nature and extent of this problem included Trading Standards Officers, Citizens Advice Bureaux, consumer organizations, restrictive trade practice material and consumer credit licensing. In devising a strategy it discounted Part II as too costly. It has attempted, however, to discourage the continued use of void terms through the licensing process, informal pressure on individual firms and requests to trade associations to draw their members' attention to the proscribed terms. In addition it engaged in a publicity campaign to make consumers more aware of those terms. Of particular interest was the attempt to draw on the resources of the legal profession. An OFT lawyer published a note on void terms[95] which drew attention to existing regulations and possible reforms. It concluded by noting the important role which legal advisors played in ensuring that their clients did not use void terms and appealed for contributions from the profession on the appropriateness of further regulation.[96]

The potential economic advantage of informal regulation in achieving a cost-effective level of regulation must be weighed against the danger of regulation becoming *ad hoc* and circumventing procedural safeguards in legislation. Achieving results in particular situations may become more important than the development of clear rules or policies. Several commentators argue that this has occurred in the Office's administration of competition policy, where negotiation and informal settlements are the dominant style of regulation.[97]

Which if any of the various theoretical explanations – public interest, economic, or capture theories – help in understanding the origins and subsequent patterns of the Office of Fair Trading? First, the contrast of the public interest and economic theory draws attention to the ambivalent role of the Director General as both a technocrat and a 'political player'. The tension between those roles seems to underlie the origins and subsequent history of the Office in the area of law reform. For example, the economic theory of regulation suggests limitations on 'scientific' techniques such as cost-benefit analysis, on their own, generating reform. The most effective way of bringing about changes may be through political pressure groups. If an issue is picked up by a group then it becomes a legitimate political objective. An example of this phenomenon is prepayments and insolvency, where the combination of pressure-group activity and continuing media exposure ensured that any proposal made by the Office might encounter a favourable legislative response. The ultimate dominance of political considerations in the policy-making process suggests also, perhaps, that the traditional civil service staffing patterns of the Office may give it advantages in the political game over other non-departmental agencies.

Jaffe commented in 1955 that 'the autonomy of "expertness" as an objective determinant of policy is, I am afraid, an illusion. Policy making is politics'.[98] While that may reflect a law professor's hyperbole it does underline the difficulties of implementing in practice the technocratic model of policy-making underlying the original conception of the OFT, and achieving significant reforms outside of politics. Whether such a model is, in any event, desirable involves difficult value judgments beyond the scope of this paper.

There are also several problems in applying capture theories to the OFT. It is necessary, for example, to identify by whom the agency has been captured. In the case of the OFT there might be several candidates – the civil service, trade associations, consumers, small business. Detailed analysis would be required of individual areas of the Office's activity to test the 'capture' hypothesis. There has been to date almost no attempt at this type of study. The only economic evaluation of codes of practice found little evidence to support or refute the application of capture theories to trade associations.[99] It seems in general implausible that capture theories will have significant power to explain the behaviour of general purpose regulatory bodies, although they may be more accurate in predicting the actions of single-industry agencies.

The economic theory has the merit of highlighting the political pressures on an agency. The literature on regulatory failure has drawn attention to the information and expertise problems facing an agency in regulatory implementation and its difficulties in measuring success.

The problem of information is partly addressed in the UK by the close central-local government cooperation in the area of consumer protection. The Office of Fair Trading is, for example, better placed than the US Federal Trade Commission to obtain reliable information on the existence of unfair trade practices. The importance of this information suggests the value of the continuing development of a sophisticated information base. Information and expertise, taken together with limitations on mandate, help to explain much of the informal style of regulation and the importance of securing the cooperation of private groups in policy implementation. Individualized bargaining may conserve resources and 'fine-tune' a broad legal mandate to accommodate the great diversity of its regulatory domain. If bargaining costs are not high, for example in dealings with a representative trade association, then informal bargaining may achieve a cost-effective level of regulation. If a bargaining agent does not exist then the media may play an important role in communicating the Office's demands to widely dispersed groups. Alternatively a media campaign may reinforce individual bargaining. The pervasiveness of this style of regulation indicates the need for greater attention to determine whether the bargaining model achieves an effective or just system of regulation.

A recognition of the information and expertise limitations on the Office in the regulation of individual trade practices suggests that greater attention might be paid to a systematic analysis of the comparative advantages of local authority regulation and the desirability of providing greater incentives for additional private regulation (for example through class actions and public interest actions). There are, for example, no compelling arguments of expertise or 'polycentricity' against the increased use of the judicial process by private individuals or groups to protect consumers' economic interests. Further research is clearly needed on the optimal balance of private and public enforcement of regulatory programmes – a matter upon which we have no coherent theory.[100] An awareness that such private actions may often be a form of political participation suggests that reforms might also be directed to overcoming the 'free rider' problems affecting the representation of consumers in the regulatory process.

Measuring success has been a continuing problem for the Office, particularly in the general area of law reform. Assuming a broad test of cost-effectiveness in remedying market failures, there are often difficulties in measuring 'effectiveness'. Obvious surrogates (for example, reductions in consumer complaints) are often neither valid nor reliable guides to changes in consumer welfare, and it is difficult to measure the benefits of greater information or intangibles such as consumer confidence in markets. There is a need for more economic research to attempt to develop measurable proxies for the general benefits of protecting consumers' economic interests. In the absence of such research there is the danger that the agency, operating in an environment hostile to regulation, may concentrate its activities on those areas where success can be most easily measured. The difficulties of measurement also highlight once again the fact that decisions on regulatory intervention may often turn ultimately on difficult value judgements based on empirical uncertainty. On whom ought the burden of proof to be placed in making these decisions – regulators or the advocates of the benefits of markets?

Finally, dramatic discussions in the theoretical literature concerning 'capture' and 'failure' may draw attention away from the necessity in this area to take a comparative institutional approach: imperfect central government regulation must be compared with imperfect markets and private law regimes, and imperfect local authority enforcement. Ultimately, 'in the real world a choice among institutional arrangements for dealing with social problems is a choice among highly imperfect alternatives'.[101] There is no first-best solution.

The Monopolies and Mergers Commission: Competition and Administrative Rationality

Paul Craig

The object of this chapter is to describe and assess the work of the Monopolies and Mergers Commission (the MMC). The role of the MMC cannot, however, be considered completely separately from that of the other main competition agencies: the Office of Fair Trading (the OFT) and the Restrictive Practices Court (the RPC). There are three main reasons why such cross-referencing is necessary. First, there are direct institutional links between the OFT and the MMC. Second, to exclude the RPC from consideration would preclude any assessment of the coherence of competition policy as a whole, and third, it is useful to compare the differing types of institutional mechanism that are used in the regulation of competition.

The chapter will be divided into two parts. In the first section the history of competition policy will be briefly reviewed, bringing into focus the political, social and economic forces which shaped this policy. An understanding of why Britain began to regulate competition in 1948 is integral to a proper appreciation of competition policy and the role of the MMC. The first section will also include a brief overview of the main substantive principles governing the present law. Without some grasp of the complexities of the current statutory framework, the issues to be considered later within the chapter would not be comprehensible. The second section of the paper will focus upon certain aspects of UK antitrust[1] policy. This will perforce be selective. The aim will be to concentrate upon those aspects of competition which have wider-ranging implications for regulation as a whole. Three main questions will be considered. First, how rational is the current institutional division of functions between the different competition agencies? Second, how far can, and how far should, the MMC proceed through rule-making as opposed to *ad hoc* discretion? The issue of how far the regulation of competition is justiciable permeates both of these questions in differing ways. Finally, what is the system of control and accountability within which the MMC operates; what are the functions of the executive and the courts within this area, and how do they interrelate with those of the MMC?

1 A Brief History of Competition Policy

The Genesis of Competition Policy

To an outsider more familiar with, for example, the antitrust laws of the United States, the competition policy of the United Kingdom might well appear to be a web of Byzantine complexity. The statutory provisions are long, complicated and technical. Different institutions adjudicate or administer discrete aspects of the law. Formal divisions are drawn between the authority of the MMC, the RPC and the OFT. In considering why UK antitrust law has evolved in this way, two central points must be borne in mind. First, our degree of commitment to competition policy has never been as strong as it has in countries such as the United States. Second, partly as a corollary to this, the fortunes of antitrust have been closely wedded to other matters of social and political choice. Nowhere are these two themes more readily apparent than in the emergence of antitrust policy.

Regulation of monopoly power and competition policy did not begin with the first modern statutory regulation of 1948. There were both common law and statutory provisions long before then.[2] However, the common law was, by the end of the nineteenth century, almost wholly ineffectual in promoting competition. For example, although it is true that the courts developed the restraint of trade doctrine, its application in the leading cases served to ensure that preservation of competitive equilibrium was not to be the prime objective. Reluctance to interfere with a bargain even if the direct effect was both to injure the economic interests of another, and to harm the competitive order, reached its apogee in the case-law on conspiracy. A horizontal price-fixing and market-allocation scheme, backed up by exclusionary tactics employed against those unwilling to submit, was held not to be an illegal conspiracy at common law.[3] Only if there were illegal ends or unlawful means, would the combination be proscribed. In the absence of malicious intent to injure one's rivals, or the presence of unlawful means such as intimidation, the defendants' actions were a perfectly legitimate exercise in trade protection.

It would, however, be misleading to represent the nineteenth and early twentieth centuries as unequivocally laissez-faire in their attitudes towards competition. Contemporaneous with general judicial and statutory abstinence, a more interventionist attitude developed towards the regulation of market power when it appeared in the form of a natural monopoly. Private companies which provided services such as water, gas, electricity, turnpikes, railways etc., usually did so on the basis of statutory regulation. It was normal in such instances for the Board of Trade, or some other department, to have direct control over the rates charged. The judiciary also intervened in certain areas where a corporation possessed a monopoly imposing an obligation to charge no more than a reasonable price;[4] the precise ambit of this doctrine was, however, unclear.[5]

Notwithstanding the piecemeal form of this regulation, it was to be some considerable time before Parliament attempted any more comprehensive control of market power. There was, to be sure, some governmental initiative shortly after the First World War but it proved shortlived. A Committee on Trusts was appointed in 1918; but recommended control only by publicity, and was mindful of the benefits which could accrue from large-scale organisation.[6] In 1919 the Profiteering Act was passed, rendering the earning of an unreasonable profit an offence. A Standing Committee on Trusts was established to administer the legislation, but its powers were weak and the Profiteering Act lapsed in 1921. The prospect of any further legislation received a further setback with the report of the Balfour Committee, which considered that there was no urgent case for immediate legislation to deal with the problems arising from market power.[7]

The reasons for the absence of intervention were eclectic. One of the most important was the altered perception of competition itself. The First World War brought many changes. During the war, industry had been forced to cooperate, and to share industrial secrets on a level hitherto unmatched. Cooperation on a 'marvellous scale'[8] had been the order of the day. Post-war prosperity failed, however, to materialize, industry found itself with excess capacity, and unemployment rose. There was a feeling that the ordinary processes of competitive equilibrium were not automatically self-correcting at either the micro or the macro level. While Keynes was pointing to the possible macroeconomic solution, a new movement based upon the concept of rationalization began to challenge hitherto orthodox beliefs concerning the micro level. Rationalization was never a sharp-edged doctrine, and its meaning could alter depending upon the personal view of the protagonist or opponent. Two of the most important aspects of the doctrine, however, were the application of more scientific methods of management, and a belief in the efficiencies of size whether achieved by merger or internal growth. Competition was no longer viewed as a necessary good. Cries of ruinous, destructive or unfair competition became increasingly common, as business attempted to justify cartelization to achieve their ends where merger or internal growth were inappropriate. Supporters of rationalization saw it also as a bulwark against socialism.[9] Rationalizers urged that the capitalist system could be preserved and revitalized provided that the main tenets of their philosophy were adopted.

Incentives to increase both plant and firm size came also from experience abroad. German and American corporations operating on a large scale were juxtaposed to the smaller, less efficient British entrepreneurs. The need to enlarge firms in order to be able to compete on the international level was a constantly recurring theme. Foreign experience began to have a more direct impact upon domestic firms through the increasing presence of both American and German corporations and individual managers within British industry.

The eventual passage of legislation after the Second World War owed its origins partly to a further change in attitude towards competition and partly to other governmental policies canvassed during or immediately after the war. As early as 1943, the Board of Trade had established a department to examine the problems involved with post-war reconstruction, the investigation of which embraced, *inter alia*, competition policy. It was argued that British industry would perforce have to become more efficient and that the continuance of restrictive agreements could be an impediment to such development. Such an approach did not find immediate favour with the Board of Trade, but the stimulus for a change of direction was given added force by the White Paper on employment policy.[10] It was felt that the object of securing full employment might be jeopardized by the existence of monopoly power and restrictive practices, both of which could lead to higher prices and profits rather than to enlarged output and increased employment.[11]

It was this link between competition policy and that of full employment which was most important in securing the passage of the first, general, modern piece of antitrust legislation: the Monopolies and Restrictive Practices (Inquiry and Control) Act 1948.

The Scope of the Legislation[12]

The title of the 1948 Act accurately conveys the intention of the framers of the legislation. Monopoly was not being proscribed or condemned. It was being investigated. To this end the Act established the Monopolies and Restrictive Practices Commission, consisting primarily of part-time members. A body outside the normal departmental framework was felt to be better suited to the investigatory nature of the work, and such an institutional choice facilitated the involvement of non-civil servants who possessed specialist expertise. The legislation applied, essentially, to those cases in which at least one-third of the goods of a particular description were supplied by one or more persons.[13] The Act specifically included oligopoly and cartels,[14] provided that the firms in question controlled the requisite share of the market. Most of the early reports of the Commission concerned cartels.[15] If a monopoly situation was found to exist, the Commission then had to determine whether it might operate against the public interest[16] and, if so, to suggest remedies. The report and recommendations were forwarded to the Board of Trade, a department of central government, which then determined what action should be taken. In addition to the power to investigate particular industries, the Commission was also empowered to undertake more general investigations. Its general report on Collective Discrimination[17] laid the groundwork for the Restrictive Trade Practices Act 1956, by identifying certain types of horizontal agreement which were potentially detrimental to competition.

The 1956 Act established a Restrictive Practices Court which continues to adjudicate upon cartel policy.[18] Cartels which engage in one of a variety of practices are required to register their agreements which will be struck down unless the participants can bring their case within one of the 'gateways'. These gateways allow for the exemption of a restriction on a wide variety of grounds.[19] The Court must be satisfied that the restriction is reasonably necessary, for example to ensure safety,[20] protect exports,[21] or prevent unemployment.[22] There is, in addition, a more general gateway which provides that a restriction should be upheld if its removal would deny to the public specific and substantial benefits resulting from either the restriction itself or any arrangements resulting therefrom.[23] Even if a restriction is within one of the gateways, it must also successfully negotiate the 'tailpiece' of the section, which states that the Court must be further satisfied that the restriction is not unreasonable having regard to the balance between the advantage resulting from a particular restriction, and any detriment to the public resulting from its operation. The jurisdiction of the Restrictive Practices Court was augmented by the passage of the Resale Prices Act 1964, which brought resale price maintenance within its ambit. Consolidating legislation has now been passed. The principal statutes governing cartels are the Restrictive Trade Practices Act 1976, and the Restrictive Practices Court Act 1976. Resale price maintenance is now regulated by the Resale Prices Act 1976.

A Monopolies Commission was retained, but its jurisdiction was restricted, after 1956, primarily to the actions of dominant firms. The position of the MMC in relation to the investigation of dominant firms is, in outline, as follows. Under the Fair Trading Act 1973[24] the Director General of Fair Trading[25] or a government minister[26] can refer to the MMC for its investigation any goods[27] or services,[28] one quarter of which are supplied by or to the same firm or by one interconnected group of companies. The legislation contemplates three possible types of monopoly reference. In the first, references are confined to fact-finding.[29] Such investigations are limited to determining whether a statutory monopoly exists and whether it is being exploited. No conclusions are reached as to whether the monopoly operates against the public interest. References limited to the facts are rare. A second form of reference is one which is limited to specific practices of dominant firms.[30] Such references have not been common.[31] Most references now take the third form, which is a public-interest reference, whereby the MMC, in addition to engaging in the fact-finding operations, also gives its opinion as to whether the monopoly is or is not against the public interest.[32] When determining whether a monopoly is likely to operate against the public interest the

MMC is instructed to take account of all relevant matters, including:[33] maintaining effective competition; promoting the interests of consumers in respect of the prices and quality of goods; promoting, through competition, new entrants into the markets; maintaining a balanced distribution of industry and employment throughout the UK; and promoting competition between UK producers in foreign markets. When the MMC have concluded their report it is sent, with their recommendations, to the Secretary of State for Trade and Industry or other government minister.[34]

In 1965 the jurisdiction of the Commission was expanded by the Monopolies and Mergers Act.

The law relating to mergers is now governed by the Fair Trading Act 1973 which applies to horizontal, vertical and conglomerate mergers. It operates where the merger creates or strengthens a statutory monopoly, or where it results in the transfer of assets exceeding a certain value.[35] A merger takes place where two enterprises cease to be distinct, which is where they are either brought under common ownership or common control, or where, as the result of arrangements between the two companies, one ceases business completely.[36]

The powers of the Monopolies Commission were augmented to include mergers for three reasons. First, the Commission's investigations into dominant firms had revealed merger activity which the powers of the Commission could not adequately deal with.[37] A procedure in anticipation of a merger was required and the then existing legislation was not directed towards this end. Second, the result of the Restrictive Trade Practices Act 1956 had been to curtail horizontal cartels; many firms which had previously colluded merged to achieve the same goals. Third, the 1950s and 1960s witnessed an intense merger boom,[38] which led to a call for greater merger regulation.

The Director General of Fair Trading has an obligation to keep himself informed of actual or proposed mergers, and to tender advice to the Secretary of State as to whether a reference should be made to the MMC.[39] An interdepartmental Mergers Panel will then investigate the proposed merger and advise the Secretary of State as to the desirability of a referral. Merger references may, as with monopoly references, be restricted to requiring the MMC to report on the existence of a proposed merger, but in practice this is always combined with a reference as to the public interest.[40] The 'definition' of the public interest is the same as that which applies in the case of monopoly.[41] An important point to note is that there is no presumption that mergers are against the public interest – if there is insufficient evidence that the merger will have deleterious effects upon the public interest, it will not be condemned even though benefits are not readily apparent. The MMC's report is forwarded to the Secretary of State, who will then decide what action should be taken.[42]

The MMC has recently acquired a new sphere of activity as a result of the Competition Act 1980. The legislation emerged from the recommendations of two reports into competition policy conducted in the late 1970s.[43] One of the conclusions of the Liesner studies was that the existing framework of the legislation did not satisfactorily cover practices of firms which were not subject to a full monopoly investigation. The object was the passage of an enactment which would secure a speedier investigation of the behaviour of individual firms than that which had hitherto been possible. The Competition Act 1980 introduced the concept of the anti-competitive practice, defined as:[44] a course of conduct which of itself, or when taken together with a course of conduct pursued by persons associated with him, has or is intended to have or is likely to have the effect of restricting, distorting, or preventing competition in connection with the production, supply or acquisition of goods or the supply or securing of services within the United Kingdom or any part of it. The difficulties of applying this vague definition, and the alternative strategies which could have been employed, will be considered later.[45] Jurisdiction over anti-competitive practices is split between the OFT and the MMC. The Director General of Fair Trading can initiate an investigation if he believes that a firm has been pursuing an anti-competitive practice. He must then publish a report stating whether he believes that there is an anti-competitive practice and whether a reference to the MMC is appropriate.[46] There are short time-limits within which such a reference must be made. After the report has emerged from the OFT and prior to any reference to the MMC there are opportunities for the firm to give undertakings as to its future conduct.[47] A reference to the MMC will follow if the Director General believes that the firm is engaging in an anti-competitive practice and fails to secure satisfactory undertakings.[48] The MMC will then determine whether the firm was engaging in a course of conduct, whether the course of conduct was an anti-competitive practice, and whether this practice operates against the public interest.[49] A report is then furnished by the MMC to the Secretary of State.[50] The remedies which are available in all these different circumstances will be considered later.[51]

2 Competition and Regulation

Institutional Choice and Regulatory Criteria: the Coherence of Competition Policy

One cannot but be struck by the diversity of regulatory techniques that currently exists in this area. This diversity manifests itself in two principal ways. On the one hand, there is institutional diversity. Cartels, or at least horizontal cartels,[52] are dealt with by the OFT and the RPC. A judicial technique prevails in the sense that the RPC is the main decision-making body. Certain types of vertical relationship are also subject to this regime, particularly vertical price-fixing. Monopolies and mergers, however, are administered by the OFT, the MMC and the Secretary of State for Trade and Industry. Market power is therefore dealt with through discretionary administration by fringe organizations, subject to the overall control of the Secretary of State. Anti-competitive practices, some of which may take the form of vertical cartels, have now also been assigned to this regulatory regime.

On the other hand, there is a difference in regulatory technique which cuts across the institutional diversity. Framers of antitrust legislation have approached their problems in one of two ways. They have attempted to define in formal terms the type of cartel behaviour or abuse of market power which they wish to proscribe or regulate. This approach is most clearly demonstrated in the legislation on cartels which is long, complex, and attempts to set out in black-letter legal terms the types of agreement (such as price fixing, market division, etc) which it wishes to catch. A similar attitude pervades the legislation on monopolies and mergers. The jurisdiction of the MMC is conditioned upon proving the requisite market share, or that the firm has assets above a certain value.[53] The economic effects of a firm or firms' behaviour may well be taken into account once the legal system has 'locked into' a particular case as, for example, in determining whether a cartel should be exempted through a gateway,[54] or whether a statutory monopoly is operating in the public interest,[55] but such effects are not the criteria through which the system initially applies.

The alternative regulatory technique is to eschew formal definitions and to adopt a criterion based upon economic effects. Thus a cartel policy devised in this way could, like Article 85(1) of the Treaty of Rome, apply to all agreements which affect trade between the member states and which have as their object or effect the restriction or distortion of competition.[56] Within United Kingdom law, the only aspect of antitrust which is effects-based in this sense is the Competition Act 1980. Our system of competition policy is therefore one in which two major elements are subjected to tests based upon form, while the other is based upon a criterion of economic effects.

The reasons for the institutional and regulatory divergence described above are largely historical. Business interests were not altogether happy with the operation of the 1948 legislation. The selection of an industry for investigation was regarded as arbitrary, firms which appeared before the Commission felt themselves to be on trial, whether justifiably so or not, and the Commission was thought of as both prosecutor and judge. In addition, it was argued that corporations had little idea as to which types of practice were regarded as suspect.

These sentiments played a major part in shaping the 1956 legislation on cartels. Discretionary administration was sacrificed in favour of a judicial regime, and the legislation which the newly created RPC had to apply attempted to meet some of the criticisms concerning lack of certainty by framing the registrable practices in formal, legal terms. The emphasis upon formalism was also designed to meet objections that the proposed legislation was not justiciable. These arguments were directed principally at the gateways, rather than initial registrability, the contention being that they required the RPC to balance complex social and economic values in a manner unsuited to judicial resolution.[57] While a formalistic approach to initial registrability did nothing in itself to meet the argument concerning the justiciability of the gateways, it did lend support to the belief that the courts were applying detailed rules set out in the enabling legislation.

Which institutional mechanism is preferable, and whether the regulatory criterion should be one of legal form or economic effects, is clearly a subject on which opinions may well differ. In retrospect, perhaps an obvious answer to the question whether a court is indeed best suited to deal with the types of task under discussion would be to argue that this depends upon the answer to the second question, concerning the appropriate regulatory technique. A judicial solution might be said to be perfectly acceptable in institutional terms provided that the substantive questions assigned to it are spelt out as clearly as possible, indicating a criterion of legal form. Now, whether one thinks that the present restrictive practices legislation is justiciable or not, it would be mistaken to conclude that a court could or should never adjudicate in a system based upon economic effects. It is important to distinguish between two different situations. On the one hand, a legal system may stipulate that economic effect is the criterion determining whether the legislation bites at all. There are a number of such systems[58] in which the courts adjudicate upon legislation framed in these terms. Even here it may well be argued that a judicial setting and adversarial proceedings are inappropriate in resolving what may be a complex, factual economic issue. It may, for example, be extremely difficult, within such a setting, to determine whether a particular type of restrictive practice is having a deleterious effect upon competition. On the other hand, antitrust legislation may require a court to weigh a broad or open-ended series of social and economic variables in order to determine whether a cartel should be exempted or whether monopolistic behaviour is in the public interest, *given* that the cartel or monopoly does have some adverse effect upon competition itself. There are relatively few instances in which the judiciary is involved in decisions of this type.[59] It is in this context that the problems of justiciability are most marked. Here the judiciary struggle to decide whether factors such as the prevention of unemployment, the enhancement of regional policy, the advancement of product safety, or a beneficial impact upon the balance of payments, should outweigh a proven detrimental effect upon competition.

The question of regulatory technique was considered in detail in the Liesner report. The advantages of a shift from a test of legal form to one of economic effects would be significant. It would enable cartels, anti-competitive practices and problems relating to dominant firms, whether behavioural or structural, to be dealt with by the same regulatory technique and a single institution could be given overall responsibility for competition policy. Greater consistency between EEC and United Kingdom law would also be possible. While the Liesner report recognized these advantages,[60] and, indeed, hypothesized about a new Competition Authority,[61] it ultimately decided against such a change. A number of reasons were given. There would be a period of uncertainty for industry and transitional provisions would be difficult to define.[62] Moreover, while an effects-based system could avoid some of the legalistic arguments which permeated the present system, there would still be difficulties in deciding when, for example, an agreement or practice had an anti-competitive effect.[63] A Competition Authority, not already answerable to Parliament, would be controversial and would require more staff and resources than the OFT and MMC.[64] A further argument was that there was less difference between systems based upon legal form and economic effect than might be imagined. In a developed effects system it will become accepted that certain forms of agreement are always anti-competitive in effect and are therefore prohibited; given that this is so, it is preferable in terms of certainty that such agreements should be proscribed immediately in terms of their form.[65]

How convincing one finds this reasoning is obviously itself a matter of opinion. A number of points can, however, be made. First, businessmen have already had to become acquainted with an effects system because of membership of the EEC. Secondly, given the large number of fringe organizations already not directly answerable to Parliament,[66] it is difficult to see why the substitution of one such body, in the guise of a Competition Authority, for two other such institutions, the OFT and MMC, should be particularly controversial.[67] Thirdly, the existence of uncertainty flowing from the new system appears both exaggerated and contradicted by the recognition that in systems based upon effects the institutions will distinguish between the heinous or innocuous qualities of different types of agreement relatively quickly.

Moreover, the argument that systems based upon legal form and economic effects tend to produce the same results involves a *non-sequitur*. It is of course true that antitrust regimes based upon economic effects might well, after a period of time, proscribe certain classes of agreement. Horizontal price-fixing agreements are a classic example of a *per se* violation; once the existence of such a price-fixing agreement is found, the deleterious effect upon competition is presumed.[68] This would appear to lead therefore to the same result as in a system which simply outlawed the legal form of horizontal price-fixing. This apparently straightforward conclusion would follow *if*, whenever the courts in a form-based system were faced with an agreement which horizontally fixed price, *however it appeared in legal terms*, they were then to proscribe the agreement. Identity of result between the two systems is, therefore, premised upon the courts, in a regime based upon legal form, being willing to look to the substance of the parties' arrangement, and not accepting at face value the parties' contentions. This is manifestly not how our own restrictive practices legislation has operated. The courts *have* accepted agreements at their face value as, for example, simple contracts of sale even though the manifest objective was price-fixing or market division.[69]

A system based upon legal form suffers, as is implicitly recognized in the Liesner report itself, from the inherent vice of formalistic legal reasoning – that of over- and under-inclusiveness. Thus, much of the report is devoted, on the one hand, to suggestions for ensuring that harmless agreements or practices are either not condemned or provided with an expedited escape route from the legislation, and, on the other, to recommendations for strengthening the legislation to reduce evasion and to increase the powers of the Director General to deal with obviously objectionable agreements or practices.[70] Not surprisingly these vices of formalism can only be cured by moderating formalism itself, and this is precisely what the recommendations of the report suggest. The remedies to cure the problems of over- and under-inclusiveness ultimately turn on an evaluation of the economic effects of the agreement. This would be undertaken by the Director General rather than the Court, and would take place at an earlier stage than that countenanced by the present legislation.[71] Moreover, the very introduction of the 1980 legislation was, as the Liesner report accepted, partially necessitated by the desire to catch practices which were only outside the restrictive practices legislation because the parties had availed themselves of escape devices, such as the formulation of a series of bilateral agreements under which only one party accepted a restriction.

Finally, the continuance of divided jurisdictions leads necessarily to rigid demarcations in jurisdictional competence. The MMC is instructed not to investigate any restrictive agreements which it finds.[72] Furthermore, when it was decided to introduce the Competition Act, difficult consequential decisions had to be taken as to whether the RPC or the MMC should assume the new power. As we have seen, the choice was to link this new power to the OFT and MMC, rather than to the RPC. The reasons for preferring this avenue were perfectly sensible:[73] the existing concern of the MMC with market power, the fact that to do otherwise would preclude the MMC from investigating any such practice which they came across in the course of a monopoly reference, and a fear that the issues were not sufficiently justiciable for the RPC. Given all this, it is still the fact that certain at least of the practices coming within the 1980 legislation are species of agreement which do not at present come within the relevant legislation on restrictive trade practices,[74] either because there is only one restriction, or because the parties have so drawn their agreement that it falls within one of the categories of excepted agreements.

The question as to the appropriate institutional mechanism and the best regulatory technique will continue to divide commentators, as it divided those who submitted evidence to the Liesner report.[75] The better view, to quote from the Liesner report,[76] is that 'there would be advantage in setting up a coherent and consistent system for dealing with the whole spectrum of competition policy', but one cannot help thinking that a valuable opportunity was missed by not adopting a bolder approach.

Rule-making v. Discretion

As we have seen, the question of whether regulatory agencies should proceed through the application of rules or *ad hoc* discretion is one which has given rise to a considerable body of literature. The enforcement of competition policy presents a particularly interesting application of this general problem. As is evident from the brief description of the legislation given above, the MMC at present operates an essentially discretionary system: provided that the monopoly or merger qualifies for a reference to the MMC, the outcome of the reference is determined by the MMC's view as to what the public interest is in that particular instance.

This approach has been criticized by Crew and Rowley,[77] who focused their attention initially upon mergers. They reviewed the effect of Williamson's work on classical welfare theory.[78] Williamson had argued that antitrust enforcement in the United States took insufficient account of the welfare benefits, in terms of scale economies, which could flow from increased size. He argued that even if such an increase in size produced a corresponding increase in market power, and hence in the ability to raise price, this would often be offset in welfare terms by cost savings generated by economies of scale.[79] Hence, before condemning a merger, the antitrust authorities should consider the welfare trade-off between the price increases and the cost savings. Crew and Rowley then considered the impact of the concept of X-inefficiency[80] upon this analysis. Put simply, X-inefficiency means that as firms increase in market power certain new costs may arise. When a firm is operating in competitive conditions the labour aspect of production is forced to co-operate fully to ensure that the firm maximizes its profits and is able to stay ahead of its rivals. However, when a firm becomes insulated against competitive forces through greater market power, management and workforce are likely to seek goals other than profit maximization, such as leisure, security or maximizing short-term income. If, therefore, antitrust authorities were to be encouraged to undertake a Williamson-style trade-off in merger analysis, they would have to weigh the costs of X-inefficiency with the costs of the resultant price increases, against the benefits of scale economies. This type of cost-benefit analysis would be extremely difficult and time-consuming. If it were to be done properly it would require complex econometric analysis for which the full evidence would probably not be available. If it were to be attempted in any less thoroughgoing fashion it would amount to a fraud. They concluded from this that the best approach for antitrust was to eschew such trade-off analysis and to concentrate upon devising rules to replace *ad hoc* discretion. Thus, for example, a rule might prohibit all mergers leading to a market share in excess of 50 per cent.[81]

The analysis of Crew and Rowley did not go unchallenged. Howe[82] responded by espousing the virtues of discretion. He argued that the difficulties of defining the relevant market, the uncertainty concerning the predictions about behaviour and performance of large firms, and problems of enforcement rendered the Crew and Rowley thesis unattractive. The advocates of rule-making responded to the Howe critique in a number of ways.[83] They pointed out that difficulties in market definition were not avoided in the pragmatic approach and accepted that, while their own approach might lead to some cases being wrong, in the sense that there would be a net welfare gain by a merger which was prevented by the hypothetical rules, the *aggregate* benefits of a rule-making system outweighed the costs of any such individual mistakes.

The question of how far the MMC actually does engage in a trade-off analysis of the type advocated by Williamson has been considered by Utton.[84] He found that out of 13 merger reports involving firms in manufacturing industry, estimates of prospective cost saving had been quantified to some extent in eight. Most of the evidence concerned forecasted savings in production. However in only two cases did the MMC give much weight to such predicted savings in its final analysis. In the remaining references, scant attention was paid to the issue, partly because the companies involved presented little documentation to back up their claims, and partly because the MMC was sceptical about the prospect of the savings being realized in practice.

Whether the MMC ought to engage in more sophisticated trade-off analysis is obviously debatable. A number of points, in addition to those which have emerged from the foregoing discussion, are of relevance.

First, given that a sophisticated trade-off analysis would necessarily be more time-consuming and costly, it would result in even fewer mergers being considered than at present. Noticeably few mergers are presently referred to the MMC, a factor which is worrying in itself.[85] Unless the resources of the MMC (and OFT) were to be significantly expanded, the diminution of merger references consequent upon acceptance of a more elaborate trade-off model would probably be unacceptable.

Secondly, the possibility of a rule-based system is dependent, partly at least, upon an acceptance of the type of factor which is to be regarded as relevant in the formulation of such rules. If the reduction of competition was regarded as the prime social detriment which antitrust policy was designed to avoid, then it might well be possible to devise rules accordingly. There would still be the difficulty of defining market power, but this is an inherent problem within any form of antitrust regulation. However, *if* the range of factors felt to be of relevance is much broader, then the problems of rule definition become more intractable. Thus, if the effects of a merger on unemployment, the balance of payments, regional policy and the like, are felt to be of integral importance, then the formulation of appropriate rules which take such factors into account, yet still yield the desired predictability of result becomes far more complex.[86] Whether, and to what extent, competition policy should be concerned with such issues is debatable. Differing views reflect divergent beliefs concerning both the importance of the welfare economics underlying antitrust and the relationship between these goals and other social, political and economic considerations. This debate is not restricted to merger policy. It is equally applicable to cartels, monopoly policy and the meaning to be given to the concept of anti-competitive practice. Whether, for example, certain business practices should be proscribed *per se* as anti-competitive,[87] and whether certain types of horizontal cartel should be similarly prohibited, with no prospect of exemption, raises analogous problems of choosing between rule-making and discretion.

Thirdly, a *via media* between strict rules and *ad hoc* discretion may be obtainable in the form of guidelines.[88] These could operate in a variety of ways. In the context of mergers it could mean that, where a proposed merger resulted in an increase in market concentration of a certain percentage, in an industry where the five-firm concentration ratio was already high (for example 70 per cent), then reference to the MMC would be automatic.[89] It could take the form of identifying certain business practices as presumptively anti-competitive. It must be admitted, however, that even the formulation of such guidelines is dependent upon agreement on two issues. Protection of competition would have to be accorded a real primacy of position among the other factors presently considered by the MMC. This in itself might necessitate alteration of the presumption which operates in merger cases so that the parties wishing to merge would have to demonstrate that their proposed merger operated positively in the public interest. Furthermore, the adoption of guidelines or rules in other areas of antitrust is dependent upon some consensus of the anti-competitive nature of the challenged practices. One of the characteristics of recent antitrust literature has been the vigorous debate concerning the deleterious or innocuous effect of certain trade practices upon the optimum allocation of resources.[90] Without a measure of agreement upon this issue the establishment even of guidelines becomes difficult.

Control and Accountability: the Relationship between the MMC, Government, Judiciary and Public

If we examine the way in which the MMC interrelates with other parts of the political and legal system, three themes are apparent. One is that the structure of our antitrust legislation vividly demonstrates the retention of ultimate control by the political arm of government. This is apparent in the role played by the Secretary of State in the initiation of monopoly and merger references, and more particularly at the remedial level. A second theme is to be found in the preference for public enforcement of competition policy and the correlatively small role accorded to the individual. The final theme is the limited role played by the judiciary. These issues will be examined in turn.

Under the original 1948 legislation, the Monopolies and Restrictive Practices Commission had no power to initiate inquiries. This power resided with the Government, and its decision to refer was primarily influenced by what it conceived to be the Commission's main function: the collation of evidence to guide the Government in framing future competition policy. The Board of Trade considered both the nature of the industry, its trade practices and representations made to the Board. Additional factors which influenced the Board were parliamentary pressure and also public disquiet following revelations concerning, for example, excessive pricing. As one writer has noted,[91] this resulted in the Commission spending some of its energies upon industries which were not of prime importance to the economy, and also of duplicating inquiries by considering the same practice in different industries.

The 'concentration' of the referral power in the hands of government caused some disquiet. It was felt that a ministry such as the Board of Trade which sponsored industry in various ways might not be the most objective institution with respect to the decision to refer. The position was altered in 1973, although distinctions must be drawn between the power to refer monopolies and mergers.

Under the Fair Trading Act 1973, the Director General has power to make *monopoly* references to the MMC.[92] There is some residual governmental power[93] but the decision to refer has remained essentially non-political. In reaching this decision the OFT will take into account conduct indicators, performance indicators, and information which is available from previous inquiries. Conduct indicators comprise: consumer complaints made to the OFT, measurement of acquisitions, evidence of price leadership or price parallelism and, where applicable, the ratio of advertising to sales. Performance indicators encapsulate, *inter alia*, the rate of return on capital and the group's contribution to inflation. Interdepartmental discussion may also play a role in the decision to refer.[94]

The principal role in the application of the Competition Act 1980 also resides with the Director General and the OFT. It is the Director General who decides whether to carry out a preliminary investigation in order to determine whether a person is pursuing an anti-competitive practice.[95] However the Secretary of State retains residual powers not dissimilar to those which he possesses under the 1973 legislation. Thus he can tell the Director General to stop a preliminary investigation and can also instruct the MMC itself not to proceed with a competition reference.[96]

Governmental influence over *merger* references is more marked. The OFT will conduct a preliminary investigation but will then submit the matter to the interdepartmental Mergers Panel. The influence of the OFT will, however, still be felt, since the Director General is chairman of the Mergers Panel. This Panel will examine proposed or actual mergers and will then make recommendations to the Secretary of State as to which mergers should be submitted to the MMC.[97] The Secretary of State is under an obligation to reach a reference decision with all due expedition, but can refer to the MMC within either six months of the merger taking place, or being made public, whichever is the later.[98]

Two general comments are apposite here. First, the retention by the Secretary of State of the sole power to make a merger reference is questionable. It might well be preferable to allow the Director General to have a concurrent power. The prevailing divergence between the reference powers for monopoly and anti-competitive practices on the one hand, and for mergers on the other, undoubtedly reflects the greater political sensitivity attendant upon merger investigations. Whether this sensitivity is warranted in terms of the policies underlying antitrust is, however, questionable. The answer to this question is rendered more complex owing to the lack of clarity as to the purposes of the merger policy itself.

Second, in deciding whether to make a monopoly reference or investigate an anti-competitive practice, the OFT obviously has to make decisions concerning the best use of their own, and the MMC's, scarce resources. Which of the many possible anti-competitive practices warrant a full MMC competition reference can present acute problems. There may well be consumer or customer complaints about the practices of a particular firm. This does not necessarily mean that those practices, or the market position of the firm, are important enough to justify an MMC investigation. Confusion of consumer protection and competition policy is always a potential problem when a single regulatory agency, the OFT, has responsibilities in both areas.[99]

On the remedial level, the central theme is that neither the OFT nor the MMC have dispositive powers in their own right. The framework established by the legislation is for a report of the MMC, whether it be upon a monopoly[100] or merger [101] reference, to be forwarded to the Secretary of State (or other relevant Minister). The appropriate Minister may then make an order by statutory instrument exercising one of a variety of powers specified in the legislation.[102] Such orders are, however, relatively rare. Most often a voluntary settlement is secured through negotiations conducted by the OFT. This is specifically provided for in the Fair Trading Act, which requires that the Director General[103] should, if so requested by the Minister, consult with the parties in order to obtain undertakings from them which meet the objections specified in the MMC's report.

The Competition Act 1980 evidences a similar distribution of power. Having completed a competition reference on an alleged anti-competitive practice, the MMC reports to the Secretary of State.[104] The whole emphasis of the subsequent section is, however, upon the negotiation of undertakings by the Director General.[105] Only if this proves unsuccessful will the Secretary of State make an order compelling the requisite action.[106] The stress placed upon negotiation is further buttressed by provisions which allow the Director General to seek undertakings after this preliminary investigation in order to render a competition reference unnecessary.[107]

Undertakings once given are then monitored by the OFT.[108] This has two aspects. On the one hand, the OFT will investigate any alleged breach of the undertaking; on the other, it will review the situation in order to determine whether circumstances have so altered as to require a modification of the original undertaking. Should an undertaking not be forthcoming the Secretary of State has a very wide range of remedies which he can impose.[109]

Discussion of the relationship between the government and the MMC at the remedial level leads naturally to the second theme: the limited role accorded to the private individual. As is evident from the above, United Kingdom competition policy concentrates upon public rather than private enforcement. Private remedies are not entirely absent. They are, however, limited. In essence a private citizen may bring a civil action for injunctive relief or damages, where a firm has contravened an order made against it as the result of an adverse report of the MMC on a monopoly or merger reference, or on a competition reference.[110] The individual, therefore, only enters the arena once an institutional decision has been taken to investigate a certain industry or practice, that industry or practice has contravened the relevant legislation and the industry has failed to comply with the subsequent order. It is of course true to say that the individual may well be the catalyst for a referral, but he or she cannot institute any proceedings should the competition authorities decline to do so. This is in marked contrast to the position in some other legal systems where the individual can actually initiate the investigative process. The most relevant example of such private enforcement is in the EEC, the competition rules of which have been held to have direct effect thereby giving rights to individuals which are enforceable within the domestic courts of the member states.[111] It may well be argued that such private enforcement aids in the effectuation of the policies underlying antitrust, particularly if the individual is provided with the added incentive of treble damages should he succeed.[112] However the whole emphasis of United Kingdom policy towards all aspects of market power is to retain a system of discretionary intervention in which authority is firmly held by public institutions and the government. While this prevails, and while negotiation and voluntary settlement are regarded as the prime aims, there is little likelihood of any movement in these directions of private enforcement.

We have seen the relationship between the MMC and the executive, and the MMC and the public. What role have the ordinary courts played within this area? Judicial review of the decisions of the OFT and MMC has been of limited significance. This may seem surprising: given that companies have no continuing 'client' relationship with the OFT and MMC, there would be no risk of upsetting future relations by seeking judicial review. The explanation must lie partly in the broad discretion possessed by the OFT and MMC in the decision whether to investigate, and in determining whether behaviour is in the public interest. Courts have, however, reviewed open-textured discretion within other areas,[113] and one might have expected some challenge to the more 'objective' aspects of the legislation, such as whether a monopolist possesses the requisite market share. Once an investigation has begun the OFT and MMC are subject to the rules of natural justice.[114] The decision whether to implement the recommendations of the MMC resides, as we have seen, with the Secretary of State. Normally this causes few problems since the Secretary of State will accept the views of the MMC on a merger reference. In one recent instance the recommendation that a merger should not be allowed to proceed was rejected,[115] causing one member to resign in protest. One of the companies involved sought judicial review of the Secretary of State's discretion, but failed.[116] The legislation, taken as a whole, was held to invest the Secretary of State with a wide discretion; although he was bound to take the views of the MMC into account he was not compelled to adopt their recommendations.

3 Conclusion

What conclusions may be drawn from the preceding discussion? More particularly, what light does competition policy throw upon general questions of public law? This is a difficult question, which is best approached upon a number of different levels.

From one perspective, consideration of British antitrust policy exemplifies in a stark form the choice which has to be made between rule-making and discretion. This has been examined in the context of mergers, but could, in an analogous way, have been considered in relation to other types of anti-competitive behaviour. Whether, for example, certain types of restrictive practice or monopolistic behaviour should be declared *per se* illegal, or whether we should investigate the particular circumstances in order to determine whether there has been a deleterious economic effect in that instance, involves similar choices between rule-making and discretion.

From a different perspective, antitrust demonstrates the way in which the choice of regulatory institution can influence the substance of the policy which that institution is to administer. The choice of a court to apply the legislation upon restrictive trade practices was, as we have seen, motivated by a number of factors: there was corporate disquiet over the system of discretionary administration which characterized the operation of the Monopolies and Restrictive Practices Commission, and a desire upon the part of government to place the administration of antitrust on a footing which would command 'respect' from those subject to it. The consequences of choosing a court emerge clearly when one reflects upon the cartel legislation. The substance of that legislation was laid down in black-letter legal terms so as to foster the impression that a court could adjudicate upon the issue with little difficulty. The fact that a criterion of legal form encourages legalistic escape devices, as well as giving rise to the problems of over- and under-inclusiveness, were ignored, while the difficulties concerning the justiciability of the gateways challenged the very assumption that these matters really were of the type which courts 'ordinarily' adjudicate upon. A further consequence of choosing a court was to reduce the extent of executive influence over both the decision to refer and the remedy to be awarded.

The administration of the Competition Act 1980 stands in stark contrast to this. Regulation is carried out by the OFT and the MMC, the criterion used is one of economic effect, and executive influence pervades differing stages of the inquiry. The spectre of the Government 'interfering' with a court is absent, as is the feeling that certainty demands legal formalism.

It would be wrong to press this link between regulatory institution and substantive policy too far. As we have seen, the MMC and OFT administer monopoly and merger references, and the criterion for the legislation to bite is one of legal form, in terms of percentage of the market, size, loss of independence, etc. Legal form and regulation by a court are not therefore inexorably linked. The connection between regulatory institution and substantive policy is nonetheless present even within this area. While the OFT and MMC can only investigate a monopoly or merger if the requisite formal criteria are satisfied, these criteria are malleable and interpreted in a flexible way. Varying definitions of both the geographic and product markets can be used in order to bring within the ambit of the legislation those whom the OFT and MMC wish to investigate. Moreover, the correlation between the type of regulatory institution and the degree of executive influence is just as strong in this area as it is in relation to investigations under the Competition Act 1980. Executive oversight reaches its apogee in the control of mergers, and is facilitated by the fact that the Government is not seen to be interfering with the judiciary, but is simply playing a role in relation to a quango or fringe organization. Furthermore, the broad range of factors which the MMC has to take into account in determining the public interest is viewed in a different light to the attempts by the RPC to adjudicate upon the gateways which involve similar considerations. Because the MMC is a fringe organization subject to executive control, it is easier to view it as part of the political decision-making process. Fears that the subject matter is non-justiciable are alleviated by the realization that the MMC is not intended to be a body which is insulated from broad political and social considerations.

Competition policy within the United Kingdom does not, however,

merely demonstrate the link between the choice of regulatory
institution and the substantive policy which it is to apply. It also
exemplifies the importance of the converse: clarity concerning the
substantive goals which antitrust is to pursue will, or should, affect
our institutional choice. This is not simply a replication of the
arguments presented above from a different perspective. It shows the
way in which such clarity will affect the choice between court or
administrative agency, and also the way in which the chosen
institution is to operate.

An example of this line of analysis may be drawn from mergers.
These are administered through the OFT and the MMC rather than
through a court for a number of reasons, in particular: a desire to
retain political control, the complex nature of the investigation as to
whether the merger will have anticompetitive results, and the equally
complex question as to whether it will be against the public interest.
However, having made this initial choice, greater clarity concerning
the objects of merger policy should have a significant impact upon the
way in which the OFT and MMC operate.

At present approximately three per cent of all mergers are referred
to the MMC for a public interest investigation. Part, at least, of the
reason for this paucity of referrals is the assumption, allegedly
encapsulated within the legislation, that mergers are not contrary to
the public interest. Thus, even though the companies concerned may
not be able to show any positive benefit flowing from the merger, it
will be allowed to proceed unless some detriment to the public interest
can be shown. The small number of mergers actually considered by
the MMC both raises doubts as to the impact of the present strategy,
and also leads one to question the suitability of the existing
presumption. One option would be to reverse this presumption,
thereby placing the 'burden of proof' upon those who wish to merge.
It would then fall to the companies concerned to show why the merger
would lead to a net benefit. This alteration was rejected by the Liesner
Report.[117] It was felt that such a change would force the OFT and the
Mergers Panel to refer almost all mergers to the MMC; that many
mergers thus referred would ultimately be approved, even under the
altered presumption; that the result would therefore be increased
delay for the parties, and significant extra work for the MMC; that
mergers would be discouraged; and that the MMC would not be able
to cope with the extra workload. While rejecting a reversal in the
presumption, *Liesner* also rejected the status quo, and recommended

instead a 'neutral position' for merger cases.[118] Their proposal involved a two-stage procedure. At stage one, the Mergers Panel would conduct a 'quick' assessment of the effect of the merger upon competition. If a merger did not have a significant effect on competition it would be cleared. Guidelines would be adopted in order both to expedite the investigative process and to achieve consistency. Only those mergers which were likely to have this significant effect would be referred to the MMC, which would then consider the potential benefits which would offset the reduction in competition and any other disadvantages which could ensue from the merger. Although the Liesner Report refers to the procedure as 'neutral', it is in fact more pro-competitive than it initially appears. Competition is given pride of place and, if a significant effect on competition is shown (or presumed from the guidelines), then the firm would be expected to provide 'convincing evidence of offsetting benefits'.[119]

The existing presumption ensures that merger policy is likely to have only a marginal or interstitial impact upon industrial concentration in the UK. This might be acceptable if the preponderance of the economic evidence pointed to the realization of significant benefits which could offset the decrease in competition resulting from a merger. However, while the reliability of this evidence is contested, much of it indicates that such benefits do not accrue. It has been found that mergers are generated more by a desire to increase market share or as a defence to prevent rivals from expanding, than as a strategy for increased industrial efficiency.[120] Even where the proponents of a merger did predict possible cost economies, these often did not materialize. Given this background, legislation implementing the *Liesner* recommendations would be welcome. Even if this were to transpire, there would still be disagreement as to whether mergers of differing types did produce anti-competitive results, an issue on which opinion is sharply divided.[121] The reforms discussed above would, however, at least force the competition authorities to consider such issues more explicitly and consistently than at present.

The final way in which the regulation of competition is important for an understanding of public law is that it demonstrates the haphazard way in which administrative institutions evolve, and the consequences which may follow from that haphazard development. The choice of a court and an administrative agency to regulate competition was influenced by a broad range of political and social factors. The retention of our dual system has rendered it more difficult to achieve a coherent antitrust policy. This is not a search for 'administrative symmetry' as an end in itself. United Kingdom law often exhibits idiosyncracies which are the result of unsystematic development. However, where the institutional diversity has contributed towards differing substantive policies, and where it prevents very similar types of behaviour from being considered by the same agency using the same criteria, then a determined effort should be made towards general reform.

The Commission for Racial Equality: Formal Investigations in the Shadow of Judicial Review

Christopher McCrudden

The Commission for Racial Equality (CRE) came into existence in June 1977. Under the Race Relations Act 1976 it is charged with the duties of working towards the elimination of discrimination, of promoting equality of opportunity and good relations between persons of different races, and of keeping under review the working of the Act. A separate body (the Equal Opportunities Commission) has comparable powers in the area of sex discrimination.[1] The CRE is given a wide discretion to assist individual complaints in the courts and industrial tribunals; powers to conduct formal investigations, to obtain information and to issue non-discrimination notices; and authority to bring legal proceedings itself against those who persistently violate the law. The Act enables the Commission to issue Codes of Practice providing practical guidance in the field of employment for the elimination of discrimination and the promotion of equality of opportunity. The Commission is also empowered to conduct research and give financial and other assistance to organizations concerned with the promotion of equality of opportunity and good relations. In practice the bulk of the money goes to local community relations councils.

The CRE is of importance to public lawyers in a number of respects: it is one of the best examples of an attempt to transplant an American-style administrative agency into Britain; it exercises powers of assistance to litigants which have proved a precedent for reform proposals in other areas; its decision to issue a code of practice and the process of consultation which it went through illustrates important aspects of rule-making in British law. This chapter, however, discusses another important aspect of the CRE's work: the conduct of formal investigations. The way in which the CRE has carried out this function exemplifies a central dilemma of enforcement, viz. whether to enforce by formal means (principally by prosecution) or seek solutions by informal negotiation and bargaining. In particular, the chapter concentrates on the way that judicial review has influenced the CRE's approach to its investigatory and enforcement functions. We shall see how judicial intervention contributed to the effective halting of one strategy based on the use of investigations and non-discrimination notices, and its replacement with another (negotiation and bargaining) in which investigations play a 'supplementary role'.[2] To appreciate how this happened, it will be useful to begin, first, with the earlier methods of anti-discrimination regulation which the Commission replaced.

1 The Genesis of Agency Enforcement in Britain (1965–1975)

The First Race Relations Board
The first Race Relations Bill was formally introduced into the House of Commons by a Labour Government in 1965. In addition to provisions concerning incitement to racial hatred, the Bill proposed to make discrimination in some limited respects a criminal offence punishable with a fine. Prosecutions were only to be undertaken with the authority of the Director of Public Prosecutions.

Considerable pressure was put on the Government to change this proposed method of enforcement. Jowell,[3] for example, argued against criminal sanctions on four grounds: the legislation did not contain the machinery to eliminate discrimination except in so far as would-be offenders would be deterred by the fear of criminal sanctions; it was difficult to persuade prosecutors to take action; it was difficult to prove a case beyond reasonable doubt; and cases might come before a jury which was not sympathetic with the aims of the law. Jowell also argued against an alternative method of civil enforcement by individual parties. This would not be effective either, he argued, for at least four reasons: aggrieved persons were unwilling to indulge in the expense or effort of instituting civil actions; a person who discriminated might be prepared to pay damages in civil cases or a fine in a criminal suit, as the price for continuing to discriminate; an immediate public hearing could exacerbate existing racial friction; and 'the opportunity of giving evidence to a civil or criminal court could be enjoyed by those with little other opportunity of obtaining an audience for the demonstration of their racial prejudices or obsessions'.[4]

Drawing on North American experience of the enforcement of anti-discrimination legislation, a number of groups constituting an incipient civil rights movement argued for a system of enforcement through a specially constituted administrative body as an alternative to the use of the criminal or civil legal process.[5] Enforcement by such a body would emphasize the elimination of discrimination in the public interest, rather than revenge or the punishment of the individual discriminator. It could also be given powers which would make it more effective than the ordinary civil or criminal processes.

Partly as a result of pressure inside and outside Parliament, significant changes were made in the Bill's anti-discrimination provisions before it became law.[6] Criminal sanctions were retained only for incitement to racial hatred. A specialized agency, the Race Relations Board (RRB), was established to investigate breaches of the legislation and secure compliance. Local conciliation committees were to be set up by the Board to investigate complaints for those who considered that they had been discriminated against. If their attempts to settle complaints by conciliation failed, the local committees were to report to the Board. If, in turn, the Board found that there had been discrimination and considered it likely that the discrimination would continue, it could refer the case to the Attorney-General and would then be empowered to bring proceedings in court seeking an injunction which would require the discrimination to cease.

Neither the Board nor the local committees, however, had the power to summon witnesses, subpoena documents, require answers to questions or issue orders. Rather than being adopted as a more effective method of enforcement, conciliation was included, according to a government spokesman, 'to avoid bringing the flavour of criminality into the delicate question of race relations'.[7] It was a continuing theme throughout the debate that the Government hoped that court litigation would not arise under the Act and actively wanted to prevent it.

A New Race Relations Board

Between 1965 and 1968 there was a well-organized campaign by a number of pressure groups (and by the Race Relations Board itself) for an extension and a strengthening of the provisions of the 1965 Act. The campaign stressed that a new Act should for the first time prohibit discrimination in housing and employment, and drew support from an influential and well-publicized report by Political and Economic Planning (PEP), an independent research organization, which found that racial discrimination in these and other areas varied in extent but was generally substantial.[8] It was argued that the weak enforcement structure of the 1965 Act should be replaced by one closer to the American agency enforcement model. In retrospect, the collapse of the incipient civil rights movement in Britain and the continuing absence of effective private enforcement bodies might be seen as another explanation for the popularity of the idea of enforcement by a public agency among concerned activists. It is arguable, however, that the existence of such a public body, once established, itself contributed to the difficulties of re-establishing a private civil rights body.[9]

A new Race Relations Act was passed in 1968, and this prohibited discrimination in both public and private employment and housing, subject to certain exceptions. The 1968 Act retained the two-tier enforcement mechanism of Race Relations Board plus local concili-ation committees. Once the Board had received a complaint, it first determined whether it had jurisdiction and whether there had in fact been discrimination, and then tried to conciliate the dispute. If this was unsuccessful the Board was empowered to bring a case against the discriminator in one of a number of specially designated county courts, in which 'race relations assessors' sat with the judge. Individuals could not take discrimination cases directly to the county courts; that was solely the responsibility of the Board. The Board was also given an additional power to initiate investigations without an individual complaint; this was limited, however, by the need for the Board to suspect that a particular person had been discriminated against.

There was a different procedure for the settling of complaints about employment discrimination. Prior to 1967, the Confederation of British Industry (CBI) and the Trades Union Congress (TUC) opposed legislation which would have prohibited discrimination in employment on the ground that it conflicted with the British tradition of 'voluntarism' in industrial relations. In this context, voluntarism involves a preference for collective bargaining over state regulation as a method of settling wages and other terms and conditions of employment; a preference for keeping industrial disputes out of court by preserving a non-legalistic type of collective bargaining; and a preference for retaining the autonomy of the bargaining parties.[10]

When the CBI and the TUC finally agreed to the inclusion of employment in the Act, it was only on condition that industry dispute procedures should be exhausted first. The procedure that was adopted in the 1968 Act required that any complaints of discrimination in employment should be dealt with, initially, not by the Race Relations Board but by the Department of Employment. If there was suitable voluntary machinery to deal with the complaint within the industry concerned, the Department would send it back to that 'industry machinery'. Only if none existed, or if the complainant was appealing against a decision of this industry machinery, did the Race Relations Board have any jurisdiction to hear the complaint. Only after that might the courts be involved. The use of industry machinery was thus a compromise between the value of self-regulation in industrial relations and the need for government intervention where the parties themselves were unable to solve the problem.

Community Relations Commission

The 1968 Act also established another institution parallel to the Race Relations Board: the Community Relations Commission. Following the passage of the Commonwealth Immigrants Act in 1962, the Government had set up the non-statutory Commonwealth Immigrant's Advisory Council (CIAC) to advise the Home Secretary on the welfare of Commonwealth immigrants in Britain and their integration into the community.[11] In April 1964, the National Committee for Commonwealth Immigrants (NCCI), was set up, again on a non-statutory basis. Its work consisted 'largely in providing advice and information. It also had an important function in assisting in the formation of local liaison committees and regional organizations.'[12] The 1965 White Paper gave its support to these local committees which it termed 'voluntary liaison committees' (vlcs). It announced that a new non-statutory National Committee for Commonwealth Immigrants would be set up, replacing both the existing NCCI and the CIAC, with increased funding and staff. The functions of the vlcs were, as the 1965 White Paper put it, 'essentially the coordination of local effort and the positive promotion of good will'. This function was contrasted with those functions of the local conciliation committees set up under the 1965 Race Relations Act which were 'to enquire into complaints of racial discrimination' and to implement 'the statutory requirements' of the Act.[13]

The 1968 Act replaced the NCCI with a statutory body, the Community Relations Commission (CRC), which was given the tasks of encouraging 'harmonious community relations',[14] coordinating on a national basis the measures adopted for that purpose by others, advising the Home Secretary on any matter referred to the Commission by him, and making recommendations to him on any matter the Commission considered should be brought to his attention. 'Community relations' was defined as 'relations within the community between people of different colour, race, or ethnic or national origin'.[15] The CRC took over the functions of the NCCI with regard to the local vlcs, now renamed 'community relations councils' (crcs).

Enforcement of the Act 1968–1975
In practice, there were deficiencies in the coverage and enforcement provisions of the 1968 Act. Discrimination, as defined by the Act, was difficult to prove.[16] The Act did not apply to the present effects of past discrimination or to unintentional discrimination. In most cases the Race Relations Board could do little until it received a complaint. It was unable to conduct a systematic planned campaign using legal enforcement against discriminatory practices. The operation of the Act demonstrated many of the limitations of a largely complaints-based approach. There appears to have been a lack of perception of discrimination by the ethnic groups themselves. Even where individuals understood that discrimination was widespread, they might not perceive it in their own particular circumstances. There appears to have been a lack of knowledge of the Board's existence or of what its functions were. There was a reluctance to complain. This appears to have been greatest, understandably, where discrimination in terms of conditions of employment, training or promotion were involved.[17] Growing unemployment was identified by the Board as a significant deterrent. These factors contributed to the low number of complaints.[18]

The limited powers given to the Race Relations Board to investigate when no complaint had been received were small compensation.

In most cases the Board waited for a specific informant to give the Board information rather than itself seek instances where this section 17 power might be used. In part, this may have been due to the discontinuance by the Board of its research function and the lack of available information.[19] The Board was, moreover, required to find a specific instance of discrimination against an identifiable person before a finding of discrimination could be made, even in a section 17 case. This had the consequence that even where it seemed that equality of opportunity was not being afforded to members of a minority group, the Board was often unwilling to intervene, without a complaint by an individual.[20] The Board did not necessarily depend on complaints from the victims themselves but in the main it did depend on fairly specific information.

The Board's investigations were further handicapped because it had no power to require relevant evidence to be given to it prior to litigation. On occasion, investigations were abandoned for lack of information without forming an opinion.[21] The lack of such powers also increased the number of decisions in which an opinion of no discrimination was formed. Although it had a wide discretion to form an opinion that there had been unlawful discrimination, it was 'inevitably reluctant to do so in the absence of convincing evidence because of the risk that their opinion [would] subsequently be rejected in the courts'.[22] Thus the frequency with which complaints were rejected was thought 'not [to] reflect the incidence of discrimination or the weakness of the complaints but rather the inability of the conciliation machinery to obtain information on its own initiative to plan an effective strategy against the most important areas of racial discrimination'.[23] The lack of such powers had the further effect of extensively delaying investigation of complaints.[24]

A number of other features of the 1968 Act proved disappointing. The two-tier structure of conciliation committee decisions being reviewed by the Board increased the time spent on investigation, and, particularly in the early years of the Board's existence, provoked some bitter controversies between Board and committees. The hope that the special enforcement provisions for dealing with employment complaints would stimulate the growth of voluntary procedures was not borne out; there were few cases in which industry machinery found discrimination; and on the whole it proved cumbersome and of questionable value to both industry and race relations groups. Finally, even when discrimination was proven the remedies available to the Board, and more particularly to the courts, were extremely limited.

Judicial Review of the Race Relations Board

Judicial review of Board decisions was exercised in few cases. Two are of importance. In *Ealing London Borough Council* v. *Race Relations Board*[25] a complaint had been investigated by the Board alleging that the Council was unlawfully discriminating on grounds of national origin in the matter of the disposal of housing accommodation. The Board formed the opinion that the complaint was well founded. It proceeded to try to secure a settlement and an assurance against repetition of such alleged discrimination. The council, however, took the view that it had committed no unlawful act and claimed a declaration to that effect. The council argued that, though they had discriminated on grounds of nationality (which was not, then, unlawful), they could not be held to have discriminated unlawfully on grounds of national origins (which was unlawful). The Board implausibly asserted that the statute on its face ruled out any challenge to the Board's opinion once the Board was satisfied that a breach of the law had occurred. More importantly, in the alternative, the Board argued that even if there was no express exclusion of the High Court the clear implication of the procedures introduced by the Act was that these should constitute the only machinery for resolving disputes arising under the legislation. The House of Lords was dismissive of both arguments. Not only was the court able to review the exercise of the Board's jurisdiction, it did so in that case.[26]

In the second case, *Selvarajan* v. *Race Relations Board*,[27] a complainant sought review of an opinion by the Board that he had not been discriminated against. At issue were the responsibilities of the Board in investigating a complaint. The Board argued that it was required only to make such enquiries as it considered necessary and not to act judicially or 'fairly'.[28] All members of the Court of Appeal agreed that the Board was not required to act judicially and that the courts should be hesitant in reviewing the exercise by the Board of its powers. Despite that, however, all were insistent that there were circumstances in which the courts would intervene, though they did not do so in this case.

2 The Development of the New Model of Agency Enforcement

Sex Discrimination Initiatives[29]

An important influence leading to the form of new legislation in 1976 was the campaign for legislative intervention to help secure greater equality between the sexes, which became prominent in the late 1960s. In 1970 an Equal Pay Bill had been introduced and passed by Parliament, and was to come fully into effect at the end of 1975. By 1973 it was becoming clear that there was little opposition to the idea of some kind of further legislative action against sex discrimination. What remained unresolved, however, was how such legislation should be enforced. Although the possibility of establishing an agency to deal with the Equal Pay Act had apparently been considered and rejected, all the subsequent privately-sponsored sex discrimination bills were in agreement that some form of anti-discrimination agency should be established, modelled on the RRB and with similar powers, though giving individuals the power to institute court proceedings on their own behalf.

The Select Committees[30] of both the Lords and the Commons were generally sympathetic to this structure though both Committees recommended that such a Board should, in addition to being the recipient and expediter of individuals' complaints, play a more positive, independent role. More explicitly, they argued that the Board should have powers to originate action in the absence of any individual complaint, to undertake enquiries into areas where the Board felt discrimination might exist, to conduct enquiries in both the public and private sectors, and to sponsor relevant research. The then Conservative Government, however, was reluctant to create a single body with what they saw as too extensive a power to investigate discrimination on its own initiative. In evidence to the Commons Select Committee, the Home Secretary argued that it would be undesirable to combine enforcement functions with the role of enquiring, reporting and generally educating public opinion.[31] The Conservative Government's Consultative Document[32] of September 1973, proposed that a new body (termed an 'Equal Opportunities Commission') should be established, but be restricted to a purely advisory role. Enforcement of the legislation was to be the preserve of individuals taking cases to industrial tribunals, as under the Equal Pay Act 1970. The Commission could conduct surveys and promote change, but it would not be able to require any direct action with respect to alleged discrimination.

The change of government in 1974 pre-empted any action on these proposals, and the incoming Labour administration soon published a White Paper[33] showing itself to be more in sympathy with the idea of establishing an enforcement rather than a campaigning agency, which it also termed an 'Equal Opportunities Commission'. The Government did not wish to leave enforcement solely to individual initiative as this could mean that the impact of the legislation would be random and relatively slow. On the other hand, to give the proposed EOC the sole responsibility to initiate legal proceedings also had drawbacks. Race Relations Board experience had indicated that any such agency would be so preoccupied with individual complaints that it would not have the time or resources properly to fulfil the positive, independent role envisaged by both Select Committees. Furthermore, with women constituting half the population, it was thought that there would be many more complaints of sex discrimination than there had been of race discrimination, and so it would have been out of the question for an agency to handle them all. If this type of intervention were to be effective, the new body had to have significant enforcement powers, and possibly some special access to the courts. The Labour Government's solution was to seek a compromise: individuals were to have access to legal redress (via the industrial tribunals or county courts), whilst the new Commission was to have a 'strategic' function of identifying and eliminating discriminatory practices 'in the public interest'.[34] The power to conduct 'formal investigations' would be given to the Commission for that purpose.

The White Paper also announced the Government's aim to 'harmonise the powers and procedures for dealing with sex and race discrimination so as to secure genuine equality of opportunity in both fields'.[35] Harmonization raised two interlinking questions. Firstly, should the procedures, coverage and enforcement provisions of the two Acts be similar? Secondly, if they should, then should a single agency with powers to deal with both race and sex discrimination be established?

With regard to the second issue, those in favour of a single agency (including the majority of the Race Relations Board, the Central Policy Review Staff (CPRS) and, initially, the Home Secretary, Roy Jenkins) argued that such an approach would be simpler, would enlarge public support for the law and would thus make it more effective and more easily enforced. Those against a unified structure (including a minority in the RRB) argued that the experience of the

United States Equal Employment Opportunity Commission (US EEOC, which has responsibilities for both race and sex discrimination) illustrated the likelihood of continuing squabbles over resources between those mainly concerned with sex discrimination and those mainly concerned with race discrimination. Others argued that racial discrimination was unique and not merely a part of a general discrimination problem.

The Government eventually decided that harmonization should not go so far as to include a single enforcement agency at that time, but that there were strong arguments in favour of adopting, almost in their entirety, the coverage and enforcement details of what was to become the Sex Discrimination Act 1975 in the new race relations legislation. Not only might this have the practical advantages of increasing public understanding of how the two Acts operated and of enabling both enforcement agencies to work on similar lines; it might also ease the passage of race relations legislation since Parliament would already have approved virtually identical enforcement provisions in the less controversial Sex Discrimination Act. In September 1975 the White Paper *Racial Discrimination*[36] was issued, proposing that almost exactly similar coverage and enforcement provisions as in the Sex Discrimination Act should be enacted to deal with racial discrimination. This led to the Race Relations Act 1976 and the establishment of the Commission for Racial Equality.

Individual Complaints

The method of adjudication of individual complaints under the 1976 Act was substantially different from that of the 1968 Act. Individuals were now permitted to take their cases directly to the county courts or industrial tribunals; they did not have to process them first through a Race Relations Board or an equivalent type of body. Non-employment complaints were heard in county courts in which race relations assessors continued to sit with the judge. Employment discrimination cases went to industrial tribunals rather than to the county courts. Before an employment case reached a tribunal there was an opportunity for another statutory body, the Advisory, Conciliation and Arbitration Service (ACAS), to attempt to conciliate in the dispute.[37]

Individuals were required to seek redress before industrial tribunals and county courts, in part because the Government did not wish the CRE to become enmeshed in extensive and laborious casework. The CRE was freed in order that it might be able to range over the entire field of discrimination and to exercise its own independent judgement and initiative. The then Home Secretary, in introducing the Sex Discrimination Bill to Parliament, made this feature of the two Bills explicit:

The general approach to enforcement is to combine the right of direct individual access to county courts, or industrial tribunals in employment cases, with the strategic role of a powerful Equal Opportunities Commission which has the responsibility and the powers to enforce the law in the public interest. . . . The commission will have power to assist individual complainants to pursue these cases, though it is our hope and intention that they would reserve this for important or significant cases and concentrate upon the strategic role.[37a]

Rather than attempt to stimulate the development of 'private attorneys general' on American lines by encouraging private bodies to assist individual complainants,[38] the Government decided to increase the role of the Commission. The Race Relations Board had argued that to require complainants to go to industrial tribunals, and even more to county courts, would place them at a serious disadvantage. Power was given to the CRE to grant assistance to individuals who wished to take proceedings under the Act. The Commission must consider applications for such assistance but with a discretion as to the type of assistance to grant, if any. Assistance might be practical or financial and could range from advice, to providing legal representation or to 'any other form of assistance which the Commission may consider appropriate'.[39] The Commission might grant assistance on the grounds that the case raised a question of principle; or that it was unreasonable having regard to the complexity of the case or the applicant's position to expect him or her to deal with the case unaided; or by reason of any other special circumstances.

Though litigation by private litigants was thus given a much greater role in the enforcement of the legislation than under the 1968 Act, it was a more strictly limited role than that played by their counterparts in the United States. Not only were private assistance-giving bodies not otherwise encouraged, but an individual was not permitted to bring proceedings with regard to discriminatory practices, discriminatory advertisements, instructions to discriminate, pressure to discriminate, or persistent discrimination. Court enforcement of these sections was only to be initiated by the Commission. The logic behind restrictions such as these on the role of individual plaintiffs drew on (and in turn reinforced) the procedural attributes of the traditional model of the private plaintiff, viz. one taking an individualized complaint and not acting 'in the public interest'. It was envisaged that the latter role would be carried out by the Commission, and (this is the important point) *only* by the Commission.

Formal Investigations

The Commission was authorized[40] to conduct formal investigations for any purpose connected with the carrying out of its statutory duties. The most important feature of these powers was that they required no complaint from an individual before they could be brought into play. It appears to have been envisaged that there would be three types of formal investigation available to the Commission. The first type was an investigation into the activities of a 'named person' alleging that those activities unlawfully discriminated. The second type was an investigation into the activities of a 'named person' but in which there was no allegation by the Commission that the person had unlawfully discriminated. The third type was an investigation not into a named person, but into a particular area of activity, for example banking, insurance etc. Again, this third type would not make allegations of unlawful discrimination.

Investigations into specific alleged acts of discrimination automatically attracted powers of subpoena; such powers were conferred only at the discretion of the Secretary of State in the case of an investigation other than into the action of a named person. If in the course of an investigation, the Commission found unlawful discrimination, it was empowered to issue a 'non-discrimination notice' requiring the person concerned to cease discriminating and to furnish information enabling the Commission to ensure that the terms of the notice were being complied with. A number of controls were written into the legislation to govern the new formal investigation power. The CRE was not to be permitted, for example, to issue non-discrimination notices without first giving notice to the recipient of the notice of its intention to do so, specifying the grounds and offering him an opportunity of making oral or written representations, or both.[41] Other controls were to prove more controversial and problematic.

Even before a formal investigation began, where the terms of reference of the proposed investigation confined it to the activities of named persons and the Commission proposed to investigate any unlawful discrimination which it believed a person may have done, the Commission was required to inform that person of its belief and its proposal to investigate.[42] In addition it was to offer him an opportunity of making oral and written representations, and of being represented by counsel or a solicitor or by some other person of his choice, subject to an objection by the Commission on the ground that the choice was 'unsuitable'.[43]

This requirement that a named person being investigated for unlawful discrimination must, even before the investigation began and still at the stage of the drawing up of the terms of reference, be given notice of the proposed terms of reference and the opportunity of a hearing was not in the Sex Discrimination Act as passed, nor in the Race Relations Bill as introduced. It was inserted in this form in the House of Lords because of the degree of opposition to an unchecked power to embark on an investigation of unlawful discrimination. The requirements included were a compromise with Conservative front bench proposals which would, in addition, have required notice and a hearing where the Commission proposed to conduct an investigation into a named person's actions *whether or not* an unlawful act was being alleged, and also given a right to legal aid at such hearings.[44]

The Government's objections to these additional Conservative proposals, neither of which was accepted, were that CRE investigations might be into wider questions of equality of opportunity and good race relations on which it should not be necessary to provide the full panoply of natural justice requirements. With regard to the legal aid proposal it was objected that it 'would create a situation whereby anyone subject to a formal investigation by the Commission would be eligible for legal aid for hearings . . . but the same person would not be eligible for legal aid to contest exactly the same case before an industrial tribunal.'[45]

Community Relations Institutions

The CRE was given a major function additional to that of being an expanded Race Relations Board, viz. that which was previously under the umbrella of the Community Relations Commission (CRC). In 1973 the Central Policy Review Staff (CPRS) had considered whether to disband the community relations machinery entirely, on the grounds that it did nothing that could not be done better by government, a strengthened Race Relations Board and voluntary community organizations. A number of criticisms had been made:

uncertainty of aim, inefficiency of operation, and inappropriate staff selection. CPRS found these criticisms to be largely justified. Despite this, it concluded that it was too late to dismantle the CRC and local community relations councils since this would, in the uneasy state of race relations then existing, be seen by many as evidence of government withdrawal from the race relations field. Instead CPRS recommended that the CRC be given a more definite set of aims through strengthening its community development role and by making better use of its research and advisory functions. It further recommended that the CRC and the RRB be amalgamated, not only because the public already did not distinguish between them, but also because the functions of the CRC and the Board were not clearly distinct under the 1968 Act, and would become even more overlapping if the other changes that it recommended in the powers of the Board and of the CRC were to be accepted.

During the preparation of the White Paper, *Racial Discrimination*, four further options were available to the Government. The first would have involved a restructuring of the CRC, but would have continued the idea of a separate national agency, funded by government, overseeing the local community relations councils (crcs). A second option would have placed the local bodies under the control of a unit in the Home Office itself. The third option would have involved a transfer of responsibility for the crcs from national to local government, with local authorities being required to take over existing community relations officers, and to integrate them in to their social services departments. Alternatively, local authorities might be required to set up race relations departments, along the lines of the existing social service departments, but separate from them.

The Race Relations Board was entirely opposed to its amalgamation with the Community Relations Commission. The reasons which had been advanced in favour of amalgamation were thought to be unconvincing.[46] The overlap between the Board and the CRC was 'insignificant'. Their work had been coordinated and 'little or no difficulty had arisen'. Second, it had been argued that amalgamation would avoid confusion in the public mind about the functions of the proposed new enforcement agency. For the Board, however, 'different approaches are required to meet different needs', and this demanded a separate organization. The Board rejected the view that public misperceptions justified amalgamation. Third, the Board did not accept that amalgamation would enable the proposed new enforcement agency to keep in touch with the local community, or prevent it from becoming too remote. 'The local network does not need to be inside . . . for the proposed new enforcement agency to be able to communicate with it; and it will have many contacts with the members of minority groups through its investigations and its involvement in the complaints process.' Fourth, to make the new enforcement body responsible for the activities of local crcs and their officers could not fail to compromise its independence and impartiality. At the same time, the crcs themselves and their officers should be in a position to speak their minds freely and openly in their localities. This independence would be compromised if the officers were employees of the new enforcement body.

Nevertheless it was eventually decided by the Home Office that in addition to its role as an expanded version of the Race Relations Board, the new enforcement agency would also be given the functions of the Community Relations Commission, including the responsibility of funding the crcs, though crc officers would not be employees of the Commission.

3 Formal Investigations: the First Generation

CRE Organization and Structure
The Commission consisted, in 1986, of 15 members who were appointed by the Home Secretary, two after consultation with employers' organizations and two after consultation with the Trades Union Congress. The membership contained two professors, four practising lawyers, a trade union general secretary, a trade union deputy secretary, one teacher/social worker, two directors of personnel, one technical director, and the vice chairman of the United Kingdom Immigrants Advisory Service. Appointments were for periods of up to five years but reappointments were possible. The Act provides that the Commission may establish a committee structure and in 1986 there were four committees of Commission members: complaints; employment; education, housing and services; and field services. These committees supervised the four operational divisions of the Commission (legal, including complaints; employment; education, housing and services; and field services). In addition there was an administrative division dealing with general services.

The Commission recruited its own staff, who were not civil servants.

However, their number, pay and conditions of service required the approval of the Treasury. In 1985 there were 200 permanent staff in post, eleven of whom were legally qualified. The Commission is funded by an annual grant-in-aid from the Home Office. For the financial year 1985–86, the grant-in-aid amounted to £9.44m of which £2.28m was expended on the salaries of Commission staff. The salaries of staff of the community relations councils amounted to £2.62m in 1985–86. The Commission is required under the Act to submit to the Home Secretary an annual report on its activities, which is laid before Parliament and published, as well as an annual statement of accounts which the Comptroller and Auditor General lays before Parliament.

Promotion and Law Enforcement

The Commission was, as we have seen, an amalgamation of the Community Relations Commission (with its research, educational/ promotional and 'spokesperson' roots) and the Race Relations Board (with its law-enforcement and complaints-resolving bias). The first years of the new Commission seem to have been dominated by the problems of making one new body out of its two predecessors.

In retrospect the organizational structure adopted after the establishment of the new Commission contributed to this tension. Two major operational divisions were established. One, the Equal Opportunities Division, was originally responsible solely for formal investigations and was staffed by a number of former Race Relations Board employees. The other, the Community Affairs and Liaison Division, was responsible for promotion, fieldwork, and community services, and was staffed by a number of former Community Relations Commission employees. The competition for posts in the new organization was exacerbated by accusations that the group of mainly white, former Board employees were being preferred over the group of mainly black, former CRC employees.

The CRE argued in public for the importance of a close relationship between the promotional side and the law enforcement side. Nevertheless, one commentator has argued that these staffing problems 'hindered the development of a coherent strategy co-ordinating the enforcement and promotional work of the Commission and, to begin with, those appointed to the CRE carried on with the work they had done before in enforcement or promotion pretty much in isolation from each other. . . .'[47] The same author pointed to what he saw as the 'somewhat contrasting' ethos of the two divisions. 'Some members of the promotional side wished the CRE to adopt a vigorous, even an aggressively campaigning style and to foster close links with the black communities, even to the extent of acting on their behalf; while those on the enforcement side felt that their role demanded the careful and objective preparation of cases against those accused of discrimination.'[48] There was therefore less of a debate over the merits of one or the other approach, than a constant jockeying for position, with both factions anxious to see that 'its' approach was given special recognition.

Complaints and Formal Investigations

So too the balance within enforcement, between formal investigations and assistance to individual complainants, was affected by the structure adopted. The Equal Opportunity Division (EOD) was, as we have seen, in effect the successor to the Race Relations Board. The position taken by the Board prior to the legislation of 1976, that it needed to have available to it the powers to carry out pro-active strategic investigations, thus carried over into the EOD. They had been asking for these powers for some time; now that they had them, they had to be seen to be used. Not surprisingly, therefore, formal investigations were regarded as the primary tool of enforcement. This approach was reflected in, and reinforced by, locating the function of assisting complainants initially not in EOD but in a separate Legal Section. Only in 1979, after a Home Office staff inspection, was this function transferred to EOD. By this time the preference of the Division for formal investigations was confirmed.

Thus, between 1977 and 1982, none of the staff (apart from the Chief Executive) could be said to have had a foot both in the promotional camp and in the formal investigation camp. No forum, therefore, naturally existed whereby a choice between strategies could be made. The main concern of EOD was whether or not to mount a formal investigation in the field; the main concern of the relevant promotional sections was whether or not to mount a promotional effort; nobody's main concern appeared to be the strategic choice between the two.

When EOD staff felt that a formal investigation was possible and desirable, a proposal went to the CRE's Equal Opportunities Committee. In the vast majority of cases the formal investigation was approved and this decision was handed on to the full Commission for formal endorsement. In effect the importance of an issue to the CRE, when endorsed by the Committee, was translated directly into a decision to mount a formal investigation. In retrospect, not enough consideration was given to alternative approaches to resolving an issue, or to the practical difficulties and resource implications of carrying out an investigation.

Investigations Initiated: 1977–1982

Between 1977 and 1982 the Commission embarked upon enquiries in 47 formal investigations. Of these 47, 29 were investigations into an allegation of unlawful discrimination against a named person (so-called 'belief' investigations[49]), 15 were investigations of a named person not alleging unlawful discrimination, and 3 were investigations into a more general situation or locality, not alleging unlawful discrimination and not naming particular persons. In two other cases, draft terms of reference were drawn up but it was decided not to embark on the investigation after hearing representations.

In part, this emphasis on 'belief' investigations was due to the CRE's view that the main reason for giving the Commission the power to conduct formal investigations was to enable it to tackle unlawful discrimination. In part, too, the Commission appears to have embarked on a number of these 'belief' investigations on the basis of specific complaints.

The Commission was at pains to stress that although it took such complaints into account, it would be wrong for the Commission to start an investigation whenever it received such evidence, for this would be so demanding on its resources that it would preclude the adoption of a coherent and effective strategy.[50] Nevertheless the CRE's early investigations were highly responsive to complaints. The Commission justified using individual complaints in certain areas as part of a general strategy. First, in some cases the Commission received evidence of possible discrimination by an organization in an area which, as part of its strategy, it had already identified as one of its priorities for investigation, and in these circumstances an investigation of that organization was seen as the best way of implementing that part of the strategy. Second, the Commission decided that the most effective method of tackling discrimination in a number of other areas was, in addition to assisting individual complainants, to initiate investigations in response to strong evidence. These were early dubbed 'responsive' investigations within the Commission.

Thus, though heavily responsive in a number of areas to individual complaints (or to general public disquiet as, for example, led to the investigation of the administration of immigration control), the Commission does appear to have been mindful of its strategic role even in these investigations. In a number of cases, for example, the Commission decided to try to broaden these responsive investigations by adopting terms of reference which went beyond the specific allegations made and thus to use a specific complaint as a peg on which to hang a more wide-ranging inquiry.

A significant number of investigations were also initiated into named persons, but without alleging unlawful discrimination (section 49(3) investigations). The then Director of the Equal Opportunity Division explained, in 1981, that in the large employment investigations it had been the policy of the Commission first

> to get the overall picture of the . . . ethnic breakdown of the workforce. Then . . . we . . . pick out . . . where the figures appear to give particular cause for concern and concentrate on those areas . . . When we moved into employment we did not necessarily have a great deal of information about particular strategic issues within particular companies. What we did believe was that there was, for example, indirect discrimination occurring in various ways throughout employment, and if we took particular spans in the vital areas we would be able to home in on those issues within those large companies.[51]

Some section 49(3) investigations involved some suspicion that discrimination was occurring, because research established that this type of discrimination occurred in similar organizations, or because it was known that the organization employed disproportionately few ethnic minority workers. Some other section 49(3) investigations were begun where it was felt that the size of the organization itself justified strategic concern and deserved to be looked at.[52]

Of the 46 investigations begun in this period (1977–82), 24 were in employment, 11 were in housing, 2 in education, 8 in the provision of goods, facilities and services, and one in immigration. Employment was the first priority of the Commission's investigation strategy because of its importance to the black community and the widespread extent of discrimination substantiated by PEP research. An additional crucial reason was, in the words of the former Director of the Equal Opportunity Division, that because 'of the way in which it is organized, employment is particularly open to investigation: indeed the whole argument for the need for investigative powers was originally formulated in the context of employment'.[53] A greater number of wide-ranging investigations were initiated in employment than in any other area and a significant number of these were named person inquiries not alleging unlawful discrimination.[54] In selecting subjects for investigation, the Commission consciously concentrated on those industries and services which they considered most important in the labour markets in which ethnic minorities are most strongly represented. It also tried to cover a wide range, both geographically and in types of employment, so that its investigations should have the widest possible impact. Clearly, too, a number of 'household names' were included.

Although employment was clearly the main area of work, and was intended to be, a number of other investigations were initiated, most notably those in education and housing. In housing a similar mix of responsive and more general investigations was also embarked on. Particular responsive investigations were undertaken with regard to local authority housing in Slough, Hillingdon, Brymbo and Walsall. Similar investigations were embarked on with regard to a number of estate agents, housing associations, accommodation agencies and individual landlords. More general investigations were begun into the allocation of local authority housing to work permit holders, the allocation of mortgage in Rochdale, and the whole range of allocation policies and practices in Hackney.

Conduct of Investigations

By mid 1981 the Commission had started 45 investigations but had published final reports in only ten. Non-discrimination notices had been issued in eight of these ten. Fieldwork had been completed in 14 other investigations and non-discrimination notices had been issued in four of these.

The time taken to complete investigations was becoming excessive. The absence of necessary statistical and other information was one reason. The decentralized nature of much of the decision-making being investigated was another. The interlocking roles of many different persons and institutions often made it difficult to allocate responsibility sufficiently clearly to warrant a legal finding of discrimination by any particular individual or institution. The information necessary was in most cases held by the respondents themselves and extracting it proved to be time consuming. When respondents were intransigent the Commission used its subpoena powers.[55] Up to May 1981 the Commission issued 40 subpoena notices in eight investigations.[56] In five of these investigations the person or persons concerned failed to comply with the notice, and the Commission had to apply to a county court for an order requiring compliance. In each case the order was granted, though not always in the precise terms applied for. The contrast between the time taken to deal with cooperative and uncooperative respondents was well illustrated in two investigations into accommodation agencies. One was fully cooperative, and the investigation lasted less than nine months. Another was 'obstructive and unhelpful' and the investigation lasted almost two years.[57]

Other delays arose from the Commission's ability to issue a subpoena order only in 'belief' investigations. In other non-'belief' investigations the Secretary of State's permission was necessary. Although the Commission did not actually have to seek such permission in any particular case, one investigation 'was delayed for very many weeks whilst we built up a case of sufficient strength had it been necessary . . . to get them [subpoena powers], and that certainly is a substantial discouragement for going for the strategic, the non-reactive, investigation'.[58]

Other problems arose from the cumbersome nature of the formal investigation machinery which the CRE operated. If the Commission decided to investigate a respondent whom it believed may have discriminated, it issued terms of reference to the respondent; offered him the right to make oral and written representations about the proposed investigation; considered any representations that were made; went through the whole procedure again if, as a result of the representations, it decided to revise the terms of reference; resolved to embark on the investigation (assuming that it still believed that the respondent may have discriminated); conducted its enquiries; issued a subpoena notice if the respondent refused to provide information, and got that notice enforced through the courts if necessary; if it found discrimination, informed the respondent of its grounds and offered him the right to make oral and written representations again; considered the representations; if it so decided, issued a non-discrimination notice; if there was no appeal against the notice, drafted a public report, offered the respondent and other interested parties the opportunity to comment on the report; revised it if necessary, and then published it.[59]

The CRE staff, commissioners and legal advisers developed these internal procedures with the possibility of judicial review very much in mind. In part this recognition was due to the experience of the Race Relations Board;[60] in part it was due to the advice of counsel, which was often sought. The Commission did not, for example, use formal investigations primarily as threat, a bargaining tool. Staff considered that it would have been heavily criticized if it had done so. Indeed, on a number of occasions those being investigated did approach the Commission, asking to negotiate a settlement at the beginning of an investigation and the Commission refused. A well-publicized row broke out when even the possibility of negotiating a settlement with Massey Ferguson at the non-discrimination notice stage was disclosed. Some Commissioners questioned the legal propriety of doing so and counsel's opinion was sought. The Commission asked whether there was an approach midway between making recommendations under section 51 and issuing a non-discrimination notice under section 58. Counsel was of the view that 'the CRE is a statutory body. It cannot assume powers wider than those granted to it by statute . . . it is not permissible for the CRE to attempt to circumvent the inconvenient pigeon-holes into which the statute has confined its powers.'[61] No agreement could therefore be negotiated lawfully where a non-discrimination notice could be issued.

Rather ironically, as will appear subsequently, the Commission believed that, if it rigidly adhered to the procedures which it considered were laid down in the Act, investigations might be delayed but that it would ultimately be successful. Thus, by 1981, although the CRE had been unable to embark on a limited number of enquiries because the respondents had been granted judicial review of their procedures, the difficulties encountered by the Commission were not substantially the excessive intervention of the courts. The Commission's consciousness of the requirements of judicial review and its apparent ability, forewarned, to fight its corner when challenged on grounds with which it was familiar was rewarded in the first cases challenging the CRE's use of its powers. In *Home Office* v. *CRE*[62] the Home Office unsuccessfully challenged the power of the CRE to investigate the administration of immigration control. In *R.* v. *CRE, ex parte Cottrell and Rothon*[63] it was argued that the CRE's procedures were unlawful on three grounds: first, that at the Commission's hearing of their oral representations (when the respondents were arguing that they had not broken the law and that a non-discrimination notice should not be issued) witnesses were not available to be cross-examined by the respondents' counsel; second, that the Commission relied on hearsay evidence, such as reports of interviews by the Commission's staff, and, third, that the two Commissioners nominated for the conduct of the investigation did not themselves carry out the enquiries but left these to the Commission's employees. All three arguments were rejected by the Divisional Court.

4 Control and Accountability

Parliamentary Scrutiny
During 1981 the Home Affairs Committee of the House of Commons carried out an appraisal of the Commission's operation and effectiveness, partly as a result of 'widespread public criticism' and partly because it had 'not been greatly impressed'[64] by the quality of evidence submitted by the Commission in the course of previous enquiries carried out by its race relations subcommittee. The Report, published in November 1981, was highly critical of the Commission and widely publicized.[65]

The Committee's view of the balance between promotion and law enforcement was heavily in favour of the Commission concentrating its resources on law enforcement. Although the Commission should continue in its dual role as an investigative and promotional body, the Committee considered that its promotional work should be 'solely dictated by the need to eradicate racial discrimination'.[66] The Commission was considered to be concentrating too many resources on types of promotional activity which did not arise from its law enforcement role.[67] It 'must not and cannot be' some sort of 'representative community body'.[68] The Commission's priority should rather be primarily to act as a law enforcement agency. Promotional work should only be undertaken where it built on experience gained through detailed investigation and research. The further promotional work was removed from being an adjunct of law enforcement 'the less effective it becomes. . . . By rushing ahead with promotional work unrelated to law enforcement, the Commission have put an unwieldy cart before an admittedly ponderous horse.'[69] The Commission should concentrate 'on coping with the backlog of investigations so that their promotional work can be undertaken on a surer foundation'.[70] The Committee was critical in this context of the lack of connection between the two operational divisions and suggested rearranging the internal divisional structure 'so that staff would not be exclusively attached to one function rather than another'.[71]

The Committee was rather more muted in its comments on the initiation of investigations. However, the CRE's own distinction between 'responsive' and 'strategic' investigations came back to haunt it. The Committee ignored or did not understand the CRE's argument that strategic considerations were furthered by relying in part on responsive investigations. The Committee criticized the number of 'responsive' investigations into small organizations: '[I]n general terms these investigations have had minimal effect, and we have some sympathy with one of those so investigated who told the sub-committee that "the CRE used a sledge hammer to put in a carpet tack" '.[72] The Committee concluded that '[i]t may well be that fewer but bigger investigations should have been begun earlier. There are unfortunately remaining one or two of the "responsive" investigations into the small fry; but by and large it is clear that the Commission have passed that unfortunate stage and are now engaged in a number of potentially significant investigations.'[73]

The major criticism of the Commission's use of its formal investigation powers related not to the initiation but to the *conduct* of investigations, and in particular the time taken to complete them. Though some delays were accepted as the fault of the statutory procedures and the uncooperativeness of respondents, the Committee concluded

that most of the causes of delay in completing investigations rest firmly within the Commission. . . . We can but conclude that the Commission have not yet developed that style of brisk and systematic investigation which might be expected of them. As they concentrate increasingly on the use of their investigative powers, the Commission must shake off their present trundling style of investigation. Allowances had in the past to be made for the novelty of the procedures employed, but by now the Commission should be experienced enough, and Parliament is entitled to expect a smarter pace.[74]

The Committee described how bodies being investigated by the Commission 'received the impression that the investigating officers did not always have a very clear idea of what they were seeking or any systematic way of obtaining it'.[75] It 'did not really know what it was looking for and therefore sought too much information'.[76] This may have arisen from the Commission's practice of getting an overview and then homing in on areas of concern. The Committee emphasized that the delays could 'seriously diminish the impact of a completed report . . . [and] seriously infringe the natural rights of the body under investigation'.[77] The Commission and Home Office were encouraged to carry out together a review of the Commission's practices in the conduct of investigations, 'with a view to ensuring that there is no repetition of the prolonged delays which have hitherto marred the Commission's investigative record'.[78]

After consultation with the CRE, the Home Office replied in April 1982,[79] accepting the need for the CRE to increase its effectiveness, improve its procedures and speed up its investigations. The CRE agreed: to review its organization, including the links and co-ordination between the divisions of the Commission; to review the procedures followed in investigations; to review its priorities of work; to improve training procedures for staff and the effectiveness of their performance; to concentrate on coping with the backlog of investigations; and to relate its promotional activities more closely to investigations and court decisions. The Home Office did not agree, however, 'that the promotional and educational work of the CRE should be as narrowly confined' as the Committee envisaged. 'Not only must the Commission undertake the law enforcement duties imposed by the Race Relations Act; it also needs to play an effective part in the wider field of combating racial disadvantage, in contributing to the general climate of opinion on racial issues and in educating people for a multi-racial society.'[80]

As a result of the Select Committee scrutiny, a working party of commissioners was established to look at formal investigations. This reported in 1982. At the same time, the Home Office offered, and the Commission accepted, the services of a Home Office researcher who conducted a more detailed review of formal investigation policy and procedures. This review was reported, separately, to the Commission in late 1982. Taken together they amounted to a set of proposals for formal investigations based on the experience of the period up to 1982. Before considering these further, however, we should turn to examine the rather different approach adopted by the courts.

Judicial Scrutiny

Controls by the judiciary were exerted on the Commission's use of formal investigations at three stages: at the beginning (stage 1), during the course of (stage 2), and at the end of the process (stage 3). However, the rationale of the *Selvarajan* and *Cottrell* cases was that the Race Relations Board and the Commission should be given a considerable leeway with regard to the operation of stage 2. In both cases the courts accepted that a process different from the judicial was legitimate, in part because of what it perceived as the 'administrative' nature of the process.[81] Issues of individual rights and responsibilities were not being finally determined.[82] There was no clear difference of structure perceived as operating between the 1968 Act Board and the 1976 Act Commission sufficient to require a different approach by the courts. More importantly, there was a clear indication of a 'hands-off' approach to judicial review of administrative action resonating through the judgments of both cases.

When the courts came to consider how they should view stage 3 (the end of the formal investigation process), it was not surprising that a wider scrutiny was felt to be appropriate. Thus, the courts were prepared to second-guess the CRE's decision, after the formal investigation process itself had ended. In *Amari Plastics* the Court of Appeal[83] held that findings as to past unlawful conduct included in a non-discrimination notice should be appealable from the Commission to a judicial body, and not just the extent and content of any non-discrimination notice, as the Commission had argued. Lord Denning in the Court of Appeal stressed (in rather exaggerated rhetoric) that freedom from judicial interference in stage 2 required intervention and scrutiny at stage 3 as a *quid pro quo*. Both he and Griffiths LJ, perhaps rather disingenuously, laid the blame for any inconveniences suffered by the Commission on Parliament: 'The machinery is so elaborate and so cumbersome that it is in danger of grinding to a halt. I am very sorry for the commission, but they have been caught up in a spider's web spun by Parliament, from which there is little hope of them escaping.'[84] The *Amari* case itself well illustrates the effect of this spider's web. The Commission's enquiries into Amari took six months in early 1979, but because of the time needed for representations by the company, the non-discrimination notice was not issued until February 1980. There then followed lengthy proceedings, culminating in 1982 in the Court of Appeal judgment. Following this, the appeal itself was heard in September and October 1983, five to six years after the alleged discrimination occurred.

When *Selvarajan*, *Cottrell* and *Amari* are taken together, therefore, a model of control emerges which insulates the formal investigation process until completion and then re-adjudicates a number of the issues, largely according to judicial methods of adjudication.

Although there was a divergence of approach among the staff of the Commission, this approach seemed generally acceptable, even anticipated. It seems to have been the case that a rather judicialized procedure had anyway been contemplated by some in the CRE and investigations were conducted with an eye to the conclusions being reached by a method ultimately acceptable to the courts. The main problems arising from the approach adopted by the courts in these cases was one of delay, rather than the creation of substantial difficulties of process or strategy.[85] It is noticeable, for example, that none of these cases was appealed beyond the Court of Appeal.

Nevertheless there is a clear resistance by the courts apparent in these cases to other than a hierarchical and unitary conception of law. This is reflected, too, in the most recent scrutiny of the Commission's formal investigation process in *R* v. *CRE, ex p. Westminster City Council* [85a], where a stage 3 appeal to an industrial tribunal or county court (both with specialized memberships, of course) was held to be replaceable in certain broad instances with a judicial review procedure before a single judge in the Divisional Court, apparently because a different institutional procedure could not have reached acceptably different substantive results.

The most profound problems for the CRE's conduct of formal investigations arose, however, from the courts' scrutiny of the initiation of investigations. Though on its face a victory for the CRE, the first case challenging the Commission's power to embark on an investigation (stage 1), *Home Office* v. *CRE*,[86] contains within it the seeds of the subsequent problems. Woolf J drew on the fact that the Commission was the product of the amalgamation of the old Race Relations Board (RRB) and the Communty Relations Commission (CRC) to draw a distinction between RRB-type investigations and CRC-type investigations. CRC-type investigations would not be scrutinized as intensively as RRB-type investigations for two main reasons. First, they were, in essence, already effectively controlled by the Secretary of State through the power to allow the CRE powers to obtain information; 'unless the Secretary of State is prepared to supply it with teeth, the commission has limited powers to obtain information'.[87] Second, only recommendations and not non-discrimination notices could be made at the conclusion, and these were 'hardly likely to substantially interfere with the functioning of those subject to this type of investigation'.[88]

This approach appears to be echoed in the hesitation articulated in the Court of Appeal's more intemperate language in *Science Research Council* v. *Nasse*.[89] Though the case involved the power of discovery available to an individual litigant who happened to be assisted by the Commission, an argument was made that discovery in proceedings under the discrimination statutes should be more restricted than in ordinary civil proceedings, in part because the statute provided a power to the Commission to hold formal investigations. Though the House of Lords rightly rejected this argument, it provided the occasion for a number of *obiter* pronouncements on the formal investigation power itself. Most extreme was Lord Denning in the Court of Appeal who referred six times in the course of his judgment to the 'inquisitional' powers of the Commission which were 'of a kind never before known to the law'.[90] The investigation powers enabled the Commission to 'interrogate employers and educational authorities up to the hilt and compel disclosure of documents on a massive scale. . . . You might think that we were back in the days of the inquisition. . . . You might think we were back in the days of the General Warrants'.[91]

The House of Lords was rather more sympathetic to the Commission in *Nasse*, with Lord Wilberforce throwing some well-deserved cold water on Lord Denning's inflammatory outburst. 'These provisions', he wrote, referring to the formal investigation powers,

may appear draconian – they did so to some extent to Lord Denning MR – but for my part I do not find it necessary to characterize them. The powers have been conferred by Parliament upon statutory bodies as part of the machinery for eliminating discrimination in situations where the parties are of unequal strength: no instance was given to us of an oppressive use of them and we should presume that they will be reasonably used for the purpose for which they were given.[92]

Despite this, however, in both *R.* v. *CRE, ex p. Hillingdon London Borough Council*,[93] and in *In re Prestige*,[94] the Commission's initiation of two formal investigations was successfully challenged. In *Hillingdon* a 'belief' investigation was in issue. The Commission's decision to conduct a formal investigation was held by the House of Lords to be ultra vires on the grounds that the terms of reference of the investigation were too wide. In order to embark on a 'belief' investigation, the Commission had to have material before it 'sufficient to raise in the minds of reasonable men possessed of the experience of covert racial discrimination that had been acquired by the Commission a suspicion that there may have been acts by the person named of racial discrimination of the kind which it is proposed to investigate'.[95] In addition, it was permissible for the Commission to infer the possibility of more widespread discrimination on evidence of specific acts: 'the circumstances may be such that [the Commission] may not unreasonably suspect that these are but instances of a more widespread discrimination of a similar kind that has not yet been uncovered'.[96] The terms of reference may lawfully be wide enough to enable the Commission to examine whether the inference was justified. But since the Commission's counsel had admitted that the Commission had no belief of the type necessary to sustain the wide terms of reference proposed by the Commission, a necessary condition was not complied with. The terms of reference did not limit the investigation to the extent of discrimination actually believed by the Commission to exist.

In *Prestige* the House of Lords considered the powers of the Commission to embark on an investigation into a named person in which unlawful discrimination was not alleged. The company relied on an interpretation of section 49(4) of the Act. This provides an opportunity, in cases where it is proposed to mount an investigation into a named person, for that person to make oral representations before the investigation commences. The Commission had previously regarded that provision as procedural in its effects, applicable only where there were specific grounds for suspecting unlawful discrimination. The company argued that the subsection went beyond imposing a procedural constraint and prevented a named-person investigation being commenced at all unless unlawful discrimination was suspected. The House of Lords agreed. The Act permitted only two types of investigation, not three as had been supposed. One type was against a named person where an unlawful act of discrimination is suspected. The second type was a general investigation without named persons.[97]

A number of explanations for the decisions in *Hillingdon* and *Prestige* might be put forward. One explanation may be that the courts reassessed their approach to the Commission and in effect, though not ostensibly, decided that the approach taken in *Cottrell* was wrong, and that a much greater scrutiny of the Commission's decisions than had previously been envisaged was now justified. On this reasoning the agency's undertaking of a formal investigation perhaps came to be seen as of much greater importance to an individual's interests than had been supposed in *Cottrell*; or perhaps the public confidence in the agency was thought in general to be low; or perhaps the preference of the Court of Appeal in *Selvarajan* and Lord Lane in *Cottrell* for a restrained approach to judicial review ran counter to the more activist Lord Diplock, the senior judge in both *Hillingdon* and *Prestige*.

A second explanation for *Hillingdon* and *Prestige* is much more particular and *ad hoc*: the facts of the *Hillingdon* and *Prestige* cases were themselves a weak basis on which to fight for the importance of strategic enforcement.[98] In *Hillingdon*, the Commission's counsel acknowledged before the House of Lords that the CRE did not have any belief of the extent of the wider discrimination alleged in the terms of reference. In *Prestige* the Commission began its investigation not alleging unlawful discrimination but subsequently issued a non-discrimination notice, without converting the investigation formally into a 'belief' investigation. Both these explanations seem likely to have played a part in the decisions but are unconvincing as complete theories either singly or together. The first explanation seems to imply a comprehensive retreat from *Cottrell*, for which there is little evidence in the opinions. The second explanation ignores the fact that while these particular attributes were alternative grounds for the opinions in the cases, the House of Lords were clear in basing their opinions on considerably wider grounds.

Rather, the basis for the opinions, and the reason for the *angst* which the cases gave rise to in the CRE, appears to have been judicial scepticism of the appropriateness of the CRE's proactive strategic role. The importance of the change from an essentially private to an essentially public enforcement role for the CRE introduced in the 1976 Act was widely misunderstood. The cases show a substantial gap between the perception held by the CRE of the CRE's role, and that held by those being investigated. Moral outrage by respondents at the conduct of the CRE resulted, and the courts appear to have responded sympathetically to those under investigation. The difference in approach between *Cottrell* and *Hillingdon/Prestige* thus becomes clearer: while the courts were content with the institutional characteristics of investigations,[99] the strategic rationale for their existence was deemed largely unacceptable, at least when pursued by the CRE. It is for this reason that the CRE felt it had to appeal to the House of Lords in both cases. Lord Diplock's criticism of the Commission in *Prestige* for taking the cases to that level betrays as much as anything a lack of appreciation of how what had been done affected the Commission's conception of its strategic role. Indeed, there was an evident unwillingness to accept the Commission's conception of its strategic role. The combined effect of *Hillingdon/ Prestige* was to call into question a substantial number of investigations.[100]

5 Formal Investigations: the Second Generation and the Shadow of Judicial Review

From the mid 1980s, formal investigations have come to be regarded by the Commission as, at best, a final resort. A combination of reasons appears to have led to this approach developing.

Reorganization
One reason was the analysis of the Home Office researcher in 1982, whose report followed the Select Committee enquiry. This report argued that the impact of investigative powers on discrimination should be maximized by using the *threat* of a formal investigation as a promotional tool and recommended that the Commission should use this approach more widely. Most potential respondents, particularly large organizations, were considered to be deeply afraid of the announcement of an investigation because it affected their public image. The report recommended that there should be a fairly lengthy pre-investigation period, during which information was gathered about the respondent, consultations were carried out inside and outside the Commission, and the potential respondent was approached both for information and to determine whether he might be amenable to a promotional approach, with the threat of investigation being employed as a lever.

A major problem which the researcher identified as arising from this approach was that the CRE might feel that it would lose credibility if it became known that it was pursuing a 'soft' option with a possible discriminator. It was argued, however, that all law enforcement agencies had to use powers of discretion if they were not to become hopelessly overloaded with work. Moreover there would always be far more possible discriminators, far more suspicions of discrimination, than could be met by formal investigations. If the credibility of the CRE rested on meeting all such suspicions with full legal action then its credibility was doomed in any case. In the long run, respect for the CRE would depend on its capacity to achieve national reductions in the level of racial discrimination. To this end, the cost-effectiveness of threatening formal investigations as opposed to actually carrying them out was too important to ignore. Other investigative bodies, such as the factory inspectorate and the pollution inspectorate, habitually used such threats to obtain non-judicial settlements, and rarely resorted to prosecution.

It was questionable, the researcher concluded, whether a named-person investigation, which did not involve an allegation of discrimination but where the Commission chose an organization on the basis of its size or because it was a household name, should ever be mounted. The lack of clarity of initial objectives tended to lead to a lengthy and open-ended style of investigation in both these and 'named person' investigations where unlawful discrimination was alleged but the terms of reference were 'broadened out' to include allegations of discrimination wider than those which originally gave rise to the investigation. In both, resources were committed without any clear idea of results or, indeed, timing. This was another reason why initial enquiries should be carried out before a more narrowly defined investigation was formally undertaken.

Formal investigations, in brief, should only be carried out when they represented the best approach to a given problem. Promotional efforts, aid to complainants and research projects might often be better alternatives and there was a need for a forum within the Commission where these alternatives could be considered. Where a finding of unlawful discrimination was unlikely to result, and subpoena powers unlikely to be necessary, there was little justification for carrying out a formal investigation. Likewise abandonment or summary termination of an investigation should also be considered when, for example, the first phase of enquiries suggested that the investigation would not be fruitful in these ways. Some investigations could be terminated with honour by the Commission taking the opportunity to issue a report recommending changes in the practices and procedures of respondents.

The integrated strategy recommended would, it was argued, be extremely difficult to carry out if the structural division between promotional and investigative staff continued. He recommended, in addition to more legal and research specialists, that a more integrated structure be adopted, with staff responsible for *both* promotional and investigative work.

This report, together with the Commission's own working party reports on investigations and structure, formed the basis for structural and organizational changes. The introduction of these reforms coincided with the appointment of a new chairman, Peter Newsam, in 1982. A legal division was created and a new Legal Director appointed. The previous two operational divisions were broken up and three new divisions created, with more integrated functions. The employment division and the education, housing and services division were given both investigative and promotional staff. The development of the new integrated structure coincided with the appointment of Directors who, with one exception, were from a 'promotion' background, and a greater emphasis was placed on promotion as a follow-up to the completion of the group of investigations commenced before 1982, and the issuing of the Code of Practice in 1984.

The Commission's priority became one of 'complet[ing] the backlog of investigative work' before commencing further investigations.[101] There was a considerable backlog which the Commission was determined to reduce by publishing as many reports as possible. Seven reports were published in 1983, eight in 1984 and six in 1985, making a total of 37 in all. In a number of investigations in which reports were issued, considerable time was required to negotiate with senior management of investigated organizations in order to reach an agreed report, or at least one which would not be appealed, or made the subject of judicial review. By the end of 1986, there was only one of the 'first generation' formal investigations still in progress[102] and that had been the subject of much litigation. Except for this investigation, the Commission had completed the backlog of its first-generation investigations, having published 20 reports in three years.

The Current Strategy

Rather ironically, in view of the Select Committee's preference for an enforcement approach using the formal investigations process, no investigations were begun in 1982 or 1983. One investigation was started in 1984 and completed almost exactly one year later.[103] The investigation is a good example of the restrictive consequences of the *Prestige* decision. It was a general investigation into the employment practices of a group of employers at a shopping centre in Leicester. It did not allege unlawful discrimination, nor were there 'named persons' in the terms of reference. The investigation disclosed a number of discriminatory practices by particular employers. Had the shopping centre been owned by one employer, the CRE's view is that it could not lawfully have been investigated, due to the *Prestige* decision. Another general investigation, into recruitment for training in chartered accountancy, was started in 1984 and published in 1986.

Since 1984, the formal investigation process has come back into play again. In 1985, draft terms of reference were drawn up and communicated to respondents in five 'belief' investigations. In two (one an education issue, one into the employment of nurses), enquiries were proceeding and one was nearing completion. In two others, representations had been heard on whether to embark on a full investigation, but decisions had not been taken by the CRE. The remaining investigation was into the MSC youth placement schemes in Birmingham. This was suspended while the local authority carried out its own enquiry. This internal enquiry reported in early 1986. The Council agreed with the Commission to adopt an equal opportunity programme to ensure that the youth training scheme was non-discriminatory. In another case a research project was commenced rather than a formal investigation. What is perhaps surprising, in the light of the previous discussion, is how little these 'second generation' investigations seem to have been threatened directly by judicial review so far. In only one, apparently, was judicial review raised openly by those being investigated during discussions with the Commission.

The effect of judicial review on the internal decision-making of the CRE is difficult to estimate. One general effect seems to have been to encourage the use of alternative types of legal proceedings. The CRE has power to take proceedings in courts and tribunals at its own initiative in relation to pressure to discriminate and discriminatory instructions. It would seem that this method of enforcement has on occasion been used where previously a formal investigation might have been begun. These proceedings have provided the occasion for wide-ranging negotiated settlements, with admissions of liability sometimes being incorporated in tribunal decisions. This emphasis on negotiated settlements is a second characteristic of the revised approach to formal investigations. Formal investigations appear now to lead much more often than before to negotiations. This is due partly to the amalgamation of promotional and enforcement staffs, partly to the perception by those being investigated that the CRE was prepared to use these powers forcefully in the past, and partly to the realization by Commissioners and staff that, in the aftermath of

Hillingdon and *Prestige*, investigations are more complicated than was previously thought. What is possible now would probably not have been politically feasible when the Commission began its work.

The power to initiate formal investigations provides, then, an incentive for bargaining. There is, however, a vital distinction between bargaining from a position of strength (where launching a formal investigation and issuing a non-discrimination notice is a real threat) and bargaining from a position of weakness. At this time, partly because of the effect of judicial review, the Commission bargains from a position of weakness, except where publicity itself is a sanction, e.g. against 'household names' which need to preserve a good image. Unless the Commission is able to face the challenge of judicial review, keep its nerve and win often enough to gain credibility for its process, then it will increasingly be seen to be negotiating with a very weak hand. The initiation of formal investigations and the issuing of non-discrimination notices are not purely symbolic therefore; they must be seen to be able to be used if a negotiation strategy is to stand any real chance of success in the medium term.

Proposals for Legislative Change

In 1983 the Commission produced a consultative document outlining a number of proposals for legislative reform of the Act under which it operates.[104] In 1985 a set of firmer proposals was published.[105] Of particular relevance are the Commission's proposals for formal investigations. There were, in effect, three changes advocated. The first was that section 49(4) should be repealed as it was unnecessary as a procedural safeguard. The Commission adopted the Home Affairs Committee's criticism that the procedure 'offers little or no worthwhile protection to a respondent; the possibility of judicial review represents a considerably more reliable safeguard'.[106] The second proposal was that the same section should be repealed so as to ensure that 'named person' investigations which did not allege unlawful discrimination should be available to the Commission in future; in effect a proposal to overturn *Prestige*. 'The Commission', it was argued, 'needs to be able to look at selected major employers to enable it to identify what practices are disadvantaging ethnic minorities. The Commission in this respect should be thought of as an inspectorate, bringing technical expertise to bear on identifying major social problems.'[107]

The third proposal was considerably more far-reaching. Under the

1976 Act, as we have seen, the Commission has the power to issue a non-discrimination notice, which is subject to appeal in the county court or industrial tribunal. In place of this power, which would be repealed, the Commission proposed that it would have a new power to take evidence of discrimination directly to a court or tribunal, seeking a finding that discrimination had occurred and appropriate remedies, including the ordering of particular changes in practice. Access to the tribunal or court by the Commission in this way would not be conditional upon a formal investigation having taken place, though in practice this 'would often be the case'.[108] The court or tribunal would not be concerned with the way in which the evidence had been obtained, but with the issues of whether a finding of unlawful discrimination should be made in this case and, if so, what remedies were appropriate. In part the proposal was justified as removing 'any suggestion that the Commission is both prosecutor and judge in the same cause'.[109] In part, it also appeared to be affected by a perception that the courts were antagonistic to formal investigations because of the CRE's power to issue the non-discrimination notice. The CRE was prepared to trade off the power of the notice, in return for increased acceptance of investigations by the public and the judiciary.

The CRE reform proposals were understandably directed at the problems the Commission has found in putting into effect their strategy. A comprehensive approach to reform would also take into account the somewhat different proposals of the EOC. In brief, its 1976 consultative paper[110] proposed that the EOC be given the additional power, similar to that proposed by the CRE, to issue a complaint in the appropriate court or tribunal alleging unlawful discrimination by any person. In contrast with the CRE, however, the EOC proposed that it *retain* the non-discrimination notice power, which would indeed be expanded to permit the Commission to order changes to practice or procedure. There are various arguments in favour of this approach. It may, for example, be more reasonable for the Commissions to soldier on with the full regulatory role envisaged in the 1975 and 1976 Acts, until a reasonable level of acceptance is won, rather than surrendering their powers. However, far fewer investigations have been attempted by the EOC, in part because of a greater preference among EOC Commissioners than among CRE Commissioners for non-adversarial approaches, and its experience is therefore less than the CRE's. This must weaken the authority of the EOC's proposals.

There are, of course, more radical methods of dealing with the underlying dissatisfactions with the current state of formal investigations, viz. the sense of the Commissions being judge in their own cause; and the sense that the judiciary are too willing to intervene. In 1986, the Northern Ireland Department of Economic Development produced a consultative document setting out its suggestions for future legislative reform of anti-discrimination legislation in Northern Ireland.[111] The Paper suggested the establishment of a Commission with two distinct arms. One arm would be a 'Directorate' with overall responsibility for conducting investigations, among other functions. At the conclusion of investigations the Directorate would form opinions or views, but it would have no power to make decisions or enter formal judgments on the matters before it. That function would fall to the second arm of the Commission: a group of three Commissioners whose task would be to consider the results of investigations by the Directorate and reach decisions. Appeals from the Commissioners would be to an Independent Appeals Tribunal, the decisions of which would be final subject only to judicial review. Although not proposed, one step further could be envisaged: to exclude judicial review altogether.

6 Conclusions

Legislators, thus, have a number of choices with regard to the role of the Commissions and of formal investigations. But the choices are broader than issues of technical institutional arrangements. We saw above how an attempt was made to place on the shoulders of the Commission the burden of carrying out functions equivalent to those of the United States anti-discrimination agencies and even some functions of those groups which act as 'private attorneys general'. Why does American enforcement appear, even now, so much more vigorous and successful? The answer appears to be that in retrospect we appear to have misperceived, or failed to follow, American experience of agency enforcement in at least five important respects. If this is correct then a number of further questions arise.

First, the United States has a variety of regulatory techniques available (pattern and practice suits, private litigation, agency enforcement, and contract compliance, among others), in a variety of different circumstances (local, state and federal). Britain could be said to have borrowed the least successful element of the United States experience (agency enforcement) and made it central. Should, then, the reform of the Commission's powers be accompanied by the development of other methods of enforcement which would operate alongside agency enforcement to a greater degree than was expected previously?

Second, Britain may have misperceived United States experience in not appreciating that the diversity and variety of techniques of enforcement, and the lack of centralization, had the great advantage of creating a multiplicity of risks for discriminators. The CRE's formal investigatory powers may, in particular, be thought to have proven an inadequate substitute for organized private litigation. The statutory agency has not been, and is unlikely to be, provided with resources sufficient for it to use its powers of formal investigation in ways which would have the scatter-gun effectiveness of the numerous privately initiated American class action suits. Should there be an attempt to stimulate a greater degree of risk to discriminators in Britain? Should the limited monopoly position which the Commission holds be further reduced?

Third, anti-discrimination law enforcement in the United States developed to the extent of attempting to impose structural reform directly on organizations. Brown and Gay[112] assessed the extent of racial discrimination and equality in employment in Britain and found that there had been no reduction in the extent of discrimination between 1975 and 1985. They placed a choice before policy-makers: to keep the Race Relations Act as an expression of what is right and wrong, 'while a substantial proportion of employers continue to hire people on the basis of their skin colour'; or to use the Act to try to stop discrimination. The choice, in other words, is whether to construct institutions of enforcement for symbolic purposes, or for instrumental purposes. As the choice implies, current British legislation is an uneasy compromise between the two. British enforcement appears to adopt the more modest task of attempting to stimulate change only indirectly, through encouraging the establishment of mechanisms within the organization which are in turn responsible for introducing change. This has not been successful. Should enforcement institutions be empowered to impose structural change more directly?

Fourth, one of the crucial roles of agencies in the United States is that of negotiating with organizations to bring about change.[113] This has been recognized to the extent that reform is often assessed in the

United States in terms of whether it provides a strengthened bargaining hand to law enforcement officials. There is a need for the various British proposals to be assessed in this way also. Yet conclusions relying essentially on predictions as to what the reactions of legal actors are likely to be in different contexts must remain tentative until further evidence is produced of what has happened under alternative institutional structures.

Finally, the British courts have proven much less sympathetic to the enforcement of race discrimination legislation than American courts.[114] The role of the ordinary courts and tribunals has given rise to a situation in which the courts rather than the agency are seen as the ultimate arbiter of the strength of the legislation, yet their decisions are limited, tortuous and ungenerous. Whether the courts should be embraced and their role extended and strengthened, or whether they should be replaced and excluded from the field, is now a matter for the most urgent consideration and the widest debate.

Cable Television: Agency Franchising and Economics

Cento G. Veljanovski

The Cable and Broadcasting Act 1984 (C & BA) has fundamentally altered the nature of British television by giving cable television, 'a deregulated status ... unprecedented in British broadcasting practice'.[1] It effectively ends the era of 'rationed television' and replaces it with a pluralistic system consisting of public and commercial broadcast TV, cable TV and satellite TV.[2] This change in television policy is part of the present Government's programme of privatization, which seeks to achieve economic growth and efficiency through the forces of private enterprise and competition.[3] The overtly economic basis for these changes in television policy is just as radical as the policy itself.

The Cable Authority has, at the time of writing, only existed for a short period. This chapter will focus on the path followed to deregulation and the consistency of the regulatory framework with stated objectives. I propose to discuss the impact and details of cable (de)regulation as they affect television.[4] Cable deregulation is based solidly on a set of interrelated economic premises and a large part of the discussion will be devoted to considering the economics of cable policy and broadcasting regulation.

1 Background

Cable Technology
A cable system is a telecommunications network which distributes video, audio and data signals by wire or cable in much the same way as the telephone.[5] Cable has a variety of uses and is not confined to television. It can be used to transmit radio programmes and data, and

where it has the ability to carry signals to and from the subscriber (known as interactive cable), it can provide a wide range of business and household services such as teleshopping, telebanking, the metering of gas and electricity consumption and the high-speed transmission of information and computer data.

The principal use of cable has been to provide pay-TV. As a television system it has two characteristics not shared by broadcast TV. First, it has almost unlimited channel capacity. In contrast, the number of channels which can be broadcast over the air are limited by the scarcity of the electromagnetic spectrum. Secondly, cable companies are able to levy a direct charge on viewers. There is thus a direct contractual relationship between the viewer and the cable company. Subscribers only receive cable programmes if they hook up to the cable system and pay a monthly subscription. Broadcast television, on the other hand, relies for the most part on advertising revenue or taxation to finance its services, although it is technically possible, though very expensive, to levy direct charges by scrambling and decoding signals. Cable television is thus multichannel pay-TV.

The channels offered by a cable system are usually marketed in tiers. For the basic subscription the viewer receives a number of channels which will typically consist of the relay of existing broadcast TV channels and others originating from the cable station. The subscriber will also have the opportunity to obtain other channels for an additional subscription. This is often referred to as 'pay-TV' as opposed to the 'basic cable' tier of channels. Pay-channels can consist of continuous feature films, twenty-four-hour news or sports programmes, ethnic channels and other special or minority interest programmes.

The Nature of the Industry

Apart from a few minor experiments, prior to 1982 the cable industry's growth was severely retarded by government regulation.[6] Under the licences issued by the Home Office, cable operators were only permitted to relay simultaneously the broadcasts of BBC and ITV channels, and they were not permitted to provide their own programmes in competition with those of the broadcast TV system. This restricted the demand for cable TV to those in areas where reception was poor or non-existent due to physical obstacles such as mountains and tall buildings. This restriction plus the improved coverage of broadcast TV has meant that the commercial sector of the cable relay business has declined during the last decade. For the year ended July 1983, the number of commercial operators fell by 7 (or 4 per cent).

The provision of cable television is almost equally divided between commercial operators and non-commercial operators, the latter consisting mainly of housing associations, local authorities and government departments. In 1983 over 2.35 million subscribers received cable TV. This figure is, however, misleading because a licence is required for broadcast relay apparatus which may consist of a master antenna serving, say, a block of flats operated by a housing association. In the year ended June 1983 there were 178 commercial operators. Most of these were very small; only 9 had more than 5,000 customers and the others had an average of 265 subscribers. The four largest companies (Rediffusion, Visionhire, Telefusion, Radio Rentals), with systems in many parts of the country, served over 90 per cent of those subscribers connected to commercial cable systems. The capital stock of most of these systems was old and outdated and had a limited channel capacity.

After deregulation a new generation of broadband cable systems have been licensed and older relay systems have been upgraded to provide programmes in competition with the terrestrial broadcast television system. These employ sophisticated technology and have the potential to supply at least 30 TV channels. By the beginning of 1987, 21 new broadband cable operator franchises had been awarded. The great bulk of these have yet to begin operation and even construction. Eight of these systems are now operating (Swindon, Aberdeen, Coventry, Westminster, Windsor, Croydon, Glasgow and Ealing) with viewers (as at 1 April 1987) totalling over 172,000, or 16.4 per cent of the number of homes passed by cable. In addition, there are ten new British national cable channels which supply the cable system with programme material (Sky Channel, Children's Channel, Screen Sport, Premiere, Music Box, Lifestyle, Arts Channel, Star, Home Video, Bravo).

The Genesis of a Policy

Prior to the C & BA, the industry was regulated by the Home Office. A cable operator required a licence from the Home Office for the reception and retransmission of off-air programmes and a separate licence from the Department of Trade and Industry (DTI) to operate relay apparatus.[7] The Home Office licence placed cable operators under significant restrictions as to the type of services they could provide. As stated above, cable companies were only permitted to distribute simultaneous sound and broadcast television programmes from authorized UK stations. The rationale behind this policy was to prevent 'destructive competition' between cable TV and the BBC/ITV duopoly which would erode the revenue base of the latter and lead to a general deterioration of programme standards. It is against the background of this highly emotive issue of programme standards that successive battles to relax the grip of the BBC on television have been fought.

The present policy toward cable TV has its roots in the report of the 1977 Royal Commission on the Future of Broadcasting (the Annan Report),[8] which considered the role that cable should play in the future development of British television. It rejected the case and need for a cable industry run by the private sector supplying programmes in competition with the BBC and ITV. Commercial cable TV was described as a 'ravenous parasite', reflecting the belief that it would merely use programme material already produced for the cinema and broadcast TV.[9] Annan recommended, instead, the development of a local community cable service.[10]

The recommendations of the Annan Report were not accepted by the then Labour Government. In the 1978 White Paper on broadcasting[11] it was stated that 'in principle there seems to be no reason why both pay television and community cable systems should not develop side by side'.[12] It recommended new legislation to provide for a number of pilot pay-TV schemes subject to 'careful regulation to guard against the possibly damaging effects which pay-TV might have on television as a whole, and on the cinema industry'.[13] The White Paper also proposed that the licensing and supervision of the industry should be transferred from the Home Office to the Independent Broadcasting Authority (IBA). The Home Office was to retain jurisdiction over technical standards for the industry.[14] Only the first of these recommendations was implemented.[15]

In 1981 the Home Office licensed 12 pilot schemes for an initial two-year period, each offering one subscription channel of feature films, although other programming was allowed. The licence provided for a quota of British and European Community material (15 per cent) and required the companies to conform to a range of taste, decency and impartiality conditions that were similar to those found in the Broadcasting Act 1981 and which governed programme standards of the ITV programme contractors.

A further step along the path to deregulation of the industry came in March 1982 with the publication of the Information Technology Advisory Panel (ITAP) report, *Cable Systems*.[16] ITAP is a group of advisors, mostly industrialists drawn from the major British electronics companies, appointed by the Government 'to ensure that Government policies and actions are securely based on a close appreciation of market needs and opportunities'. It has no official status or power to make policy, although it is housed in the Cabinet Office. The ITAP report made the following set of recommendations:[17] removal of the present restrictions on programming; formation of a new statutory body to regulate the industry; development by the industry of an effective system of self-regulation; and the Government to disclose the broad outlines of its future policy by mid-1982. The theme of the ITAP Report was that the Government should move rapidly:

We believe that only through a set of speedy, positive and radical regulatory changes can the United Kingdom obtain the benefits offered by developments in cable technology. . . . for British industry a late decision is the same as a negative decision.[18]

The ITAP report had considerable influence on the Government and, it is reported, the Prime Minister, who took a personal interest in the matter. The expansion of the cable industry became a matter of urgency. Since any decision to allow expansion would have profound implications for broadcasting policy, a committee of inquiry chaired by Lord Hunt of Tanworth was set up in early 1982 to report within six months.[19] The inquiry's terms of reference made it quite clear that cable would be deregulated – the committee was to consider the issues in light of 'the Government's wish to secure the benefits which cable technology can offer'. The Hunt Inquiry was asked to consider the extent and form of regulation, taking into account 'the wider public interest, in particular the safeguarding of public service broadcasting'.[20]

The Hunt Report gave the go-ahead for what many saw as a free-for-all in the cable industry. Cable TV, argued Hunt, was to be regarded as different from broadcasting – as a form of electronic publishing – and therefore should not be subject to the same type of programme controls which applied to public service broadcasting. The Hunt Report did, however, see grounds for some regulation of the industry, because the cable operator was likely to have an 'effective local monopoly'.[21] It thus proposed 'certain liberal groundrules', the licencing of cable providers and operators, and oversight of the industry to be administered by a new Cable Authority. The general tenor of the Hunt Report was that cable expansion should be privately financed and should be allowed to take place with the minimum of government intervention. A widespread view at the time of the publication of the Hunt Report was that the proposed safeguards and controls on the industry 'were liberal to the point of invisibility'.[22] The Cable White Paper published in April 1983[23] endorsed nearly all the main recommendations of *Hunt* and was itself described as a Magna Carta for the industry.

The White Paper proposed the interim licensing of up to 12 new cable systems before the enactment of the C & BA. The reason for this unusual move was 'to maintain the momentum already achieved'.[24] In October 1983 the Department of Trade and Industry and the Home Office established an Independent Cable Advisory Panel (ICAP) to advise the Government on franchise applicants for interim licences. The applicants were to be evaluated by a private consult-ancy firm whose report ICAP was also required to assess. The Guidance Notes for this round of licencing were published in July,[25] and applications were to be submitted just over one month later with a decision to be announced in November 1983. The ICAP received 37 applications and in the end awarded 11 interim franchises in early 1984. The Government also invited applications from existing cable systems to offer additional programme services, attracting 11 applications to provide new programme services in 166 areas.[26]

Evaluation of the Policy Process

The Government's approach to cable deregulation evolved not as part of broadcasting reform but as part of an industrial strategy which was based on some dubious premises. The emphasis has been on the speedy implementation of cable expansion, with some unfortunate consequences. Peter Fiddick, writing in the *Guardian*, described the Hunt Report 'as part of a political process so swift and so foggy as to be unprecedented'.[27] The then Minister for Information Technology made a virtue of this when he rejected pleas in the Commons for a more considered approach with the memorable rebuff that he would not delay matters any further by 'another winter of debate, spring of reflection and a summer of reappraisal'.[28] Un-fortunately, the Government's policy did not in the end even have the virtue of speedy and decisive implementation. The interim franchising process is an example. The companies were rushed into submitting their applications. Government then took a considerable time to evaluate them. The applicants were given only a scant idea of the criteria which would be used and were told ominously that their licences would be issued subject both to technical conditions yet to be written by the DTI and to any conditions that the new Cable Authority thought fit to impose on them. A considerable period of uncertainty followed when it was announced that, due to delay in the enactment of the Telecommunications Bill, the Government did not have the legal authority formally to award cable licences, but would instead issue 'letters of intent' – which those companies who were awarded interim franchises (or more accurately their financial backers) found unacceptable.[29] Interim licences were, in the event, awarded under the British Telecommunications Act 1981, but ad hoc changes in other government policies, most notably the Chancellor of the Exchequer's decision to remove the tax allowance on investment in cable laying, have adversely affected the commercial attractiveness of cable investment. Important aspects of the policy are still undergoing revision (such as the decision that all cable systems be interactive and that the whole franchise area be cabled) in ways that should have been evident to the Government earlier because they conflicted so markedly with the principle that cable regulation should be economically sound and alive to commercial realities.

The other notably unattractive feature of the way deregulation has proceeded is the Government's failure to see cable television as part of the telecommunications industry and its failure to formulate an integrated policy for the whole sector. The problems of failing to do this have again been illustrated by subsequent developments in broadcasting, cable and satellite television sectors. Cable, satellite and terrestrial broadcast TV are to a large degree competing technologies which deliver essentially the same product to viewers. Inevitably, developments in one of these industries will affect the others. The incremental and ad hoc progress of the Government's deregulation of television and its ill-thought-out basis has given rise to many problems. For example, the direct broadcast by satellite (DBS) project has floundered twice because of the Government's insistence that an expensive British-designed satellite be used, and the possibility that the BBC might be permitted to compete with the ITV system for advertising revenue. A related development is the Home

Secretary's move to search for alternative means of financing the BBC other than by the licence fee. A Home Office committee of inquiry, the Peacock Report, supplied a novel set of recommendations.[30] Although the Committee had been asked a narrow question concerning financing of the BBC, the Committee's recommendations will, if accepted, have profound effects on the whole television sector and will undermine the public service broadcasting concept (see part 2 below).

2 Traditional Grounds for Broadcasting Regulation

The C & BA, together with other changes such as the prospects of new satellite television channels and advertising on the BBC, marks a radical change in the philosophy underpinning the regulation of television in Britain over the last sixty years. In order to evaluate cable policy it is necessary to discuss the basis of the old and new policies.

Public Service Broadcasting
Britain's broadcasting policy has been dominated by several resilient ideas which have been fashioned into the concept of public service broadcasting. The first set of propositions derives from the early history of the BBC. The BBC began as a private company formed by radio manufacturers to promote the sale of their sets by offering a radio service. The issue at the time was how this industry was to be regulated, given the limited number of frequencies and the danger that competition between radio stations would lead to the type of radio interference which had occured in the US. The compromise solution was to create first a private and then a state-owned monopoly.[31] This solution was adopted largely for administrative convenience. The idea behind the arrangement was that the problem of radio interference was best solved if the entire broadcasting service was placed in the hands of a single organization and, moreover, the limited channel capacity meant that genuine competition was not feasible. As was pointed out in chapter 2, at the time, the transformation of the BBC into a public corporation was an institutional innovation in government involvement in the economy and the successful operation of the BBC served as a model for the later period of nationalization.

The public service broadcasting concept couples the above technical and administrative arguments with a concern for the quality of television programmes and a paternalistic vision of the role of television in a democratic society. First, it is argued that television has a tremendous power to persuade and influence and therefore must be controlled in the public interest to ensure that programmes are impartial and standards maintained. This philosophy was largely the brainchild of John Reith, the first Director General of the BBC. Prior to the introduction of commerical broadcast TV, the BBC gave viewers what it thought they needed and displayed a 'lofty in-difference to what people wanted'.[32] The hallmarks of the BBC were its self-evolved duty (but also contained in the BBC's Charter) to inform, educate and entertain, and – what must be regarded as Reith's most remarkable feat – a determination to keep the BBC largely free from political interference. Although the BBC pre-dominantly reflected the values and tastes of a particular segment of the middle class (epitomized by the expression 'a BBC accent'), it is undeniably true that it acquired a very high international and domestic reputation as the best television in the world. The 1978 White Paper echoed this assessment when it declared that 'the BBC is arguably the single most important cultural organisation in the nation'.[33]

A related argument, which underpins the public service broadcast-ing notion, is that programme standards can only be maintained at their high level if competition from the private sector is severely limited. Over the years the BBC has become a master of this type of claim. In its submission to the Hunt Inquiry it argued that cable television would be 'socially divisive, sacrifice hard-won programme standards and coarsen popular tastes'.[34] The claim, which can be called the *destructive competition rationale* for broadcasting regulation, has both a financial and an artistic component. It is argued that unrestrained competition from commercial television would erode the financial basis of the BBC and force it to engage in competition for ratings and revenue. The artistic argument is that overt competitive pressures of the type just outlined would destroy the ability of the BBC to produce programmes of artistic merit, which are experi-mental, high-risk and which only appeal to minority audiences. The net result is seen as an unadventurous public television network indistinguishable from advertiser-supported television. This idea was expressly advanced by the Annan Committee, which recommended that different forms of television should not compete for the same source of revenue. Hence the BBC is financed by the licence fee, ITV by advertising, and cable TV by subscription.

Another feature of the public service broadcasting concept, which is a feature of all telecommunications systems in advanced countries, is the goal of universal service. Both the BBC and IBA (which owns the transmitters for the ITV network) have pursued construction programmes designed to bring television to the whole country. At present around 98 per cent of the population can receive BBC television and radio. This necessarily involves massive regional cross-subsidization of services. Competition would undermine the financial base for this policy.

Thus the public service broadcasting concept is hostile to the introduction of commercialism in television and favours restricting competition from new forms of telecommunications. Greater competition would, it has been argued, lower standards and erode the revenue base of the BBC and ITV programme companies. And if there is any doubt about the truth of these statements, say the supporters of the status quo, look at television in the United States.

The Concept Appraised

It is worth spending some time examining these claims, if only to show their limitations when applied to cable television and indeed broadcast TV. Consider first the technical and administrative arguments concerning the spectrum. These justifications for the BBC's monopoly are open to challenge on two grounds. First, it is true that free competition among radio and TV stations would result in congestion of the airwaves. This congestion is not, however, the result of the scarcity of frequencies or commercialism, but the absence of property rights in frequencies. If television stations were given ownership rights in particular frequencies, which were legally enforceable and could be traded, then the problem of radio interference would be alleviated or else resolved through private litigation.[35] In any case, the technical problems of frequency management do not, standing alone, provide grounds for a BBC monopoly, or (since 1954) the BBC/ITV duopoly, of broadcast TV. This scarcity is an artificial one created by the government.[36]

The concept of public service broadcasting is left with one remaining plank: the fear that programme standards will deteriorate. This involves two quite separate contentions. The first is paternalistic – it asserts that people should not be given what they want but what they need. This argument is hard to evaluate since there can be little doubt that broadcast TV can have a powerful influence on opinion and does at times serve an educative function. The question that has to be addressed is whether the present structure of programme regulations and the existing organization of broadcasting are needed to give effect to programmes which are educative and uplifting. One need not deny the case for some form of programme regulation (although this may be hard to reconcile with a policy which espouses a free-choice market ideology), to question the basis of the present system of broadcast TV regulation. When there is a single broadcasting organization, then the argument that it has a duty to maintain programme standards becomes convincing because of its monopoly over an important channel of communications. However, when the monopoly is weakened, the case for paternalism is similarly weakened.

The second charge is that there are inherent structural defects in markets for television programming and distribution which necessitate government involvement. Competition between a small number of commercial-advertiser-supported TV stations will tend to lead to a high degree of similarity in programming and mass audience programmes.[37] The danger of this is highest when there are only two channels because revenue can be maximized by splitting the audience. This is achieved if both channels show similar programmes at the same times. It can also arise because of advertising as a method of financing television. Advertiser-supported television does not sell programmes to viewers. It sells advertising time, or more accurately audiences, to advertisers. Its primary customer is, therefore, the advertising agency and it must persuade those agencies that it has the largest audience. Thus, advertiser-supported TV stations compete for mass audiences, which may lead to common denominator programmes and wasteful duplication of programme types.

In a rather ironic sense the BBC has had to compromise its own position by adopting a programme policy which mimics that of its competitor. The battle for ratings forces the BBC to act as if it were an advertiser-supported (but regulated) channel. The reason for this is partly historical. When the ITV network came on the air, the BBC lost about 75 per cent of its audience to the new channel, and this sent shock waves throughout the Corporation. Today there is active competition between the two organizations for audiences which results in each organization capturing about 50 per cent of the audience with year-to-year fluctuations. The BBC behaves in this way because Parliament will not increase the licence fee if the BBC is not seen to offer a significant proportion of the viewing public what they want.[38] Rating competition thus tends to make the output of the two organizations indistinguishable in terms of the type and quality of programmes. Obviously, given the detailed programme regulations imposed on the ITV system, the most undesirable effects of ratings competition have been ameliorated. Nonetheless, there remain considerable doubts about the extent to which the programmes shown reflect the preferences of the viewers (as opposed to those of the advertisers and the regulators) and the degree to which a separate public broadcasting system is needed if a commercial but regulated TV system is capable of profitably showing the same range and quality of programmes. Casual empiricism indicates that the output of the BBC and ITV systems are virtually indistinguishable. If the ITV system can do this profitably then the question 'Why the BBC?' is inevitably asked by the critics of the present system.

Wasteful duplication of programme types is thus an inherent inefficiency in any television system consisting of a small number of channels financed by advertising and/or dominated by ratings competition. But again, the small-channel nature of the British broadcasting system is not inevitable but itself an artificial restriction arising from the public service principle. A system consisting of numerous channels would diminish the prospect of identity in programming and would probably be commercially feasible, but not under the present system of programme regulations and public service requirements. Moreover, the incentives on the BBC to compete for audiences with ITV can be avoided either by divorcing the funding of the BBC from considerations based on audience size or else by forcing the commercial stations to show programmes which are not mass appeal and therefore not revenue maximizing. The Broadcasting Acts have sought to achieve this by giving the IBA wide powers to regulate the programmes shown on the ITV network and by requiring the programme companies to show certain types of educational and current affairs programmes. The present programme controls do attempt to widen the viewers' choice by requiring complementary programming between the first and second channels of both the BBC and ITV systems. The second public channel (BBC 2) and the second commercial channel (Channel 4) are required to provide a complementary programme schedule to BBC1 and ITV respectively. Thus, the Broadcasting Act 1981 requires Channel 4, inter alia, 'to ensure that the programmes contain a suitable proportion of matter calculated to appeal to tastes and interests not generally catered for by ITV'.[39]

The public service broadcasting concept has greatly influenced successive governments' policies towards all technologies which have posed a potential threat to the BBC/ITV duopoly, even though the technical and commercial features of alternative methods of distributing TV programmes have been radically different. The concept is now perceived as highly contentious and its applicability to cable and other pay-TV systems is seen as dubious. This is because cable TV has technical and institutional features radically different from broadcast television. The potentially unlimited channel capacity of cable systems and the direct contractual relationship between cable operator and viewer are critical factors undermining the relevance of the public service broadcasting concept. This was recognized by those who argued that cable TV should be treated as an electronic publisher. The White Paper also accepts that there is something fundamentally different about cable TV. It states that the heavy programme regulation of broadcasting reflects the fact that it is 'intended for all and available for all', whereas reception of cable TV requires initiative in offering services 'and then of the individuals offered the opportunity, to pay the subscription involved and take up the service'.[40]

These two differences are not only noteworthy in themselves but have an important effect on programme standards and variety. The direct link between consumer and cable operator afforded by pay-cable ensures that the programmes shown cater to a greater extent for the preferences of viewers (rather than those of the regulator or advertisers). Thus, cable TV is more likely to be a system that maximizes consumer welfare in terms of programmes shown than the existing organization of broadcast TV.[41] The fear concerning cable TV is not its ability to cater better for consumer demand for programmes, but its effect in fragmenting audiences and thus damaging the ability of ITV and the BBC to finance the high-budget programmes that are seen as the hallmark of public service broadcasting.

3 Cable Liberalization

The C & BA marks a sharp break with the tenets of public service broadcasting. The decision to permit the expansion of cable services is not, however, based on the rejection of the public service concept, but on a set of interrelated and often conflicting economic and industrial objectives.

Privatization and Liberalization

The rhetoric of cable policy is that of the Government's programme of privatization and liberalization. Privatization of state monopolies and the opening up of industries to competition (so-called liberalization) has replaced public investment as a macroeconomic tool in the hands of the Conservative Government. The idea is that through the forces of private investment and competition, industry will perform more efficiently and supply consumers with the goods and services that they demand at competitive prices.[42] Cable expansion is to be 'privately financed and market-led'[43] and this, states the White Paper, means that 'the Government has both a duty to enable the new technology to flourish and fulfil its potential unfettered by unnecessary restrictions'[44] and an obligation 'to create the opportunities which will enable cable development to happen provided a market exists for it'.[45]

The rhetorical basis of liberalization in the cable and telecommunications sectors is that competition will ensure that consumer welfare is maximized. Hunt proclaimed that 'Cable television is . . . all about widening the viewer's choice', and more explicit statements can be found in Government statements elsewhere.[46] It is not, however, clear that the Government's privatization programme is based on a clear appreciation of this point. The most obvious departure from the pursuit of consumer welfare lies in the use of privatization to generate revenue for the Government. Liberalization policies also reveal confused thinking and ad hoc accommodation to conflicting objectives. The conceptual flaw underlying liberalization involves quite a fundamental misunderstanding of the true nature of competition. Competition is not measured by the number of firms in an industry, but the extent to which a firm lacks a protected position in the market it serves. It is, as stated above, competition in the interests of consumers which eliminates excess profits, inefficiencies, and poor-quality services and products. The corollary to this is regulation in the interests of consumers, not in order to protect the old technologies against the new under the cloak of fears about 'destructive competition'.

Employment and Technology-Forcing

It is evident that cable policy is concerned with more than competition and consumer welfare as defined above. The key to the present system of regulation as found in the C & BA and the terms of cable franchises, is easy to identify. Cable policy was initially seen as a key component to the Government's industrial policy aimed at revitalizing British industry and pulling the economy out of its depression. In the post-war period Britain's telecommunication industries have experienced considerable decline and their share of world trade in telecommunications equipment has dropped, and still continues to fall dramatically. Rejuvenation of the telecommunications industry is seen by the Conservative Government as a way of modernizing Britain's industry, creating jobs and exports and placing Britain at the forefront of product development.[47] The Government's early strategy was to achieve this by forcing those cable companies who were awarded interim franchises to invest in the most advanced technology. They were required to build interactive cable systems and cable providers were encouraged to build systems with more sophisticated architecture by the award of longer franchises. These technical requirements increase the costs of a cable system considerably. But, more significantly, they amount to a rejection of the principle that cable expansion is to be market-led. Moreover, this departure from efficiency-based economic principles is not adequately justified either in terms of the failure of the industry itself to decide on the best technology or in terms of the superior wisdom, and (we must assume) business acumen, of those Ministers and civil servants in the DTI who have decided these technical standards for the industry. One can be forgiven for citing this as another example of what can be termed 'the Concorde mentality' – that is, an undue fascination with high technology and a poor appreciation of market principles. These requirements also seem to fly in the face of commercial reality, because, on present estimates, interactive cable is a product without a market. Very few of the over 5,000 cable systems in the US generate any income from non-TV sources, and those which do have an interactive capability do so not because of compelling commercial considerations but because of pressure from franchise authorities.

This policy of *technology-forcing* is anti-consumer. The net effect of these requirements is to dissipate the cable operators' monopoly rents (i.e. profits in excess of a normal rate of return) in over-capitalized systems that are built to provide unremunerative services. Instead of the regulatory framework keeping subscription rates low, the subscriber is effectively subject to a form of indirect taxation (through higher subscription rates or a hidden tax if the costs become so high that a cable system in a particular area is not commercially viable) so as to finance unremunerative advanced technology.

There is another more practical reason to question this aspect of cable policy. The benefits that are assumed to flow from it are increased employment, industrial expansion and greater exports. That these effects will occur is based on curious economic assumptions. The first is that the increased capital costs that the Government is forcing on to cable investors will not deter the rate of cable development. The second is that cable investment will generate jobs of sufficient quantity and type to lower significantly the unemployment rate.[48] At this early date there are already signs that the flawed nature of these assumptions have been recognized. Despite the Government's rhetorical efforts to maintain momentum, the cable boom has dissipated, with investors being much more cautious, partially as a result of the Government's own erratic and uncoordinated policies. The DBS project, which was to be financed first by the BBC and then a consortium of the BBC, ITV companies and other media interests, has collapsed twice, largely as a result of the Government's insistence that a more expensive British satellite be used. The adverse effects of technology-forcing are slowly beginning to dawn on the Government. There is, at the time of writing, a clear retreat from this approach. The Cable Authority, for example, has announced that the franchise applicant's 'contribution to advanced technology' will not have as great an influence in the criteria for the award of cable licences as it did for the interim franchises.[49]

Key Safeguards and Destructive Competition

Another aspect of cable policy which has given rise to a divergence between the Government's words and deeds are the restrictions that have been placed on direct competition between cable operators and broadcast television and the public telecommunications companies. A number of safeguards have been created which are designed to ensure that broadcast TV and telecommunications operators are not impoverished by competition from cable.

The logic underlying some of these safeguards is extremely curious, especially in respect of cable's non-TV uses which would directly threaten the business of British Telecom and Mercury plc (the new private long-distance telephone company). Pared to its bare essentials, the Government has both contrived the threat and then imposed an inefficient restriction on competition to guard against its realization. More specifically, those who obtained interim franchises were required to build interactive cable systems which could provide the full range of business and other interactive services now offered by BT at 'marginal prices' because the capital costs of the system would be financed by entertainment. In this way, cable would emerge as a competitive threat to BT's undoubted monopoly of local telephone services and thus assist OFTEL (the new regulatory agency formed to regulate BT) in its efforts to prevent BT from abusing its monopoly position. However, there is a fallacy in all this. To force the cable companies to invest in interactive technology is to contrive costly competition, and far from creating a fully competitive environment, it will retard the growth of cable. Ironically, the Government, having artificially set out to create a competitive threat to the public telecom networks, has forbidden outright competition between cable and telecom systems in the short run. Cable companies must enter into collaboration with BT and Mercury if they wish to provide what are, in effect, competitive voice-telephone and data services. These restrictions are designed to prevent erosion of the telecom companies' revenue base and will last for 12 years, the length of the initial franchises. In short, had the technology of cable systems been left to the industry, there might not have been the need for safeguards to be imposed on the cable industry in relation to telecoms. The (cable systems) telecommunications licence does, however, have certain pro-competitive provisions which attempt to ensure open access to cable systems by third parties (so-called value added network services or VANS).[50]

The BBC/ITV system is protected by a number of provisions in the C & BA which are more justifiable given its public service obligations. Section 12(3) of the C & BA restricts the time devoted to advertising for programmes 'calculated to appeal to the tastes and interests which are generally catered for by ITV' to the maximum time that ITV can advertise (currently a maximum of 7 minutes in an hour).

Less defensible is the largely redundant ban on 'pay-per-view' for those national sporting events which are 'listed' by the Home Secretary under section 14(2)(a) of the C & BA. The basis for this restriction is the fear that if cable operators were permitted to levy a separate charge for national sporting events they could outbid BBC and ITV for the television rights. This would deprive a substantial proportion of the population of these programmes because cable does not have national coverage. However, under the C & BA, the mere fact that the events are listed precludes the cable companies from purchasing exclusive rights to those events in circumstances where the BBC or ITV network wish to purchase them.

The market has also been denied a full role in determining programme production and standards. These restrictions are based on paternalistic and moralistic concerns and outright economic protectionism. The White Paper, although acknowledging the differences between broadcasting and cable, rejects, as 'at the very least premature', the idea that cable can be treated as a 'kind of electronic magazine rack' because it will not 'offer the same unlimited possibilities for the expression of opposing viewpoints as the written word'.[51] The Act gives the Authority the power to ensure that cable programmes do not offend good taste and decency, or incite crime or racial hatred. News must be impartial and accurate and a range of other restrictions on programmes are imposed by statute.[52] In addition, the Authority is required to draw up a code regarding the showing of violence when children may be watching and 'such other matters concerning standards and practices for programming as the Authority considers suitable'.[53] Most of the sections have been lifted directly from the Broadcasting Act 1981, although the programming controls are not as stringent or as extensive as those which the IBA must administer, such as vetting of programmes and advertisements and limits on the time devoted to different types of programmes and advertisements.[54] Nonetheless, the Authority will have considerable potential censorship powers. The Victorian morality which the Conservative Government has espoused is nowhere better captured than in the cable White Paper's self-righteous declaration that '"adult [i.e. pornographic] channels" have no place on the sort of cable system which the Government wishes to see develop.'[55]

The C & BA safeguards are also protectionist. They are either designed to restrict competition between cable and broadcast television or to protect the domestic film industry from foreign (i.e.

American) competition. Section 7 makes it clear that cable operators will have to include a significant and increasing proportion of 'programme matter which originates within the European Community' (EC). The White Paper states that 'the Government is not in favour of artificial barriers to international trade which hinder the normal working of market forces.'[56] However, it continues, to allow free trade in programmes will do 'irreparable harm to the British film industry' if cable operators 'opt for cheap overseas material'.[57] While the Act limits the quota to EC material it is quite clear that the restriction is aimed at the American film industry and in fact the Interim Guidance Notes use the phrase 'British material' rather than EC material.

4 The Cable Authority

Form and Functions

The method chosen to regulate the cable industry is similar in form to that now applied to commercial broadcasting. The industry is to be overseen by a new Cable Authority. The Authority was set up on 1 December 1984 and given its powers on 1 January 1985. It takes over the functions which were previously the responsibility of the Home Office, although some continuity has been maintained by the appointment of Jon Davey as Director General of the Authority – he had previously been Secretary to the Hunt Committee and heavily involved in the interim franchising process. The Authority is to be small (between 5 and 10 members, including Chairman and Deputy Chairman), self-financing and a central government body. The membership of the Authority is determined on a personal basis and there will be no representation of particular groups.[58] The first Chairman of the Authority is Richard Burton, a former corporate executive.

The Authority has two functions: to license cable operators and, flowing from this, to see that licence terms are complied with, regulations observed and the public interest served. The Authority's remit is not confined to television or radio uses of cable. It also has a 'responsibility to promote the development of interactive services'. Once franchises have been granted, the Cable Authority is, to paraphrase the White Paper, to adopt a light, flexible, reactive posture which emphasizes oversight of the industry rather than detailed regulation.[59] Detailed regulation of the industry was rejected because this would conflict with the idea that cable expansion should be market-led and because a large bureaucracy might overregulate and stultify both initiative and diversity.[60] The Authority and the C & BA are built on the premise that it is only by having a small authority exercising minimum regulation and with 'a wide measure of discretion' that it can respond to a dynamic industry such as cable.

Why a New Central Agency?

In the White Paper the case for a new national cable authority is stated as being 'conclusively strong, and widely accepted'.[61] The reasons for this are cogently stated. First, to continue to allow the Home Office to license cable operators would violate 'the established principle of British broadcasting policy that the Government should be distanced from decisions about the application of general obligations ... to individual programmes'.[62] Moreover, if rules were established by 'administrative authorisation', as they would be if the Home Office retained responsibility, Parliament would be deprived of the opportunity to consider them in any detail and investors, argued the White Paper, would not be assured of the greater stability brought about by the new legislation.

The C & BA retreats in significant areas from this idea of arms-length control by the Government. A number of provisions give the Home Secretary considerable scope for involvement in determining the type of material shown on cable TV. Section 12 gives the Home Secretary power to list events of national importance (mostly sporting events such as the Derby and the Oxford and Cambridge boat race) which cannot be exclusively acquired by the cable companies. Section 12 requires the CA to prevent the broadcasting of advertisements on behalf of political organizations or directed at political ends or having any relation to any industrial dispute. Section 13 of the Act gives the Home Secretary the power to require cable operators to retransmit regional BBC and ITV channels in their respective areas.

Regulation of the industry by local authorities was rejected, although the Act makes provision for consultation with local groups and franchise areas are to be made up of 'recognisable communities'. In part this was based on the US experience where cable franchises are awarded by city municipalities. This practice has not been satisfactory, being 'beset by delays, excessive demands ... and unrealistic promises'.[63] Suggestions of corruption have not been uncommon. If cable franchising were in the hands of local authorities the lack of uniform conditions would, according to the White Paper, deter investment. A national cable authority could not eliminate all these inefficiencies, but would be 'well placed to form a fair and critical judgement'.[64]

The White Paper also considered whether responsibility should be handed over to the IBA or to the newly established Office of Telecommunications (OFTEL) which is charged with regulating the privatized British Telecom and other telecom companies. Both these alternatives were rejected. While both the IBA and OFTEL will play important roles in regulating the cable industry, the key decisions are to be made by the Authority.

The Government's reluctance to transfer responsibility to the IBA was based on a straightforward reason. The ever-present danger in the regulatory field is that of agency capture (or, as it is referred to in the English civil service, 'going native') – the prospect that a regulatory authority will serve the interests of industry rather than the public or consumers at large. This is not without precedent in British broadcasting experience. The Pilkington Committee on Broadcasting in 1960 identified the problem when it described the IBA's predecessor (the Independent Television Authority or ITA) as 'a friend and partner' of the independent television programme companies.[65] It is to prevent the type of 'contractual relationship' which existed between the ITA and the ITV programme companies that the Cable Authority will be required to adopt a reactive style. It could be argued that by transforming the IBA into a more broadly-based regulatory agency it would be less liable to capture because of the diversity and conflicting pressures of its client industries. This, however, ignores the fact that the older client industry would have greater influence in the agency and, therefore, would tend to obtain greater concessions. This was stressed in the White Paper, which feared that the IBA 'would see cable too narrowly in broadcasting terms' and would favour existing commercial broadcasters to the detriment of cable investment.[66] The IBA would also find it hard to adopt a reactive approach to one part of the television industry and an aggressively proactive approach to another.

Nonetheless the IBA will have a role to play in the regulation of cable. It must be consulted by the Authority when drawing up its code of advertising practice, and complaints about unjust and unfair treatment and unwarranted interference with privacy will be considered and adjudicated by the Broadcasting Complaints Board.[67]

Placing the cable industry under the umbrella of OFTEL was ruled out because it is run as a non-ministerial department and staffed by civil servants. The White Paper argued that it would not be desirable that this body should engage in general assessments about sensitive issues concerning the attractiveness of rival programme packages, taste and decency and political impartiality. OFTEL will nonetheless play an important part in the regulation of the industry because of the two-tiered system of franchising. In addition to a cable operator's franchise, a cable provider licence will be needed by the company or consortium building the cable system. The cable provider will have to satisfy the DTI that it is suitable and must comply with the technical conditions specified in the licence drawn up by the DTI. OFTEL will be responsible for monitoring compliance, ensuring that the construction timetable is adhered to, and that all parts of the franchise area are wired and capable of receiving cable. Moreover, OFTEL will also be responsible for issues concerning interconnection and the provision of interactive services over cable systems, especially since British Telecom and Mercury have been given rights to provide data and voice services over cable systems.

5 Cable Franchising

As already noted, the industry is regulated by a two-tiered system of licensing. The cable operator is the company which packages and markets the services supplied by the cable system. It will require a licence from the Cable Authority. The cable provider (the owner of the physical cable system), whether or not this is the same person or company as the operator, will also need a licence from the Secretary of State for Trade and Industry to run a 'cable programme service'.[68] The award of a cable operator's franchise by the Authority is seen as the 'key decision'.[69] The Authority will award operating franchises after considering the applications of those who tender. Although it is not stated in the Act, the implication is that the bidding process will be open and more than one applicant will be encouraged to apply. The Authority will be expected to select that applicant which in its opinion offers the best service for the area concerned. The Authority has announced that it plans to award five new franchises every four months. The first round of licensing by the Authority occurred in early 1985.

Justification for Franchising

The principal justification for franchising is that the cable industry will consist of 'a geographical patchwork of private monopolies'.[70] It has been widely accepted that due to the high infrastructure costs (in excess of £30 million per cable system) each area will only support one profitable cable system. If cable is such a natural monopoly then the competitive duplication of wires in the same area is wasteful; it will increase subscription rates and will generate destructive competition between rival cable companies until the losses are sufficient to drive all but one cable system out of the market. In short, competition will not be feasible, efficient or desirable because the market could be supplied most cheaply by one cable system.

The monopoly provision of cable services can lead to certain abuses which harm consumers. The traditional (economic) argument against monopoly is that it restricts output and overcharges consumers. If a cable operator does have significant market power, consumers will have less choice (relative to the services that they are willing to pay for and which can profitably be supplied), and, for those services which are available, they will have to pay a price which gives the operator monopoly profits. Secondly, cable companies may have programming power. As the owner/operator of a multi-channel cable system, the cable company may be able to dictate which type of programmes are to be shown and who has access to the system. Thus in many countries commercial television is usually subject to a range of regulations designed to encourage diversity and 'merit' programming. In addition to these static inefficiencies, firms may often invest resources to acquire and maintain their market power through such activities as lobbying, predatory practices and investment in unnecessary capital to deter the entry of new firms.

Whether or not cable is a natural monopoly remains an unanswered question.[71] The White Paper assumed that it was and this provided the justification for franchising cable operators. While it is true that in North America there are relatively few instances of cable systems directly competing in the same area, this is just as likely to be the result of franchising, which creates a legal monopoly immune from direct competition, as it is of the cost conditions in the industry that make genuine competition unprofitable. The White Paper recognized the possibility that franchising could create monopoly power and recommended that the Authority would need to consider whether to grant more than one franchise in each area.[72] This recommendation finds no expression in the Act. The Authority's guidance notes do envisage the possibility of multiple franchises for the same area but only in 'extraordinary circumstances'.[73] The Act makes provision for access by other programmers to be a matter taken into consideration when awarding the franchise,[74] but says nothing about the control of other manifestations of monopoly, such as high subscription charges.

Control of Market Power by Franchising

Apart from the contentious status of cable as a natural monopoly, the effectiveness of franchising in terms of protecting consumers from monopoly abuses was not adequately discussed in either Hunt or the White Paper. The inadequacy of the present structure of regulation is shown when the issues concerning the control of market power by franchising are considered more fully.

The control of monopoly by franchising is based on a simple idea – the exclusive right to supply a service is awarded to one applicant in an open bidding procedure, and thus replaces competition in the market with competition for the right to serve the market on terms specified by a regulatory agency. If the franchising scheme is structured correctly, it can channel competitive pressures in a way that induces applicants to offer and bind themselves to terms and conditions which approximate to those prices, terms and services that would be offered in a more competitive industry.

Franchising can only achieve regulatory objectives if it satisfies certain conditions. Foremost amongst these are (a) that the licence is awarded by competitive bid, by (b) an agency which has the competence and expertise to choose the best applicant, on the basis of (c) criteria that are known and clearly understood by all potential applicants and (d) the criteria taken into account are consistent with regulatory objectives. If the regulatory objective is to maximize consumer welfare, then the franchising process must ensure that consumers obtain the maximum benefits from cable expansion.

One method of franchising which appears to satisfy many of these requirements is the so-called Chadwick auction.[75] In a Chadwick auction the legal right to be the sole supplier is awarded to the applicant that undertakes to sell its services to subscribers at the lowest price. This type of auction relies on competition at the licensing stage to eliminate monopoly prices and practices. Applicants are told that the franchise will be awarded on the basis of one criterion – the promise to supply a service of a given quality at the lowest price. Provided there are a sufficient number of applicants and that they do not collude, rivalry between them will ensure that monopoly profits are eliminated.

This method of franchising is appealing for several reasons. First, it deals directly with the problem of potential monopoly abuse. Competition for the franchise ensures that monopoly rents are passed on to consumers in the form of lower prices for services that they actually want and are not dissipated in complying with regulations and conditions which satisfy the wishes of the regulatory authority but no one else. Secondly, it is simple and relies almost exclusively on the self-interest of the applicants to define the terms of the franchise and reveal the information necessary to choose the best applicant. The Cable Authority merely has to compare bids in terms of one objective variable – price. Thirdly, it reduces to a minimum the role played by the agency, removes its ability to impose onerous terms on the industry which have nothing to do with the control of monopoly and, perhaps most importantly, it minimizes the likelihood that the agency will be captured by the industry since the agency has little discretion.

Practical Difficulties with Franchising
The simplicity and attractiveness of franchising, even the Chadwick auction, is unfortunately illusory for industries such as cable.[76] In principle, franchising is most effective for industries which produce relatively homogeneous products or services, such as gas, electricity and water. For industries such as cable television, where quality differences and variety are critical factors and where pricing schemes are complex, franchising needs to be experimental and to change in the light of new market information. It will not be possible to restrict bidding to one easily measured term. Nor can all the terms of the licence be determined by the freewheeling bids of those seeking to operate a cable system. The bids will be complex and multi-dimensional, varying in terms of system design, programmes offered and pricing schemes. The Cable Authority will inevitably have to set down a range of (arbitrary) uniform conditions, terms and technical standards which all successful applicants must adhere to and it will have to exercise considerable discretion in the assessment of those terms which are left open to the applicant. Whatever system is selected, the Cable Authority is faced with the problem of developing

criteria for the selection of bids which are difficult to compare. The award of franchises will tend to involve a large subjective element and will often look arbitrary and ad hoc and the regulatory agency will have considerable scope to introduce terms and conditions which have very little to do with the control of monopoly. This may be intentional, or incidental, e.g. where (as will often be the case) the regulatory agency has inadequate information.

The method of television franchising in Britain does not meet the criteria for an effective franchising scheme listed above.[77] The C & BA gives the Authority extremely wide latitude to determine the criteria for the award of franchises. Section 7 requires the Authority to take into account 'all matters appearing to them to be relevant' and sets out a number of specific factors which the Authority must take into account: range and diversity of programmes, proportion of European Community programmes, educational programmes, programmes calculated to appeal to and involve those in the local community, programmes for the deaf, programmes produced other than by the applicant, and the provision of related services. A noteworthy feature is that these conditions nearly all relate to programming and are couched in vague language: the Authority is 'to take into account all matters appearing to them to be relevant',[78] and the specific duties in section 7 and elsewhere are qualified by such phrases as 'increased proportion'[79] and 'adverse to the public interest'.[80]

These terms can take on very different meanings depending on the attitude of the regulatory agency. For potential applicants it will be difficult to determine what weight the Authority will give to each of the section 7 considerations and to challenge the Authority's decisions since the C & BA has been worded so as to give it the widest discretion.[81] Moreover the Cable Authority is not bound to give reasons for its decisions and it may well decide not to spell out its selection criteria in any detail in an effort to retain the greatest flexibility. The IBA's public announcements concerning the award of ITV programme contracts are usually expressed in the most general and vague terms (although more details are given by the IBA for local independent radio licences). This tendency has already been borne out in both the interim and the Authority's first round of licensing where the guidance notes add very little to the vague provisions of the C & BA. The National Consumer Council was 'profoundly un-impressed' by the procedure that the Government had used for deciding who should be given interim franchises. Not only had the

Government refused to disclose in advance even the non-confidential parts of the franchise bids, but it had been 'impossible to find out what criteria it was using in granting franchises.'[82]

In practice, television franchising is a method of regulation that is based on vague and unstated criteria. As such it has more in common with a patronage system than a competitive-bid process designed to allow market forces to determine who is the best applicant and what are the best terms.

Franchising can also generate considerable uncertainty. The factors that have already been discussed – obscure criteria, unilateral modification of licence terms and unpredictable changes in government policy – combine to increase the risks of cable investment and reduce the effectiveness of intervention by the Authority. This will not only reduce the willingness of industry to invest in cable expansion but will also impair the effectiveness of the Authority in promoting efficiency and consumer welfare. Specifically, regulatory uncertainty will be reflected in one or all of the following consequences: a reduced number of applicants for each franchise (thus making the bidding thin, with consequent monopoly distortions in the terms and no necessary guarantee that the applicant selected is the best); discounting of the success and profitability of cabling (with the effect that applicants are not willing to design the best systems or make promises that seem unduly risky); and finally, increased subscription charges because cable investors require a higher rate of return to compensate for anticipated and costly regulatory changes.[83]

So far there has been very little competition for licences. In the interim franchising round, only one application was received for most of the 36 different areas which attracted bids. Similarly in the first round of the Authority's franchising there was only one applicant for each of the five areas. The reasons for this are obviously varied, but regulatory uncertainty must certainly have been a critical factor.

There are also more general difficulties with franchising as a regulatory technique for the cable industry. First, there is the possibility of overbid: that is, the tendency to make unrealistic promises which have to be revised in the light of experience. The tendency for overbid is a function of several factors – the criteria and uncertainty surrounding the selection process, the expected scope for renegotiating a franchise once it has been awarded, and the nature and severity of the penalties for infringing the original terms of the franchise. In addition, overbid will occur because the future is unknown and subject to unpredictable changes that may alter significantly the profitability of promises originally made. This problem is compounded when applicants are encouraged by the Cable Authority to make commercially unrealistic promises in order to gain an advantage in the franchising process. The White Paper states that the Cable Authority, when awarding franchises, should not force operators to make unrealistic promises, but 'should take into account what the market will bear.'[84] The Government's desire to get cabling off to a quick start and the preference it will give to those willing to employ 'advanced technology' will, however, inevitably cause overbid, followed by a period of licence revision, extended deadlines and renegotiations.

Sanctions and Enforcement

The ability of the Cable Authority to prevent overbid and to ensure that promises made are promises kept depends in part on the nature and severity of the penalties for non-performance. The White Paper rejected financial penalties because the Authority 'will be reaching mainly qualitative judgements'.[85] The C & BA permits the Authority to impose a regulatory regime for infringements of programme standards and non-renewal or revocation of the licence as the ultimate sanction when this is in the 'public interest'.[86] The former requires the cable operator to submit its programme schedule for advanced vetting by the Authority.

The powers given to the Authority under the Act do not represent a sufficiently finely-tuned deterrent. In relation to the control of programme content, the Authority does not have the powers which the IBA has, and must, again unlike the IBA, operate reactively. For major infractions the threat of revocation of a licence is so draconian as to be ineffective as a serious threat except for the most outrageous breaches. To draw on the IBA experience again, an ITV programme contract has yet to be revoked and it is unlikely that an agency will find this an attractive response since it would admit that the wrong applicant had been chosen and it would not be clear that a transfer of the system could be achieved without a serious disruption in services. The Cable Authority is also less likely to revoke a licence than the IBA because many cable operators will be owners of the cable system and hence the disruption in service and problems in transferring assets to the new operator will be more serious.

Cable operator franchises are awarded initially for 15 years and renewed every eight years thereafter but with no presumption that the existing operator will be re-awarded the franchise. In determining the 'optimal' length of a franchise, there are two considerations which operate in opposite directions. The White Paper recognized that 'the franchise period should be sufficiently long to encourage investment and to enable programme and other services to establish themselves'. It acknowledged, however, that 'the longer the period, the greater would be the danger that monopolistic abuses might start to develop'.[87] But this is not an easy calculation to make since the first factor requires knowledge of the time-stream of revenue and costs and the risks that the industry confronts, all of which are unavailable. The original proposal of the Government was for eight-year franchises, the same as are awarded to the ITV programme companies. If this had been carried through, it would have created an anomaly since the programme companies are not required to invest in the transmission system, whereas cable operators would most likely own the cable system. Moreover, the nature of cable investment is such that investment is heavily geared and profits are not really earned until well into the accounting life of the system. Thus a franchise of relatively short duration would have considerable effect on the financing and attractiveness of cable investment. On the other hand, infrequent refranchising impairs the ability of the cable authority to regulate the behaviour of existing operators. Refranchising, with no promise that the incumbent operator will be awarded the franchise, will not only constrain operators from behaving monopolistically, but the rival bids will reveal important information to the agency about costs, revenue and other factors associated with the operation of cable systems and the technological opportunities available to the industry.

Another major issue is parity between the existing operator and new applicants. Existing operators can be expected to have an advantage over new applicants when franchises come up for renewal for two principal reasons. First, given their dealings with the Cable Authority over the period of the first franchise, they will have a greater feel for the factors which will most influence those officials making the decision. The second consideration may, however, be more important. The existing cable operator may have a cost advantage arising from his investment in the cable system. A component of the costs of cable systems will be sunk, in the sense that they have no scrap or resale value. The existence of sunk costs enables the existing operator to offer more favourable terms and thereby undercut new applicants for his franchise area, who will have to invest in a whole system and must base their bid on the full costs of that investment.[88]

The present regulatory framework leaves both the problem unresolved and the Cable Authority without any clearly stated policy on how to deal with the very real possibility that when franchises come up for renewal there will be no competition. The White Paper did not examine Hunt's proposal that if a cable operator who also owns the cable system loses his franchise, he should 'sell or lease his infrastructure on a pre-determined basis to another operator'.[89] This would make refranchising more competitive, even though the valuation of assets will be difficult and may involve some arbitrariness.

The preceding issues are more than theoretical niceties introduced for completeness. Bidding for ITV franchises has generally been thin. In the three rounds of ITV franchising the largest number of applicants for any one area has been three, many have not been contested and very few of the original companies have been displaced. This does not bode well for cable franchising since the part played by sunk costs in ITV franchising is considerably less (because the IBA owns the transmission system), although asset valuation problems and disputes over studios and equipment have occurred when the franchise has not been awarded to the existing programme contractor.

6 Conclusions

The C & BA represents a watershed in television regulation in Britain by permitting cable TV to compete directly with the BBC/ITV system. Although the style of regulation is still very much in the IBA mould, it is, as the White Paper is at pains to stress, much lighter and less detailed. The path followed toward deregulation has, however, revealed some difficulties. The first is the Government's failure to adopt a coherent and consistent approach to the deregulation of telecommunications. Although it has taken bold steps, the strategy has been ad hoc, without a clearly understood objective, and has displayed a lack of coherence that has damaged the success of the policy. In the above discussion it has been shown that in important areas the Government has rejected the idea that the development and

form of the industry should be totally market-led or that it should
have as its primary goal the efficient protection of consumers. These
rejections have not been accompanied with reasons or adequate
justifications. It could be argued that in terms of the changes wrought
by the C & BA, this criticism, though valid, is misguided, given the
interim nature of many of the departures from the fully competitive
ideal and the political realities of framing radical policies in the face of
stiff opposition from powerful vested interests. Nonetheless, one can
still be sceptical as to whether the Cable Authority will be an effective
institution and whether franchising is able to ensure that the industry
operates efficiently. These concerns, which must await the assessment of time, are captured in the *Financial Times* leader which
concluded that the Cable Authority's task will be a difficult one: 'In
attempting to balance between a sense of public decency, market
forces, and the need to provide a real alternative service it is liable to
fall flat on its back.'[90]

13

Financial Services: The Self-Regulatory Alternative?

Alan C. Page

The principal aim of governmental regulation of the financial system as a whole is the maintenance of financial and economic stability:

> While financial regulation has many purposes, some of which change with market conditions and political ideologies, it has one goal which is of overriding importance: to maintain stability in financial markets and to guarantee that vicissitudes in economic activity do not undermine the economic health of nations and the world economy. Other goals, such as those of maintaining low interest rates, allocating credit to favoured groups, protecting the financially unsophisticated, and curbing monopoly power are of lesser importance. A regulatory system that achieved these while failing to maintain financial and economic stability would be a clear failure.[1]

This broad aim yields two narrower-range objectives: control of monetary conditions, which all governments attempt because of the perceived relationship with inflation; and the avoidance, through their prudential supervision, of failures on the part of individual financial institutions, and in particular banks, which might in turn lead to a more general collapse in financial confidence. However, although these objectives remain constant, the instruments for their attainment do not. Two developments in particular have stood out for some time as sources of change. The first is increasing domestic and international competition between financial institutions and markets; and the second is the steady erosion of the boundaries between institutions, together with the emergence, or creation through mergers, of financial services conglomerates, so that individual financial and investment services are no longer identified exclusively with particular kinds of institutions. This makes the task of monetary control, with its traditional concentration upon banks, more difficult;

and it has compelled the revision, sometimes too late to prevent failures occurring, of prudential regimes.

These developments have also had a major impact on an additional objective, that of investor protection, in which prudential supervision plays a key role. In the wake of a series of collapses among licensed dealers in securities, Professor Gower was commissioned by the Secretary of State for Trade in 1981 to conduct a review of the protection required by investors. At the time his appointment was widely regarded as little more than 'a political sop'. The government had to do something, but it was not clear that the political will existed to effect major reform. But by 1984, when Part I of Professor Gower's Report was published, a marked shift in political attitudes had occurred.[2] Partly this was the result of the steady succession of further scandals in the insurance and commodity markets. More importantly, it stemmed from the wave of change which engulfed the Stock Exchange following the removal in 1983 of its rule book from the scope of the restrictive practices legislation and the abatement of the proceedings which were then pending before the Restrictive Practices Court.[3] The removal of the restrictions on the outside ownership of member firms led to the rapid emergence of financial services conglomerates combining conflicting interests which had to be addressed if investors were not to be prejudiced. At the same time, existing protective devices such as the Exchange's single-capacity dealing system which required stockbrokers to act only as agents and stockjobbers only as principals, were set to disappear. Accordingly, new ways of protecting investors had to be found.

This chapter concentrates largely upon the organization of government in relation to investor protection, and to a lesser extent its organization in relation to prudential supervision, using its organization in respect of monetary control as a point of comparison. The concentration will be upon investor protection because it is the new regime introduced by the Financial Services Act 1986 which has most relevance for a study of regulation by agency, not least because of the proposal which continues to be put forward that a Securities and Exchange Commission should be set up for the United Kingdom. The concentration will be upon organization rather than functioning because the new regime is not yet in operation. Nevertheless, it is possible, from an analysis of the considerations which have shaped the way in which government is being organized in relation to this objective, to identify the main features of the system, and, above all, the style of regulation which is being adopted, a style which is markedly at variance with that commonly associated with regulation by agency. Having done this I want to turn to the issues of control and accountability which are raised by the emphasis placed on self-regulation or practitioner-based regulation, rather than govern-mental regulation, as the primary means of protecting investors.

1 Government and the Financial System

Monetary control is the responsibility of the Treasury, assisted by the Bank of England. The Treasury is a small, high-level policy-making department responsible for the determination and coordination of overall economic policy. This responsibility developed from its traditional responsibility for government expenditure and its financing. It conforms to the standard pattern of central government organization, in that it is a department staffed by civil servants and headed by a Minister responsible to Parliament. Its smallness aids communication within the department, but, correspondingly, limits its regulatory capacity. Regulation tends, therefore, to be handled through other departments and organizations on which the Treasury relies for the execution of its policies.[4]

The Bank of England, unlike the Treasury, does not form a part of central government. It is a legally separate entity, a public corpor-ation incorporated by Royal Charter in 1694 and taken into public ownership by the Bank of England Act 1946. Its responsibilities include the execution of monetary policy and advising on its formulation. While I hesitate to describe the Bank, which has claimed for itself the status of 'a nationalized institution' rather than a nationalized industry,[5] as a mere agency, the relationship between the Treasury and the Bank may be treated as an example, albeit a rather singular one, of the traditional department/agency relation-ship.

The Treasury and the Bank are also involved in the prudential supervision of financial institutions. The Treasury is responsible, for the supervision of building societies through a statutory body, the Building Societies Commission, which is in turn served by a non-ministerial government department, the Registry of Friendly

Societies; while the Bank is responsible for the supervision of banks under the Banking Act 1987. The Bank also has a more diffuse responsibility for watching over the good order of the financial system as a whole.[6] In addition the Department of Trade and Industry (DTI), which again is a normal government department, is responsible for companies, including insurance companies, unit trusts and, more generally, for the statutory aspects of the supervision of the securities markets.

Responsibility for prudential supervision, however, is not confined to government departments or agencies like the Bank of England: a part in the supervision of financial institutions is also played by what the financial services legislation terms 'self-regulating organizations' (SROs). The Stock Exchange, for example, stipulates financial requirements for member firms which are similar in purpose and content to those laid down by the Bank of England and the DTI in respect of banks and insurance companies respectively, and its arrangements for their financial surveillance were tightened in the same way as those in respect of banks and insurance companies after a number of firms became insolvent and others got into difficulties.[7] In 1976, following an internal governmental review of arrangements for the supervision of the securities markets, the Bank of England assumed responsibility for overseeing this and other non-statutory aspects of their supervision.

Pending the bringing into operation of the new financial services regime, the pattern of governmental organization in respect of investor protection is almost identical. Investor protection is the responsibility of a number of organizations, some governmental, among which the DTI and the Bank are again prominent, others, for example the Stock Exchange and the Panel on Takeovers and Mergers, non-governmental, administering a mixture of governmental and self-regulation. Like most systems of regulation this system developed in an ad hoc, piecemeal way. Its defects were summarized by Professor Gower:

Complication, uncertainty, irrationality, failure to treat like alike, inflexibility, excessive control in some areas and too little (or none) in others, the creation of an elite and a fringe, lax enforcement, delays, over-concentration on honesty rather than competence, undue diversity of regulations and regulators, and failure overall to achieve a proper balance between Governmental regulation and self-regulation. . . .[8]

In the light of these defects Professor Gower recommended that this system should be abandoned and replaced by a new and more comprehensive system of regulation 'based so far as possible on self-regulation subject to government surveillance'.[9]

The framework for this new system of 'practitioner-based, statute-backed regulation' is provided by the Financial Services Act, which prohibits the carrying on, or purpoted carrying on, of investment business without authorization of exemption.[10] Under the Act, the power of authorization is vested in the Secretary of State, but he is empowered to transfer this and other functions to a practitioner-based agency designated by him which matches a number of criteria laid down in the legislation.[11] The Government's White Paper, *Financial Services in the United Kingdom: A New Framework for Investor Protection*,[12] envisaged the creation of two agencies, a Securities and Investments Board (SIB), covering the regulation of securities and investments, and a Marketing of Investments Board (MIB), covering the marketing of investments such as life assurance and unit trusts. After the White Paper was published, these two agencies were established, the latter in the form of an organizing committee (MIBOC), but they were subsequently merged to form a single agency, recognized by the legislation, the SIB. The SIB will in turn operate through a number of SROs recognized by it. Five SROs are likely to be recognized – the Securities Association (created through a merger of The Stock Exchange and the International Securities Regulatory Organization (ISRO)), the Association of Future Brokers and Dealers (AFBD), the Investment Management Regulatory Organisation (IMRO), the Life Assurances and Unit Trust Regulatory Organisation (LAUTRO), and the Financial Intermediaries, Managers and Brokers Regulatory Association (FIMBRA). The Act makes provision for the recognition of professional bodies through which firms whose main business is the practice of their profession will be able to obtain authorization to carry on investment business.

What is thus being set up is a three-tier pyramid with the SROs at the bottom, the Board above them in the middle, and the Secretary of State at the top. However, it is likely that the significance of the constituent parts of this pyramid will be in inverse proportion to the extent of their statutory recognition and definition. Neither the Board nor the SROs will have been established by the legislation. The Board has been be set up by the industry itself as a registered company with a view to meeting the criteria laid down, while the SROs are being formed, or reorganized, with a view to recognition by the Board. The direct regulatory significance of the Board will thus depend partly on how successful investment businesses are in forming or joining SROs and hence in obtaining authorization through membership of them rather than directly from the Board. The Board's preference is for firms to obtain authorization through membership of an SRO or SROs, and if this preference is realized, as seems likely, its direct regulatory responsibilities will be limited and the main regulatory burden will fall on the SROs.

It is not too great an exaggeration to see this projected increase in the role of self-regulation as the culmination of the enormous efforts on the part of government and self-regulating organizations alike which has gone into building a belief in the self-regulatory mechanism and its continued place in the protection of investors. Earlier important results of this effort were the establishment, at the initiative of the Bank of England, of the Panel on Takeovers and Mergers in 1968 to interpret and administer the City Code, and, following the Bank's agreement noted above to develop its surveillance of the securities markets, the establishment of the Council for the Securities Industry (CSI) in 1978, again on the Bank's initiative, as a voluntary representative body with general responsibility for the non-statutory aspects of the supervision of the securities market.

This emphasis on self-regulation should not be allowed to obscure the fact that the criminal and civil law are intended to play a prominent part in the protection of investors. Existing offences have been redefined and provision made for civil remedies for loss due to breach of the Act's provision or of the rules of business conduct laid down by the Board or SROs. With regard to regulation, however, the question I want to address here is why has the government expended the effort which, as I have documented elsewhere,[13] it has expended in fostering the self- regulatory habit? Put another way – why has self-regulation been preferred to governmental regulation by a statutory agency?

2 Self-Regulation v. Governmental Regulation

Explaining the reasons for the proposed structure, the White Paper stated that self-regulation within a statutory framework had a number of advantages. It offered the best possibility of combining adequate investor protection with a competitive and innovative market: Regulation was more likely to be effective if there was significant practitioner involvement in devising the rules, enforcing them and encouraging the observance of high standards of conduct. A private sector body able to make and enforce rules would have greater flexibility in its operation than a body unable to change its rules other than by parliamentary legislation. Practitioners were best equipped to spot breaches of the rules and take swift and effective enforcement action. A private sector body could be established and brought to a high degree of readiness by the time the legislation received the royal assent; the legislation and the practical preparation could go forward together rather than consecutively. Finally, day-to-day regulatory action would be distanced from government.[14]

In the main this is a familiar litany and a not altogether convincing one: for example, governmental bodies have been set up and their organization altered in the expectation that parliamentary approval will be forthcoming; equally, it is not inconceivable that private law-making will encounter delays and, if speed is required, parliamentary legislation may be changed very quickly. No doubt there are other reasons which could be advanced to explain the Government's preference for self-regulation. One reason is numbers. To a large extent the legislation is about intermediaries rather than about institutions and there are far more intermediaries – an estimated 15,000 – than there are institutions. Self-regulation accordingly fits with the Government's emphasis on less government, and indeed, this was one of the reasons why Professor Gower did not provisionally recommend the setting up of a Securities Commission.[15] However, self-regulation has been encouraged as much under Labour as Conservative governments and the Government has set up new regulatory agencies, albeit in a somewhat attenuated form, in areas such as telecommunications and data protection. Again, direct regulation by government would be more costly; but the greater the proportion of the cost to be borne by the regulated – and the intention is that they should bear the whole of the cost – the weaker an explanation this becomes.[16] Finally, it might be pointed out that the setting up of a Securities Commission has been consistently opposed by the City, but as the speed of change has increased, this opposition has become more muted and the possibility that a Commission might be set up eventually cannot be ruled out.

An additional insight into why self-regulation may appeal both to organizations and to government may be gained by looking more closely at its attractions from the point of view of the former. Two attractions in particular stand out. First, self-regulation holds out the prospect of preserving the autonomy and independence of the organization. The point here is not so much that organizations attach importance to the maintenance of their freedom from outside control, for that is to be expected, but that self-imposed investor protection provides a ready justification for an organization's continued autonomy – to the extent that there is a need to protect investors, that need is already being met by the organization itself. Secondly, it might be expected that self-regulation, i.e. regulation by one's peers, might be administered in a more sympathetic and understanding manner than governmental regulation. Something of the contrast anticipated here was evident in the introduction to the first edition of the present City Code, which stated that the choice before the City was either 'a system of voluntary discipline, based on the Code and administered by the City's own representatives or regulation by law enforced by officials appointed by Government'. In more general terms the Inter-Bank Research Organisation expressed the view in 1972, in the course of a report on the future of London as an international financial centre, not only that the regulatory regime should remain as liberal and as flexible as possible, but that any new regulatory bodies should have 'a genuine understanding of the City's problems', and that in particular their staff 'should be more like the staff of the Bank of England and the Takeover Panel in experience and outlook than traditional Whitehall civil servants'.[17]

The first of these attractions explains the emphasis which has been placed on the independence of the self-regulatory system from government, and I propose returning to it in the next section which considers the controls to which self-regulation is subject. The second attraction, however, does suggest one reason why self-regulation appeals not only to the organizations but also to government. If the objectives set by government for the financial services sector – that it should be efficient and fully competitive internationally, with maximum freedom for market forces to stimulate competition and encourage innovation[18] – are to be met, two things are necessary. First, the regime itself must not be unduly restrictive; in particular it must be competitive internationally. Hence Professor Gower's observation that:

it would be lamentable if our regulations were so strict in comparison with those of other countries that London ceases to be the world's centre for financial services that it still is. If the constraints imposed here are unduly severe, market makers will move elsewhere.[19]

Secondly, the regime must be administered in a manner which contrasts with that associated with normal governmental administration. A style of regulation is required which is expert, and hence understanding and sympathetic, which is informal rather than formal, and which is flexible rather than inflexible. One of the reasons why self-regulation appeals more than traditional government regulation is accordingly because it is thought more likely to display these qualities. This explains, I think, the reference in the White Paper to self-regulation within a statutory framework as offering 'the best possibility of linking adequate investor protection with a competitive and innovative market',[20] although it is not a consideration upon which too great a stress can be laid for fear of destroying the credibility of governmental regulation as an alternative.

Self-regulatory organizations, and their representatives, have also argued that there is a connection between regulatory style and international competitiveness. In its response to Professor Gower's Report, the influential City Capital Markets Committee suggested that 'the tradition of self-regulation in UK capital markets is envied elsewhere in the world and provides an inducement for foreign firms to set up operations in London', and it went on to emphasize the importance of achieving 'effective investor protection . . . without a cumbersome legal and bureaucratic structure';[21] the Association of Investment Trust Companies pointed out that they remained 'strong advocates' of self-regulation because a system of statutory regulation would be not only less effective but would also 'impede innovation, reducing the ability of the City to compete with financial markets overseas';[22] and the CSI argued that governmental regulation would 'inevitably tend towards over-detailed regulation and rigid interpretation of rules'.[23]

As a conscious practitioner of the style of regulation sought, and as one of the chief architects of the new regime, the Bank of England has consistently put forward the same view. Its view was outlined in evidence to the Wilson Committee:

We do in certain instances see the need for statutory regulation. In other instances we think that the flexible system of non-statutory regulation that we have, sometimes welded with the other, provides by far the best answer and, indeed, is part of the reason for the success of London as a financial centre.[24]

Part of the success achieved in world markets, the Bank has gone on to argue,

is clearly attributable to the relatively light regulatory touch that has been applied; inventiveness and enterprise were not impaired. This underlines that we must continually be sensitive and alert to steer clear of regulation that is so comprehensive that nothing can be done, so to speak, without planning permission.[26]

In his Discussion Document Professor Gower, too, observed that the retention by government of discretionary powers over matters of recurring detail was likely to lead to:

their exercise by relatively junior staff acting in accordance with rules derived from past precedents which destroy flexibility, prevent desirable initiatives and constitutes a code of estoric law and lore largely unknown to those it affects.[26]

And one of the reasons why he refrained from provisionally recommending the establishment of a Securities Commission was because of the risk of 'the creation of a large bureaucracy staffed . . . by a less experienced and dedicated team than that of the Department of Trade'.[27]

The general tenor of this analysis, that one of the key reasons why self-regulation is preferred by government as well as by organizations is because it is less likely to impair international competitiveness, is confirmed by Professor Gower's analysis of the disadvantages of the Department and the advantages of a Commission as vehicles for carrying out the functions assumed by government in relation to the new system. Among the disadvantages of the Department, which he stressed could be overcome, he included its relative remoteness, the lack of direct commercial experience and of specialization on the part of civil servants produced by the rapidity of their turnover which, together with manpower shortages, lead 'to a tendency to seek reasons for not exercising powers and discretions and to delays in coming to decisions' and more generally to 'ossification'.[28] A Commission, on the other hand, could be expected

to keep in closer touch with what is going on, to develop greater expertise and commercial and professional know-how and to provide a career structure offering the prospect of greater specialisation, better special salary scales and greater movement to and from commerce and the profession. . . . It should, therefore, ensure a more flexible and business-like approach . . .[29]

He recommended that the governmental role should be left to the Department, but that if a substantial volume of day-to-day regulation and supervision were to be involved then it should be undertaken by a Commission. An expanded role for government of course implies a reduction in the role for self-regulation, and the assumption of the role by a Commission thus makes sense in terms of Professor Gower's analysis of its advantages because, if self-regulation fails, the benefits which are sought initially through it are more likely to be achieved by means of a Commission rather than the Department.

The same reasoning was evident in the responses to Professor Gower's Report. In general those who wanted the governmental role entrusted to the Department wanted as large a role for self-regulation as possible, and a correspondingly reduced role for governmental regulation. Thus the City Capital Markets Committee argued that the role of self-regulation should be increased, with a consequent upgrading in the role proposed for the CSI and a reduced role for government which could be left to the Department.[30] Those, on the other hand, who favoured a Commission either wanted self-regulation restricted or a greater amount of independent regulation, as did the TUC and the National Consumer Council, or else, like the Accepting Houses Committee, were preparing a fall-back position in the event that self-regulation was to be superseded. Similarly, the Wilson Committee, which had considered the issue earlier, argued that the creation of an independent statutory Commission would not be the right way to proceed because the need for a shift in the balance between self-regulation and governmental regulation had not been demonstrated.[31] Changing the balance in favour of increased governmental regulation would undoubtedly have resulted in the establishment of a Commission rather than the enlargement of the administrative responsibilities of the Department.

Regulatory styles do of course vary. The Panel on Takeovers and Mergers is a good example of a self-regulatory agency which has been forced to adopt what the City Capital Markets Committee describes as 'a more legalistic approach' as its list of rulings has grown.[32] Nevertheless, although the new regime is not yet in operation, and although the debate between the proponents of self-regulation and of a Commission has not been concluded, it is possible to derive from this analysis some idea of the regulatory style which is being sought. Like the Bank of England's supervision of the banking sector, it will be a style which will be statutorily underpinned but which will not involve recourse to detailed legal provisions.[33] The role of law in enhancing investors' rights I have mentioned. Below I look at the role of the courts as a check on the Board and government. But so far as the functioning of the Board is concerned, the scope for law, other than in terms of the conferral of broad powers, and for legal techniques, will be restricted; and the contrast with 'regulation by agency' will thus be considerable. Moreover, it is a style the scope of which seems set to increase, for the argument that there is a connection between regulatory style and international competitiveness applies across the whole range of financial services. Which is presumably why the Government is planning to transfer responsibility for the regulation of unit trusts – one of the DTI's main responsibilities – to the new Board.[34]

To sum up: self-regulation is regarded as having advantages over governmental regulation, but they are not necessarily those upon which most emphasis was placed in the White Paper. From the point of view of both self-regulating organizations and government, the main advantage of self-regulation is not that it will, for example, lead to higher standards of business conduct, though it may do so, but that it is thought less likely than is governmental regulation to inhibit innovation and international competitiveness and thus frustrate the goals which the government has set for the financial services sector. This need not preclude the setting up of a Commission, but if one is to be set up the emphasis is again likely to be on expertise, informality and flexibility, rather than simply on the establishment of an agency with comprehensive legislative, judicial and executive functions along the lines of the United States' model.

3 The Control of Self-Regulation

Turning to the control of self-regulation, a useful starting point is the traditional department/agency relationship as exemplified by the relationship between the Treasury and the Bank of England in the field of monetary policy. The relationship between the two is complex: the Radcliffe Committee on the Working of the Monetary System said of it that it was 'not easy to describe in formal language with any great precision'.[35] The Bank of England Act gives the Crown the power to appoint the court of directors and the Treasury a power, which has never been exercised, to give the Bank directions in the national interest. But these formal powers give little indication of the extent of the control exercised by the Treasury over the Bank in respect of monetary policy. Thus the setting of interest rates and the management of the gilt-edged market, which were previously regarded as part of 'the affairs of the Bank', and hence, under section 4(2) of the Act, as matters for the Bank subject to any direction which might be given by the Treasury, are now firmly controlled by the Treasury.[36]

Another illustration of the Bank's subordination to the Treasury in this area is the consistent rejection ever since the resumption of an active monetary policy in 1951 of the possibility that the Bank should be given greater independence in the formulation and execution of monetary policy. The Wilson Committee, following the Radcliffe Committee before it, insisted that:

the deliberate ceding of part of an elected government's sovereign powers to a separate non-elected institution insulated from party political pressures . . . would be contrary to the British system and tradition of government . . . we do not accept that there is anything about monetary policy to distinguish it sufficiently from other forms of macro-economic policy to justify taking it out of the hands of elected governments.[37]

However, the opposing idea – that the Bank's ultimate subordination to government should be underlined by merging it with the Treasury – has also been rejected. The Wilson Committee thought that the Bank should not be more fully integrated into government. As had the Radcliffe Committee, it saw advantages in retaining the Bank 'as a separate organisation with a life of its own, giving advice and making proposals over a range of areas. The Bank makes an important contribution not simply to the quality but also to the variety of advice available to government.'[38]

This idea that independence, or more precisely a legally separate existence, is essential to the proper performance of the Bank's advisory function, while attacked by some commentators as quite indefensible,[39] has not surprisingly been strongly defended by the Bank itself. In evidence to the Select Committee on the Nationalised Industries, the Governor argued that because the Bank was a corporate entity, it was 'independent, self-governing, not under the control of any Minister'. The value of that independence, he continued, was that it enabled the Bank to form an entirely independent view of matters coming within its sphere, a view influenced by the market conditions in which it lives and within which government departments do not live. It believes that that view is valuable to Ministers as a counterbalance to other opinions. . . .[40]

This emphasis on ultimate political control, albeit combined with sufficient freedom to enable functions to be performed, has not been as readily apparent in respect of the Bank's activities in relation to prudential supervision or investor protection, although the Johnson Matthey affair has led to a greater emphasis on Treasury control in the area of banking supervision.[41] Instead the emphasis has been primarily on the coordination of the activities of the Bank and the DTI (rather than the Bank and the Treasury) through the Joint Review Body (JRB) which was set up as a liaison committee between the two institutions following the internal governmental review conducted between 1974 and 1976. The JRB is charged with the general oversight of all aspects of the supervision of the securities markets including the identification of any gaps or deficiencies in the combination of statutory and self-regulatory control.[42]

When we turn to the relationship between government generally and the new investor protection regime, we find the relative weighting accorded to 'independence' and 'control' almost completely reversed. One of the attractions of self-regulation, as we saw, is that of autonomy, and the price to be exacted for undertaking self-regulation on the scale now being attempted is the freedom to get on with the job.

[I]f the industry is voluntarily to set up, run and pay for its own regulatory agencies, it must be assumed that government will genuinely stand back. Some ultimate statutory base there must be, some degree of broad responsibility to Parliament by the Secretary of State, and some arrangements for appeal. But beyond that, I am sure that a counterpart to the willingness by the securities industry to undertake the heavy burden and responsibilities of regulation itself, is that the government must not intrude itself on the detail.[43]

Is this, however, a price that government can afford to pay, or be seen to pay? Control remains important for two reasons. First, organizations' powers may be abused to the detriment of their own members, third parties or the public at large. Despite the emphasis now being placed on competitiveness, there is a long tradition of restrictive practices in the financial services sector. Hence the observation of the Wilson Committee that: 'Even if it were practical, we do not regard it as acceptable that the regulation of financial institutions, particularly those as important as the Stock Exchange and Lloyd's, should be left entirely to the institutions themselves.'[44]

Secondly, a failure of regulation threatens to be as economically damaging as over-regulation. As the Secretary of State pointed out:

Our regulatory framework must command the confidence of users, both here and abroad. It does not take many scandals to sully the reputation of a multitude of decent traders. There can be no conflict of interests in this matter between producer and provider on the one hand and the customer on the other. Unless the markets command the confidence of potential customers, here and abroad, they will not attract the business they need to prosper and develop.[45]

To what controls, then, will self-regulation in the field of investor protection be subject?

The controls which will apply differ between the Board and the SROs through which it will operate. To take the Board first, as we have seen the whole system of self-regulation within a statutory framework depends upon the delegation by the Secretary of State of his powers to the Board. The Financial Services Act sets out a number of requirements which the Board has to meet before a delegation order transferring powers to it can be made. Of the requirements set out, the most important are those relating to the composition of its governing body and its rules. Its constitution must provide for its chairman and the other members of its governing body to be appointed by the Secretary of State and the Governor of the Bank of England acting jointly. Its rules and regulations must afford investors adequate protection, and must comply with the principles embodied in the legislation. Moreover, the likely effects on competition of its rules, regulations and guidance must not exceed those necessary for the protection of investors. In addition, it must have a satisfactory system for monitoring and enforcing compliance with the obligations imposed upon persons regulated by it, effective arrangements for the investigation of complaints and it must be able and willing to promote and maintain high standards of integrity and fair-dealing in the carrying on of investment business.[46] These requirements will continue to apply after a delegation order has been made. Should they cease to be met, the transferred powers may be resumed[47] and exercised directly by the Secretary of State, or, as is more likely, by a

Commission appointed for this purpose. In principle, therefore, the subsequent operation of the Board should be subject to a measure of control.

The arrangements for the control of SROs are similar to those in respect of the Board, the main differences being that control will stem initially from the power to recognize rather than the power to transfer, and when the Secretary of State transfers his powers to the Board they will be recognized and their subsequent operation monitored by the Board rather than by the Secretary of State. Thus there are again requirements as to its composition, rules and procedures which an SRO will have to meet as a condition of recognition. The composition of its decision-making bodies must secure a proper balance between the different interests of its members, and between the interests of the organization or its members and the interests of the public. Its admission, expulsion and disciplinary procedures must be fair and reasonable and include adequate provision for appeals. Its membership requirements must ensure that its members are fit and proper persons to carry on the kinds of investment business which it regulates, and it must have rules preventing members from carrying on other kinds of investment business unless they are separately authorized. Its rules and powers must afford investors protection at least equivalent to that afforded in respect of directly authorized investment businesses. The likely effects on competition of its rules and guidance must not exceed those necessary for the protection of investors. And it must meet the same requirements as the Board in relation to the monitoring and enforcement of compliance by its members with the obligations imposed upon them, the investigation of complaints and the promotion and maintenance of standards.[48]

Once an SRO has been recognized, the Board will be responsible for ensuring that these requirements continue to be met. It will have powers to obtain information and conduct investigations which will assist it in this task. It will also have a range of sanctions at its disposal. It will be able to seek a compliance order from the courts directing the organization to comply with any requirements with which it is in breach.[49] It will be able to alter an organization's rules and restrict the kinds of investment business which its members are authorized to carry on by virtue of their membership of the organization.[50] And it will be empowered to revoke a recognition order.[51] The Act provided that this power is exercisable in the event of any of the requirements outlined above, except that relating to the competitive effect of the SRO's rules and guidance, ceasing to be met, or a failure by the organization to comply with any of its obligations under the legislation. Safeguards are provided. For example, a recognition order may not be revoked, or a restriction order made, without notice being given and an opportunity afforded for representations to be made. But these safeguards may be dispensed with if this is considered essential in the interests of investors.[52]

A number of features of these controls merit further comment. The first is the special regime which the Act establishes for the application of competition policy. As we have noted, there is a long tradition of restrictive practices in the financial services sector and competition policy thus has a potentially important role to play in this area. Agreements or practices, which do not stem from the rules, regulations or guidance of the Board or SROs will be subject to the provisions of the Fair Trading Act 1973, the Restrictive Trade Practices Act 1976 and the Competition Act 1980. But the rules, regulations and guidance of the Board and SROs, together with practices stemming from them, will be exempt from those provisions. Moreover, whether the conditions for exemption are satisfied, namely that their anti-competitive effects do not outweigh those necessary for the protection of investors, is to be decided by the Secretary of State and not by the Director General of Fair Trading (DGFT) and the Restrictive Practices Court. True, the Secretary of State must obtain and have regard to the advice of the DGFT, but he is not to be bound by it.[53]

The Government describe these arrangements as a more appropriate basis for the application of competition policy in the financial services sector than the procedures currently laid down in the restrictive practices legislation, citing the 1983 agreement with the Stock Exchange as an example of the benefits of flexibility.[54] That agreement was defended on the grounds that the proceedings before the Restrictive Practices Court were an obstacle to urgently required changes, and that the Court was not a suitable forum in which to decide the issues involved.[55] There is an irony here in that this latter argument was one of the grounds upon which the original restrictive trade practices legislation was opposed, the then Labour Opposition arguing that the compatibility of an agreement with the public interest was not a justiciable but instead a policy question which fell to be determined by the Government.[56] When the Government in effect adopted this argument in defending its agreement with the Stock Exchange, the Labour Opposition were forced to argue that, on the contrary, the Court did have a valuable role to perform in determining such issues.

The upshot, however, is that the application of competition policy is to be firmly the subject of political rather than judicial control. It is noteworthy, however, that this result has not met with an unqualified welcome. The City Capital Markets Committee argued that the criteria to be taken into account by the Secretary of State should be spelled out in the legislation, thus rendering his decisions amenable to judicial review.[57] As providing a framework for decision-making and a protection against abuse of powers, the law is seen, in some quarters at least, as having a role to perform.

Secondly, the tension between independence and control is clearly illustrated by the compromise over the powers which the Board should have to require an SRO to change its rules. Professor Gower proposed that rule changes should be notified to the Secretary of State who would be empowered to revoke or amend them if he was satisfied that this was necessary for the protection of investors or the orderly conduct of business.[58] This proposal was opposed by, among others, the Stock Exchange and the CSI (but not by its lay members) on the ground that it would diminish the incentive for practitioners to regulate themselves and hence the effectiveness of self-regulation.[59]

Under the Act, the power to effect rule changes is more tightly circumscribed. First, the Secretary of State is empowered to direct the Board to take steps to ensure that the anti-competitive effects of its rules, regulations or guidance do not exceed those necessary for the protection of investors.[60] Similarly, when the anti- competitive effects of an SRO's rules or guidance are adjudged excessive, he may either direct the Board to revoke its recognition order or, through the Board, cause the SRO to take remedial action or change its rules.[61] Secondly, the Secretary of State can direct the Board and SROs to take any action necessary to comply with the United Kingdom's international obligations.[62] Finally, the Board is empowered to direct an SRO to alter, or itself alter, its rules should they not afford investors protection equivalent to that afforded in relation to directly authorized businesses.[63] This last power was introduced in response to criticism that the Bill as originally drafted would have left the Board in too weak a position in its dealings with SROs. In return for conceding the power to impose rule changes, SROs have been given the right to make a judicial application to have any imposed rule changes set aside.[64]

The same tension was evident in relation to the requirements in respect of the admission, discipline and expulsion of members. As we have seen, these must be 'fair and reasonable' and include 'adequate provision for appeals'.[65] The result here, however, as presaged by the Stock Exchange's agreement with the Government in 1983, was always likely to be more clear-cut. As regards the *admission* of members, the Stock Exchange agreed to establish a Membership Appeals Committee, composed entirely of lay members, with the power to review and override any decision to reject an application for membership which complies with the rules of the Exchange. By doing so, it effectively brought to an end the almost complete freedom it had enjoyed in this respect for nearly two centuries.[66]

As regards *expulsion*, the power to expel members for breach of an organization's rules has long been regarded as the key to self-regulation. The Select Committee on Foreign Loans observed of the London Stock Exchange in 1878 that:

So long as the Stock Exchange has the power of expelling one of its members without appeal or redress, it can be bound by no law which it does not choose to obey. When it loses that power the means of self-government are gone, and the Society as at present constituted is at an end.[67]

Organizations, however, have never enjoyed the same degree of freedom in relation to the expulsion of their members as they have in relation to their admission. The common law in particular imposes a number of procedural safeguards upon the exercise of their powers. Observance of the rules relating to the discipline of members can be insisted upon, and they will not be interpreted so as to permit the rules of natural justice to be disregarded. This aspect, however, has been effectively overtaken by organizations' own rules which go some way beyond the requirements of natural justice strictly construed, most notably in the provision of internal appeals. Alleged breaches of the Stock Exchange's Rules, for example, are investigated by ad hoc Investigative Committees, and may lead to proceedings before a standing Disciplinary Committee from which an appeal lies to a standing Disciplinary Appeals Committees, with penalties being reviewed finally by the Council itself. The Disciplinary and Disciplinary Appeals Committees are composed of Council members who are not members of the original Committee of Investigation, and the reports of the Disciplinary and Disciplinary Appeals Committees are considered by the Council in the absence of their members. The Disciplinary Committee is normally assisted by a legal assessor, and the defendant may also be legally represented both here and before the Appeals Committee.

What is now being required, however, is a 'suitably independent' appeals procedure,[68] which again strikes at the autonomy previously enjoyed by self-regulating organizations in this field. Professor Gower described the lack of an independent appeal as objectionable, and as likely to conflict with the United Kingdom's obligations in international law.

In this day and age it is just not acceptable . . . that people can be excluded from bodies, which are not mere social clubs but agencies on which their livelihood depends, without a right to seek to persuade an independent arbiter that they were wrongly excluded.[69]

The Stock Exchange initially opposed the introduction of an independent appeal on the grounds that it would weaken its authority and that the appellate body would be too cautious, but it conceded the case as part of the agreement with the Government to the extent that lay members now constitute a majority on the existing Disciplinary Appeals Committee.[70]

Finally, we may note that the public interest in disciplinary procedures is not confined to the protection of members. It also extends to ensuring that rule-breakers are excluded, and disciplinary procedures may thus be looked at from the point of view of whether they are efficient for this purpose. Do they enable rule-breakers to be got rid of, or do they present major obstacles thereto? The emphasis placed on these two aspects of the public interest has varied. Under the Prevention of Fraud (Investments) Act 1958, the Financial Services Act's predecessor, the emphasis is on the protection of applicants and licence-holders through a specially constituted tribunal, although this has not prevented the revocation of licences.[71] In the case of the Insurance Companies (Amendment) Act 1973, on the other hand, the Government argued that the provision of an appeal against a finding that an individual was not a fit and proper person might prejudice the attainment of the primary purpose of the legislation, which was the protection of policy-holders.[72] Current practice, as exemplified by the establishment under the Financial Services Act of a Financial Services Tribunal to which persons refused authorization or whose authorization is revoked by the Board may appeal, emphasizes the value of specially constituted tribunals as a means whereby errors may be corrected without relinquishing control over decision-making.[73]

4 The Question of Accountability

Over the last twenty years, government has resorted increasingly to self-regulation as an alternative to direct regulation by itself. The financial services sector provides the clearest examples of this, but the same tendency is evident in other areas such as consumer protection. The realization that government may thus no longer be disinterested gives rise to two fears. First, because its role as sponsor of self-regulation may conflict with its role as guardian of the public interest, there is a fear that self-regulation may be subject to less external supervision and control than it ought to be; secondly, there is a fear, which goes in the opposite direction, that resort to self-regulation may mean that government is able to deny any responsibility for the control which it may in fact exercise. Both of these fears underline the importance of ensuring that government is not allowed to evade accountability in respect of its encouragement, use and control of self-regulation. In relation to both fears, however, the position under the proposed system will be complicated by the interposition of the Board between government and the SROs which are likely to play the primary role in the protection of investors.

An idea of the difficulty which the interposition of the Board poses may be gained from an examination of the relationship between the Treasury and the Bank in relation to monetary policy. We saw in relation to monetary policy that the Bank's functions are defined as advisory and administrative. However, as the Wilson Committee pointed out, the dividing line between policy and administration is often indeterminate and the Bank's advice may be sufficiently authoritative to determine policy.[74] This in turn raises the possibility either of the Treasury being accountable for matters which it does not control, or of there being no accountability at all.

The position in respect of Treasury control we have already looked at. With regard to accountability the Bank is subject to less parliamentary scrutiny than it would be were it a department such as the DTI headed by a minister responsible to Parliament. Until 1968 such parliamentary scrutiny as did obtain was through ministers, but, with the Bank being treated in the same manner as the nationalized industries, accountability was confined to those matters over which ministers had powers, and did not extend to matters of day-to-day administration. The Bank itself did not publish accounts, and according to the Radcliffe Committee its annual report was a by-word for meagreness.[75] The position in this respect has improved: the bank's annual report is now fuller, and incorporates a report on the exercise of its powers under the banking legislation, and accounts have been published since 1971. These changes are traceable to a recommendation of the Select Committee on the Nationalised Industries within the order of reference of which the Bank was first brought in 1968, though many of its functions were excluded from scrutiny.[76] As an 'associate public body', the Bank is now subject to examination by the Treasury and Civil Service Select Committee. This increase in the scope for scrutiny, coupled with the abandonment of the earlier restrictions on the scope of select committee investigations, at a time when the Bank's responsibilities have increased, is of obvious importance in providing a means of reducing the opacity of relations between the Bank and government, thereby ensuring that the authorship of decisions is not concealed and that lines of responsibility do not become blurred.

Applying this analysis to the Board, as we have seen, the Secretary of State will be able to exercise a degreee of control over the Board itself. However, the control which he will be able to exercise over the Board in its dealings with SROs will be much more limited. Nor will there be any provision for parliamentary scrutiny of the Board equivalent to that which we have just seen in relation to the Bank. The Board will be obliged to report annually to the Secretary of State who will lay its report before Parliament,[77] but it is unlikely to be treated as an associated public body and it will thus escape scrutiny by the Trade and Industry Select Committee. Whether this means that government will be able to distance itself effectively from the working of the system is not a question I want to pursue further here. The question I do want to address is whether there is any other sense in which the system, and in particular the SROs upon which it is based, may be described as accountable.

There is of course one respect in which they always have been accountable, namely to their own members. In addition, however, self-regulation has been progressively redefined to encompass the public interest, the interests of users as well as practitioners, of non-members as well as members. Self-regulation itself has come to carry connotations of accountability. This redefinition of self-regulation can of course be seen as part and parcel of the effort which we saw has gone into building a belief in the self- regulatory mechanism and its continued place in the protection of investors. It covers a number of different forms of accountability.

At its simplest it involves the provision of information about the activities of self-regulatory organizations. The Stock Exchange, for example, provides an immeasurably greater amount of information about its activities than it did fifteen years ago,[78] and, according to the Wilson Committee, self-regulation generally should become as open as possible 'so as to demonstrate its fairness and effectiveness'.[79] In line with this emphasis the White Paper stated that the Government would expect the Boards 'to foster public awareness of their existence and their activities'.[80] Allied to the provision of information is consultation with users and consumers of the facilities and services provided by the organization and its members. Under pressure from major users, principally over the level of commissions, the Stock Exchange in 1975 established a Chairman's Liaison Committee made up of nine representatives of market users and three other members of the financial community to act as a forum for the discussion of issues of general concern, and the more recent changes, according to the Secretary of State, were designed to 'allow the influence of Stock Exchange users to be felt at the centre of policy-making in the exchange'.[81]

An alternative or additional method of taking outside opinion into account while at the same time trying to inspire confidence that organizations are motivated by wider considerations than the purely sectional interests of their members, involves the appointment of lay members to their governing bodies. Following the agreement with the Government, five lay members were appointed to the Council of the Stock Exchange, and under the terms of the agreement outsiders were to eventually constitute 25 per cent of the Council's membership. Lay members were appointed by the Council with the approval of the Governor of the Bank of England, the requirements of the Bank of England's approval being designed to inspire confidence that lay members are indeed independent. The members of the governing body of the Board, too, must include non-practitioners, and, as we have seen, the composition of the decision-making bodies of an SRO

must secure a proper balance between the interests of the organization or its members and the interests of the public.[82]

The penultimate form of accountability involves the provision of
mechanisms for the settlement of disputes between members and
outsiders. The lead in this respect belongs to the Stock Exchange,
which from 'its early days . . . considered complaints from clients
against their members and enforced the same high standards as it did
in dealings between members'.[83] Undoubtedly it did so partly for the
self-interested reason that it wanted to shield its own rules from too
close judicial scrutiny, but again the device is of more widespread
potential application. Thus, as we have seen, it will be a condition of
the designation of the Board and the recognition of SROs that they
have effective arrangements for the investigation of complaints.[84]

All of these, it should be stressed, are relatively weak forms of
accountability. With the exception of the last, they imply no
restriction on an organization's freedom of action, only that it should
take outside opinions and interests into account. The same is not
necessarily true of the final form of accountability, namely membership of bodies such as the CSI or recognition by the Board. Thus the
Wilson Committee was of the view that the CSI represented an
'undoubted improvement' on the extent of the Stock Exchange's
public accountability: changes could not be made without the CSI's
approval, it would be able to press for changes, and it would be able to
subject the Exchange to the 'continual informed scrutiny which is
necessary if non-statutory regulation is to command general acceptance'.[85] That the relationship between the CSI and its member
organizations did not develop in this way before it ceased its activities
seems clear: Professor Gower described it as 'not yet very effective'
and, in relation to the Stock Exchange, as 'to some extent . . . its
partner and dependent'.[86] Whether the new Board will represent an
improvement in accountability in this respect remains to be seen.
Clearly, one of its acid tests will be whether it does.

5 Conclusion

By way of conclusion it may be asked whether the system of self-
regulation within a statutory framework described here is unique to
the financial services sector or whether it could be applied to other
areas. The fact that it has been deliberately fashioned over the last

twenty years suggests that it is not confined in its scope to the financial services sector. So long as the conditions of effective self-regulation are satisfied, viz. the individuals whose conduct is the object of control belong to an organization which is sufficiently motivated to regulate their conduct and which has effective sanctions at its disposal for this purpose,[87] there is no reason from the point of view of efficiency why self-regulation should not be adopted as an alternative to direct governmental regulation or regulation by agency.

Considerations of accountability, however, may militate against too rapid a rush to embrace the self-regulatory alternative. As we have seen, the controls which obtain over self-regulation do not in part depart from the conventional pattern of powers exercisable by ministers responsible to Parliament, but they have also involved the development of new and indigenous forms of accountability. The key question which the example of the financial services sector raises is whether these external controls, including governmental controls exercisable over self-regulation, are sufficient, or whether a system has evolved which is slanted heavily towards indigenous forms of accountability, and which, including the Bank of England within the scope of the system as one of its chief architects, is substantially insulated, if not from governmental pressure, then certainly from the parliamentary pressures which the Wilson Committee saw as so fundamental to the development and execution of monetary policy.

Part III

14
Conclusions: Regulation and Public Law

Modern British administration is concerned with at least five different governmental functions. One is the prevention of undesirable behaviour and the securing of desirable behaviour in particular areas of public and private life. An example of this is the regulation of health and safety at work, or the prevention of race discrimination in employment. A second is providing state facilities for the reaching of compromises between parties. An example of this is provided by the institution of ACAS. A third is the provision of services and the redistribution of goods. Examples of this are the provision of social security benefits, education, and the health service. A fourth, standard-setting function is involved in attempting to settle those disputes with respect to which the law is unsettled. A fifth, more mundane function is grievance remedying, i.e. settling those disputes with respect to which the law is more settled. Many of the disputes arising in the social security area would also fall into this category. Many of these different government functions have been the focus of discussions in this book.

Academic administrative law has adopted at least three approaches to the study of these functions: first, a conceptual or doctrinal approach; second, a more theoretical approach. A third approach, which concentrates more on the empirical context of law has, in the administrative law area, given rise to at least two major variants. One is a more functional variant; another is an institutional variant. In this book, we have concentrated on the extent to which governmental functions are carried out by one particular institution of government: the regulatory agency. However, our case studies and the earlier chapters do not aim to view regulatory agencies primarily from the institutional approach only. Rather we have attempted to meld the three approaches together into a more coherent view of agencies in their diversity, grounded in law and fact but conscious of theory.

We have also avoided concentrating on the study of these bodies primarily from a grievance-remedying approach. There is a danger of distorting the way we view administrative law, of skewing it towards grievance-settling to the detriment of research on the other functions of government and law. Concentration on those institutions mainly devoted to the settling of grievances would lead, for example, to some rather significant exclusions. Once other functions are considered, other institutions must surely be deemed as important as those more traditionally considered. The function of preventing undesirable behaviour brings the HSE and the Gaming Board to mind. The facilitative function brings ACAS into prominence. The provision of services raises the importance of the CA. We have aimed our selection of case studies to illustrate the wide variety of governmental functions associated with regulatory agencies.

This book has been concerned to examine the strengths and weaknesses of agency performance and to consider the place of these bodies within the British constitutional structure. We are concerned, in particular, with whether agencies can be more fully integrated into the constitutional scheme. The earlier chapters examined why agencies are chosen rather than other institutions. We outlined the operational choices frequently faced by such bodies and pointed out a number of failings to which agencies are often said to be susceptible. The growth of agencies in British government was traced and we considered whether there were criteria which could be used to evaluate agency performance. We argued that the legitimacy of specific agency actions, or the agency itself, could be assessed under at least five criteria: adherence to its legislative mandate; the degree of accountability and control exercised over it; the degree of due process accorded by it; its expertise; and its efficiency. The limitations of these criteria were considered and illustrated.

In Part II, our contributors addressed many of these issues in detailed accounts of eight regulatory schemes. The variety of agencies, tasks, operational styles, schemes of oversight and problems which they illustrate is considerable, and it may be argued that each agency operates in such a highly specific context that it is fanciful to draw lessons from, say, the Gaming Board and attempt to apply them to the CRE. We think that this scepticism goes too far. There are a number of problems peculiar to each agency, of course, but common themes do emerge from the studies and broad lessons can, we think, be drawn.

One theme which emerges is the vagueness of the mandate under which most agencies operate. In the case of the GB, ACAS, OFT, MMC and the CA, our contributors laid particular stress on this point. It might be thought extraordinary that the majority of agencies discussed in this book are not told what they are supposed to be doing. On the other hand, vagueness of mandate tends to reflect Parliament's allocation of a complex, specialist and flexible function to that body. Indeterminacy of mandate may thus be seen not only as not unusual for regulatory agencies, but likely to be the norm. Such indeterminacy makes assessment of agency performance (at least by reference to statutory criteria) highly problematic. It should be recognized, nevertheless, that indeterminacy of practical objectives does not justify lack of clarity about arrangements for control and accountability, or participation. Increased efforts should therefore be made to spell out to whom, in what respects and by which procedures, agencies are to be held accountable. Such provisions could also increase the openness with which controls over agencies are operated. We discussed whether administrative rule-making might provide a means of rendering statutory objectives more precise. In the case of agencies such as the MMC, CAA, HSE and ACAS, we saw that important tasks have been carried out through codes of practice and administrative rules of differing types. Rule-making powers and the legal effects of rules should, however, be more fully dealt with in the statute establishing the agency.

The absence of secure agency legitimacy in the British constitutional structure emerges as a second theme. The consequent attempts at a variety of methods of accountability and control over the agencies were discussed by a number of contributors. In the discussion of the GB, a highly discretionary scheme of regulation subject to low levels of accountability and control was noted. The GB's task has not been made significantly more difficult by the interventions of government, Parliament or the courts. With most other agencies the story is considerably different. In contrast with the GB, ACAS has faced political changes that have put its survival at issue and judicial review (particularly in relation to recognition procedures) has severely cramped one of its most important tasks. The HSE has managed to limit areas of contentious review but in large part by adopting a consensual approach which has arguably restricted agency innovation. The CAA's scheme of written ministerial policy guidance may have provided a means of effective compromise between accountability and agency initiative but this system of control itself failed to survive a combination of judical review and ministerial scrutiny. In the case of the OFT and the MMC, ministers retained a degree of control over agency actions. The study of the CA illustrated the difficulties of establishing clear controls in an area of conflicting objectives and incoherent governmental strategies. Where deregulation has taken place, or, as in the financial services field, a degree of 'self-regulation' has been relied on, external controls are almost necessarily a weak form of legitimation and the benchmarks of expertise, efficiency and effectiveness have to be relied on instead.

Also in the context of accountability, we have sought to illuminate the relationship between the courts and regulatory agencies, but without concentrating unduly on it. As we have seen, the courts are important, indeed vital, for their standard-setting function. However, they are worthy of study by administrative lawyers not only as a source of standards but also as institutions themselves. Too little work has been done on the procedural mechanisms of the courts, partly, we suspect, because civil procedure has seldom been taken seriously enough as an academic subject. This defect has a continuing effect on the quality of studies of other institutions. In Part I, we emphasized a number of institutional characteristics of the courts and the potential effect these have on their competence in operating judical review. We considered why institutional design and tradition tend to make the relationship between courts and agencies a difficult one. We pointed to the need for the judiciary to recognize the value of forms of control and accountability other than judicial review (internal, ministerial and parliamentary), when reviewing the activities of agencies. Courts, it was suggested, might not always be the most competent bodies or in the best position to review agency actions or decisions. A call was made for a more developed and explicit approach to judicial review. The studies of specific agency regimes, we think, reinforce these points. Lawyers, we argued, should resist the temptation to focus exclusively on legal values, to assume the omni-competence of the judiciary and to ignore the role of non-judicial institutions in interpreting the law. Lawyers should be more willing to trade-off legal and other forms of effective oversight and to recognize the value of non-judicial procedures of scrutiny.

A third theme which emerges from the studies is the difficulty which agencies have encountered in arriving at procedures that are seen to achieve an acceptable balance between the participation of parties affected by a decision, and the effective pursuit of statutory objectives. Such a tension may be seen to be particularly likely in the case of bodies such as agencies which possess specialist policy-making powers and exercise judgment, yet are often expected to act in a manner modelled on the courts. In the case of the GB, the kinds of decision made in gaming regulation are not wholly consistent with the supply of full information to applicants. In the case of ACAS, the judiciary's notions of due process were not consistent with ACAS's view of what constituted effective agency action. The useful device of administrative rule-making also gives rise to a host of participatory dilemmas. For the HSE, the tension between due process and effectiveness emerged in the course of agency rule-making. Large, organized interests tended to be consulted rather than the small, disorganized and less willing employers and workers. Yet there are indications that the very group not consulted may be the group creating the greatest health and safety hazards.

The problem of how best to reconcile expertise with other values is a fourth theme which runs throughout the studies. Most of the agencies discussed in the case studies were created as experts or specialists. The need to preserve powers of expert judgement free from undue constraints was frequently mentioned. Particularly in relation to ACAS and the CRE, however, the judiciary have not been conspicuously sensitive to agency realities in exercising review. They have not been seen as intervening in a manner which enhances effective agency action. They appear to have failed to establish a clear basis for intervening (or failing to intervene) in the decisions of expert bodies. One alternative proposed may be for the courts to develop a more coherent notion of respective institutional competence.

A related issue raised by the studies is the problem of how to render polycentric issues manageable by an agency. An agency such as the CAA which employs trial-type procedures to decide complex regulatory issues has a particularly severe problem in that respect. We saw that the CAA, by using policy statements and rules in combination with case decisions, has had some success on this front. Justiciability is a theme which runs through the discussion of the MMC. The agency has been able to consider the economic effects of a firm's behaviour, but only after that behaviour has been tested against a standard of legal form. Craig suggested that the use of guidelines might provide a means (albeit not an unproblematic one) of reconciling these factors. Agencies, then, can employ processes commonly associated with the courts when involved in polycentric decision-making. Success demands, however, astute use of ancillary procedures such as rule-making and disclosure of policy guidance.

A fifth theme encountered in the studies centres on the problem of assessing effectiveness in the context of agency action. The problem which recurrs most frequently is that of assessing effective *enforcement*. The HSE, OFT and CRE have had to balance promotional and campaigning activities with enforcement through more formal legal processes. How to target effectively the limited agency resources which agencies have at their disposal, and how to establish clear regulatory priorities are issues which recurr repeatedly in the studies. It would seem that agencies could do more to co-ordinate case-by-case enforcement with rule-making strategies. Rules could thus be related more closely to those forms of activity that are to be anticipated in the field, and greater efforts could be made to identify those subject to regulation who are to be the particular targets of agency action.

The issue of effectiveness is also closely related to the level of regulation and the overall regulatory strategy that is chosen in the particular field. The degree of 'self-regulation' relied on was an issue raised particularly in relation to ACAS, HSE, CA and the financial services agencies. Where 'self-regulation' prevails, there is a special case for developing means by which its effectiveness can be assessed and demonstrated. However, the need for clarification of agency aims and objectives emerges as a precondition for the adequate testing of effectiveness by an agency in such circumstances. Where, as with the CA, such clarity is not provided by the parent statute, the agency or overseeing Department might take steps to provide such clarification by more open disclosure of rules and policies.

Finally, a theme emerges which could well come to dominate academic administrative law in Britain in the 1990s, as it has already done in the United States. This is the issue, not of *how* to regulate, but of *whether* to regulate at all. It is an issue which is likely to percolate more and more explicitly into the field of public law. Though our contributors have not sought to focus on this issue systematically, except in the context of the regulation of cable television, it is an issue which underlies many of the discussions. Whether to regulate should not, however, be divorced from consideration of the methods to be used when Government reasseses the scope and stringency of regulation. The themes which emerge from this book are thus intimately connected with the question of whether to regulate. Just as public lawyers can no longer ignore economics and political science, so economists and political scientists can no longer afford to neglect public law.

15

Suggestions for Further Reading

This chapter aims to avoid repeating references that are readily available in existing texts on administrative law. On the British administrative law literature see J. Beatson and M. H. Matthews, *Administrative Law: Cases and Materials* (1983, Oxford) and C. Harlow and R. Rawlings, *Law and Administration* (1984, Weidenfeld and Nicolson). Nor does it offer an exhaustive literature review on such institutions as tribunals – that task has been accomplished admirably by Richard Rawlings' ESRC study, *The Complaints Industry: A Review of Socio-Legal Research on Aspects of Administrative Justice* (1986, Economic and Social Research Council). Our object is to point to specific areas of work of relevance to regulation by agency. For reasons given in the text, the richest source on such topics is the United States literature. We will, however, draw on such United Kingdom material as exists. In this rapidly developing field we focus on recent works rather than set down a guide to established writing.

1 General Discussions of Regulation

On this topic particularly, much of the literature comes from the United States. A useful review of justifications for regulation is contained in S. Breyer, *Regulation and its Reform* (1982, Harvard). Approaches to regulation are dealt with in detail in B. M. Mitnick, *The Political Economy of Regulation* (1980, Columbia) and more briefly in R. Cranston, 'Regulation and Deregulation: General Issues' (1982) 5 *UNSW Law J.* 1. Economic questions and readings are set out in A. Ogus and C. G. Veljanovski, *Readings in the Economics of Law and Regulation* (1984, Oxford). The classic economic text is A. E. Kahn, *The Economics of Regulation: Principles and Institutions* (1970, John Wiley).

A number of North American studies are frequently referred to on the legal, political and economic aspects of regulation, notably: S. Breyer and R. Stewart, *Administrative Law and Regulatory Policy*, 2nd edn (1985, Little Brown); G. Stigler, 'The Theory of Economic Regulation' (1971) 2 *Bell J. of Econ. and Man. Sci.*; G. Stigler, *The Citizen and the State: Essays on Regulation* (1975, Univ. of Chicago); G. Kolko, *The Triumph of Conservatism* (1963, Quadrangle); G. Kolko, *Railroads and Regulation* (1965, Princeton); T. J. Lowi, *The End of Liberalism* (1969, Norton); B. M. Owen and R. Brauetigan, *The Regulation Game* (1978, Ballinger); S. Peltzman, 'Towards a More General Theory of Regulation' (1976) 19 *J. of Law and Econ.* 211; R. A. Posner, 'Theories of Economic Regulation' (1974) 5 *Bell J. of Econ. and Man. Sci.* 335; J. Q. Wilson, *The Politics of Regulation* (1980, Basic Books); W. Friedman (ed.), *Public and Private Enterprise in Mixed Economies* (1974, Stevens); E. Bardach and R. A. Kagan, *Going by the Book: The Problem of Regulatory Unreasonableness* (1982, Temple).

On the development of regulation in the USA, see T. K. McGraw, 'Regulation in America: A Review Article' (1975) 49 *Bus. Hist. Rev.* and *Prophets of Regulation* (1984, Harvard). A. Shonfield's *Modern Capitalism* (1965, Oxford) takes a broad comparative view, and British perspectives on American developments are provided by R. J. Williams, 'Politics and Regulatory Reform: Some Aspects of the American Experience' (1979) 57 *Pub. Admin.* 55, and N. Lewis and I. J. Harden, 'Privatisation, De-regulation and Constitutionality: Some Anglo-American Comparisons' (1983) 34 *NILQ* 297. An American perspective on an aspect of British regulation is provided by D. Vogel, *National Styles of Regulation: Environmental Policy in Great Britain and the United States* (1986, Cornell).

2 Agencies and the Administrative Process

The North American literature on regulatory institutions is vast. Good starting points are J. Dickinson, 'Commissions', in *Encyclopaedia of the Social Sciences* (1931, Macmillan), vol. 4, pp. 36–40, and James M. Landis' classic defence of the expert agency in *The Administrative Process* (1938, Yale). Reference is made to earlier British practices in R. E. Cushman, *The Independent Regulatory Commissions* (1941, OUP, New York) which gives a very full review of institutional issues; see also B. Schwartz, *The Professor and the Commissions* (1959, Knopf). The best known statement of the agency 'life-cycle' theory is found in M.

H. Bernstein, *Regulating Business by Independent Commission* (1955, Princeton). Other well-known American works lead towards a discussion of the crisis in legitimacy faced by the agencies: E. S. Redford, *The Regulatory Process* (1969, University of Texas); W. L. Carey, *Politics and the Regulatory Agencies* (1967, McGraw-Hill); H. J. Friendly, *The Federal Administrative Agencies. The Need for Better Definition of Standards* (1962, Harvard); L. L. Jaffe, 'Effective Limits of the Administrative Process: A Re-evaluation' (1954) 67 *Harv. L. Rev.* 1105; and J. O. Freedman, *Crisis and Legitimacy* (1978, Cambridge U.P.). Key readings are given in R. L. Rabin (ed.), *Perspectives on the Administrative Process* (1979, Little Brown).

Canadian work on agencies is exemplified by H. N. Janisch, 'The Role of the Independent Regulatory Agency in Canada' (1978) *UNB LJ* 27; H. N. Janisch, 'Policy Making in Regulation: Towards a New Definition of the Status of Independent Regulatory Agencies in Canada' (1979) *Osgoode Hall LJ* 17; Law Reform Commission of Canada, *Independent Administrative Agencies* (1980 and 1985, LRCC); F. F. Slatter, *Parliament and Administrative Agencies* (1982, LRCC). Anglo-American comparisons are drawn in B. Schwartz and H. W. R. Wade, *Legal Control of Government* (1972, Oxford).

3 The Machinery of Government in Britain

A series of works considers the development of regulatory institutions in Britain and deals with the traditions of public ownership and control in this country. Principal examples are M. E. Dimock, *British Public Utilities and National Development* (1933, Chester); W. A. Robson, *Nationalised Industry and Public Ownership*, 2nd edn (1962, Allen and Unwin); H. Parris, *Constitutional Bureaucracy* (1969, Allen and Unwin); D. C. Hague *et al.*, *Public Policy and Private Interests: the Institutions of Compromise* (1975, Macmillan); F. Stacey, *British Government 1966–1974: Years of Reform* (1975, Oxford Univ. Press); W. Thornhill, *The Modernization of British Government* (1975, Pitman). Some of the historical roots are considered in D. Roberts, *Victorian Origins of the British Welfare State* (1960, Yale), and O. MacDonagh, 'The Nineteenth Century Revolution in Government: A Reappraisal' (1958) 1 *Hist. J.* 52; H. J. Laski, W. I. Jennings and W. A. Robson, *A Century of Municipal Progress* (1935, Allen and Unwin); F. M. G. Willson, 'Ministers and Boards: Some Aspects of Administrative Development since 1832, (1954) 32 *Pub. Admin.* 43. An analysis of different methods available for obtaining redress for grievances (including regulatory agencies) against central government, local authorities, nationalized industries and the police is provided by P. Birkinshaw, *Grievances, Remedies and the State* (1985, Sweet and Maxwell), P. Birkinshaw, 'Departments of State, Citizens and the Internal Resolution of Grievances' [1985] *Civil Justice Q.*15 and P. P. Craig, *Administrative Law* (1983, Sweet and Maxwell). See also C. Turpin, *British Government and the Constitution* (1985, Weidenfeld and Nicolson).

A recent and stimulating study is T. Prosser, *Nationalised Industries and Public Control* (1986, Blackwell).

4 'Quangos', Fringe Bodies and Agencies

On means of classifying agencies, fringe bodies and quangos, see N. Chester, 'Public Corporations and the Classification of Administrative Bodies' (1953) 57 *Pol. Stud.* 34 and 'Fringe Bodies, Quangos and All That' (1979) 57 *Pub. Admin.* 51; C. Hood, 'Keeping the Centre Small: Explanations of Agency Type' (1978) 26 *Pol. Stud.* 30; G. Jordan, 'Hiving-Off and Departmental Agencies' (1976) 21 *Pub. Admin. Bulletin*; N. Johnson, 'Quangos and the Structure of Government' (1979) 57 *Pub. Admin.* 379.

Reviews of fringe bodies are contained in G. Bowen, *Survey of Fringe Bodies* (1978, Civil Service Department) and Sir L. Pliatsky, *Report on Non-Departmental Bodies*, Cmnd 7797 (1980, HMSO). Advice on the creation of fringe bodies is given by the Civil Service Department in *Non-Departmental Bodies: A Guide for Departments* (1981, CSD) and by the Cabinet Office and Treasury in *Non-Departmental Bodies: A Guide for Departments* (1985, Cabinet Office).

The word 'quangos' was invented by Anthony Barker who edited the study *Quangos in Britain* (1982, Macmillan) and co-authored the seminal D.C. Hague, W. J. M. Mackenzie and A. Barker, *Public Policy and Private Interests: The Institutions of Compromise* (1975, Macmillan).

The political attack on quangos was largely based on the charge of patronage: see P. Holland, *Quango Quango Quango* (1979, Adam Smith Institute) and P. Holland and M. Fallon, *The Quango Explosion* (1978, CPC). For a defence, see The Outer Circle Policy Unit, *What's Wrong With Quangos?* (1979, OCPU). See also C. Hood, 'The Politics of Quangocide' (1980) 8 *Policy and Politics* 247.

5 Agencies, Public Law and Politics

Until recently public lawyers have been slow to deal with the issues raised by agency government. A pioneering work was W. A. Robson's *Justice and Administrative Law*, 3rd edn (1951, Stevens).

A broader view of 'policy-oriented' as well as 'court-substitute' tribunals was urged by B. Abel-Smith and R. Stevens' *In Search of Justice* (1968, Heinemann), and see also J. A. Farmer, *Tribunals and Government* (1978, Weidenfeld and Nicolson). These issues are discussed in relation to one agency in R. Baldwin, *Regulating the Airlines* (1985, Oxford).

For studies that look at the political significance of agency government and which deal with the corporatist arguments, see J. T. Winkler, 'Law, State and Economy: The Industry Act 1975 in Context' (1975) *Brit. J. of Law and Society* 103; T. Smith, *The Politics of the Corporate Economy* (1979, Martin Robertson); D. Coombes, *Representative Government and Economic Power* (1982, Heinemann); O. Newman, *The Challenge of Corporation* (1981, Macmillan); E. Kamenka and A. E. Tay (eds), *Law and Social Control* (1980, Arnold); J. J. Richardson and G. Jordan, *Governing Under Pressure* (1979, Martin Robertson).

A thought-provoking review of the way in which governments choose decision-making bodies is G. Ganz, 'Allocation of Decision-making Functions' [1972] *Public Law* 215. The same author has examined procedural aspects of regulation in 'The Control of Industry by Administrative Process' [1967] *Public Law* 93 and in *Administrative Procedures* (1974, Sweet and Maxwell).

6 Regulatory Reform, Deregulation and Privatization

Much of the modern American writing on regulation deals with deregulation, regulatory reform and 'least restrictive' regulation. See, for example, Breyer (*op. cit.*); L. J. White, *Reforming Regulation* (1981, Prentice Hall); Mitnick (*op. cit.*); M. Derthick and P. J. Quirk, *The Politics of Deregulation* (1985, Brookings); S. I. Tolchin and M. Tolchin, *Dismantling America* (1985, OUP). On the machinery that President Reagan has created for deregulating by means of cost-benefit testing and new regulations, and for Anglo-American comparisons, see R. Baldwin and C. G. Veljanovski, 'Regulation by Cost-Benefit Analysis' (1984) 62 *Pub. Admin.* 51.

A paper by British public lawyers that looks *inter alia* at the distinction between privatization and deregulation is N. Lewis and I. Harden, 'Privatisation, De-regulation and Constitutionality: Some Anglo-American Comparisons' (1983) *NILQ* 207. G. Teubner attempts to situate these issues within a more broadly based social theory in two Working Papers of the European University Institute Law Department: 'After Legal Instrumentalism?' (No. 100, April 1984) and 'Substantive and Reflexive Elements in Modern Law' (No. 14, June 1982).

Rationales and justifications for privatization are explored in M. Williams, 'Privatisation's Progress: What is the Government's Denationalisation Programme For? (1985, Brunel University Economics Department); J. A. Kay and D. J. Thompson, *Privatisation: A Policy in Search of a Rationale* (1985, Institute for Fiscal Studies, Working Paper 69); C. G. Veljanovski, *Selling the State* (1987, Weidenfeld and Nicolson). Economists have produced a number of recent studies of privatization, notably: J. Kay, C. Meyer and D. Thompson (eds.), *Privatisation and Regulation – the U.K. Experience* (1986, OUP); J. Vickers and G. Yarrow, *Privatisation* (1985, Centre for Policy Studies); J. LeGrand and P. Robinson (eds), *Privatisation and the Welfare State* (1984, Allen & Unwin); D. Steel and D. Heald (eds), *Privatising Public Enterprises* (1984, RIPA); D. Heald and D. Steel, 'Privatising Public Enterprises – an Analysis of the Government's Case' (1982) 53 *Political Quarterly* 333; D. Heald, 'Will the Privatisation of Public Enterprises Solve the Problem of Control?' (1985) 63 *Pub. Admin.* 7; P. J. Curwen, *Public Enterprise* (1986, Wheatsheaf). See also A. Henney, *Regulating Public and Privatised Monopolies* (1986, Public Finance Foundation); K. Ascher, *The Politics of Privatisation: Contracting Out in the NHS and Local Authorities* (1985, Macmillan); Royal Institute of Public Adminstration, *Contracting Out in the Public Sector* (1977, RIPA); P. Dunleavy, 'Explaining the Privatisation Boom: Public Choice versus Radical Approaches' (1986) 64 *Pub. Admin.* 13; C. Graham and T. Prosser, 'Privatising Nationalised Industries: Constitutional Issues and New Legal Techniques' (1987) 50 *Modern Law Review* 16.

The Government's arguments for disburdening and deregulation are set out in Department of Trade and Industry, *Burdens on Business* (March 1985, HMSO), in the White Paper *Lifting the Burden*, Cmnd

9571 (July 1985, HMSO) and in the White Paper *Building Business, Not Barriers*, Cmnd 9784 (1986, HMSO).

7 Studies of Particular Regulatory Regimes

Only a limited number of British regulatory systems have been studied in detail from a socio-legal perspective. An early look at control by a court and problems of justiciability is R. B. Stevens and B. S. Yamey, *The Restrictive Practices Court* (1965, Weidenfeld and Nicolson). R. Baldwin's *Regulating the Airlines* (1985, Oxford) analyses the Civil Aviation Authority and its predecessors, and the same author has considered the judicial response to such agencies in 'A British Independent Regulatory Agency and the "Skytrain" Decision' [1978] *Public Law* 57. Administrative practice by various equality agencies is reviewed in C. McCrudden, 'Law Enforcement by Regulatory Agency: The Case of Employment Discrimination in Northern Ireland' (1982) 45 *MLR* 617; G. Appleby and E. Ellis, 'Formal Investigations: the Commission for Racial Equality and the Equal Opportunities Commission as Law Enforcement Agencies' [1984] *Public Law* 236; P. Byrne and J. Lovenduski, 'The Equal Opportunities Commission' (1978) 1 *Women's Studies Inter. Q.* 131; and V. Sacks, 'The Equal Opportunities Commission – Ten Years On' (1986) 49 *Modern Law Review* 56. The idea for these agencies was originally proposed by J. Jowell in 'The Administrative Enforcement of Law Against Discrimination' [1965] *Public Law* 119. The match between regulatory method and issue-type is discussed in N. Lewis, 'IBA Programme Contract Awards' [1975] *Public Law* 137; A. Briggs and J. Spicer, *The Franchise Affair* (1986, Century); W. G. Carson, *The Other Price of Britain's Oil* (1982, Martin Robertson); R. Cranston, *Regulating Business* (1979, Macmillan) and R. Cranston, *Consumers and the Law*, 2nd edn (1984, Weidenfeld and Nicolson). See also M. Clarke, *Regulating the City* (1986); A. C. Page, 'Self-Regulation and Codes of Practice' (1980) *JBL* 24; A. C. Page, 'Self-Regulation: The Constitutional Dimension' (1986) 49 *MLR* 141; M. Elliot, 'ACAS and Judicial Review' (1980) 43 *MLR* 580.

Particular attention is paid to enforcement and the process of negotiating compliance in K. Hawkins, *Environment and Enforcement* (1984, Oxford), G. Richardson *et al.*, *Policing Pollution* (1983,

Macmillan), and A. Peacock (ed.), *The Regulation Game* (1984, Blackwell).

8 Agencies and Governmental Control

For many years American scholars have been concerned to redress the deficiencies of regulatory agencies by changing control mechanisms. In 1941 R. E. Cushman proposed the use of planning agencies with powers to direct regulatory agencies – see *The Independent Regulatory Commissions* (1941, OUP, New York). Suggestions have continued to flow; see, for example, L. L. Jaffe, 'The Independent Regulatory Agency – A New Scapegoat' (1956) 65 *Yale LJ* 1068 (on presidential direction); L. J. Hector, 'Problems of the CAB and the Independent Regulatory Commissions' (1960) 69 *Yale LJ* 931 (on separating different agency functions), and L. L. Fuller, *The Morality of Law* (1966) (on planning by non-adjudicating bodies). The most influential proposals in recent years have focused on ways to structure either presidential or congressional powers of direction. Notable discussions are: R. D. Arnold, *Congress and the Bureaucracy* (1980, Yale); L. N. Cutler and D. Johnson, 'Regulation and the Political Process' (1975) 84 *Yale LJ* 1395; G. O. Robinson, 'The Federal Communications Commission, An Essay on Regulatory Watchdogs' (1978) 64 *Virginia Law Review* 169; H. M. Bruff and E. Gellhorn, 'Congressional Control of Administrative Regulation: A Study of Legislative Vetoes' (1977) 90 *Harv. L. Rev.* 1369; H. M. Bruff, 'Presidential Power and Administrative Rulemaking' (1979) 88 *Yale LJ* 451; and C. Byse, 'Comments on a Structural Reform Proposal: Presidential Directives to Independent Agencies' (1977) 29 *Admin. L. Rev.* 157.

In this country, governmental controls over the Civil Aviation Authority have been considered by R. Baldwin in 'A Quango Unleashed: The Abolition of Policy Guidance in Civil Aviation Licensing' (1980) 58 *Pub. Admin.* 287 and in *Regulating the Airlines* (1985, Oxford). N. Lewis has considered the issue more generally in 'Who Controls Quangos and the Nationalised Industries?' in J. Jowell and D. Oliver (eds), *The Changing Constitution* (1985, Oxford), and in 'De-Legalisation in Britain in the 1980s' in P. McAuslan and J. F. McEldowney (eds), *Law, Legitimacy and the Constitution* (1985, Sweet and Maxwell). See also G. Ganz, *Government and Industry* (Professional Books, 1977); A. J. Doig, 'Public Bodies and Ministerial Patronage'

(1978) 31 *Parl. Affairs* 86. There exists an extensive literature on government control of the nationalized industries; for a guide see T. Prosser, *Nationalised Industries and Public Control* (1986, Blackwell); I. Harden and N. Lewis, *The Noble Lie: The Rule of Law and the British Constitution* (1986, Hutchinson).

9 Agency Capture

A detailed review of theories of life-cycle, capture and regulatory origin is given in B. M. Mitnick, *The Political Economy of Regulation* (1980, Columbia). A useful volume devoted to industry/agency relations is P. J. Quirk, *Industry Influence in Federal Regulatory Agencies* (1981, Princeton). The classic early account of agency life-cycles is M. H. Bernstein, *Regulating Business by Independent Commission* (1955, Princeton). For other life-cycle theories, see L. L. Jaffe, 'The Effective Limits of the Administrative Process: A Re-evaluation' (1954) 67 *Harvard L. Rev.* 1105; W. L. Cary, *Politics and the Regulatory Agencies* (1967, McGraw-Hill); E. S. Redford, *Administration of National Economic Control* (1952, Macmillan); A. Downs, *Inside Bureaucracy* (1967, Little, Brown).

The standard work on agency origins, and one sympathetic to the 'public interest' theory (in which regulation offers a response in the public interest to market failures), is R. E. Cushman, *The Independent Regulatory Commissions* (1941, Oxford). The 'economic theory' sees regulation as an item sought by industry for its own protection: see G. J. Stigler, 'The Theory of Economic Regulation' (1971) 2 *Bell J. of Econ. and Man. Sci.* 3; R. A. Posner, 'Theories of Economic Regulation' (1974) 5 *Bell J. of Econ. and Man. Sci.* 335; and W. A. Jordan, 'Producer Protection, Prior Market Structure and the Effects of Government Regulation' (1972) 15 *J. Law and Economics* 151. Economic historians have looked at these matters in detail; see G. Kolko, *Railroads and Regulation 1877–1916* (1965, Princeton); P. W. Macavoy, *The Economic Effects of Regulation* (1965, MIT). For approaches emphasizing the political, bureaucratic and behavioural aspects of agency behaviour see: S. Peltzmen, 'Towards a More General Theory of Regulation' (1976) 19 *J. Law and Economics* 211; R. G. Noll, *Reforming Regulation: An Evaluation of the Ash Council Proposals* (1971, Brookings) and 'The Economics and Politics of Regulation' (1971) 57 *Virginia Law Review*

1016; P. L. Joskow, 'Pricing Decisions of Regulated Forms: A Behavioural Approach' (1973) 4 *Bell J. of Econ. and Man. Sci.* 632.

10 The Limits of the Trial-Type Process

Agencies that employ trial-type procedures often find that a tension exists between such processes and the requirements of planning or policy-making and political control. Some have argued that many agencies are given incompatible powers. This was argued by Louis J. Hector on his resignation from the Civil Aeronautics Board: see L. J. Hector, 'Problems of the CAB and the Independent Regulatory Commissions' (1960) 69 *Yale LJ* 931. Other commentators have been more optimistic but have considered procedural limitations. Thus: L. L. Fuller, 'The Forms and Limits of Adjudication' (1978) 92 *Harv. L. Rev.* 353; B. B. Boyer, 'Alternatives to Administrative Trial-Type Hearings for Resolving Complex Scientific Economic and Social Issues' (1972) 71 *Mich. L. Rev.* 111; and J. L. Jowell, *Law and Bureaucracy* (1975, Dunellen).

The ability of bodies using trial-type procedures to develop coherent policies through case-law or rules is discussed in H. Friendly, *The Federal Administrative Agencies: The Need for Better Definition of Standards* (1962, Harvard) and by D. L. Shapiro, 'The Choice of Rulemaking or Adjudication in the Development of Agency Policy' (1965) 78 *Harv. L. Rev.* 921. How decision-makers can best go about their tasks in such situations is an issue addressed in D. J. Gifford, 'Decisions, Decisional Referents and Administrative Justice' (1972) 37 *Law and Cont. Prob.* 3.

For British experience see R. B. Stevens and B. S. Yamey, *The Restrictive Practices Court* (1965, Weidenfeld and Nicolson), R. Baldwin, *Regulating the Airlines* (1985, Oxford) and J. Beatson, 'A British View of Vermont Yankee' (1981) 55 *Tulane LR* 435. On the strengths and weaknesses of tribunals see R. Rawlings' ESRC study and authorities cited therein.

11 Discretionary Justice

The legitimacy of agencies that make decisions depends to a large degree on the extent to which those decisions are seen as appropriate and fair. One influential argument has asserted that administrative rule-making provides the best hope of controlling arbitrariness. K. C. Davis' *Discretionary Justice* (1969, Illinois) is the classic text, with its proposals on the confining, structuring and checking of discretion. This thesis is appraised in R. Baldwin and K. Hawkins, 'Discretionary Justice: Davis Reconsidered' [1984] *Public Law* 570. D. J. Gifford looks at the particular problems of agencies in 'Discretionary Decisionmaking in the Regulatory Agencies: A Conceptual Framework' (1983) 57 *Southern Calif. L. Rev.* 101. The concept of discretion, its legal control and the limitations of rights-based decision-making are notably discussed in J. L. Jowell, 'The Legal Control of Administrative Discretion' [1973] *Public Law* 179; D. J. Galligan, 'The Nature and Function of Policies within Discretionary Power' [1976] *Public Law* 332, and *Discretionary Powers* (1986, Oxford); R. M. Titmuss, 'Welfare "Rights" Law and Discretion' (1971) 42 *Pol. Q.* 42; M. Adler and A. Bradley (eds), *Justice, Discretion and Poverty* (1986, Professional Books); M. Adler and S. Asquith, *Discretion and Welfare* (1981, Heinemann) and D. Donnison, 'Against Discretion', *New Society*, 15 September 1977, p. 534. A. J. Reiss (Jr) reviews 'Research in Administrative Discretion' at (1970) 23 *J. Leg. Ed.* 69, and Jerry L. Mashaw makes the case for bureaucratic rationality in *Bureaucratic Justice* (1983, Yale). Studies of the operation of discretion in particular bodies can be found in S. Weaver, *Decision to Prosecute* (1977, MIT), R. A. Katzmann, *Regulatory Bureaucracy* (1980, MIT), and A. Stone, *Economic Regulation and the Public Interest* (1977, Cornell).

12 Administrative Rule-making

Much of the literature on discretion is relevant in considering the appropriateness of rules. A valuable introduction that deals with the concept of rules is W. Twining and D. Miers, *How To Do Things With Rules*, 2nd edn (1982, Weidenfeld and Nicolson). On the history of rules and delegated legislation see C. K. Allen, *Law and Orders*, 3rd edn (1965, Stevens). The prevalence of informal administrative rules in modern government and the problems of control in Britain are discussed in R. Baldwin and J. Houghton, 'Circular Arguments: The Status and Legitimacy of Administrative Rules' [1986] *Public Law* 239 and G. Ganz, *Quasi-Legislation* (1987, Sweet & Maxwell).

The circumstances in which an agency should proceed by means of rules or adjudication is the topic of D. L. Shapiro, 'The Choice of Rulemaking or Adjudication in the Development of Agency Policy' (1965) 78 *Harv. L. Rev.* 921, and G. O. Robinson, 'The Making of Administrative Policy: Another Look at Rulemaking and Adjudication and Administrative Procedures Reform' (1970) 118 *U.Pa. L.R.* 485. On the nature of particular rules, their accessibility, effectiveness and precision, see C. S. Diver, 'The Optimal Precision of Administrative Rules' (1983) 93 *Yale LJ* 65, and I. Ehrlich and R. A. Posner, 'An Economic Analysis of Legal Rulemaking' (1974) 3 *Leg. Stud.* 257.

Different approaches to rule-making and discretion are discussed in B. Schwartz and H. W. R. Wade, *Legal Control of Government* (1972, Oxford), by S. Kelman in *Regulating America, Regulating Sweden* (1971, 1981, MIT), and by I. Harden and N. Lewis in *The Noble Lie: The Rule of Law and the British Constitution* (1986, Hutchinson).

13 Organizations and Decision-making

One issue is whether agency policy-making should properly proceed by means of comprehensive rationality or muddling-through. Advocates of muddling-through (a process of adjustment based on past performance) argue that comprehensive rationality (decision-making based on a full review of relevant factors and policies) is unrealistic in complex policy areas: see C. E. Lindholm, 'The Science of Muddling-Through' (1959) 19 *Pub. Admin. Rev.* 79, and P. Braybrooke and C. E. Lindblom, *A Strategy of Decision* (New York, 1963, 1970). The counter argument is put by Y. Dror in 'Muddling-Through – Science or Inertia?' (1964) 24 *Pub. Admin. Rev.* 153. A discussion of the relative merits of these models and their application to regulation is to be found in C. S. Diver, 'Policymaking Paradigms in Administrative Law' (1981) 95 *Harv. L. Rev.* 393. Another issue is the extent to which empirical and theoretical research from other disciplines is able to illuminate administrative behaviour. See, for example, the discussions by K. C. Davis, 'Behavioural Science and Administrative Law' (1964) 17 *J. Leg. Ed.* 137; P. H. Schuck, 'Organisation Theory and the Teaching of Administrative Law' (1983) 33 *J. Leg. Ed.* 13; R. A. Katzmann, 'Judicial Intervention and Organisation Theory: Changing Bureaucratic Behaviour and Policy' (1980) 89 *Yale LJ* 513. Classic reviews of the relevant social science literature are provided by H. Simon, *Administrative Behavior*, 3rd edn

(1976, Collier Macmillan), and P. M. Blau and W. R. Scott, *Formal Organisations* (1963, Routledge).

14 Implementation

The fields of pollution and safety are particularly productive of enforcement studies. Often cited is W. G. Carson's work on the Factory Inspectorate in the 1970s. See his 'White Collar Crime and the Enforcement of Factory Legislation' (1970) 10 *B.J. Crim.* 383 and 'The Conventionalisation of Early Factory Crime' (1979) 71 *J. Soc. Law* 37. Two books in this area have arisen from work at the Centre for Socio-Legal Studies, Oxford: G. Richardson *et al.*, *Policing Pollution* (1983, Macmillan) and K. Hawkins, *Environment and Enforcement* (1984, Oxford). See also N. Gunningham, *Pollution, Social Interest and the Law* (1974, Martin Robertson). An American study is J. Mendeloff, *Regulating Safety* (MIT, 1979).

More generally see R. A. Katzman, *Regulatory Bureaucracy* (1980, MIT); R. A. Kagan, *Regulatory Justice: Implementing A Wage and Price Freeze* (1978, Russell Sage); J. H. Skolnick, *Justice Without Trial* (1966, Wiley); C. S. Diver, 'A Theory of Regulatory Enforcement' (1980) 28 *Pub. Policy* 257; E. Bardach, *The Implementation Game* (1977, MIT); J. L. Pressman and A. Wildavsky, *Implementation*, 2nd edn (1979, University of California Press); and R. T. Nakamura and F. Smallwood, *The Politics of Policy Implementation* (1980, St Martins Press).

15 Critical Approaches to Public Law

Until recently, public lawyers in Britain have been slow to relate public-law issues to broader political and constitutional questions. (For notable exceptions, see W. A. Robson, *Justice and Administrative Law* (1928, Stevens), W. I. Jennings, *The Law and the Constitution* (1938, University of London Press) and J. D. B. Mitchell, 'The Causes and Effects of the Absence of a System of Public Law in the United Kingdom' [1963] *Public Law* 95.) Patrick McAuslan has commented on administrative lawyers' poor record in 'Administrative Law and Administrative Theory: The Dismal Performance of Administrative Lawyers' (1978) 9 *Cambrian L.R.* 40, and Tony

Prosser has urged a revised approach based on the key concepts of participation and accountability in 'Towards a Critical Public Law' (1982) 9 *J. Law and Society* 1 and in his *Nationalised Industries and Public Control* (1986, Blackwell).

The literature is now more rich. There is a text and materials book that takes the contextual approach: C. Harlow and R. Rawlings, *Law and Administration* (1984, Weidenfeld and Nicolson). And a number of recent volumes look at the nature of the modern constitution with an eye to issues in public law; see in particular J. Jowell and D. Oliver (eds), *The Changing Constitution* (1985, Oxford); P. McAuslan and J. McEldowney (eds), *Law, Legitimacy and the Constitution* (1985, Sweet and Maxwell) and I. Harden and N. Lewis, *The Noble Lie: The Rule of Law and the British Constitution* (1986, Hutchinson). See also H. Arthur, 'Rethinking Administrative Law: A Slightly Dicey Business' (1979) 17 *Osgoode Hall LJ* 1 and H. Arthurs, *Without the Law: Administrative Justice and Legal Pluralism in Nineteenth Century England* (1985, Toronto).

A series of prominent articles deals with more particular issues in a critical manner. Patrick McAuslan's 'Administrative Law, Collective Consumption and Judicial Policy' (1983) 46 *MLR* 1, focuses on the judiciary's tendency to translate issues into matters of individual rights. A caution about the drift away from legal principle is contained in M. Loughlin, 'Procedural Fairness: A Study of the Crisis in Administrative Law Theory' (1978) 28 *University of Toronto LJ* 215. The relationship between economic policy, the machinery of government and the law is explored in T. C. Daintith, 'Regulation by Contract: the New Prerogative' (1979) 32 *CLP* 31, 'Public Law and Economic Policy' (1974) *JBL* 9 and 'Legal Analysis of Economic Policy' (1982) 9 *J. Law and Society* 191; A. Page, 'Public Law and Economic Policy: The United Kingdom Experience' (1982) 9 *J. Law and Society* 255; I. Harden and N. Lewis, 'Privatisation, Deregulation and Constitutionality: Some Anglo-American Comparisons' (1983) 34 *NILQ*; and J. T. Winkler, 'Law, State and Economy: The Industry Act 1975 in Context' (1975) 2 *Brit. J. Law and Society* 103. A review of recent British literature on complaints can be found in R. Rawlings, *The Complaints Industry: A Review of Socio-Legal Research on Aspects of Administrative Justice* (1986, ESRC). In Britain there are a number of works that may be referred to by lawyers who are concerned to draw on the literatures of political and social theory. Mention should be made of: J. Winkler, 'Corporatism' (1976) 17 *B.J. Sociol.*; E. Kamenka and E. Tay, 'Beyond Bourgeois Individualism: The Contemporary

Crisis in Law and Legal Ideology' in E. Kamenka and R. S. Neale (eds), *Feudalism, Capitalism and Beyond* (1975, Arnold); R. M. Unger, *Law in Modern Society* (1976, Free Press); B. Jessop, 'The Transformation of the State in Postwar Britain' in M. Castells and R. Scase (eds), *The State in Western Europe* (1979, Croom Helm); G. Poggi, *The Development of the Modern State* (1978, Stanford); H. Hecklo and A. Wildavsky, *The Private Government of Public Money*, 2nd edn (1981, Macmillan); W. Connolly (ed.), *Legitimacy and the State* (1984, Blackwells).

16 The Legitimacy and Effect of Judicial Review

The issue of the legitimacy of judicial review of administrative action in Britain is considered in P. Cane, *An Introduction to Administrative Law* (1986, OUP); C. Harlow and R. Rawlings, *Law and Administration* (1984, Weidenfeld and Nicolson); P. Craig, *Administrative Law* (1983, Sweet and Maxwell) and H. W. R. Wade, *Constitutional Fundamentals* (1980, Stevens). J. A. G. Griffith, *The Politics of the Judiciary*, 3rd edn (1985, Fontana) takes a particularly sceptical view of the benefits of judicial review.

A number of discussions draw attention to the problems of justiciability and polycentricity and the difficulties that adjudicatory bodies have in dealing with many-centred, multi-dimensional problems. The broad issues are considered in J. Jowell, *Law and Bureaucracy* (1975, Dunellen); G. Marshall, 'Justiciability' in A. G. Guest (ed.), *Oxford Essays in Jurisprudence* (1961, Oxford); R. S. Summers, 'Justiciability' (1963) 26 *MLR* 530; D. L. Horwitz, *The Courts and Social Policy* (1977, Brookings); P. Weiler, 'Two Models of Judicial Decision-making' (1968) 46 *Can. Bar Rev.* 406; and A. Chayes, 'The Role of the Judge in Public Law Litigation' (1976) 89 *Harv L. Rev.* 1281. An excellent set of readings taken from the American literature is to be found in R. M. Cover and O. M. Fiss, *The Structure of Procedure* (1979, Foundation Press). A recent review of these issues is to be found in J. T. Lieberman (ed.), *The Role of Courts in American Society* (Final Report of the Council on the Role of Courts) (1984, West Pub. Co.). Discussion of some of these matters in relation to particular agencies and courts is to be found in R. B. Stevens and B. S. Yamey, *The Restrictive Practices Court* (1965, Weidenfeld and Nicolson) and R. Baldwin, *Regulating the Airlines* (1985, Oxford).

What happened when lawyers obtained the upper hand within one agency is described in fascinating detail in P. Nonet, *Administrative Justice: Advocacy and Change in a Government Agency* (1969, Russell Sage). B. Ackerman and W. T. Hassler explore the extent to which courts can remedy organizational failure in *Clean Coal, Dirty Air* (1981, Yale). C. Harlow examines the effect of judicial review in the British context in 'Administrative Reaction to Judicial Review' [1976] *Public Law* 116, as does S. Melnick, *Regulation and the Courts* (1983, Brookings) in the American context. An interesting warning of the need for civil servants to be aware of the increasing scope of British judicial review is given by the Treasury Solicitor, Sir Michael Kerry, in 'Administrative Law and the Administrator' (1983) 38 *Management in Government* 168.

More theoretical treatments of the idea of the 'rule of law' – from which one strand of justification for judicial review arises in Britain – may be found in E. P. Thompson, *Whigs and Hunters* (1975, Allen Lane); F. Hayek, *The Constitution of Liberty* (1960, Routledge); J. Raz, 'The Rule of Law and its Virtue', in *The Authority of Law* (1979, Oxford); and J. Jowell, 'The Rule of Law Today' in Jowell and Oliver (eds), *op. cit.*

An earlier American study of the relationship between the courts and agencies is M. M. Shapiro, *The Supreme Court and Administrative Agencies* (1968, Free Press). A frequently cited American article that gives an overview of the role of judicial review within a broadly conceived conception of administrative law is R. B. Stewart, 'The Reformation of American Administrative Law' (1975) 88 *Harv. L. Rev.* 1667. A more recent book setting judicial review of administrative action in the context of American constitutional law is J. L. Mashaw, *Due Process in the Administrative State* (1985, Yale). An article by an author associated with Critical Legal Studies which provides a critique of the ideology of American administrative law is G. E. Frug, 'The Ideology of Bureaucracy in American Law' (1984) 97 *Harv. L. Rev.* 1276.

Further philosophical and jurisprudential explorations from an American point of view may be found in R. Dworkin, *Law's Empire* (1986, Fontana), R. Dworkin, *A Matter of Principle* (1985, Harvard), and J. H. Ely, *Democracy and Distrust: A Theory of Judicial Review* (1980, Harvard).

Notes

Chapter 1: Regulatory Agencies

1. See A. Barker (ed.), *Quangos in Britain* (1982); D. C. Hague, W. J. M. MacKenzie and A. Barker, *Public Policy and Private Interests: The Institutions of Compromise* (1975).
2. G. Bowen, *Survey of Fringe Bodies* (Civil Service Department 1978).
3. Sir L. Pliatsky, *Report on Non-Departmental Bodies*, Cmnd 7797 (1980).
4. J. F. Garner, 'New Public Corporations' [1966] *Public Law* 324.
5. F. Slatter, *Parliament and Administrative Agencies* (1980), pp. 1–19. Slatter's work has influenced this section considerably. See also Law Reform Commission of Canada (LRCC) Working Paper No. 25, *Independent Administrative Agencies* (1980), pp. 34–5. See also C. Hood, 'Keeping the Centre Small: Explanations of Agency Type' (1978) 26 *Pol. Stud.* 30.
6. R. B. Reich, reviewing J. P. Wilson's *The Politics of Regulation*, in *The New Republic*, 14 June 1980, at p. 38.
7. *Ibid.*
8. Hood, *loc. cit.*
9. See the discussion of the pros and cons of both in R. A. Katzmann, *Regulatory Bureaucracy* (1980), chapter 3.
10. Incrementalism is associated with the work of C. Lindblom. See 'The Science of Muddling Through' (1959) 19 *Pub. Admin. Rev.* 79. A useful discussion of the relative merits of these models in their application to regulation may be found in C. S. Diver, 'Policymaking Paradigms in Administrative Law' (1981) 95 *Harv. L. Rev.* 393.
11. H. Simon, *Administrative Behaviour*, 2nd edn (1957, Free Press), pp. 39–41, 80–84.
12. For example, as reflected in the White Paper, *The Reorganisation of Central Government 1970–71*, (1970), Cmnd 4506.
13. LRCC, *op. cit.*, p. 9.
14. Reich, *op. cit.*, p. 36.

Chapter 2: The Rise of Regulatory Agencies

1. LRCC, *op. cit.*; see also G. Ganz, 'Allocation of Decision-making

Function' [1972] *Public Law* 215.

2. See H. Parris, *Constitutional Bureaucracy* (1969); F. M. G. Willson, 'Ministers and Boards: Some Aspects of Administrative Development Since 1832' (1954) 32 *Pub. Admin.* 43; P. Craig, *Administrative Law* (1983), chapter 2.

3. See O. MacDonagh, *Early Victorian Government* (1977), pp. 107–8.

4. *Ibid.*

5. Willson, *loc. cit.*, pp. 52–3.

6. *Ibid.*, p. 46.

7. *Ibid.*, p. 48.

8. See H. Parris, *Government and the Railways in Nineteenth Century Britain* (1965).

9. M. E. Dimock, *British Public Utilities and National Development* (1933).

10. P. W. J. Bartrip, 'State Intervention in Mid-Nineteenth Century Britain – Fact or Fiction?' (1983) *Journal of British Studies* 63.

11. See also, e.g., N. Lewis, 'IBA Programme Contract Awards' [1975] *Public Law* 317.

12. Cd 9230 (1918).

13. See H. Morrison, *Socialisation and Transport* (1933).

13a [1968] AC 997 (HL).

14. Cmnd 3638 (1967).

15. Department of Employment functions were hived-off to the Manpower Services Commission (1973), the Health and Safety Commission (1974) and the Advisory, Conciliation and Arbitration Service (1975). See G. Jordan, 'Hiving-Off and Departmental Agencies' (1976) 21 *Public Administration Bulletin*.

16. B. Abel-Smith and R. Stevens, *In Search of Justice* (1968), p. 228; see also J. A. Farmer, *Tribunals and Government* (1974), p. 186.

17. *Committee on Administrative Tribunals and Enquiries*, Cmnd 218 (1957), para. 105. For a detailed literature review on tribunals, see R. Rawlings, ESRC study, *op. cit.*

18. Farmer, *op. cit.*, p. 185.

19. R. B. Stevens and B. S. Yamey, *The Restrictive Practices Court* (1965), p. 41.

20. *Report of the Committee on Carriers' Licensing* (1965), para. 2.55.

21. See in general R. E. Wraith and G. B. Lamb, *Public Inquiries as an Instrument of Government* (1971) and, for references and materials, J. Beatson and M. H. Matthews, *Administrative Law: Cases and Materials* (1983), chapter 17.

22. See the Franks Committee, *Report on Administrative Tribunals and Enquiries*, Cmnd 218 (1957), para. 267.

23. See Wraith and Lamb, *op. cit.*, chapter 2.

24. See, e.g., Outer Circle Policy Unit, *The Big Public Inquiry* (1979), outlined at (1979) *JPL*, 501; J. Beatson, (1981) 55 *Tulane L. Rev.* 435;

D. G. T. Williams, 'Public Local Inquiries – Formal Administrative Adjudication' (1980) 29 *ICLQ* 701; G. Ganz, *Administrative Procedures* (1971), chapters 4–6; P. P. Craig, *Administrative Law* (1983), pp. 173–92; *Bushell* v. *Secretary of State for the Environment* [1981] AC 75.

25. For a more recent view see Lewis, *loc. cit.*

26. R. E. Cushman, *The Independent Regulatory Commissions* (1941), pp. 5–10.

27. J. M. Landis, *The Administrative Process* (1938), p. 30.

28. *Ibid.*, p. 4.

29. See T. K. McGraw, 'Regulation in America' (1975) 49 *Business History Review* 159.

30. For the last 25 years of criticism see, e. g., J. O. Freedman, *Crisis and Legitimacy* (1978); P. W. MacAvoy (ed.), *The Crisis of the Regulatory Commissions* (1970); L. J. Hector, 'Problems of the CAB and the Independent Regulatory Commissions' (1960) 69 *Yale LJ* 931; S. Breyer and R. Stewart, *Administrative Law and Regulatory Policy*, 2nd edn (1985), pp. 13–162.

31. See Trevor Smith, *The Politics of the Corporate Economy* (1979), chapters 6 and 7.

32. See M. Williams, 'Privatisation's Progress: What is the Government's Denationalisation Programme For?' Brunel University Economics Department mimeo.

33. See J. A. Kay and D. J. Thompson, *Privatisation: A Policy in Search of a Rationale* (1985, IFS); C. G. Veljanovski, *Selling the State* (1987).

34. See e.g. K. Hartley and M. Huby, 'Contracting-Out in Health and Local Authorities: Prospects, Progress and Pitfalls', *Public Money*, Sept. 1985, p. 23.

35. On the distinction between privatization and deregulation see N. Lewis and I. Harden, 'Privatisation, De-regulation and Constitutionality: Some Anglo-American Comparisons' (1983) *NILQ* 207.

36. See e.g. the White Paper *Lifting the Burden*, July 1985, Cmnd 9571, Annex 1.

37. Department of Trade and Industry, *Burdens on Business*, March 1985 (HMSO).

38. Above, n. 36.

39. *Ibid.*, para. 1.8.

40. See R. Baldwin and C. G. Veljanovski, 'Regulation by Cost-Benefit Analysis' (1984) 62 *Pub. Admin.* 51.

41. Cmnd 9794, May 1986.

42. *Ibid.*, p. 12. The Department of Employment also publishes *A Guide to Full Compliance Cost Assessment* (1986).

43. See S. Breyer, *Regulation and its Reform* (1982), chapter 8.

44. Interview (1985).

45. See R. Baldwin and J. Houghton, 'Circular Arguments: The Status

and Legitimacy of Administrative Rules' [1986] *Public Law* 239.
46. See T. C. Daintith, 'Regulation by Contract: The New Prerogative' (1979) *CLP* 41; 'Legal Analysis of Economic Policy' (1982) 9 *JL Soc.* 191.
47. See Daintith, *loc. cit.* (1979); O. Newman, *The Challenge of Corporatism* (1981), pp. 94–5; J. Jowell, 'Public Regulation by Contractual Means: Trends and Implications', Conference on Comparative Administration and Law, May 1984.
48. Quasi-non-governmental organization. See A. Barker, 'Quango: A Word and a Campaign' in A. Barker (ed.), *Quangos in Britain* (1982).
49. A. Sherman, *The Newest Profession* (1978).
50. P. Holland, *Quango Quango Quango* (1979); *Costing the Quangos* (1980).
51. See e.g. Association of Scientific, Technical and Managerial Staffs, and Society of Civil and Public Servants, *Who Cares About Quangos?* (1979); A. Davies, *What's Wrong With Quangos?* (Outer Circle Policy Unit, 1979).
52. Barker, *op. cit.*, p. 3.
53. G. Bowen, *op. cit.*
54. Sir L. Pliatsky, *op. cit.*
55. Barker, *op. cit.*, p. 228.
56. See C. Hood, 'Keeping the Centre Small: Explanations of Agency Type' (1978) 26 *Political Studies* 1; 'The Machinery of Government Problem' (1979) 28 *Studies in Public Policy* and 'Governmental Bodies and Governmental Growth' in Barker (ed.), *op. cit.*
57. Barker, *op. cit.*, Appendix.
58. See R. Baldwin, 'A Quango Unleashed: The Abolition of Policy Guidance in Civil Aviation Licensing (1980) *Pub. Admin.* 287.
59. Local Government (Interim Provisions) Act 1984.
60. See *Report of the President's Committee on Administrative Management* (The Brownlow Committee) (1937, Washington, DC).
61. For a review see J. O. Freedman, *Crisis and Legitimacy* (1978); see also L. L. Jaffe, 'The Independent Regulatory Agency – A New Scapegoat (1956) 65 *Yale LJ* 1068.
62. See O. Newman, *The Challenge of Corporatism* (1981), p. 149.

Chapter 3: The Evaluation and Oversight of Regulatory Agencies

1. Mashaw, *Due Process in the Administrative State*, p. 16.
2. Stewart, 'The Reformation of American Administrative Law' (1979) 88 *Harvard Law Rev.* 1667 at p. 1675.
3. See, e.g., the case of *R. v. CRE ex parte Hillingdon LBC* [1982] AC 779.
4. See K. C. Davis, *Discretionary Justice* (1969), p. 39.
5. See Stewart, *loc. cit.*, p. 1695. The Law Reform Commission of Canada in Report 26: *Independent Administrative Agencies: A Framework for Decision Making* (1985).

6. See LRCC, 1985, pt III. LRCC (1985) urges clear, plain and unambigous objectives for agencies (pt I).

7. *Ibid.*

8. See R. Baldwin and K. Hawkins, 'Discretionary Justice: Davis Reconsidered' [1984] *Public Law* 570.

9. On the accountability of quangos as a whole, see Lewis 'Who Controls Quangos and the Nationalised Industries?' in J. Jowell and D. Oliver (eds), *The Changing Constitution* (1985).

10. Select Committee on the Parliamentary Commissioner for Administration, *Report on Non-Departmental Public Bodies* (MC 1983–4, 619) (1984).

11. Fourth report from the Select Committee on the Parliamentary Commissioner for Administration, *Observations by the Government*, Cmnd 9563 (1985).

12. Section 6.

13. Parliamentary Commissioner for Administration, *Annual Report 1983* (MC 1983–4, 322).

14. See R. Baldwin, *Regulating the Airlines* (1985), p. 272.

15. See R. Wilding, 'A Triangular Affair: Quangos, Ministers and M.P.s', in A. Barker (ed.), *Quangos in Britain* (1982) and N. Johnson, 'Quangos and the Structure of Government' (1979) 57 *Pub. Admin.* 379.

16. See L. R. Cutler and D. R. Johnson, 'Regulation and the Political Process' (1975) 84 *Yale LJ* 1395.

17. American Bar Association Commission on Law and the Economy, *Federal Regulation: Roads to Reform* (1979).

18. See R. Baldwin and C. Veljanovski, 'Regulation by Cost-Benefit Analysis' (1984) 62 *Pub. Admin.* 51.

19. Cmnd 9571 (1985, HMSO). See *Building Business, Not Barriers*, Cmnd 9794 (1986).

20. See R. Baldwin, *Regulating the Airlines* (1985), esp. chapters 6, 9, 13, 14.

21. See Baldwin, *op. cit.*, chapter 14.

22. *Ibid.*

23. See R. Baldwin, 'A Quango Unleashed: The Abolition of Policy Guidance in Civil Aviation Licensing' (1980) 58 *Pub. Admin.* 287.

24. See e.g. C. Byse, 'Comments on a Structural Reform Proposal: Presidential Directives to Independent Agencies' (1977) 29 *Admin. L. Rev.* 157; L. Jaffe, 'The Independent Regulatory Agency – A New Scapegoat' (1956) 65 *Yale LJ* 1068; E. S. Redford, *The President and the Regulatory Commissions*, Report to the President's Advisory Committee on Government Organisation (1960).

25. Law Reform Commission of Canada, Working Paper 25, *Independent Administrative Agencies* (1980, Ontario), p. 85.

26. See LRCC, *Final Report on Independent Administrative Agencies* (1985), chapter 2.

27. See LRCC, 1985, pt II.

28. See Stewart, *loc. cit.*, p. 1791.

29. A. Davies, *op. cit.*, p. 172.

30. Labour Research Department, quoted in *The Guardian*, 4 June 1986.

31. *The Guardian*, 29 July 1980.

32. Davies, *op. cit.*, p. 173.

33. LRCC, chapter 4.

34. A. Davies, 'Patronage and Quasi-Government; Some Proposals for Reform' in A. Barker (ed.), *Quangos in Britain*, p. 167, at 169.

35. *Ibid.*, p. 174.

36. See Stewart, *loc. cit.*, p. 1793.

37. See Mashaw, *op. cit.*, pp. 22–3.

38. N. Lewis, 'IBA Programme Contract Awards' [1975] *Public Law* 317, 339.

39. See R. Baldwin, M. Cave and T. Jones, 'Independent Local Radio Franchising: Questions of Legitimacy' (1986), Brunel University Economics Department mimeo.

40. For a review of administrative rules in Britain see R. Baldwin and J. Houghton, 'Circular Arguments: The Status and Legitimacy of Administrative Rules' [1986] *Public Law* 239, and Ganz, *Quasi-Legislation* (1987).

41. *Ibid.*

42. *Bates* v. *Lord Hailsham of St Marylebone* [1972] 1 WLR 1373.

43. For a defence of expertise see J. M. Landis, *The Administrative Process* (1938).

44. See e.g. National Consumer Council, *Air Transport and the Consumer: A Need for Change* (1986), chapter 6.

45. R. A. Katzmann, *Regulatory Bureaucracy* (1980), p. 9.

46. *Ibid.*, p. 9.

47. *Ibid.*, p. 107.

48. *Ibid.*

49. *Ibid.*, p. 9.

50. LRCC, *op. cit.*, chapter 3, Recommendation No. 19.

51. Compare R. A. Posner, 'Utilitarianism, Economics and Legal Theory' (1979) 8 *J. Leg. Stud.* 103 and R. M. Dworkin, 'Is Wealth a Value?' (1980) 9 *J. Leg. Stud.* 191.

52. See R. Baldwin and C. G. Veljanovski 'Regulation by Cost-Benefit Analysis' (1984) 62 *Pub. Admin.* 51.

Chapter 4: The Courts and Regulatory Agencies

1. *The Economist*, 21 May 1977 (editorial: 'All honourable men').

2. Johnson, 'Accountability, Control and Complexity: Moving Beyond Ministerial Responsibility' in A. Barker (ed.), *Quangos in Britain*, p. 215.

3. Law Reform Commission of Canada, *Final Report on Independent Administrative Agencies* (1985), chapter 1.

4. *Ibid.*, chapter 2.

5. See, e.g., *Ministry of Housing and Local Government* v. *Sharp* [1970] 2 QB 223.

6. A notable exception is Harlow, 'Administrative Reaction to Judicial Review' [1976] *Public Law* 116.

7. Kerry, 'Administrative Law and the Administrator', 38 *Management in Government*, August 1983, No. 3, p. 168.

8. Woolf, 'Public Law – Private Law: Why the Divide? A Personal View' [1986] *Public Law* 220 at 222.

9. *The Financial Times*, 6 May 1986.

10. J. Beatson, 'Financial Services: Who will Regulate the Regulators?' (forthcoming).

11. **IBA**: *R.* v. *IBA, ex p. the Rank Organisation plc*, CA, 26 March 1986; *R.* v. *IBA, ex parte Whitehouse, The Times*, 4 April 1985 (CA), *The Times*, 14 April 1984 (QBD); *AG (ex rel McWhirter)* v. *IBA* [1973] QB 629. **Gaming Board**: *De Keller* v. *Gaming Board, The Times*, 28 April 1983; *Playboy Club of London* v. *Gaming Board*, SJ 216/80, 14 July 1980; *Rogers* v. *Sec. of State for the Home Dept.* [1973] AC 388; *R.* v. *Gaming Board, ex p. Benaim and Khaida* [1970] 2 QB 417. **Health and Safety Commission/Executive**: *R.* v. *Health and Safety Executive, ex p. British Aerosol Manufacturers Assoc.* (QBD, Crown Office List, unreported, 3 December 1985); *R.* v. *Health and Safety Executive, ex p. Spelthorne Borough Council, The Times*, 18 July 1983. **Civil Aviation Authority**: *Laker Airways Ltd* v. *Department of Trade* [1977] QB 643; *R.* v. *CAA, ex p. British Airways Board* (QBD, Crown Office List, unreported, 21 September 1983). **Office of Fair Trading**: *R.* v. *DGFT, ex p. FH Taylor & Co. Ltd* [1981] ICR 292. **Monopolies and Mergers Commission**: *R.* v. *MMC, ex p. Elders IXL Ltd, Financial Times Law Reports*, 2 May 1986; *R.* v. *MMC, ex p. Argyll Group plc* [1986] 2 All ER 257 (CA); *R.* v. *Sec. of State, ex p. Anderson Strathclyde plc* [1983] 2 All ER 233; *Hoffman-La Roche & Co.* v. *Secretary of State for Trade and Industry* [1975] AC 295. **Advisory, Conciliation and Arbitration Service**: *Powley* v. *ACAS* [1978] ICR 123; *Grunwick Processing Laboratories Ltd* v. *ACAS* [1978] AC 655; *Engineers and Managers Assoc.* v. *ACAS* [1978] ICR 875 (Ch), [1979] ICR 637 (CA), [1980] ICR 215 (HL); *United Kingdom Assoc. of Professional Engineers* v. *ACAS* [1979] 2 All ER 478 (CA) [1981] AC 424 (HL); *National Employers Life Assurance Co.* v. *ACAS* [1979] ICR 620. **Commission for Racial Equality**: *Home Office* v. *CRE* [1981] 2 WLR 703; *London Borough of Hillingdon* v. *CRE* [1982] AC 779; *R.* v. *CRE, ex p. Cottrell and Rothon* [1980] 1 WLR 1580; *In re Prestige* [1984] ICR 473; *R.* v. *CRE, ex p. Westminster City Council* [1985] IRLR 426.

12. Woolf, *op. cit.*, pp. 221–2.

13. Norton-Taylor, 'Ministers Fear Court Intervention Here to Stay', *The Guardian*, 14 January 1986. See also McAuslan and McEldowney (eds), *Law, Legitimacy and the Constitution* (1986, London), p. 35.

14. Blom-Cooper, 'Lawyers and Public Administrators: Separate and Unequal' (The Child Lecture), pp. 19, 13.

15. Kerry, 'Administrative Law and the Administrator', 38 *Management in Government*, August 1983, No. 3, pp. 168, 169–70, 176.

16. H. Young, 'Judges and the Exercise of Power', *The Guardian*, 31 October 1985.

17. *The Economist*, 23 February 1985.

18. One of the best examples is *Home Office* v. *CRE* [1981] 2 WLR 703. Others include *R.* v. *HSE, ex p. Spelthorne BC, The Times*, 18 July 1983, and *R.* v. *CAA, ex p. British Airways Board* (unreported, 21 September 1983).

19. T. Prosser, *Test Cases for the Poor* (CPAG, 1983), p. 85.

20. J. Mashaw and R. A. Merrill, *Administrative Law: The American Public Law System* (1985, West), p. 267.

21. Law Reform Commission of Canada, Working Paper 25, *Independent Administrative Agencies* (1980), p. 153.

22. Though see *Padfield* v. *Minister of Agriculture, Fisheries and Food* [1968] AC 997.

23. Ackerman and Hassler, *Clean Coal, Dirty Air* (1981, Yale), p. 25.

24. Breyer, 'Alternative Approaches to Regulatory Reform: Judicial Review' (paper for Conference on Comparative Administration and Law, May 1984), p. 39.

25. *Laker Airways Ltd* v. *Department of Trade* [1977] QB 643.

26. Blom Cooper, *op. cit.*, p. 13. See also Kerry, *op. cit.*, p. 177.

27. Law Reform Commission of Canada, Working Paper 25, *Independent Administrative Agencies* (1980), p. 153.

28. E.g. Interception of Communications Act 1985, s.7(8): 'The decisions of the Tribunal (including any decisions as to their jurisdiction) shall not be subject to appeal or liable to be questioned in any court.'

29. McAuslan, 'Administrative Law Implications of the Rates Bill 1983' (unpublished paper 1983), p. 10.

30. Financial Services Act 1986, s.187.

31. See *The Guardian*, 18 March 1985.

32. An example is the establishment of British Telecom by the Telecommunications Act 1984, especially s.52, which gives a new Director General of Telecommunications power to give assistance to certain legal proceedings.

33. See e.g. H. Collins, *Marxism and Law* (Oxford, 1982).

34. See C. Harlow, *op. cit.*

35. Mashaw and Merrill, *op. cit.*, p. 270.

36. McCrudden has examined this issue in the context of anti-discrimination law in 'Anti-discrimination Goals and the Legal Process' in Young and Glazer (eds), *Ethnic Pluralism and Public Policy* (1983), from which the following is drawn.

37. Weiler, 'Two Models of Judicial Decision Making', (1968) 45 *Canadian Bar Review* 420.

38. *Ibid.*, p. 423.

39. *Ibid.*

40. *Bromley LBC* v. *Greater London Council* [1983] 1 AC 768.

41. M. Stonefrost in a paper presented to the Administrative Law and Administrative Process seminar (Oxford University Faculty of Law and SSRC Centre for Socio-Legal Studies), 2 March 1983.

42. D. Horowitz, *The Courts and Social Policy* (1977, Brookings Institution), p. 45.

43. *Ibid.*

44. J. A. G. Griffith, 'Judicial Decision-Making in Public Law' [1985] *Public Law* 564 at 582.

45. Stonefrost, *op. cit.*

46. Breyer, 'Alternative Approaches to Regulatory Reform: Judicial Review' (Paper for Conference on Comparative Administration and Law, May 1984), p. 37.

47. Stonefrost, *op. cit.*

48. Breyer, 'Alternative Approaches to Regulatory Reform: Judicial Review' (paper for Conference on Comparative Administration and Law, May 1984), p. 33.

49. R. S. Summers, 'Pragmatic Instrumentalism in Twentieth Century American Thought – A Synthesis and Critique of our Dominant General Theory about Law and its Use' (1981) 69 *Cornell Law Review* 861, 923.

50. *R.* v. *Secretary of State for the Environment, ex p. Brent LBC* [1982] QB 593.

51. Woolf, *op. cit.*, pp. 236–7.

52. *Op. cit.*, at 582.

53. Cmnd 9797 (1986).

54. Para. 9.95.

55. Para. 9.99.

56. J. K. Lieberman (ed.), *The Role of Courts in American Society* (The Final Report of the Council on the Role of Courts) (1984, West).

57. [1984] 3 All ER 935 at p. 950.

58. [1983] 2 All ER 262.

59. [1983] 2 All ER at p. 267.

60. *The Financial Times*, 28 February 1986 (the House of Lords refused leave to appeal).

61. See further *Chief Constable of North Wales* v. *Evans* [1982] 3 All ER 141 (HL).

62. See Lord Diplock in *IRC* v. *Nat. Fed. of Self-Emp. and Small Bus.* [1981] 2 All ER 93 at 107.

63. See *The Times*, 2 July 1982, quoted in J. Beatson and M. Mathews, *Administrative Law: Cases and Materials*, pp. 61–2.

64. This is not to say that other factors do not also play a part in the exercise of judicial review. We do not discount the possibility, for example, that the particular subject-matter of the dispute (immigration, students, local government) may play an important part. Rather, we aim to try to winnow out those sets of value premises which we consider play a part and which could provide a coherent justification for the content of a rule-of-law justification in this context. We are not concerned at the moment in selecting which of any is the best justification. Rather we are concerned to provide a critique of the standard-setting justification as it currently seems to operate in the context of administrative law. We do not argue that all judges have the same set of values; nor that they are unchanging; nor that they must be supplied in all cases; nor that they are necessarily consistent.

65. Wade, *Constitutional Fundamentals* (Stevens, 1980).

66. Griffith, *op. cit.*

67. Arthurs, 'Rethinking Administrative Law: a Slightly Dicey Business' (1979) 17 *Osgoode Hall LJ* 1. See also H. W. Arthurs, *Without the Law: Administrative Justice and Legal Pluralism in Nineteenth Century England* (Toronto, 1985).

68. Breyer, 'Alternative Approaches to Regulatory Reform: Judicial Review' (paper for Conference on Comparative Administration and Law, May 1984), p. 14.

69. *Anisminic Ltd* v. *Foreign Compensation Commission* [1969] 2 AC 147.

70. *Council of Civil Service Unions* v. *Minister for the Civil Service* [1985] AC 374.

71. *Notts. CC* v. *Sec. of State for the Environment* [1986] AC 240 (HL).

72. *Khawaja* v. *Secretary of State for the Home Department* [1984] AC 74.

73. McAuslan, 'Administrative Law, Collective Consumption and Judicial Policy' (1983) 46 *Mod. Law Rev.* 1.

74. Sir John Donaldson's statement in *R.* v. *Boundary Commission for England* [1983] 1 All ER 1099 should be more generally applied: 'Since a very large number of people are interested in this appeal and since it is most unlikely that our decision . . . will meet with universal approval, it is important that it should at least be understood. In particular it is important that everyone should understand what is the function and duty of the courts' (p. 1102).

75. Mashaw and Merrill, *op. cit.*, p. 176.

76. *Ibid.*, p. 174.

77. *Ibid.*, p. 224.

78. *Ibid.*, p. 229.
79. *Ibid.*, p. 224.
80. *Ibid.*, pp. 224–5.
81. Beatson, 'A British View of *Vermont Yankee*' (1981) 55 *Tulane Law Review* 435.
82. See also *R.* v. *Independent Broadcasting Authority, ex p. the Rank Organisation plc* (unreported, CA, 26 March 1986).
83. Where unwilling to intervene, however, there are powerful statements of the need to protect and enhance administrative action and of the desirability of trying to prevent judicial review becoming an undue burden on administrators; see e.g. Lord Diplock in *Bushell* v. *Secretary of State* [1981] AC 75; Woolf J. in *R.* v. *HSE, ex p. Spelthorne BC, The Times*, 18 July 1983 and *R.* v. *Secretary of State for the Environment, ex p. the GLC* (unreported, 3 April 1985).
84. *Nottinghamshire CC* v. *Secretary of State for the Environment* [1986] AC 240; *CCSU* v. *Minister for the Civil Service* [1985] AC 374.
85. Chapter 2, recommendation no. 16.
86. In *Preston* v. *Inland Revenue Commissioners* [1985] 2 All ER 327 (HL), expertise was heavily drawn on by the House of Lords, e.g. by Lord Templeman (at p. 337), when discussing the availability of judicial review even where there was an appeal structure provided in the legislation. See also *Grunwick Processing Laboratories Ltd* v. *ACAS* [1978] AC 655.
87. [1986] 2 All ER 257 (CA). See also the approach sympathetic to the MMC taken by Mann J in *R.* v. *MMC, ex p. Elders IXC Ltd, The Financial Times*, 2 May 1986.
88. p. 263.
89. p. 266.
90. *R.* v. *Boundary Commission for England, ex p. Foot* [1983] 1 All ER 1099, Sir John Donaldson MR, pp. 1110, 1116.
91. Stewart, 'The Reformation of American Administrative Law' (1975) 88 *Harvard Law Rev.* 1667.
92. J. H. Ely, *Democracy and Distrust* (1980, Harvard), p. 103.
93. J. L. Mashaw, *Bureaucratic Justice: Managing Social Security Disability Claims* (1983).
94. *The Guardian*, 31 October 1986.

Chapter 5: The Gaming Board for Great Britain

1. See generally D. Miers, 'The Regulation of Commercial Gaming' (1984) 11 *Journal of Law and Society* 33–66. I am grateful to the Editors and Publishers for permitting me to draw upon that article.
2. Lord Stonham, HL Deb. vol. 293, col. 854 (20 June 1968).

3. Lord Stonham, HL Deb. vol. 274, col. 1156 (19 May 1966).
4. Mr J. Callaghan, HC Deb. vol. 758, col. 1175 (13 February 1968).
5. Lord Stonham, HL Deb. vol. 293, *op. cit.*, col. 857.
6. Gaming Act 1968, Schedule 2, para. 4(6).
7. S. Breyer, *Regulation and Its Reform*, (1982, Harvard), p. 131ff.
8. Mr J. Callaghan, HC Deb. vol. 766, col. 315 (12 June 1968).
9. Lord Stonham, HL Deb. vol. 293, *op. cit.*, col. 856.
10. [1970] 2 QB 417.
11. [1973] AC 388 (HL)
12. S. A. de Smith, *Judicial Review of Administrative Action*, 4th edn J. Evans (1980, Stevens), pp. 184–5.
13. [1964] AC 40; de Smith, *ibid.*, pp. 176–7.
14. See also Lord Denning, in *R.* v. *Commissioner of the Police for the Metropolis, ex parte Blackburn* [1968] 2 QB 118.
15. *Royal Commission on Gambling, Final Report* (1978, Cmnd 7200; Chairman: The Lord Rothschild; hereafter as *Rothschild*), para. 19.68.
16. *Rothschild*, para. 19.69 (emphasis added).
17. See D. Miers, 'Malpractices in British Casino Management' in M. Clarke (ed.), *Corruption* (1983, Francis Pinter), pp. 24–38.
18. *Rothschild*, para. 19.20.
19. (1970) 28 *Cambridge Law Journal* 178.
20. See *Rothschild*, para. 18.18 and *Report of the Gaming Board for Great Britain 1978* (1979, HC 11), para. 28.
21. Lord Stonham, HL Deb. vol. 296, col. 464 (August 1968). The policy was implemented in the Gaming Clubs (Licensing) Regulations 1969, 1969 S.I. No. 1110.
22. Schedule 2 para. 18. This test applies also to the renewal of a licence.
23. HL Deb. vol. 293, *op. cit.*, col. 854.
24. Gaming Board for Great Britain, *Licensing of Gaming Clubs (including Bingo Clubs)*, Memorandum of Advice under the Gaming Act 1968 for the 1986 Licensing Sessions, para. 5 (this repeats previous years' advice).
25. See the discussion in Miers, note 1 above, pp. 44–7.
26. Note 24 above, para. 21.
27. *Report of the Gaming Board for Great Britain 1986* (1987, HC 263), Appx II.
28. See, *Report of the Gaming Board for Great Britain 1982* (1983, HC 311), para. 34; Monopolies and Mergers Commission, *Pleasurama PLC and Trident Television PLC and Grand Metropolitan PLC* (1983, Cmnd 9108), chapter 3; and Miers, note 1 above, pp. 50–1.
29. Lord Stonham, HL Deb. vol. 293, *op. cit.*, col. 858.
30. S. Breyer, 'Analysing Regulatory Failure: Mismatches, Less Restrictive Alternatives, and Reform' (1979) 92 *Harvard Law Review* 549, 573.

31. S.16(4). There are other formalities which must be complied with if the cheque is to be lawful under s.16; see generally D. Miers, 'The Provision of Credit for Gaming', *The Society for the Study of Gambling Newsletter*, No. 3 (April 1983), 8–14.

32. These are discussed in detail in Department of Trade, *Scotia Investments Ltd* (1980, investigation under s.165(b) of the Companies Act 1948), para. 18.11ff. See also *Rothschild*, paras 18.63–18.65 and, for the attitude of one casino proprietor, V. Lownes, *Playboy Extraordinary* (1983, Granada), pp. 159–63.

33. *R. v. Crown Court at Knightsbridge, ex parte Marcrest Ltd* [1983] 1 All ER 1148, 1154.

34. *Report of the Gaming Board for Great Britain 1984*, (1985, HC 443), Appx II.

35. *Report of the Gaming Board for Great Britain 1986, op. cit.*, Appx I. This figure of 85 has remained relatively stable over the past 5 years for which figures have been given.

36. K. Hawkins, *Environment and Enforcement* (1984, Oxford University Press), p. 129.

37. R. Schwartz and H. Wade, *Legal Control of Government* (1972, Oxford University Press), p. 32.

38. See C. Veljanovski, chapter 12 of this book.

39. Lord Stonham, HL Deb. vol. 293, *op. cit.*, col. 861. See also HL Deb. vol. 274, col. 1156 (19 May 1966).

40. Lexis transcript SJ 216/80 (14 July 1980).

41. *Ibid.*, p. 5.

42. *Ibid.*

43. A phrase used by R. Kagan and J. Scholz in 'The "Criminality" of the Regulatory Enforcement Strategies' in K. Hawkins and J. Thomas (eds), *Enforcing Regulation* (1984), pp. 67–95, to describe those entrepreneurs whose compliance with the law is influenced only by what they perceive they can afford to lose if caught; see text *infra*.

44. Note 40 above, p. 6.

45. British Casino Association, Code of Conduct (1980), para. 2.

46. Described in Miers, note 17 above, and Lownes, *op. cit.*, pp. 156–65.

47. 'The Political Economy of Regulation' (1982) 5 *University of New South Wales Law Journal*, 29–60, 31.

48. See, e.g. R. Baldwin, *Regulating the Airlines* (1985, OUP); B. Behrman, 'Civil Aeronautics Board' in J. Wilson (ed.), *The Politics of Regulation* (1980, Basic Books), pp. 75–120.

49. See, e.g., Hawkins, *op. cit.*, and Richardson *et al.*, *Policing Pollution* (1982, OUP).

50. Note 30 above.

51. These may of course feature in such other contexts as private law; e.g. D. Harris and C. Veljanovski, 'Remedies under Contract Law' (1983)

5 *Law and Policy Quarterly* 87.

52. R. Kagan, 'On Regulatory Inspectorates and the Police' in *Enforcing Regulation, op. cit.*, pp. 45–6.

53. *Ibid.*

54. Kagan and Scholz, *op. cit.*, p. 67.

55. On the role of (and the constraints upon) the Gaming Board in determining the conditions of the market, see generally Monopolies and Mergers Commission, *Pleasurama PLC and Trident Television PLC and Grand Metropolitan PLC, op. cit.*.

56. In 1986 the Board was specifically invited by the Home Office to consider the relaxation of controls over gaming, but concluded that they needed strengthening. *Report of the Gaming Board for Great Britain 1986, op. cit.*, para. 13.

57. *Report on the Gaming Board for Great Britain 1986, op. cit.*, paras 19–23.

58. de Smith, note 12 above, p.189. See, e.g., the decision of the Court of Appeal in *ex parte Marcrest, op. cit.*, and of the Divisional Court in *R. v. Crown Court at Knightsbridge ex parte International Sporting Club* [1982] 1 QB 304.

59. A. Page, 'Legal Analysis of Economic Policy – II' (1982) 9 *Journal of Law and Society* 225.

60. See, e.g., T. Daintith, 'Legal Analysis of Economic Policy – I' (1982) 9 *Journal of Law and Society* 191; N. Lewis and P. Wiles, 'The Post Corporatist State?' (1984) 11 *Journal of Law and Society* 65, and T. Prosser, 'Towards a Critical Public Law' (1982) 9 *Journal of Law and Society* 1.

Chapter 6: The Advisory Conciliation and Arbitration Service

1. Roy Lewis, 'Collective Labour Law', in G. S. Bain (ed.), *Industrial Relations in Britain* (1983, Blackwell), p. 369.

2. Jon Clark and Lord Wedderburn, 'Modern Labour Law: Problems, Functions and Policies' in Lord Wedderburn, R. Lewis and J. Clark (eds), *Labour Law and Industrial Relations: Building on Kahn-Freund* (1983, Clarendon Press), pp. 130–44.

3. Lewis, *op. cit.*, pp. 371–3.

4. Clark and Wedderburn, *op. cit.*, p. 131.

5. K. W. (Lord) Wedderburn, 'The Employment Protection Act 1975: Collective Aspects' (1976) 39 *Modern Law Review*, 174.

6. R. Lewis and R. Simpson, 'Disorganising Industrial Relations: An Analysis of Sections 2–8 and 10–14 of the Employment Act 1982' (1982) 11 *Industrial Law Journal* 227–46.

7. B. C. M. Weekes, 'ACAS – An Alternative to Law?' (1979) 8 *Industrial Law Journal*, 147–59.

8. Clark and Wedderburn, *op. cit.*, p. 131.

9. Otto Kahn-Freund, *Labour and the Law*, 3rd edn (ed. and intro. by P. Davies and M. Freedland; 1983, Stevens), p. 53; K. W. (Lord) Wedderburn, 'Industrial Relations and the Courts' (1980) 9 *Industrial Law Journal* 71–4.

10. Otto Kahn-Freund, 'Industrial Relations and the Law – Retrospect and Prospect' (1969) 7 *British Journal of Industrial Relations* 305.

11. W. Paynter, 'Is There a Future for Conciliation and Arbitration?' (December 1972), *Personnel Management* 18–21; ACAS, *First Annual Report 1975* (1976, HMSO), p. 4.

12. EPA 1975, Schedule 1, para. 11(1).

13. M. Jones, L. Dickens, B. Weekes and M. Hart, 'Resolving Industrial Disputes: The Role of ACAS Conciliation' (1983) 7 *Industrial Relations Journal* 14; John Lockyer, *Industrial Arbitration in Great Britain – Everyman's Guide* (1979, IPM), p. 59.

14. ACAS is required to appoint a panel of experts to assist industrial tribunals with equal-pay-for-work-of-equal-value claims. Equal Pay Act 1970, s.2A(4).

15. The controversy over union membership at GCHQ led the TUC to withdraw from the tripartite National Economic and Development Council as a gesture of protest. Although it reviewed its membership of other public bodies, including ACAS, it did not withdraw from them. Its boycott of NEDC ran from March to December 1984.

16. In 1984 ACAS became involved in civil service disputes for the first time. These concerned proposals to privatize the Crown Agents and shiftworking in computer areas of the Department of Health and Social Security.

17. W. A. Brown (ed.), *The Changing Contours of British Industrial Relations: A Survey of Manufacturing Industry* (1981, Blackwell), p. 49; Weekes, *op. cit.*, p. 152.

18. ACAS, *Annual Report 1984* (1985, HMSO), p. 22.

19. ACAS, *Annual Report 1985* (1986, HMSO), p. 96.

20. Jones *et al.*, *op. cit.*, p. 16.

21. ACAS, *Annual Report 1985*, *op. cit.*, pp. 96, 101. The Service also established private and informal contact in another 379 disputes, and claims to have been in touch with the parties 'in virtually all lengthy stoppages and in other important disputes and when it did not assist directly in their resolution, served as a channel of communication or sounding board for the parties' (*ibid.*, p. 23).

22. L. Dickens and D. Cockburn, 'Dispute Settlement Institutions and the Courts' in R. Lewis (ed.), *Labour Law in Britain* (1986, Blackwell).

23. Jones *et al.*, *op. cit.*

24. E. Armstrong and R. Lucas, *Improving Industrial Relations: The Advisory*

Role of ACAS (1985, Croom Helm), pp. 74–7 and 101–4.

25. Weekes, *op. cit.*, pp. 155–7.
26. ACAS, *Annual Report 1979* (1980, HMSO), p. 68.
27. ACAS, *Annual Report 1985*, *op. cit.*, p. 47.
28. *Ibid.*, p. 46.
29. W. E. J. McCarthy and N. D. Ellis, *Management by Agreement* (1973, Hutchinson), pp. 115–16; Clark Kerr, *Labor and Management in Industrial Society* (1964, Doubleday), p. 180.
30. Royal Commission on Trade Unions and Employers' Associations, *Report*, Cmnd 3623 (1968, HMSO), para. 198.
31. K. W. (Lord) Wedderburn, 'Labour Law and Labour Relations in Britain' (1972) 10 *British Journal of Industrial Relations* 275.
32. B. Weekes, M. Mellish, L. Dickens and J. Lloyd, *Industrial Relations and the Limits of Law* (1975, Blackwell), chapter 5.
33. L. Dickens, 'ACAS and the Union Recognition Procedure', (1978) 7 *Industrial Law Journal* 160–77.
34. Wages Councils Act 1979, s.6 and s.10.
35. J. Purcell, *Good Industrial Relations: Theory and Practice* (1981, Macmillan), chapter 1.
36. Elements of the Donovan–CIR reform package can, however, be detected in, for example, the checklist ACAS provides as 'a reminder of those principles which have long been generally accepted as a basis for good industrial relations' in its publication *Improving Industrial Relations: A Joint Responsibility* (1981).
37. See, for example, J. H. Goldthorpe, 'Industrial Relations in Great Britain: A Critique of Reformism' in T. Clark and L. Clements (eds), *Trade Unions Under Capitalism* (1977, Fontana).
38. EPA 1975, s.6.
39. Kahn-Freund, *Labour and the Law*, *op. cit.*, p. 61.
40. EPA 1975, s.6(11).
41. Weekes *et al.*, *op. cit.*
42. P. Elias, 'Fairness in Unfair Dismissal: Trends and Tensions' (1981) 10 *Industrial Law Journal* 201–17.
43. CAC, *Annual Report 1978* (1979, HMSO), p. 15.
44. H. Gospel, 'Disclosure of Information to Trade Unions' (1976) 5 *Industrial Law Journal* 223–36.
45. L. Dickens and G. S. Bain, 'A Duty to Bargain? Union Recognition and Information Disclosure' in R. Lewis (ed.), *Labour Law in Britain*, *op. cit.*
46. Weekes *et al.*, *op. cit.*, p. 181; CIR, *Small Firms and the Code of Industrial Relations Practice*, Report no. 69 (1974, HMSO).
47. EP(C)A 1978, Part V.
48. L. Dickens, M. Jones, B. Weekes and M. Hart, *Dismissed: A Study of Unfair Dismissal and the Industrial Tribunal System* (1985, Blackwell), pp. 232–8.

49. P. Elias, 'Closing in on the Closed Shop' (1980) 9 *Industrial Law Journal* 211; G. Pitt, 'Code of Practice on Closed Shop Agreements and Arrangements' (1981) 10 *Industrial Law Journal* 45–6; C. D. Drake, 'Code of Practice on Picketing' (1981) 10 *Industrial Law Journal* 47.

50. ACAS Council commented on the Consultative Document issued in March 1983 proposing changes to the Truck Acts and other legislation. ACAS felt the second Consultative Document issued in late 1984 reflected many of the Council's points (*Annual Report 1984, op. cit.*, p. 13).

51. EA 1980, s.3(7).

52. Wedderburn, 'The Employment Protection Act 1975: Collective Aspects', *op. cit.*, p. 169.

53. ACAS, *Annual Report 1985, op. cit.*, p. 110.

54. *Ibid.*

55. Department of Employment, 'Work of the Industrial Tribunals and the Employment Appeal Tribunal', *Employment Gazette* (February 1986), 48.

56. R. Upex, 'Conciliation Agreements' (1982) 11 *Industrial Law Journal* 124–6; J. McIlroy, 'Conciliation' (1980) 9 *Industrial Law Journal* 179–83.

57. See Dickens *et al.*, *Dismissed, op. cit.*, chapter 6.

58. *Moore* v. *Duport Furniture Products Ltd* [1982] IRLR 31 (HL).

59. *Slack* v. *Greenham (Plant Hire) Ltd* [1983] ICR 554.

60. *Gilbert* v. *Kembridge Fibres Ltd* [1984] ICR 188.

61. Dickens *et al.*, *Dismissed, op. cit.*, p. 174.

62. ACAS, *Annual Report 1984, op. cit.*, p. 85.

63. For example, J. Gregory, 'Equal Pay and Sex Discrimination: Why Women are Giving up the Fight' (1982) 10 *Feminist Review* 75–89.

64. Dickens *et al.*, *Dismissed, op. cit.*, pp. 180–81.

65. ACAS, *Annual Report 1980* (1981, HMSO), p. 138.

66. *Ibid.*, p. 89.

67. A. Flanders, 'The Tradition of Voluntarism' (1974) 12 *British Journal of Industrial Relations* 354.

68. Weekes *et al.*, *op. cit.*, chapter 5.

69. See Dickens and Bain, *op. cit.*

70. ACAS, *Annual Report 1979, op. cit.*, pp. 134–8.

71. *Grunwick Processing Laboratories Ltd* v. *ACAS* [1978] ICR 231 (HL).

72. *UKAPE* v. *ACAS* [1979] ICR 303 (CA).

73. Dickens, 'ACAS and the Union Recognition Procedure', *op. cit.*

74. See *ibid.*; Dickens and Bain, *op. cit.*; ACAS, *Annual Report 1980, op. cit.*, p. 83.

75. ACAS, *Annual Report 1980, op. cit.*, pp. 86–7.

76. *UKAPE* v. *ACAS* [1979] ICR 303 (CA).

77. *Ibid.*

78. ACAS, *Annual Report 1980, op. cit.*, pp. 137–8.
79. *UKAPE* v. *ACAS* [1980] ICR 201 (HL); *EMA* v. *ACAS* [1980] ICR 215 (HL).
80. M. Elliott, 'ACAS and Judicial Review' (1980) 43 *Modern Law Review* 585–6.
81. R. Simpson, 'Judicial Control of ACAS' (1979) 8 *Industrial Law Journal* 69.
82. Cf. Lord Denning's comments concerning the Commission for Racial Equality. See chapter 11 of this book.
83. See Kahn-Freund, *Labour and the Law, op. cit.*, pp. 17–18.
84. Wedderburn, 'The Employment Protection Act 1975: Collective Aspects', *op. cit.*, p. 183.
85. P. L. Davies, 'Failure to Comply with Recognition Recommendation' (1979) 8 *Industrial Law Journal* 57–8; B. Doyle, 'A Substitute for Collective Bargaining? The Central Arbitration Committee's Approach to Section 16 of the Employment Protection Act 1975' (1980) 9 *Industrial Law Journal* 158.
86. *Powley* v. *ACAS* [1977] IRLR 190, 195.
87. Lord Salmon, approving the view of Lord Denning, *ACAS* v. *Grunwick Processing Laboratories Ltd* [1978] IRLR 38, 44.
88. J. A. G. Griffith, *The Politics of the Judiciary*, 2nd edn (1981, Fontana), pp. 205–6.
89. ACAS, *Annual Report 1980, op. cit.*, pp. 99–100.
90. R. J. Price and G. S. Bain, 'Union Growth in Britain: Retrospect and Prospect' (1983) 21 *British Journal of Industrial Relations* 60.
91. Dickens and Bain, *op. cit.*
92. D. Winchester, 'Industrial Relations in the Public Sector' in G. S. Bain (ed.), *Industrial Relations in Britain, op. cit.*

Chapter 7: Health and Safety at Work

1. See *Safety and Health at Work*, Report of the Committee 1970–2, Cmnd 5034 (1972) (The Robens Report, hereafter 'Robens').
2. *Ibid.*
3. *Ibid.*, paras 28–39; Chapter 5.
4. *Ibid.*, para. 28.
5. *Ibid.*
6. *Ibid.*, para. 118.
7. *Ibid.*, para. 254.
8. *Ibid.*, para. 255.
9. For criticism of Robens' philosophy see N. Gunningham, *Safeguarding the Worker* (1984), chapter 11 and pp. 348–54; A. D. Woolf, 'Robens Report – the Wrong Approach' (1973) 2 *Industrial Law Journal* 88; P.

Kinnersly, *The Hazards of Work* (1973); J. Nichols and P. Armstrong, *Safety or Profits* (1973).

10. See J. Locke, 'The Politics of Health and Safety', Alexander Redgrave Memorial Lecture (1981), p. 18.
11. *Ibid.*, pp. 21–2, 33.
12. Robens, p. 63.
13. For background to the MSC see the White Paper, *Employment and Training: Government's Proposals*, Cmnd 5250 (1973).
14. The position was reversed by the Employment Protection Act 1975, which made the MSC a Crown body and staff became civil servants.
15. *Ibid.*, para. 66.
16. Health and Safety at Work Etc Act 1974 (HSW Act), s.2(3).
17. *Ibid.*, s2(2)(c).
18. *Ibid.*, s.2(1).
19. *Ibid.*, s.2(4). See also Safety Representatives and Safety Committee Regulations 1977, SI 1977, No. 500.
20. On health and safety consultation see P. Davies and M. Freedland, *Labour Law: Text and Materials*, 2nd edn (1984), pp. 230–7.
21. See HSC/E, *Plan of Work 1985/6 and Onwards* (Plan of Work 1985/6), Annex 2.
22. See Locke, *op. cit.*, p. 28.
23. HSW Act, s.50.
24. HSW Act, s.16(2).
25. Locke, *op. cit.*, p. 28.
26. Department of Trade and Industry, *Burdens on Business* (March 1985); see also the White Paper, *Lifting the Burden*, Cmnd 9571 (1985).
27. Locke, *op. cit.*, p. 34.
28. Robens, chapter 5, p. 40.
29. *Ibid.*, para. 142.
30. See chapter 11 on the CRE in this book.
31. See HSE, *Guide to Making Regulations and Preparing Approved Codes of Practice* (1984).
32. See C. D. Drake and F. B. Wright, *Law of Health and Safety: The Approach* (1983), p. 124.
33. HSC, *Plan of Work 1985/6, p. 20*.
34. See HSE, *Director General's Report 1979–80*, p. 16.
35. See HSC, *Plan of Work 1981–2*, p. 9.
36. Interview 1985. See also: W. G. Carson, 'White Collar Crime and the Enforcement of Factory Legislation' (1970) 10 *B.J. Crim.* 383; 'The Conventionalisation of Early Factory Crime' (1979) 7 *Int. J. Soc. Law* 37; P. Bartrip and P. Fenn, 'The Administration of Safety: The Enforcement Policy of the Early Factory Inspectorate 1844–64' (1980) 58 *Pub. Admin.* 87; N. Gunningham, *op. cit.*, chapter 4.
37. See HSC, *Plan of Work 1985–6*, paras 23, 242.

38. See references at note 9 above.

39. See Robens, para. 254.

40. *Ibid.*, para. 215(b).

41. The number of general factory inspectors fell from 742 to 627 in the period 1979 to 1984. HSC, *Plan of Work 1985–6*, Table 6. On law versus enforcement resources, see Gunningham, *op. cit.*, p. 320.

42. See HSC, *Annual Report 1978–9*, para. 7.

43. HSW Act, s.2(2)(c).

44. *Ibid.*, s.11(2)(b).

45. HSC, *Annual Report 1978–9*, para. 7.

46. HSC, *Plan of Work 1985–6*, pp. 3–4.

47. Health and Safety Executive, *Manufacturing and Service Industries Report* (1983), p. 1.

48. HSC, *Plan of Work 1985–6*, para. 149.

49. *Ibid.*, Annex 2(d).

50. *Ibid.*, para. 108.

51. HM Factory Inspectorate, *Five Year Programme 1984–89* (1983), pp. 3–4.

52. HSC, *Plan of Work 1985–6*, para. 48.

53. *Ibid.*, para. 53.

54. HSC, *Plan of Work 1985–6*, pp. 32–3.

55. *Ibid.*, paras 122, 246.

56. See Gunningham, *op. cit.*, pp. 358–61.

57. House of Lords Select Committee on Science and Technology, *Report on Occupational Health and Hygiene Services*, HL (1983–4) 99–I, para. 13.19.

58. *Ibid.*, p. 46.

59. *Ibid.*, para. 54.

60. *Ibid.*, para. 13.17.

61. See evidence of TUC to the House of Lords Select Committee on Science and Technology at HL (1983–4) 99–II, pp. 94–131, and General, Municipal, Boilermakers and Allied Trades Union evidence to the same committee.

62. See note 45 above, p. 107.

63. HSC, *Plan of Work 1985/6*, para. 246.

64. The HSE has resolved that all its decisions will be unanimous. See G. K. Wilson, *The Politics of Safety and Health* (1985), p. 114.

Chapter 8: Civil Aviation Regulation

1. For a more detailed account see R. Baldwin, *Regulating The Airlines: Administrative Justice and Agency Discretion* (1985).

2. D. Corbett, *Politics and the Airlines* (1965), pp. 26–32; H. J. Dyos and

D. H. Aldcroft, *British Transport* (1974), chapter 13. See also the Hambling Report, *Government Financial Assistance to Civil Air Transport Companies*, Cmnd 1811 (1923).

3. See Report of the Maybury Committee, *The Development of Civil Aviation in the United Kingdom*, Cmd 5351, (1937) (hereafter 'Maybury').

4. *Ibid.*

5. Royal Commission on Transport, *Final Report*, Cmd 3751 (1930).

6. See Maybury, paras 106, 125, 126.

7. See *Report of the Committee of Inquiry into Civil Aviation*, Cmnd 5685 (1938) (The Cadman Committee).

8. *Ibid.*, para. 46.

9. Air Navigation (Licensing of Public Transport) Order 1938, No. 613.

10. *The Times*, 14 March 1945.

11. See H. Morrison, *Socialisation and Transport* (1933).

12. See Mr Lennox-Boyd, HC Deb. vol. 422 col. 662, 6 May 1946.

13. HC Deb. vol. 422, col. 623, 6 May 1946.

14. This was the exception to the Corporation monopoly as set out in section 14(4) of the Civil Aviation Act 1946 and section 15(3) of the Air Corporations Act 1949.

15. B. Abel-Smith and R. Stevens, *In Search of Justice* (1968), p. 228. See also J. A. Farmer, *Tribunals and Government* (1974), p. 186.

16. Mr D. Sandys, HC Deb. vol. 618, col. 1231. The case-law of road passenger cases was hoped to be emulated – see HL Deb. vol. 232, col. 595.

17. See ATLB, *Second Report* (1962) para. 8(d), *Decision on European Routes*, 23 November 1961.

18. See ATLB, *Second Report* (1962), para. 8.

19. See S. F. Wheatcroft, *Air Transport Policy* (1964), p. 165.

20. ATLB, *Ninth Report* (1969), para. 46.

21. ATLB, *Fifth Report* (1965), para. 7.

22. See Wheatcroft, *op. cit.*, p. 150.

23. *Report of the Select Committee on Nationalised Industries* (British European Airways), HC 673 (1967).

24. *Ibid.*, Pt IV, p. 56.

25. Cmnd 4018 (1969).

26. *Ibid.*, chapter 19.

27. *Ibid.*, para. 1002.

28. *Ibid.*, para. 1031.

29. *Ibid.*, para. 640.

30. For an account see Baldwin, *op. cit.*, pp. 89–90.

31. For a useful review of these see S. Breyer, *Regulation and Its Reform* (1982), chapter 1.

32. For criticism of the 'empty box' of the excessive competition justification, see Breyer, *op. cit.*, pp. 29–32.

33. See the Edward's Report, *Air Transport in the Seventies*, Cmnd 4018 (1969), paras 1006–7.
34. *Ibid.*, para. 1008.
35. See Mr M. Noble, introducing the Second Reading of the 1971 Civil Aviation Bill, HC Deb. vol. 814, col. 1173 (29 March 1971).
36. See R. Baldwin, 'A Quango Unleashed: The Abolition of Policy Guidance in Civil Aviation Licensing (1980) 58 *Pub. Admin.* 287.
37. See *Laker Airways Ltd* v. *Department of Trade* [1977] QB 643. Also R. Baldwin, 'A British Regulatory Agency and the "Skytrain" Decision' [1978] *Public Law*, 57.
38. See HC Deb. vol. 926, col. 29, Mr E. Dell (14 February 1977).
39. For such an account see Law Reform Commission of Canada, Working Paper 25, *Independent Administrative Agencies* (1980).
40 Application 1B/24 340 etc., 23 March 1979, para. 45.
41. For an insider's account of the decline of CAA independence after 1977, see P. Reid, 'Regulating Airlines: Why the Arms-Length Approach has Failed' in T. Harrison and J. Gretton (eds), *Transport U.K. 1985* (1985).
42. See D. J. Gifford, 'Discretionary Decision-making in the Regulatory Agencies: A conceptual Framework' (1983) 57 *Southern California L. Rev.* 101.
43. See comments of Mr J. Nott at HC Deb. vol. 973, col. 47.
44. Decision 1B/24 240. See also decisions Alc 180, September 1972; A 9643, 3 October 1972.
45. Decision 1A/20107, 3 December 1974, para. 38. See also decision A/ 15946, 10 October 1973.
46. Civil Aviation Publication 420, CAA (1979).
47. See Breyer, *op. cit.*, chapter 11.
48. *Ibid.*, p. 185.
49. Useful discussions of aviation policy are contained in Civil Aviation Authority, *Airline Competition Policy*, CAP 500 (1984) and the Department of Transport's White Paper *Airline Competition Policy*, Cmnd 9366 (1984).

Chapter 9: The Office of Fair Trading

* Research for this chapter was facilitated by a grant from the University of Newcastle upon Tyne Research Fund. I wish to acknowledge gratefully this assistance.
1. See J. M. Landis, *The Administrative Process* (1938). See the discussion by L. Jaffe, 'The Illusion of the Ideal Administration' (1973) 86 *Harv. L. Rev.* 1183.
2. See e.g. Sir John Methven, 'Keynote Address' in K. D. George and C.

Joll, *Competition Policy in the U.K. and E.E.C.* (1975) and G. J. Borrie, 'The Work of the British Office of Fair Trading' in M. Cappelletti and B. Garth (eds), *Access to Justice,* Vol. III: *Emerging Issues and Perspectives* (1979), p. 497.

3. See *Hansard*, HC 848 (1972–73), cols 453–8 (Fifth Series).
4. Fair Trading Act 1973, s.2.
5. *Ibid.*, Pt II.
6. *Ibid.*, s.3. Part VII of the Act outlines the procedures of the Committee, and for a detailed discussion of its role see below at pp. 188–90.
7. *Ibid.*, s.22(2).
8. *Ibid.*, Pt III.
9. *Ibid.*, s.124(1).
10. S.124(3). See HL Deb. vol. 343, cols. 1491–3.
11. See Paul Craig, chapter 10 of this book.
12. Fair Trading Act 1973, s.2(2).
13. See D. P. O'Brien, 'Competition Policy in Britain: the Silent Revolution' (1982) 27 *Antitrust Bulletin* 217.
14. HC Deb. vol. 848, cols 453–4 (Sir Geoffrey Howe).
15. See, e.g., *The Reorganisation of Central Government 1970–71* (1970), Cmnd 4506.
16. The following account draws heavily on William Roberts, 'The Formation of Consumer Protection Policy in Britain 1945–73' (Kent University Ph.D. thesis, 1975), and an interview with a civil servant involved in the preparation of the Fair Trading Act.
17. *Final Report of the Committee on Consumer Protection* (The Molony Committee), Cmnd 1781 (1962).
18. See, for example, The Trade Descriptions Act 1968 and the Merchandise Marks Acts 1887–1953, and Breyer, *Regulation and its Reform* (1982), p. 6.
19. See, e.g., Parliamentary Debates Commons, Fair Trading Bill 1973, Standing Committee B, Session 1972–73, cols 69–70, 104–23, 125–7.
20. *Ibid.*, at col. 62 (Mr P. Emery, Under Secretary of State, Trade and Industry) and see also cols 58–62.
21. Note 19 above, cols 113–14, 125–7 (Sir Geoffrey Howe).
22. For example, Jeremy Mitchell (Director, Consumer Affairs Division) and J. K. Humble (Assistant Director, Consumer Affairs Division). Mitchell had been Deputy Research Director and Director of Information at the Consumers Association and was Secretary of the Social Science Research Council. Humble had held a position in the Local Government Trading Standards Inspectorate.
23. See *Annual Report of Director General of Fair Trading 1973–74,* p. 13.
24. There was strong opposition within the Civil Service to the introduction of outsiders when the Office was set up in 1973. Sir John Methven made it a condition of his appointment that he could bring

in outsiders (Informant).

25. R. G. S. Brown and D. R. Steel, *The Administrative Process in Britain*, 2nd edn (1979), p. 108.

26. Informant. Part of the research involved interviews with past and present senior executives of the Office of Fair Trading and a former civil servant involved in the background and drafting of the Fair Trading Act 1973. Where I have referred specifically to information provided by these individuals I have used the term 'informant'. I would like to acknowledge the help which these individuals provided in preparing this chapter.

27. See S. Breyer and R. Stewart, *Administrative Law and Regulatory Policy*, 2nd edn (1985).

28. This is the description used by the Office but it is not included in the *Report on Non-Departmental Public Bodies* (The Pliatzky Report) (1980), Cmnd 7797.

29. Breyer and Stewart, *op. cit.*, pp. 130–81.

30. Fair Trading Act 1973, s.125.

31. The classification drawn from The Pliatzky Report, *op. cit.*, p. 175.

32. See on the background to the NCC, Department of Prices and Consumer Protection, *National Consumers' Agency* Cmnd 5726 (1974).

33. See M. J. Trebilcock, 'Winners and Losers in the Modern Regulatory State: Must the Consumer Always Lose?' (1975) 13 *Osgoode Hall LJ* 619.

34. The *locus classicus* on the free-rider effect is M. Olson, *The Logic of Collective Action* (1965, Harvard).

35. Consumer Credit Act 1974, s.1.

36. This description was suggested to me by a senior member of the consumer protection branch of the Office.

37. See, e.g., J. F. Pickering and D. C. Cousins, 'The Economic Implications of Codes of Practice' (unpublished research report, Department of Management Sciences UMIST, 1980); see also A. I. Ogus and C. K. Rowley, 'The cost- effectiveness of Pt. III of the Fair Trading Act 1973 and Licensing under the Consumer Act 1979' (unpublished research paper 1982).

38. See generally Breyer, *op. cit.*, pp. 4–7; G. J. Stigler, 'Regulation: The Confusion of Means and Ends', chapter 10 in G. J. Stigler, *The Citizen and the State: Essays on Regulation* (1975).

39. See L. Jaffe, *op. cit.*, p. 1188.

40. Informant.

41. *Annual Report of the Director General of Fair Trading 1973–74*, pp. 9,19.

42. See Pickering and Cousins, *op. cit.*, pp. 48–54 and see also J. Mitchell, 'A Systematic Approach to Analysing Consumer Complaints' (1977) *J. Consumer Studies and Home Economics* 1, p. 3.

43. See generally A. Hirschman, *Exit, Voice and Loyalty* (1971, Harvard).

44. See G. Priest, 'A Theory of the Consumer Product Warranty' (1981)

90 *Yale LJ* 1297, and I.D.C. Ramsay, *Rationales for Intervention in the Consumer Marketplace* (Office of Fair Trading, Occasional Paper, 1984), p. 49.

45. The Price Marking (Bargain Offers) Order 1979 has been subject to much criticism and has been reviewed by the Office; see *Office of Fair Trading, Review of the Price Marking (Bargain Offers) Order 1979* (1981) and *Review of Legislation on False and Misleading Price Information*, Report of the Interdepartmental Working Party (1984).

46. See Price Commission, *The Pricing of Beds* (HC 650, 1978); Office of Fair Trading, *Review of the Price Marking (Bargain Offers) Order 1979*, Appendix C, paras 3.4–3.5, 3.10. See also R. Pitofsky, 'Beyond Nader: Consumer Protection and the Regulation of Advertising' (1977) 90 *Harv. L. Rev.* 661 at 667–9.

47. Pitofsky, *op. cit.*

48. 1972–73 was described as 'The Year of the Consumer's Charter' in *The Times*, 6 September 1973.

49. This literature is outlined in Ramsay, *op. cit.*, pp. 25–37.

50. Informant.

51. J. D. Gribbin, 'Recent Antitrust Developments in the United Kingdom' (1975) 20 *Antitrust Bulletin* 373 at 394.

52. See *Annual Report of the Director General of Fair Trading 1973–74*, p. 15.

53. See Parliamentary Debates (HC) (1972–73) Standing Committee B, Fair Trading Bill, cols 436–8, 463–6 (Sir Geoffrey Howe); Parliamentary Debates (Lords) (1972–73) 21 June 1973, cols 1497–9.

54. Fair Trading Act 1973, s.3(5).

55. *Ibid.*, s.81.

56. See Parliamentary Debates (HC) (1872–73), Standing Committee B, Fair Trading Bill, cols. 436–8.

57. Over 12 months in a number of cases.

58. *Annual Report of the Director General of Fair Trading 1982*, p. 45.

59. Informant. The Committee was, for example, only given three months in which to report on a reference. Fair Trading Act 1973, s.20(1).

60. See Consumer Protection Advisory Committee, *A Report on Practices Relating to the Purported Exclusion of Inalienable Rights of Consumers and Failures to Explain their Existence* (1974, HMSO).

61. This became known as 'The Heal Project' since it was conducted by Geoffrey Heal, Professor of Economics at Sussex University. The OFT have not published the findings of that study.

62. Informant.

63. HC (*Hansard*) 1972–73 vol. 848, col. 459 (Sir Geoffrey Howe).

64. See generally Pickering and Cousins, *op. cit.*, and G. M. Woodroffe, 'Government Monitored Codes of Practice' (1984) 7 *J. Consumer Policy* 171.

65. Pickering and Cousins, *op. cit.*, pp. 19–27.

66. For example, in relation to used cars. See *Annual Report of the Director General of Fair Trading 1982*, p. 11.

67. See Office of Fair Trading, *Home Improvements*, A Discussion Paper, 6.1–6.8 (1982); *Home Improvements: A Report by the Director General of Fair Trading*, paras 12.1–12.7 (1983).

68. Pickering and Cousins, *op. cit.*, p.265.

69. *op. cit.*

70. *Jenkins* v. *Lombard North Central PLC* [1984] 1 WLR 307, Goff LJ. p. 313.

71. See *Report of the Committee on Consumer Credit* (The Crowther Committee), Cmnd 4596 (1971), vol.1, 6.3.2–6.3.15 and 7.2.1–7.2.11; *Reform of the Law on Consumer Credit* Cmnd. 5427 (1973). See generally R. M. Goode, *Consumer Credit* (1978, Sweet & Maxwell), pp. 37–46.

72. Crowther, *op. cit.*, 6.1.19–6.1.20 and 6.3.3.

73. Consumer Credit Act 1973, s.25. G. J. Borrie, 'Licensing Practice under the Consumer Credit Act' [1982] *J. Bus. L.* 91.

74. Consumer Credit Act 1973, s.25(2)(d).

75. *Annual Report, Director General of Fair Trading 1982*, p. 49.

76. See, for example, *Annual Report, Director General of Fair Trading 1980*, pp. 31–3; *1982*, pp. 19–21.

77. Informant and Borrie, *op. cit.*, note 73.

78. *Annual Report, Director General of Fair Trading 1980*, p. 31.

79. See Goode, *op. cit.*

80. National Consumer Council, *Consumers and Debt* (1983, NCC), p. 98.

81. See, for example, *Jenkins* v. *Lombard North Central PLC*, above; *Elliott* v. *Director General of Fair Trading* [1980] 1 WLR 977.

82. Fair Trading Act, s.34. See *Attorney General* v. *Harris* [1961] 1 QB 74.

83. The use of press releases to give publicity to assurances received judicial approval in *R.* v. *Director General of Fair Trading, ex parte F.H. Taylor & Co. Ltd* [1981] ICR 292.

84. See generally, G. J. Borrie, *The Development of Consumer Policy – Bold Spirits and Timorous Souls* (1984, Stevens), pp. 73–4.

85. See P. Craig, *Administrative Law* (1984, Sweet & Maxwell), pp. 380–3; I. Ehrlich and R. Posner, 'An Economic Analysis of Legal Rulemaking' (1974) 3 *J. Legal Studs*. 257.

86. See Craig, *op. cit.*, p. 476.

87. The Ogus and Rowley paper, *op. cit.*, provides a framework.

88. Extract from Director General's paper to the Consumer Affairs Minister 1983 (on file with author).

89. *Annual Report of the Director General of Fair Trading 1982*, p. 22.

90. See Ramsay, *op. cit.*, pp. 25–34.

91. The Office recently obtained an assurance from Sinclair Electronics.

92. *Annual Report of the Director General of Fair Trading 1982*, p. 10.

93. *Ibid.*

94. See, e.g., 'Tough Warning for Unfair Debt Collectors', *Office of Fair Trading press release*, 25 February 1981.

95. G. Vaughan-Davies, 'Void Terms in Consumer Contracts: Should Their Use be a Criminal Offence?', *Law Society's Gazette*, 3 August 1983, pp. 1978–9.

96. *Ibid.*, p. 1979.

97. J. Kay and T. Sharpe, 'The Anti-Competitive Practice' (1982) 3 *J. Fiscal Studies* 191.

98. L. Jaffe, 'The Independent Agency – A New Scapegoat' (1955–6) 65 *Yale L.J.* 1068 at p. 1070.

99. Pickering and Cousins, *op. cit.*, pp. 175–6.

100. See R. Stewart and C. Sunstein, 'Public Programs and Private Rights' (1982) 95 *Harvard L. Rev.* 1195.

101. R. Posner, 'The Federal Trade Commission' (1969–70) 37 *Univ. Chic. L. Rev.* 47 at p. 89.

Chapter 10: The Monopolies and Mergers Commission

1. The words antitrust or antitrust policy will be used synonymously with competition or competition policy throughout this chapter.

2. *Davenant* v. *Hurdis* (1599) Moore 576; *Darcy* v. *Allen (The Case Of Monopolies)* (1602) 11 Co. Rep. 84.

3. *Mogul S.S. Co. Ltd* v. *McGregor Gow* [1892] AC 25. See also *Sorrell* v. *Smith* [1925] AC 700.

4. *Bolt* v. *Stennett* (1800) 8 TR 606; *Allnut* v. *Inglis* (1810) 12 East 527; *AG* v. *Simpson* [1901] 2 Ch. 671, 718–19; *Nyali Ltd* v. *AG* [1955] 1 All ER 646, 651; [1956] 2 All ER 689, 694.

5. Difficulty is caused by the cases mentioned in note 4 above in so far as they use the term 'public' in a variety of senses. They usually encompass situations in which the property in question is in some sense dedicated to a public use, or where special privileges have been granted by the government.

6. Cmd 9236 (1918).

7. Committee on Trade and Industry, Cmd 3282 (1929).

8. Hannah, *The Rise of the Corporate Economy* (1976), pp. 32–3.

9. *Ibid.*, pp. 36–8.

10. Cmd 6527 (1944).

11. G. C. Allen, *Monopoly and Restrictive Practices* (1968), p. 62.

12. Whish, *Competition Law* (1985); Merkin and Williams, *Competition Law: Antitrust Policy in the United Kingdom and the EEC* (1984); Korah, *Competition Law of Britain and the Common Market*, 3rd edn (1982); *Chitty on Contracts*, 25th edn (1983); Swann, *Competition and Consumer Protection* (1973); Wilberforce, Campbell and Elles, *Restrictive Trade Practices and Monopolies*, 2nd edn (1965).

13. Monopolies and Restrictive Practices (Inquiry and Control) Act 1948, s.3.
14. S.3(2).
15. For discussion see Allen, *op. cit.*, and Rowley, *The British Monopolies Commission* (1966).
16. The public interest was 'defined' in s.14 of the 1948 Act.
17. Cmd 9504 (1955).
18. In addition to the literature mentioned in note 12 above, see also Stevens and Yamey, *The Restrictive Practices Court* (1965); Hunter, *Competition and the Law* (1965); Swann, O'Brien, Maunder and Howe, *Competition in British Industry* (1974).
19. Restrictive Trade Practices Act 1956, s.21.
20. s.21(1)(a).
21. s.21(1)(f).
22. s.21(1)(e).
23. s.21(1)(b).
24. Cunningham, *The Fair Trading Act 1973* (1974).
25. Fair Trading Act 1973, s.50. There are certain limits to the Director's power of reference.
26. Fair Trading Act 1973, s.51.
27. s.6.
28. s.7.
29. s.48.
30. s.49(2).
31. Any references are now more likely to be brought under the Competition Act 1980.
32. S.49.
33. Fair Trading Act 1973, s.84.
34. s.54.
35. s.64.
36. s.65.
37. See *Wallpaper* (1964) HC 59; *Matches* (1952–3) HC 161.
38. See Hannah, note 8 above; Hannah and Kay, *Concentration in Modern Industry* (1977); Hart, Utton and Walshe, *Mergers and Concentration in British Industry* (1973); Walshe, *Recent Trends in Monopoly in Great Britain* (1974).
39. Fair Trading Act 1973, s.76.
40. s.69.
41. s.84.
42. ss.72–3.
43. *A Review of Restrictive Trade Practices Policy*, Cmnd 7512 (1979); *A Review of Monopolies and Mergers Policy*, Cmnd 7198 (1978).
44. Competition Act 1980, s.2(1).
45. See below, pp. 214–17.

46. Competition Act 1980, s.3.
47. s.4.
48. s.5.
49. s.6.
50. s.8.
51. See below, pp. 219–21.
52. Many vertical agreements are outside the Restrictive Trade Practices Act 1976, because of exemptions within the legislation. See particularly s.9(3), Sched. 3, para. 2.
53. Fair Trading Act 1973, ss.6, 7, 64.
54. Restrictive Trade Practices Act 1976, s.10.
55. Fair Trading Act 1973, s.84.
56. See also Sherman Act, ss.1, 2 (United States). The antitrust legislation of, e.g., Germany, France, Australia and Sweden is also based upon an effects approach.
57. HC Deb. vol. 350, col. 404, 12 April 1956. See also the decision in *Texaco Ltd* v. *Mulberry Filling Stations Ltd* [1972] 1 WLR 814, given by Ungoed-Thomas J.
58. See, e.g., United States, Australia and the EEC.
59. Cf. Art. 85(3) of the EEC Treaty.
60. Cmnd 7512 (1979), para. 7.6.
61. *Ibid.*, para. 7.5.
62. *Ibid.*, para. 7.7(i) and (iii).
63. *Ibid.*, para. 7.7(iv).
64. *Ibid.*, para. 7.7(v) and (vii).
65. *Ibid.*, para. 7.7(ii).
66. See *Report on Non-Departmental Public Bodies*, Cmnd 7797 (1980).
67. This is particularly so, given that other recommendations of the Liesner Report were designed to strengthen the power of the OFT; see Cmnd 7512 (1979), chapter 7.
68. See, e.g., Sullivan, *Antitrust*(1977), chapter 3.
69. See, e.g., *Schweppes Ltd* v. *Registrar of Restrictive Trading Agreements* [1965] 1 WLR 157; *Registrar of Restrictive Trading Agreements* v. *Schweppes (No. 2)* [1971] 1 WLR 1148; *Re Cadbury Schweppes Ltd's Agreement* [1975] 2 All ER 307. For comment see Craig [1975] *ASCL* 482. See also *Re Automatic Telephone and Electric Co. Ltd Agreement* [1964] 2 All ER 873.
70. Cmnd 7512 (1979), chapter 7 of which provides a summary.
71. *Ibid.*, para. 7.10–7.47.
72. Fair Trading Act 1973, s.10.
73. Cmnd 7512 (1979), paras 7.33–7.38.
74. *Ibid.*, paras 7.21–7.26.
75. *Ibid.*, Annex C.
76. *Ibid.*, para. 7.45. Not all of the recommendations were accepted by the government. See Cmnd 7512 (1979), paras 7.46–7.49.

77. 'Antitrust Policy: Economics versus Management Science', *Moorgate and Wall Street*, Autumn 1970.

78. 'Economics as an Antitrust Defense: the Welfare Trade-offs' (1968) 58 *American Economic Review* 18.

79. Williamson did, however, accept that there were various reasons why these cost savings might not be realized.

80. Leibenstein, 'Allocative Efficiency vs. X-Efficiency' (1966) 56 *American Economic Review* 392.

81. Note that Crew and Rowley feel that such a rule-based system could then be administered judicially, note 77 above, pp. 33–4.

82. 'Anti-Trust Policy: Rules or Discretionary Intervention', *Moorgate and Wall Street*, Spring 1971.

83. Crew and Rowley, 'Anti-Trust Policy: The Application of Rules' *Moorgate and Wall Street*, Autumn 1971.

84. 'British Merger Policy' in George and Joll (eds), *Competition Policy in the U.K. and E.E.C.* (1975), chapter 4.

85. *Ibid.*, pp. 97–8; Merkin and Williams, note 12 above, pp. 247–8.

86. The 1969 and 1978 Merger Guidelines take into account just such a broad range of factors.

87. See *Review of Restrictive Trade Practices Policy*, Cmnd 7512 (1979), paras 6.1–6.13.

88. For the use of guidelines in the United States, see Sullivan, *Antitrust* (1977), pp. 620–1; Areeda, *Antitrust Analysis*, 3rd edn (1981), pp. 911–13, 976–80, 1023–4.

89. A suggestion made by Utton, note 84 above, p. 117.

90. See e.g. Bork, *The Antitrust Paradox* (1978).

91. Allen, note 11 above, p. 64.

92. s.50.

93. Fair Trading Act 1973, ss.12, 50(6), 51, Schedules 5 and 7.

94. Trade and Industry, 25 July 1974.

95. Competition Act 1980, s.3.

96. ss.3(5), 7(2).

97. The factors which influence the Mergers Panel are similar to those which the MMC would consider.

98. Fair Trading Act 1973, ss.64(4)(5).

99. Kay and Sharpe, 'The Anti-Competitive Practice' (1982) 3 *Fiscal Studies* 191, 198.

100. Fair Trading Act 1973, s.54.

101. s.72.

102. ss. 56, 73.

103. s.88.

104. Competition Act 1980, s.8.

105. s.9.

106. s.10, especially s.10(3).

107. s.4.

108. Fair Trading Act 1973, s.88(4); Competition Act 1980, s.9(4).

109. Fair Trading Act 1973, Sched. 8, Pts I and II. See generally, Merkin and Williams, note 12 above, Chapter 10.

110. Fair Trading Act 1973, s.93(2); Competition Act 1980, s.9(4). Failure to register a restrictive agreement is a breach of statutory duty under the Restrictive Trade Practices Act 1976, s.35(2).

111. 127/73, *BRT* v. *SABAM* [1974] ECR 57 and 313. In *Garden Cottage Foods* v. *Milk Marketing Board* [1983] 2 All ER 770, the House of Lords held that, assuming that an individual citizen of the United Kingdom affected by a breach of Article 86 of the EEC Treaty could bring an action, damages could be claimed in our courts for a breach of Article 86 of the EEC Treaty.

112. Sullivan, *Antitrust* (1977), chapter 9(C) & (D); Elzinga and Breit, *The Antitrust Penalties* (1976).

113. For the general principles of judicial review see Craig, *Administrative Law* (1983), chapters 10 and 11.

114. *Hoffmann-La Roche & Co.* v. *Secretary of State for Trade and Industry* [1975] AC 295. See also *R.* v. *Monopolies and Mergers Commission, ex p. Elders IXL Ltd* [1987] 1 All ER 451; *R.* v. *Monopolies and Mergers Commission ex p. Mathew Brown plc* [1987] 1 All ER 463.

115. *Charter Consolidated – Anderson Strathclyde*, Cmnd 8771 (1982).

116. *R.* v. *Secretary of State for Trade and Industry, ex p. Anderson Strathclyde* [1983] 2 All ER 233.

117. *A Review of Monopolies and Mergers Policy*, Cmnd 7198 (1978), paras 5.13–5.17.

118. *Ibid.*, paras 5.18–5.21.

119. *Ibid.*, para. 5.20(ii).

120. Meeks, *Disappointing Marriage* (1978); Cowling *et al. Mergers and Economic Performance* (1980). See also Newbould, *Management and Merger Activity* (1970); Hannah and Kay, *Concentration in Modern Industry* (1977).

121. For example the sharp contrast between the White House Task Force on Antitrust Policy (1968) and Bork, *The Antitrust Paradox* (1978).

Chapter 11: The Commission for Racial Equality

1. There is a growing literature on both bodies. Two of the more recent are Appleby and Ellis, 'Formal Investigations: the Commission for Racial Equality and the Equal Opportunities Commission as Law Enforcement Agencies' [1984] *Public Law* 236; Sacks, 'The Equal Opportunities Commission – Ten Years On' (1986) 49 *Mod. Law Rev.* 560.

2. See CRE Evidence to the House of Commons, Employment Committee

(HC 131, 1986), Q. 58 (Mr Newsam).

3. Jowell, 'The Administrative Enforcement of Laws Against Discrimination' [1965] *Public Law* 119.

4. *Ibid.*, p. 167.

5. B. Heinemann, *The Politics of the Powerless* (1972), *passim*.

6. Race Relations Act 1965.

7. Official Report, HL Deb. vol. 286, col. 1006, 26 July 1965.

8. Political and Economic Planning, *Racial Discrimination* (1967).

9. Dummett and Dummett, 'The Role of Government in Britain's Racial Crisis' in L. Donnelly (ed.), *Justice First* (1969), pp. 25–78.

10. A. Flanders, 'The Tradition of Voluntarism' (1974) 12 *British Journal of Industrial Relations* 352 at p. 354.

11. S. Patterson, *Immigration and Race Relations in Britain 1960–1967* (1968), pp. 114–15.

12. White Paper, *Immigration from the Commonwealth*, Cmnd 2739 (1965), para. 65.

13. *Ibid.*, para. 71

14. Race Relations Act 1968, s.25.

15. Race Relations Act 1968, s.25(3).

16. See A. Lester and G. Bindman, *Race and Law* (1972), p. 100.

17. See RRB Report for 1969–70 (HC 309, 1970), para. 46; RRB Report for 1970–71 (HC 448, 1871), para. 65.

18. There seem to have been a number of additional factors which may also help to explain the relatively low number of complaints, given the degree of discrimination which had earlier been demonstrated, e.g. the effect of alternative dispute-settlement procedures, especially the enactment of unfair dismissals legislation, which appears to have had some effect on the number of complaints of discriminatory dismissal. See RRB Report for 1972 (HC 297, 1973), para. 29; RRB Report for 1974 (HC 409, 1975), para. 32; RRB Report for 1975–76 (HC 3, 1976), para. 40.

19. See Nuffield Foundation, 'Problems and Prospects of Socio-Legal Research' (proceedings of a seminar, Nuffield College, Oxford, June–July, 1971) (March 1972), *passim*.

20. See RRB Evidence to House of Commons Select Committee on Race Relations, *The Organisation of Race Relations Administration* (HC 448, 1975), Q. 252; RRB Report for 1971–2 (HC 296, 1972), paras 77–80. But see contra, RRB Report for 1973 (HC 144, 1974), para. 42.

21. See, e.g., RRB Report for 1973 (HC 144, 1974), p. 40 (case 3) and para. 42. This was particularly the case where section 17 investigations were concerned; see West Midlands Conciliation Committee, Evidence to the House of Commons Select Committee, Employment (HC 312, 1975), Q. 291.

22. Lester and Bindman, *Race and Law*, p. 305.

23. *Ibid.*, pp. 305–6.

24. House of Commons Select Committee on Race Relations, Employment, Report (HC 448, 1975), para. 19.

25. [1972] AC 342.

26. See more detailed criticism by Hucker, 'The House of Lords and the Race Relations Act: A Comment on *Ealing* v. *Race Relations Board*' (1975) 24 *ICLQ* 290.

27. [1975] 1 WCR 1686.

28. P. 1693.

29. Byrne and Lovenduski, 'The Equal Opportunities Commission', 1 *Women's Studies Int. Q.* 131 (1978), provide an excellent account of the development of the idea of agency enforcement with regard to sex discrimination, and the following is adapted from this account.

30. See the Second Report from the House of Lords Select Committee on the Anti-Discrimination Bill (HL 104, 1972/3); Report from the House of Commons Select Committee on the Anti-Discrimination (no. 2) Bill (HC 333, 1972/3).

31. House of Commons Select Committee Report (HC 333, 1972/3), para. 321.

32. Department of Employment, *Equal Opportunities for Men and Women* (Consultative Document) (1973).

33. White Paper, *Equality for Women*, Cmnd 5724 (1974).

34. *Ibid.*, para. 81.

35. *Ibid.*, para. 24.

36. Cmnd 6234 (1975).

37. A different procedure was introduced to enforce the general duty of non-discrimination in the public sector of education. Here the only sanction was action by the Minister responsible, Race Relations Act 1976, s.19.

37a Official Report, 889 HC, 26 March 1975, cols 521-2 (Mr Jenkins).

38. Runnymede Trust, *Racial Discrimination: Developing a Legal Strategy Through Individual Complaints* (April 1982).

39. Race Relations Act 1976, s.66.

40. RRA 1976, s.48(1).

41. RRA 1976, s.58.

42. RRA 1976, s.49.

43. RRA 1976, s.49(4)

44. See, e.g., proposed New Clause 3, Official Report, 914 HC, 8 July 1976, col. 491 (Mr Mayhew).

45. Official Report, 374 HL, 4 October 1976, cols 1003-4.

46. See RRB, 'The Issue of the Amalgamation of the Community Relations Commission with Law Enforcement Functions', 25 July 1975 (unpublished); RRB, 'Comments on the White Paper, *Racial Discrimination*' in RRB, *Report for January 1975–June 1976* (HC 3, 1976). This last statement contains the fullest argument and is the one quoted in this paragraph.

47. Layton-Henry, *The Politics of Race in Britain* (1984), p. 139.
48. *Ibid.*
49. RRA 1976, s.49(4).
50. House of Commons, Home Affairs Committee, Race Relations and Immigration Sub-Committee, Session 1980–1981, *The Operation and Effectiveness of the Commission for Racial Equality*, Minutes of Evidence, HC 259 (i), Memorandum of the Commission for Racial Equality, para. 4.4. (Hereafter 'Select Committee Evidence'.)
51. Sanders, 'Anti-Discrimination Law Enforcement in Britain' in K. Young and N. Glazer (eds), *Ethnic Pluralism and Public Policy* (1983), p. 65.
52. E.g. Unigate, Abbey National investigations.
53. Sanders, *op. cit.*, p. 65.
54. E.g. Chubb, National Bus Co., Prestige, Phillips and Unigate investigations.
55. RRA 1976, s.50.
56. Select Committee Evidence, Q. 112.
57. Select Committee Evidence, Commission for Racial Equality, 'Length of Time Taken by Formal Investigations' (hereafter 'Length of Time'), paras 3 and 4.
58. The Select Committee Evidence, Q. 436.
59. Sanders, *op. cit.*, p. 80.
60. 'Length of Time', para. 2.
61. CRE, 'Review of the Race Relations Act 1976: Proposals for Change' (1985) (hereafter 'Proposals'), p. 34.
62. *Home Office* v. *CRE* [1982] QB 385.
63. *R.* v. *CRE, ex p. Cottrell and Rothon* [1980] 1 WLR 1580.
64. House of Commons Home Affairs Committee, Commission for Racial Equality (hereafter 'Select Committee Report'), HC 46 (session 1981–2), November 1981, para. 1.
65. *Ibid.*
66. *Ibid.*, para. 14.
67. *Ibid.*, para. 15.
68. *Ibid.*, para. 18.
69. *Ibid.*, para. 16.
70. *Ibid.*
71. *Ibid.*, para. 17.
72. *Ibid.*, para. 43.
73. *Ibid.*, para. 44.
74. *Ibid.*, para. 60.
75. *Ibid.*, para. 46.
76. *Ibid.*, para. 54.
77. *Ibid.*, para. 55.
78. *Ibid.*, para. 60.

79. *Home Office Response to Home Affairs Committee*, Cmnd 8547 (1982).
80. *Ibid.*, para. 4.
81. Scarman LJ in *Selvarajan* [1975] 1 WLR at p. 1700; Lord Lane CJ in *Cottrell* [1980] 1 WLR at p. 1586.
82. Lawton, LJ in *Selvarajan* [1975] 1 WLR at p. 1697.
83. *CRE* v. *Amari Plastics Ltd* [1982] QB 1194.
84. *Ibid.*, p. 1203. See also the comment in 1 *Civil Justice Q.* 301–5 (1982).
85. Non-discrimination notices were issued without any appeal in eleven investigations. In the ten investigations in which there were appeals against non-discrimination notices, the notices were quashed in two cases, and modified in six, either as a result of the industrial tribunal decision or in a compromise agreed to by the parties. In one case the appeal was dropped, and the *Westminster* case is still outstanding.
85a [1985] ICR 872.
86. *Home Office* v. *CRE* [1982] QB 385.
87. *Ibid.*, p. 397.
88. *Ibid.*, p. 397.
89. *Science Research Council* v. *Nasse* [1979] QB 144 (CA).
90. *Ibid.*, p. 170.
91. *Ibid.*, p. 172.
92. [1980] AC 1028 at p. 1064.
93. *R.* v. *Commission for Racial Equality, ex p. London Borough of Hillingdon* [1982] AC 779.
94. *In re Prestige* [1984] ICR 473.
95. [1982] AC at p. 791.
96. [1982] AC at p. 787.
97. See further, Munroe, 'The Prestige Case: Putting the Lid on the Commission for Racial Equality' (1985) 14 *Anglo-American L. Rev.* 187.
98. See above, p. 255.
99. See above p. 256.
100. At least three investigations were regarded by the CRE as ultra vires as a result of *Hillingdon*, and at least six as a result of *Prestige*. See *CRE Annual Reports* for 1983 and 1984.
101. *CRE Annual Report*, 1982, p. 25.
102. Westminster investigation. See *R.* v. *CRE, ex p. Westminster City Council* [1985] ICR 872.
103. Beaumont Leys investigation.
104. CRE, *Race Relations Act 1976: Time for a Change?* (July 1983). On this document, see Lacey, 'A Change in the Right Direction?: The CRE's Consultative Document' [1984] *Public Law* 186; Bindman, 'Amending the Race Relations Act' (1983) 80 *Law Soc. Gaz.* 2349; Appleby and Ellis, 'Amending the Race Relations Act – Proposals of the Commission for Racial Equality' (1983) 2 *Civil Justice Q.* 313.
105. CRE, *Proposals, op. cit.*

106. Select Committee Report, *op. cit.*, para. 51.

107. Para. 3.4.13.

108. Proposal 13.

109. Para. 3.5.5.

110. Equal Opportunities Commission, *Legislating for Change?: Review of the Sex Discrimination Legislation* (1986).

111. Department of Economic Development, *Equality of Opportunity in Employment in Northern Ireland: Future Strategy Options* (1986).

112. Brown and Gay, *Racial Discrimination 17 Years After the Act* (1985, PSI), p. 33.

113. R. Marshall, C. B. Knapp, M. H. Liggett and R. W. Glover, *Employment Discrimination: The Impact of Legal and Administrative Remedies* (1978), *passim*.

114. Contrast *EEOC* v. *Shell Oil Co.*, 104 S. Ct. 1621 (1984), with *Hillingdon*, for example.

Chapter 12: Cable Television

1. S. Day-Lewis, 'Go-Ahead Urged for Cable TV', *Daily Telegraph*, 13 October 1982.

2. See Home Office, *Direct Broadcast by Satellite* (1981, HMSO), Cable & Broadcasting Act 1984, Part II.

3. M. Beesley and S. Littlechild, 'Privatisation: Principles, Problems and Policies' (1983) 143 *Lloyds Bank Rev.* 1.

4. The non-broadcasting aspects are discussed in C. G. Veljanovski, 'UK Cable Policy in the Eighties' (1983) 4 *Fiscal Studies* 29.

5. For more detailed descriptions of cable technology, see C. G. Veljanovski and W. D. Bishop, *Choice by Cable: The Economics of a New Era in Television* (1983, Institute of Economic Affairs), chapter 2; J. Howkins, *New Technologies, New Policies* (1982, British Film Institute).

6. P. M. Lewis, *Community Television and Cable in Britain* (1979, British Film Institute). Also R. Hutchinson, *Cable, DBS and the Arts* (1985, Policy Studies Institute).

7. Previously, cable relay companies required up to three licences: a licence from the Home Office under the Wireless Telegraphy Act 1949, s.1, to allow the reception and distribution of off-air programmes; a licence from BT, or the Secretary of State for Trade and Industry after consultation with BT (British Telecommunications Act 1981, s.15), to install and operate a telecom system; and, for those pilot cable systems offering their own programme material, a third licence was required from the Home Secretary under the Post Office Act 1969, s.89.

8. *Report of the Committee on the Future of Broadcasting*, Cmnd 6752 (1977), paras 14.34–14.56.

9. *Ibid.*, para. 14.50.
10. A number of community cable systems were licenced in the early seventies. See Lewis, *op. cit.*, and Veljanovski and Bishop, *op. cit.*, pp. 34–9.
11. *Broadcasting*, Cmnd 7296 (1978).
12. *Ibid.*, para. 175.
13. *Ibid.*, para. 178.
14. *Ibid.*, para. 181.
15. The 1978 Broadcasting White Paper also recommended that a new agency be established, to be called the Open Broadcasting Authority, to oversee the new fourth channel (C4). This recommendation was not implemented.
16. Cabinet Office, *Cable Systems* (1982, HMSO).
17. *Ibid.*, para. 8.11.
18. *Ibid.*
19. *Report of the Inquiry into Cable Expansion and Broadcasting*, Cmnd 8679 (1982).
20. *Ibid.*, App. 1.
21. *Ibid.*, para. 8.
22. Leader, *The Sunday Times*, 17 September 1982.
23. *The Development of Cable Systems and Services*, Cmnd 8866 (1983).
24. *Ibid.*
25 Home Office, *Cable: Interim Licensing of Pilot Projects: Guidance Notes* (July 1983).
26. Home Office, *New Programme Services and Existing Systems – Guidance Notes on Licensing Procedure* (July 1983).
27. P. Fiddick, 'Rescuing Cable Television from Its Shameful Beginnings', *The Guardian*, 18 October 1982.
28. Official Report, 1281 HC, 13 June 1983, col. 788 (K. Baker).
29. The original intention of the DTI was to issue pilot project licences under Clause 7 of the Telecommunications Bill.
30. *Report of the Committee on Financing of BBC* (Peacock Inquiry), Cmnd, 9824 (1986).
31. R. H. Coase, *British Broadcasting: A Study in Monopoly* (1950, Longmans).
32. S. Young, 'The Paternal Tradition in British Broadcasting 1922–?', Watt Club Lecture, Heriot-Watt Univ. (1983), p. 2.
33. Note 11 above, at para. 42.
34. A. Milne *et al.*, *The Cable Debate – A BBC Briefing*, September 1983.
35. Market allocation of frequencies was first approved in L. Herzel, 'Public Interest and the Market in Color Television' (1951) 18 *Univ. Chicago L. Rev.* 802. Also R. H. Coase, 'The Federal Communications Commission' (1959) 2 *J. Law and Econ.* 1; A. S. De Vany *et al.*, 'A Property System for the Market Allocation of the Electromagnetic Spectrum' (1969) 21 *Stan. L. Rev.* 1499.
36. *Report of the Independent Review of the Radio Spectrum* (30–960 MHz.), Cmnd

9000 (1983). Although the Report is sceptical of pricing approaches to spectrum management, it is highly critical of the way the Home Office has allocated frequencies and its administrative procedures. The DTI is seriously examining deregulating the spectrum – see *Deregulation of the Radio Spectrum in the UK* (1987, HMSO).

37. See generally R. G. Noll, M. J. Peck and J. J. McGowan, *Economic Analysis of Television Regulation* (1973, Brookings); B. M. Owen, J. H. Beebe and W. G. Manning, *Television Economics* (1974, Heath).

38. The controversy in 1985–86 over the licence fee amply illustrates the problems and incentives created for similar programming by the BBC. H.C. Parliamentary Debates (BBC Financing), 19 December 1984, vol. 70(33) at 247. The internal efficiency of the BBC is another matter receiving careful attention: Home Office, *Two Studies Concerning the British Broadcasting Corporation* (1979).

39. Broadcasting Act 1981, s.11.

40. White Paper, para. 130.

41. This argument is developed in more detail in Veljanovski and Bishop, *op. cit.*, chapter 4, and the references cited in note 32 above.

42. *The Future of Telecommunications in Britain*, Cmnd 8610 (1982); C. Veljanovski, *Selling the State: Privatisation in Britain* (1987, Weidenfeld & Nicolson).

43. White Paper, para. 217.

44. *Ibid.*, para. 87.

45. *Ibid.*, para. 10.

46. Hunt, p. 3.

47. On telecommunications as a major growth sector, see the ACARD Report (*Technological Change: Threats and New Opportunities for the United Kingdom* (1980)). See also K. Baker, HC Deb. vol. 33, col. 494, 2 December 1982, and *The Economist*, 'The Wiring of Britain', 6 March 1982, p. 11.

48. For OECD doubts see *Telecommunications – Pressures and Policies for Change* OECD (1983); NEDO, *The Crisis Facing UK Information Technology* (1984).

49. Cable Authority, *Preliminary Guidance Notes on the Grant of Franchises* (1984), para. 3.

50. 'Draft Telecommunications Licence for Cable Operators', DTI (1985).

51. White Paper, para. 140.

52. C & BA, s.10.

53. C & BA, s.11.

54. See Broadcasting Act 1981, s.2(b).

55. White Paper, para. 137. See also M. O. Wirth *et al.*, 'Demand for Sex-oriented Cable TV in the USA – Community Acceptance and Obscenity Law' (1984) 8 *Telecommunications Policy* 314.

56. White Paper, para. 120.

57. *Ibid.*, para. 122. The restrictions are almost identical to those recommended by the Wilson Committee: *Statistics, Technological Developments and Cable Television – Third Report of the Interim Action Committee on the Film Industry*, Cmnd 7855 (1980), para. 70.

58. White Paper, para. 46. Members of the Board are Paul Johnson (author), Professor James Ring (physicist, member of the IBA 1974–81, member of the Hunt Committee, Deputy Chairman of the Authority), Peter Paine (TV executive) and Elizabeth Brown (marketing).

59. White Paper, para. 40.

60. *Ibid.*, para. 190.

61. *Ibid.*, para. 40.

62. *Ibid.*, para. 41.

63. *Ibid.*, para. 40.

64. *Ibid.*

65. Pilkington Report, *Report of the Committee on Broadcasting*, Cmnd 1753 (1960), para. 572; see also P. Johnson, 'The Dallas Affair', *The Spectator*, 20 July 1985, p. 20.

66. White Paper, para. 40.

67. Broadcasting Act 1981, Pt III; C & BA, s.28.

68. Telecommunications Act 1984, s.58.

69. White Paper, para. 57.

70. J. Mitchell, 'The Information Society: Private Monopolies and the Consumer Interest' (1983) 54 *Political Quarterly* 160. For more technical economic discussions of natural monopolies, see W. W. Sharkey, *The Theory of Natural Monopoly* (1982, CUP) A. E. Kahn, *The Economics of Regulation* (1971, Wiley).

71. On cable as a natural monopoly, see E. M. Noam, 'Economies of Scale in Cable Television', Columbia Graduate School of Business (1983); B. M. Owen and P. R. Greenhalgh, 'Competitive Policy Considerations in Cable Television Franchising' (1982, Economists Inc.); G. K. Webb, *The Economics of Cable Television* (1983, Heath); T. W. Hazlett, 'Private Monopoly and the Public Interest: An Economic Analysis of the Cable Television Franchise' (1986) 134 *Univ. Penn. Law Rev.* 1335. S. M. Besen *et al.*, 'Economic Policy Research on Cable Television: Assessing the Costs and Benefits of Cable Deregulation' in P. W. MacAvoy (ed.), *Deregulation of Cable Television* (1977, American Enterprise Institute).

72. White Paper, para. 62.

73. See note 49 above.

74. C & BA, s.7.

75. E. Chadwick, 'Results of Different Principles of Legislation and Administration in Europe; of Competition for the Field, as Compared

with Competition within the Field of Service' (1859) 22 *J. Royal Stat. Soc.* 22; H. Demsetz, 'Why Regulate Public Utilities?' (1968) 11 *J. Law and Econ.* 55.

76. O. E. Williamson, 'Franchise Bidding for Natural Monopolies – in General and with Respect to CATV' (1976) 7 *Bell J. Econ.* 73.

77. N. Lewis, 'IBA Programme Awards' [1975] *Public Law* 317; S. Domberger and J. Middleton, 'Franchising in Practice: The Case of Independent Television in the UK' (1985) 6 *Fiscal Studies* 17; S. Domberger, 'Economic Regulation Through Franchise Contracts' in J. A. Kay, C. Mayer and D. Thompson (eds), *Privatisation and Regulation: The UK Experience* (1986, OUP), Ch. 14. ￼

78. C & BA, s.7.

79. *Ibid.*

80. *Ibid.*, s.8(3).

81. See M. F. Barton, 'Conditional Logit Analysis of FCC Decisionmaking' (1979) 10 *Bell J. Econ.* 399.

82. National Consumer Council, *Annual Report and Accounts 1983/84*, p. 13.

83. P. Stylianos and J. Silva-Echenique, 'The Profitability and Risks of CATV Operations in Canada' (1983) 15 *Applied Econ.* 745.

84. White Paper, para. 44.

85. White Paper, para. 76.

86. C & BA, s.17.

87. White Paper, para. 72.

88. Economists now refer to this as making the market more contestable. Baumol *et al.*, *Contestable Markets and the Theory of Industry Structure* (1982, Harcourt, Brace, Jovanovich). Cf. W. G. Shepard, 'Contestability vs. Competition' (1984) 74 *Am. Econ. Rev.* 572.

89. Hunt, para. 87.

90. *The Financial Times*, 2 December 1983

Chapter 13: Financial Services

* This chapter was completed before the Financial Services Bill had completed its parliamentary stages. The Act was duly passed and is being brought into force during the course of 1987.

1. Edwards, 'Financial Institutions and Regulation in the 21st Century: After the Crash?' in Verheirstraeten (ed.), *Competition and Regulation in Financial Markets* (1981), p. 1.

2. *Review of Investor Protection*, Cmnd 9125 (1984) (hereafter the *Gower Report*).

3. Restrictive Trade Practices (Stock Exchange) Act 1984.

4. *Report of the Committee to Review the Functioning of Financial Institutions*, Cmnd 7937 (1980) (hereafter the *Wilson Report*), Evidence, Vol. 5,

p. 52; *First Report from the Select Committee on Nationalised Industries, The Bank of England* (1969–70; HC 258), q. 298.

5. *Ibid.*, q. 188.

6. The *Wilson Report, op. cit.*, para. 1260.

7. *Ibid.*, para. 1137; Gower, *Review of Investor Protection: A Discussion Document* (1982), para. 3.23.

8. *Disc. Doc. op. cit.*, para. 10.04.

9. The *Gower Report, op. cit.*, para. 10.03.

10. Financial Services Act, s. 3.

11. *Ibid.*, s. 114, Sched. 7.

12. Cmnd 9432 (1985).

13. 'Self-Regulation: The Constitutional Dimension' (1986) 49 *MLR.* 141.

14. Cmnd 9432, *op. cit.*, para. 5.2.

15. *Disc. Doc., op. cit.*, para. 7.08.

16. Cmnd 9432, *op. cit.*, para. 5.14.

17. *The Future of London as an International Financial Centre* (1972), pp. 1–38, para. 102.

18. HC Deb, vol. 64, col. 50 (16 July 1984).

19. *Disc. Doc., op. cit.*, para. 7.01.

20. Cmnd 9432, *op. cit.*, para. 5.2.

21. *The Review of Investor Protection and its Implications for the Capital Markets* (3 April 1984), p. 1.

22. *Review of Investor Protection* (Gower Report) (27 April 1984), para. 5.

23. Views of the CSI on the Report by Professor Gower (25 April 1984), para. 9.

24. Evidence, vol. 4, 153.

25. McMahon, 'Responsibilities of the Private and Public Sectors' (1984) 24 *BEQB*, 501.

26. *Op. cit.*, para. 6.02.

27. *Ibid.*, para. 7.09.

28. The *Gower Report, op. cit.*, para. 3.08.

29. *Ibid.*, para. 3.09.

30. Note 21 above.

31. *Op. cit.*, para. 1195–1200.

32. Comments on Financial Services White Paper (28 February 1985), p. 9.

33. Cooke, 'The Role of the Banking Supervisor' (1982) 22 *BEQB*, 547.

34. Cmnd 9432, *op. cit.*, para. 9.6.

35. *Report of the Committee on the Working of the Monetary System*, Cmnd 827 (1959) (hereafter the *Radcliffe Report*), para. 761.

36. Moran, 'Monetary Policy and the Machinery of Government' (1981) 59 *Pub. Admin.* 47.

37. *Op. cit.*, para. 1278; the *Radcliffe Report, op. cit.*, paras 767–8.

38. *Op. cit.*, para. 1279; the *Radcliffe Report, op. cit.*, paras 761 and 770.

39. See, e.g., Day, 'The Bank of England in the Modern State' (1961) 39 *Pub. Admin.* 15.

40. *First Report from the Select Committee on Nationalised Industries, op. cit.*, q. 120; see also q. 1030.

41. See Page, 'Self-Regulation: The Constitutional Dimensions' (1986) 49 *MLR*, 141 at 161.

42. The *Wilson Report, op. cit.*, paras 1161–2; *Disc. Doc., op. cit.*, para. 3.34. The Wilson Committee recommended a number of changes: *Report*, paras 1111–19.

43. McMahon, *op. cit.*, pp. 501–2; see also Walker, *op. cit.*, p. 500.

44. *Report, op. cit.*, para. 1108; see also the *Gower Report, op. cit.*, paras 2.03–4.

45. HC Deb. vol. 64, col. 50 (16 July 1984).

46. Financial Services Act, s. 114, Sched. 7.

47. s. 115(3).

48. s. 10, Sched. 2.

49. s.12.

50. s.13.

51. s.11.

52. s.11(3)–(6), 13(7).

53. s.122.

54. Cmnd 9432, *op. cit.*, para. 8.3.

55. See, e.g., HC Deb. vol. 49, col. 203 (22 November 1983) and the *Wilson Report, op. cit.*, paras 364–6.

56. Stevens and Yamey, *The Restrictive Practices Court* (1965), pp. 16–19.

57. Comments on Financial Services White Paper, *op. cit.*, pp. 8–9.

58. The *Gower Report, op. cit.*, para. 6.36; see earlier *Disc. Doc., op. cit.*, para. 8.04.

59. Sixth Annual Report of the CSI (1984), Appx A, para. 38.

60. Financial Services Act, s.121(3).

61. *Ibid.*, s.120(4).

62. *Ibid.*, s.192.

63. *Ibid.*, s.13(1).

64. *Ibid.*, s.13(5).

65. *Ibid.*, Sched. 2, para. 2.

66. In *Weinberger* v. *Inglis* [1919] AC 606, the Stock Exchange Council successfully claimed the right, so long as they did not act arbitrarily or capriciously, to decide whom they would elect or re-elect to membership; see also *Cassells* v. *Inglis* [1916] 2 Ch. 211.

67. *Report from the Select Committee on Foreign Loans* (HC 367; 1875), p. xlviii.

68. SIB/MIBOC, *Regulation of Investment Business: The New Framework* (1985), para. 2.5.

69. The *Gower Report, op. cit.*, para. 6.13. The obligations referred to are those under Article 6(i) ECHR; *Report, op. cit.*, para. 6.20.

70. The Stock Exchange's commentary on the principal proposals of Professor Gower's *Discussion Document* (1982), p. 13. See also the CSI's *Fifth Annual Report* (1983), Appx A, paras 6(a) and 7.

71. The *Gower Report, op. cit.*, paras 6.22–6.23.

72. See, e.g., HL Deb. vol. 340, col. 907 (22 March 1973). The finding that an individual was not a fit and proper person has been challenged on two occasions, both of which illustrate the limitations of judicial review. In the first case (Second Report of the Parliamentary Commissioner for Administration (1976–77, HC 116), Appx B), the PCA recommended that the Department should reconsider its decision, although it is doubtful whether the circumstances outlined amounted to a breach of the duty to act fairly. In the second case ((1981) 21 ECHR Decisions and Reports 5), the applicant accepted the legality of the decision and simply wanted to challenge its merits, which in the absence of an appeal could not be done.

73. Financial Services Act, ss.96–101, Sched. 6.

74. *Report, op. cit.*, para. 1269.

75. Cmnd 827, *op. cit.*, para. 366.

76. Special Report from the Select Committee on Nationalised Industries, *The Committee Order of Reference* (1967–68; HC 298).

77. Financial Services Act, s.117.

78. The *Wilson Report, op. cit.*, para. 1116.

79. *Ibid.*, para. 1109.

80. Cmnd 9432, *op. cit.*, para. 6.7.

81. HC Deb. vol. 49, col. 188 (22 November 1983).

82. Financial Services Act, Sched. 7, para. 1(3)(b); Sched. 2, para. 5.

83. Morgan and Thomas, *The Stock Exchange: Its History and Functions* (1969), p. 166. On the position today, see the *Wilson Report, op. cit.*, para. 1136. The City Capital Markets Committee has suggested that the procedure should be better publicized so that small investors are more aware of it.

84. Financial Services Act, Sched. 7, para. 4; Sched. 2, para. 6.

85. *Op. cit.*, para. 1168.

86. *Disc. Doc., op. cit.*, para. 6.03.

87. Ferguson and Page, 'The Development of Investor Protection in Britain', (1984) 12 *IJLS* 287 at 297–300.

INDEX